Ernest Duvergier de Hauranne

From an engraving (1871)

The Lakeside Classics

A FRENCHMAN
IN LINCOLN'S AMERICA

Huit Mois en Amérique:
Lettres et Notes de Voyage, 1864–1865

By Ernest Duvergier de Hauranne

Translated and Edited by RALPH H. BOWEN
With Introduction and Notes by RALPH H. BOWEN
and ALBERT KREBS

VOLUME TWO

The Lakeside Press

R. R. DONNELLEY & SONS COMPANY

CHICAGO

Christmas, 1975

This Book
Is Gratefully Dedicated
to the Memory of
ALLAN NEVINS

PUBLISHERS' PREFACE

THE 1975 edition of *The Lakeside Classics* is the second volume of *A Frenchman in Lincoln's America*. In Volume I, which was our last year's selection, we left the author, Ernest Duvergier de Hauranne, in Chicago musing upon the moral fiber of Americans as evidenced in their financial and romantic dealings. He found much to admire.

The beginning of the present volume finds him still in Chicago in the final days of the presidential election of 1864. After learning with satisfaction of Lincoln's victory, he continues the story of his journeys, returning to France by way of Martinique in the early spring of the following year.

Duvergier de Hauranne was young, well-to-do, well educated and from a distinguished French family. His father, an author and a member of King Louis-Phillippe's cabinet for many years, financed his trip to America primarily so that he might learn by first-hand observation about political institutions in this country. The curious mind of the young man led him to make astute observations on many other phases of the American character.

The accounts in these two volumes appeared first as a series of articles in the highly-regarded French publication, *Revue des Deux Mondes*, and as a book, *Eight Months in America*, in 1866. An abridged edition in French was published in 1966 by Albert Krebs, Conservateur at the Bibliotheque Nationale. Mr. Krebs also participated in the editing of the current Donnelley edition of the book.

Professor Ralph H. Bowen, the translator and primary editor of these two volumes, saw the need for a translation of the complete book, and with the encouragement of the able American historian Allan Nevins and Professor Claude Fohlen of the Sorbonne, produced the present work.

As we noted last year, Professor Bowen has taught at Columbia College, Columbia University; Elmira College, State University of New York on Long Island; the University of Nantes, France; and Northern Illinois University at DeKalb, where he has been Professor of History since 1960. He has received both Fulbright Research and Ford Foundation Grants and has written a number of books and articles on history.

Sources and references for the maps which appear in this edition were researched and verified by the Donnelley Cartographic Services. With this information, Robert Williams of Chicago prepared the routes and calligraphy. This is the fourth edition for which Mr. Williams has provided maps.

Again the type was generated by the Donnelley Electronic Graphics Division on computerized electronic equipment which includes the use of a cathode ray tube. Printing by offset lithography and binding were done by the Donnelley Crawfordsville (Indiana) Manufacturing Division.

Our thanks are extended to the institutions who opened their archives to Professor Bowen and Mr. Krebs for the selection of illustrations. They are individually identified at each reproduction.

* * *

To comment about our own business for the benefit of those readers who may be interested, we shared in 1975 the problems of our own industry and industry in general throughout the world. Shortages in materials and supplies, except energy, suddenly disappeared. Our customers and our Company were left with considerable inventories of paper which are being gradually reduced. While our sales and profits continued to grow in 1975, we had more than adequate capacity in most areas of our business and continued to feel the effects of the recession. The printing industry is a lagging indicator; that is, its ups and downs trail general economic conditions by six to twelve months. It is our firm belief that we have been well served by continued heavy investment in advanced technology, modernized facilities and development of good people. Our expanded sales force, constantly gaining skill and experience, is ever alert to opportunities to keep our plants busy and profitable. Competition is especially keen during times like these, with great downward pressure on prices in the marketplace. Not every potential customer can or wants to take advantage of our superior service at a price which will produce an adequate return on investment. We have been able to grow because of the many customers who have wisely taken a longer term view of the value of our services.

Our new gravure plant in Gallatin, Tennessee, our new telephone directory composition facility in Elgin, Illinois and the new Eastern financial printing facilities in New York and Lancaster, Pennsylvania are in various stages of start-up and successful operation. New press capacity is now on-stream at Old Saybrook, Connecticut, further to be supplemented by presses bought from Williams Press which has discontinued magazine production.

Some years ago, we embarked on a gradual reorganization to bring the sales and manufacturing of our major categories of products together under one senior executive. Further progress in organization was made in 1975. There is a group vice president for each of our major product categories: catalogs, magazines, books and directories. These in turn report to the Executive Vice President, a new position. This has proven an effective way to direct and coordinate our efforts in these different fields.

Gaylord Donnelley attained his 65th birthday in May of 1975 and retired as Chairman of the Board in accord with our Company's retirement policies. He will continue to serve on our Board of Directors and is Chairman of the Executive Committee of the Board. Gaylord's many great contributions to our business were the subject of a special story in the Summer issue of The Donnelley Printer. We would be pleased to send copies of this to any of our readers on request to the Company. Gaylord continued the tradition of family dedication and leadership that began with the founding of the Company by Richard Robert Donnelley in 1864 and was continued by his father, Thomas E. Donnelley, and in this generation by his brother Elliott and his brother-in-law, General Charles C. Haffner, Jr. The Donnelley family has given this Company its unique characteristics of integrity, quality and service and of dedication to our employees, to our customers, to our stockholders and to our nation. Gaylord's strict sense of ethics, his sense of responsibility and his warm regard for the well-being of others have characterized his leadership. The 50th volume of this series, issued in 1952, pays tribute in the Publishers' Preface to his father, Thomas E. Donnelley.

Gaylord has maintained the traditions of *The Lakeside Classics*; he has been instrumental in their selection and has written much of the Publishers' Preface during his years of leadership. He will continue in these activities even though retired. The following extract from the Publishers' Preface of 1952 is included here so that many new readers of this series may acquire a better appreciation of these efforts.

When Mr. [Thomas E.] Donnelley decided, in 1903, to issue a small book as an expression of good wishes at Christmastime to the patrons and other friends of the Press, he intended also to show that a machine-made book could better reflect the ideals of the book-making industry than could the then prevalent so-called "editions de luxe," usually printed on handmade paper and on hand presses.

[Early books in the series covered a broad range of American subjects including memorable speeches, but] the publication in 1911 of the Autobiography of the late Gurdon S. Hubbard . . . brought such enthusiastic praise from its readers that the publishers realized that by reprinting titles containing the personal relations of our frontiersmen and early settlers, they would add greatly to the interest of the series and would be making a real contribution toward a wider knowledge of the early history of the West.

. . . [The series] is now confined to a field where many

of the titles have long been out of print and are extremely
rare, and which are little known except to historians spe-
cializing in the early West or the collectors of Americana.
. . . The book must be a personal relation in order that
the reader may feel the reality of first-hand information;
it must be sufficiently scarce so as to be fresh to the average reader; . . . and above all, it must be of human interest
to hold its readers who range in taste from the most discriminating bibliophiles and collectors of Americana to
that recipient who expresses his enthusiastic praise by
writing annually that "it is the only book I read the entire
year."

While 1975 has not been an easy year for our
Company, we face a somewhat uncertain future
with confidence and guarded optimism. In doing so,
we are ever mindful of the many loyal customers,
suppliers, employees and other friends who have
made our present strength and success possible. To
them, warm thanks and best wishes for a Merry
Christmas, and a Happy New Year.

THE PUBLISHERS

Christmas 1975

CONTENTS

ILLUSTRATIONS

MAPS

HISTORICAL INTRODUCTION

AS READERS of the first volume of this account will already have realized, Ernest Duvergier de Hauranne was one of the most sympathetic and likable, as well as one of the youngest—he celebrated his twenty-second birthday during his trip—of the European travelers who visited America during the mid-nineteenth century. Alert, open-minded, fascinated by the land and its people, he had the first-rate journalist's eye for telling detail. But more than that, he was equipped with a political philosophy sympathetic to, but also critical of, egalitarian democracy (for which he was indebted in large part to Alexis de Tocqueville, his father's close friend and his own teacher and model).

Best of all, he came prepared to like the country and its people, despite their reputation for violence and raw pushiness. He was almost entirely free of the sour social snobbery that permeates so many Britishers' accounts of their American travels. Never taking Europe or himself too seriously, he had a delightful sense of humor that not only helped him absorb the shocks of travel in a half-settled country disrupted by civil war, but lent a sparkling quality to his pages. His sensitive, compassionate and admiring comments about black people, Indians, about American women and about recent immigrants place him in a class by himself so far as social insight goes, and almost make him sound like an enlightened contemporary. His writing about the destruction of the environment for quick pecuniary profit has an especially topical flavor, as do his comments about the threats to the quality of life in a *laissez-faire* society devoted to rapid industrialization and personal enrichment.

Duvergier de Hauranne's account does, of course, share many of the qualities typical of French visitors to nineteenth-century America. Following in the footsteps of Lafayette and Tocqueville, a succession of travelers arrived in the 1840s and 1850s, inkstands full and notebooks at the ready, to observe and record the half-inspiring, half-appalling folkways of that new species, *Homo democraticus*. Some were in search of the picturesque, the grotesque, the vulgar, the primitive or the grandiose. Romantics came to seek the Noble Savage in his primeval forest or the panther in his lair (usually located not far from Schenectady, New York). Others came to anthropologize on Manhattan Island or among the Brahmins of Boston, among the descendants of Penn and Franklin or among the belles of Baltimore. Few cared to go south of the Potomac or west of the Alleghenies. A standard itinerary including these eastern cities, optionally extended to include Saratoga Springs, Lake Champlain, Niagara Falls, and perhaps Richmond, Charleston and New Orleans, became more or less *de rigueur*, like the great continental art centers and watering-places that marked the stops on an eighteenth-century Englishman's Grand Tour.

One of the best narratives of this kind of tour is Jean-Jacques Ampère's *Promenade en Amérique* (Paris, 1855, 2 vols.), written by the son of the famous physicist and investigator of electricity. Like Ernest

Duvergier de Hauranne, who came a decade later,
Ampère was a close family friend and enthusiastic
disciple of Tocqueville; both men came with well-
annotated copies of *Democracy in America* in their
luggage, both were doing "follow-up" studies,
checking on the predictions of their great predecessor and model; both studied America with the theoretical bias of Tocqueville's aristocratic liberalism,
though, as we shall see, Duvergier de Hauranne, at
any rate, was thoroughly converted in the course of
his visit to an advanced form of democratic republicanism, a conversion that made him a political ally
(after his return to France) of Léon Gambetta and
Georges Clemenceau. Both were sons of well-
to-do and distinguished families—Duvergier de
Hauranne's father had been a noted historian and
a cabinet minister under the Orleanist monarchy
of King Louis-Philippe (reigned 1830–1848)—and
had been given an excellent education. He had a
good command of English, plenty of pocket-money
and numerous letters of introduction that opened
all doors from Beacon Hill to Capitol Hill and the
White House. Both came with some apprehensions
about the crude manners of the Americans, and
both were quickly won over by the warm hospitality and the egalitarian vitality of the new land.

But here the resemblances end. Duvergier de
Hauranne, arriving in New York from Liverpool by
way of Cork, Ireland, on June 15, 1864, dutifully
made the rounds of New York society, went to take
the waters at Saratoga and admired the splendors of
Niagara Falls. But one senses a certain impatience
in his account of these places, described in the early

part of the first volume of *A Frenchman in Lincoln's America*, and the pace of his writing noticeably quickens when he starts to explore the St. Lawrence, the wilds of the Ottawa, the Indian villages and mining towns of Lake Huron and Lake Superior. He paints with rapid, sharp strokes the cities of Milwaukee, Rock Island, Dubuque and St. Paul, sketching with an almost photographic vividness the trainloads of German, Bohemian and Scandinavian immigrants with whom he shared unventilated passenger coaches and steamboat lounges and describing the natural scenery with a freshness and verve that delighted the eminent French critic Sainte-Beuve.

Descending the Mississippi to St. Louis, he came abruptly into contact with the violent hatreds aroused in the border states by civil conflict and military rule. After watching some political rallies—the election campaign of 1864 was by now well under way—one of which (supporting the Democrats) was broken up by the military, he gave up his earlier plan to cross the prairie to Kansas and instead returned to New York.

After a brief visit to Boston, where he was shown around by his friend, Senator Charles Sumner, he took the train north to Portland and went on by way of the White Mountains and the Québec town of Sherbrooke to Montréal. The first volume of his travels closes with his journey via Toronto and Detroit to Chicago as to be on hand for the November elections in the metropolis of the upper Midwest where he expected the campaign—and with it the success of the Union cause—to be decided, for by

now he was a thoroughgoing Republican and Abolitionist, convinced that the fate of American democracy hung upon the re-election of Abraham
Lincoln. He was fascinated, too, by the political
spectacle offered by the Democratic National Convention in Chicago (though he did not actually get
there in time to see it with his own eyes) and by the
meetings, parades, flamboyant oratory and unre-
strained newspaper comment that accompanied the
electioneering of both major parties. Well aware
that both parties were guilty of misrepresentation,
humbug, rabble-rousing, fraud, violence and intimi-
dation—all of which he conscientiously described—
he remained detached enough to give us a remark-
ably accurate and shrewd picture of the democratic
political mores in the great metropolis on the shores
of Lake Michigan, where many of the things he described can (it is said) still be observed at election
time.

On November 9 he learned with great satisfaction
that Lincoln had been re-elected and that the voters
had gone to the polls in an atmosphere of calm. But
he was now eager to return from Chicago to New
York. Travelling this time by way of the Ohio valley and Pittsburgh, he found that Columbus offered
little entertainment on Sunday, but Pittsburgh on a
week-day proved to be rather interesting. "This is
one of the most unusual cities, not only in America,
but in the whole world." Not far from Pittsburgh,
the "land of petroleum" proved to be equally fascinating, though he complains eloquently of having
to slog through deep mud to and from primitive
hotels that were jammed with speculators and oil

men. Regaining the railroad after a hair-raising midnight ride on horseback over uncertain country roads he went on to Buffalo, "an immense city whose uniformity is utterly depressing." At last he got back to New York, but only for a brief stay. He hurried on to Boston, where he had been previously, but only long enough for a quick look around.

This time he chose to linger for a full two weeks; he soon made a number of interesting acquaintances and came to have a higher opinion of Boston than of any other city in America. Longfellow, Edward Everett and Wendell Phillips were the most eminent of the celebrities he met, and he notes that Phillips was "one of the most fascinating and original speakers I have ever listened to." Nor was his visit exclusively devoted to meeting the intelligentsia of the male sex; he writes charmingly of attending a meeting of a women's literary circle in the company of Julia Ward Howe. He was much impressed with Harvard and certain of its faculty members, including the celebrated naturalist, Louis Agassiz. On his way back to New York, where he arrived December 19, he made a long detour through Pittsfield, Massachusetts, from which he traveled by sleigh to visit the nearby Shaker community in New Lebanon, New York.

After the rather gloomy sobriety of the Shaker Sabbath, New York was more lively, and he was invited to a round of Christmas and New Year's parties at which he was able to make further clinical observations on youthful life-styles and courtship customs. But the vulgarity of New York's newly rich rubbed him the wrong way, and he soon came

to dislike the city more than ever. "Returning to
this American Babylon, I feel that sense of disgusted familiarity which one has on returning in the
early morning to the mud and filth of Paris after
travelling all night. One so quickly gets used to
places and things that it feels as though I were coming home." He made two unsuccessful trips to New
Jersey hoping to meet General George B. McClellan, but the defeated Democratic candidate was
away from home on both occasions. So our traveler
was obliged to fill up his diary with thoughts about
Sherman's march through Georgia which was just
then being reported in the newspapers.

The first of January, 1865, fell on a Sunday, "a
day devoted to immobility and boredom," so the
New Year's Day festivities took place on Monday.
As a visitor to society in New York, Duvergier de
Hauranne found he could meet his obligations by
making some twenty-five calls and accepting the
same number of glasses of sherry, most of which he
was able to pour into the potted palms when no one
was looking. Except for attending a mildly amusing
session of a "dancing class"—actually an opportunity for young women to flirt with their "beaux"—he
found fashionable people rather tiresome and did
not enjoy himself much at the various formal holiday balls to which he was invited. Thanks to his
introductions, however, he was able to make the
acquaintance of some of the old aristocratic Dutch
families and to observe the contrasts between their
ways and the more flamboyant manners of the rising
tycoons of finance, business and journalism whom
he mostly disliked on sight.

Nor did the social whirl distract him for long from the great political and military events being reported in the press. When Sherman's forces occupied and reorganized Savannah, he was much interested to learn that there had been little resistance by irreconcilable Confederates and also that there had been many secret Unionists in the city throughout the war. He considered these to be hopeful signs pointing to a relatively painless reintegration of the Southern states into the national community once hostilities came to an end. Since Duvergier de Hauranne was convinced that slavery was the only important issue dividing the North and South, he believed that its abolition would remove the only real obstacle to national unity, so logical and necessary on all other grounds. Hence he was optimistic about the chances for a quick and easy reconstruction of America's national unity.

Early in January, 1865, Congress began debate on the proposed Thirteenth Amendment and other matters connected with slavery. In order to follow these developments at close hand Duvergier de Hauranne hastened off to Washington and took an uncomfortable room on the sixth floor of Willard's Hotel, which was crowded at the moment with all manner of soldiers, politicians and businessmen. He visited Congress with some regularity, profiting from his friendship with Senator Charles Sumner to make the acquaintance of the leading anti-slavery congressmen.

Despite all the courtesies extended to him as a distinguished foreign visitor—he was given a seat on the floor of the House—he found the quality of de-

bate disappointing. There had been, he believed, a
decline in the standards of American oratory since
the days of Clay, Everett and Webster; what was left
of this great tradition had degenerated into "a tireless and tiresome verbosity." He commented also
on the qualities and failings of the newer, plebeian
type of politician being sent to Congress from the
West (a term he uses to include the whole of the
United States west of the Alleghenies)—their great
physical size and strength, their intimidating energy, their gregariousness, their impatience with social niceties and the exact use of language. He notes
the growth of anti-slavery opinion and the simulta-
neous losses of the Democrats both in the country
and in Congress; the abolition of slavery was now,
he thought, a foregone conclusion; the only uncertainties had to do with the method and the timing
of emancipation; but he foresaw that these problems would not be easy to solve, particularly the
ones relating to the structure of the Southern economy and society.

Meanwhile he was calling on eminent persons
like Seward, Lincoln's Secretary of State, Admiral
Farragut, General Butler (whom he found rather
impressive if somewhat disturbing on account of his
ambition)—and, of course, Sumner and other members of Congress.

Among these he noted two groups: "the Easterners who are much like us Europeans" and "the
Westerners who . . . are more countrified but . . .
[have more] originality . . .".

He had not yet seen Lincoln. Though he had
overcome his earlier doubts about the President's

real stature as a statesman, he was still not sure that so poorly educated a person would be interesting to talk to. He was at a loss to understand why Lincoln was so often ridiculed by the press both in America and in Europe and used several pages of his journal to refute the slanders then current about the private life of Mr. and Mrs. Lincoln, praising their modesty, simplicity and honesty. "How can one take any stock in the reputation he has in Europe for ineptness?" Above all, he admired Lincoln's character, his goodness and "that virtue of perseverance and determination which is, moreover, the American virtue *par excellence*."

Finally, on January 20, 1865, he was introduced to Lincoln by Sumner. It was a brief conversation of perhaps fifteen minutes, held in an interval between other callers who had come to seek special favors for themselves or their relatives, and it does not appear that anything particularly memorable was said.

Still, Duvergier de Hauranne was impressed not only by Lincoln's physical presence but by the power of his mind. "I took away with me the mental picture of a man who is not very brilliant, not very aristocratic, not at all royal in his manner, but full of good qualities, unpretentious, able and hardworking." The next day he attended a public reception at the White House where he saw the President "distributing handshakes to everyone in sight with a stiff, regular motion like a piece of clockwork."

At the end of January, Duvergier de Hauranne eagerly seized an opportunity to inspect the Federal battle lines near Richmond. In New York he had met Brigadier-General Régis de Trobriand,[1] thanks to an introduction given him before leaving France by the young Duc de Chartres, who had met the General in 1861 when he and his elder brother, the Comte de Paris, princes of the deposed House of Orléans, served with the Union forces. General de Trobriand was a naturalized American of French birth who had been a successful journalist and drama critic for the New York *Courrier des Etats-Unis* for a number of years before becoming a citizen in 1861. He had invited our young traveler to visit his headquarters near Hatcher's Run on the extreme left flank of the Army of the Potomac. This tour of inspection lasted a week and is the subject of a long chapter filled with details of military life.

Duvergier de Hauranne describes the voyage down the wintry Potomac into lower Chesapeake Bay, then on past Fort Monroe and Yorktown to City Point, Grant's great supply depôt and headquarters on the James River. From there he took the military railroad that had been built over hill and dale for twenty miles to Patrick Station. A little farther along, outside the Federal entrenchments, looking north toward Petersburg and Richmond, he found the headquarters of the First Brigade, Third Division, Second Corps of the Army of the Potomac, where his host, General de Trobriand, had made space for him adjacent to his headquarters.

The weather was bitterly cold. He greatly admired the ingenuity with which the troops contrived

[1] The latter's memoirs of his post-war service on the Indian frontier, *Army Life in Dakota*, were published in 1941 as Volume 39 of *The Lakeside Classics*.

to make heated shelters, using only their axes and
pocket-knives, and he gives many illuminating details about camp life, the manning of the outposts,
the occasional fraternization, the Confederate prisoners and deserters, the runaway slaves and the
black troops of the Union forces, and there is a fine
account of a rather boozy military review at which
he met de Trobriand's superior officer, General Andrew A. Humphreys, and a number of other high-
ranking commanders of that sector. He made some
telling comparisons with French military practice,
noting that the American units remained chronical-
ly below strength because of the failure to have a
replacement battalion from which they could be
brought back up to strength after battles. "An
army," he reflected, "is an abyss into which men are
thrown by the thousand; they come out by the hundred if they come out at all."

On the way back to Washington he tells us more
about the difficulties officers and soldiers going on
leave encountered in finding space on the steamer
to Annapolis and on the trains; each man was expected to shift for himself, though he paid no fare,
and taverns at railway junctions were closed by order of the War Department whenever troops were
passing through—this made it extremely difficult for
them to get hot food or keep warm while waiting
for a connecting train. Since he himself was traveling in the company of a general officer, these re-
strictions were waived, but the trip was strenuous
nevertheless.

Once back in the capital he proceeded to bring
himself up to date on the tentative, unofficial peace

negotiations that were in progress, and he retails the gossip he had picked up from the party of Francis P. Blair, Sr., who was just back from a mission to the Confederate government, whom he met at Annapolis Junction on his return from the Army of the Potomac. As a trained lawyer and economist, Duvergier de Hauranne's comments on the economic position of the Confederacy were shrewd and to-the-point.

Duvergier de Hauranne was disappointed at his inability to see with his own eyes what was going on behind the Confederate lines, but he was able to take some accurate soundings of the Southern state of mind in these closing weeks of the Civil War by spending a few days in Baltimore, where the upper classes were still for the most part in sympathy with the Southern cause. He was there, in fact, on January 31, 1865, when Congress approved the text of the Thirteenth Amendment and sent it to the states for ratification. The congressional debates, and his conversations with pro-Southern ladies at a society ball, prompted him to summarize his impressions and ideas on American slavery, its economic significance and moral effects on both slaves and slave-owners. Needless to say, his judgments were strongly adverse to the South's "peculiar institution," for he had by this time, thanks in part to the influence of Sumner and other Bostonians, become a staunch Abolitionist; yet his criticism of Southern white society is, on the whole, temperate and he was deeply impressed by the dedication and heroism of the South's defenders.

In Philadelphia he found the moral atmosphere

(compounded of working-class self-help, prison reform, utilitarian education and municipal improve-
ment) much more to his liking; again he was taken
in hand by prominent citizens who conscientiously
showed him the new reservoir, the Cherry Hill penitentiary and Girard College for sheltering and educating orphan boys both white and black (though
the two were segregated in classes and living quarters). Returning to New York February 8, he made
a final round of social calls, packed his trunks and
left for Havana on the *Morro Castle* a week later; his
ship sailed in the midst of a blinding snowstorm
and he was almost arrested on suspicion of being an
escaping Rebel agent by a plain-clothes police inspector when he boarded the ship. He spent over a
month in Cuba and Martinique enjoying the mild
climate and recovering from the rigors of winter
travel in wartime America, then returned to France
on the *Impératrice Eugénie*.

For the next few years he continued to write on
politics, the American scene, the arts and the future
of democracy, contributing to the *Revue des Deux
Mondes* (in which his account of his American travels first appeared as a series of articles in the months
between August, 1865, and April, 1866). In 1869 he
published two books on the need for liberal reform
in France. He served with distinction as a captain of
infantry in the Franco-Prussian war of 1870, was
wounded and received the Legion of Honor for
bravery. A wartime friend of the republican leader
Léon Gambetta, Duvergier de Hauranne won the
election in July, 1871, to his father's former seat
in the Chamber of Deputies, representing the

Département du Cher. This conversion to moderate republicanism—he took his place with the parliamentary group known as the Left Center—apparently was accompanied by a break with his family, who continued to support the cause of the Comte de Paris, the Orleanist claimant to the throne. He was regarded as a rising young man of great promise and took an active part in public life both inside and outside the Chamber.

But his health (never robust) seems to have given way under the strains of political and journalistic activity; there are indications that his marriage in 1873 was unhappy and he left no descendants. A severe bout of pneumonia contracted in Wisconsin, when someone bribed the conductor to eject him from a sleeping berth he had reserved, obliging him to spend a cold night on the open platform between coaches, may have done permanent damage to his lungs. Then, as a result of over-exertion in behalf of his friend Gambetta in the great constitutional crisis of 1876, Duvergier de Hauranne fell gravely ill. He lived long enough to witness the great republican triumph in the elections of May 16, and his health even improved briefly for a few weeks, but a sudden relapse occurred in the late summer and he died on August 16. Had his career been prolonged, there are many indications that he might have become a major republican statesman, perhaps of the stature of Georges Clemenceau with whom he had a great deal in common, including residence in the United States and an intimate understanding of America and its experiment in popular government.

Published first as a series of articles and then

(1866) as a two-volume book under the title *Huit mois en Amérique*, Duvergier de Hauranne's conclusions on the meaning of what he had seen in the New World did not escape either praise or blame. On one hand his book was lavishly praised for its acute observation and vivid reporting style by the eminent author and critic Sainte-Beuve, who even went so far as to compare him favorably with Tocqueville as a reporter and stylist. (See *A Frenchman in Lincoln's America*, Vol. I, Historical Introduction, pages xxiii–xxvi.) On the other hand, his hostile treatment of slavery came under attack from partisans of the Confederacy and in particular from Edward Lee Childe, a Southerner resident in Paris and a friend of the writer Prosper Mérimée. Childe vehemently attacked Duvergier de Hauranne for generalizing from too few facts and from untypical situations, accusing him (quite unjustly) of having frequented only "the intellectually superior, cultivated and well-behaved people." Childe's four long articles were published between December 18, 1866, and January 10, 1867, in the ultra-conservative *Gazette de France* under the title "The Question of America: A Reply to M. Ernest Duvergier de Hauranne." He went on to defend the Southern plantation system against the Abolitionist critique which Duvergier de Hauranne had adopted:

He continually pushes slavery into the foreground because this is a more certain way of playing upon popular sympathies by repeating time and again that the blacks are whipped and mistreated, by holding up the heart-rending spectacle of that society which he has never seen, of those cruelties invented or exaggerated by the imagination of a [Harriet] Beecher Stowe or the bitterness of a Sumner. He takes pleasure in spreading out before us the hideous spectacle of a father selling his children and he gives free rein to his indignation. Mrs. Stowe likewise was able to pile up, in the course of a brief narrative dealing with a small cast of characters, a number of atrocious acts whose reality I do not deny, but which were rare, committed in isolation and promptly punished by universal reprobation.

He is completely mistaken when he says: "You know that there are in the Southern states strict laws that even forbid teaching a Negro to read." I lived in Virginia in 1856, and I saw the daughters of a general [Robert E. Lee] who since then has played a great role in the ranks of the Confederates, teaching young Negroes to read every day and instructing them in their religious duties. I know that this was done everywhere in the South on the plantations. There was no law that required it to be done, but neither was there any law that forbade it. The only state where the law prohibited such teaching was South Carolina because for many years the emissaries of the Abolitionists swarmed through the countryside distributing to the Negroes appeals to rebel and urging them to cut the whites' throats. [There were, in fact, laws in most of the Confederate States that made it a crime to teach a black person to read; these laws were not strictly enforced, and many plantation families ignored them.] Our young author ought to remember, however great may be his indignation against the South, that the ancestors of the present planters are far from being the only guilty ones. Some of the biggest fortunes of the northern United States and of England have had their origins in the Negro slave trade.

To these attacks and to a large number of others Duvergier de Hauranne replied (in the same journal) on January 7, 1867:

. . . I will not attempt to deny that I left Europe already inclined to support the abolitionist cause. . . .

But veracity compels me to say that I did not fall into any abolitionist "trap." It was only after quite a long period of uncertainty, of which my book itself must bear many traces, that I deliberately aligned myself with the party of Republicans devoted to the Federal Union against those self-styled conservatives who would place slavery before the Union. It is true that I did not wait so long before forming with one of the most honorable leaders of the abolitionist party [Sumner] those relations of respect and friendship which arouse Mr. Childe to so much indignation and pity. . . .

As for the Civil War, its causes are doubtless manifold, and it would be an exaggeration to say that everything turned upon the philosophical question of Abolition. But it is nonetheless certain that one will find the slavery issue at the bottom of all those considerations of interest or antipathy which drove the two factions to take up arms against each other. Nor is it any less a matter of public knowledge that the South was the first to open fire with cannon, that it tore the nation's flag to shreds without any provocation and that it voluntarily severed its ties with that Federal Constitution whose privileges are now being claimed on its behalf. . . . The South is conservative of nothing but slavery, and there is no principle of liberalism that exempts people from obeying the laws. . . .

I will release Mr. Childe from any charitable obligation to attribute my illusions to my youthful frivolity. If it is true that I was mistaken, I have at least the advantage of sharing my error with the vast majority of the American people.

Perhaps we may best conclude this introduction by citing a passage or two from a long and hitherto unpublished letter written by our author from the

Château d'Herry, the family home near Bourges, on
June 30, 1865, to his military friend and host, General Régis de Trobriand: [2]

My Dear General,

      I often think of you and our long conversations at
your fireside in the camp of the Army of the Potomac;
indeed, more often than one might think, judging from
the inexplicable silence I have observed since the month
of January. I recall leaving you with a promise to send
news of New York and Havana. Then you had no further
word from me—no more than as though I had taken a
final plunge into the Gulf Stream or the Caribbean Sea. I
will tell you right now by way of excuse, and before giving any other extenuating circumstances, that I am in general quite likely to experience this sort of eclipse, and
that you must not attribute it to forgetfulness but to one
of those irresistible attacks of laziness which become all-powerful tyrants for those who form the habit of yielding
to them—they make a person busy himself always with
tomorrow's tasks while putting off till tomorrow the
things he should do today. Besides, you are not the only
person towards whom I feel guilty. I have in my portfolio
two letters from the Comte de Paris and the Duc de
Chartres who have been awaiting a reply from me since
the month of November last. To repair this neglect, I
shall have to seize upon the propitious moment when
they present themselves vividly to my memory. Perhaps I
shall have to wait six months for this. For with lazy people nothing but the initial impulse exists, and whatever is postponed for a moment is likely never to be done.
      That is why I am taking advantage, in order to write to

    [2] Made available to Albert Krebs by kind permission of the
late Waldron K. Post of Bayport, Long Island, New York,
the owner of the original. Mr. Post was the grandson of General de Trobriand.

you, of a moment when my thoughts—which I have been trying to concentrate upon a tedious piece of work (preparing for publication my travel notes themselves)—irresistibly carry me back to that fireplace that flares up and crackles and roasts everyone's frontal parts while his behind is a lump of ice and the wind sighs in the tall pines. Nor do I forget your pipe on which you were always puffing, nor the small glasses so frequently replenished, nor the pale features of your good old Muller [probably the general's orderly] peering in through the barely opened door with his gray beard, his fur cap and his enormous Siberian hood. What a strange life I led for those five days! You will probably laugh at me, you who found it odd to be sleeping under a roof, who scorned to sleep on a mattress and laughed at featherbeds as foolishness! In my memories your headquarters seems to me one of those weird, fantastic places where one doubts that one has ever been—which, viewed from afar, seem much more like the illusions of a dream than solid reality.

And so it is with my whole journey. There is such a sharp, clear separation between the random life I led and my old way of life, now resumed, that it is impossible to join them together, for one or the other of them always takes on the appearance of a strange, unlikely experience. After a year of nomadic life I could scarcely imagine that it was possible to live otherwise, so far from my mind was the picture of "home"—so far as to seem almost legendary. On the train from Nantes to Paris, in a car filled with officers returning from Mexico whom their native air made half-crazy with joy, I was the only one who felt like a foreigner in his own country and had no clear idea of what he would find at the end of his journey. My thoughts dwelt involuntarily on some hotel where I might spend the night and when I knocked at the door of my father's house it seemed to me that I had fallen from another planet, that I was being brought back to life in some dimly remembered [these two words were written in English] former existence. I had to undergo several days of this singular hesitation between two worlds, learn to recognize people and things, and connect the present with the past. I was like a person who sees things he had forgotten since childhood. Finally I got across the bridge from one continent to the other, and so now, my dear General, it is you and your camp and your country that I see through a veil, surrounded by a cloud of myth that threatens to hide you even more completely.

When we were living under canvas you told me that your greatest solace was to remember and to cause to pass in procession before your hearth like Chinese shadows the events of your whole life. In truth, that is ones natural inclination when in solitude. I have become aware of this during these long days I am now obliged to spend lying on my steamer-chair immobilized—not by the gout—but by my doctor's orders. I've been lost in my dreams and, no matter what I attempt to do, everything evaporates in daydreams—so much so that I am lost in a fog: instead of explaining to you the "extenuating circumstances" as I promised, I am trying my judge's patience by afflicting him in advance with boredom.

After mentioning that he had been ill in Cuba and then pestered for three weeks in Paris by acquaintances to whom he was forced to recite twenty times over a speech he prepared for the purpose on American politics, he went on to say that:

I have gotten used to letting my inkwell get dry, and since then, during a trip I made to the seashore near Nice and afterwards here in the bosom of my family, I have felt nothing but a growing disinclination to take up paper and pen to the point where I've almost forgotten how to write. I will add that I have been ill for two weeks, but that I think I am now on the mend.

Finally, speculating about his friend's role in the last battles from Richmond and Petersburg to Appomattox, Duvergier de Hauranne hopes that he is safe and sound and that he will be able to carry out the plans they had discussed together, including a possible reunion in France. Or, failing that, our author expressed his hope that on his next visit to Long Island, perhaps in ten years' time, he would find his friend planting carrots and cabbages.

We regret that the pressure of affairs and his failing health prevented Duvergier de Hauranne from making this second visit to America. He and General de Trobriand never met again. But Duvergier de Hauranne did not forget either him or his other American friends, and through his contribution to the theory and practice of democratic republicanism in France after 1871 he did something to embody the respect and admiration he had learned for the best aspects of American life in the new republican society of France. Had it not been for a venal railroad conductor on the Milwaukee-LaCrosse line one cold night in late August, 1864, he might have lived to forge still more solidly the bonds that will always join together those who love freedom in France and America.

RALPH H. BOWEN
Professor of History
Northern Illinois University
DeKalb, Illinois

ALBERT KREBS
Conservateur
Bibliothèque Nationale, Paris

ACKNOWLEDGMENTS

THE EDITOR is grateful to a number of persons without whose aid this book would be much more imperfect than it is; none of these people, however, is responsible for its imperfections. In the first place thanks are due to Susan H. Bowen for preparing preliminary drafts of many chapters and for her valuable criticism of the entire manuscript. Research for the notes and for the identification of the many individuals whom the author refers to by their last names only was performed on a high level by two students of Northern Illinois University, Renae D. Fisher and David St. John; the latter's extensive and accurate knowledge of the military history of the Civil War proved extremely helpful at many points. Many especially difficult problems were successfully solved by Terry Sternberg's research in the contemporary press and other sources, and she is also responsible for locating a considerable share of the illustrations. Winifred Evans, Joan Luzbetak and Renae D. Fisher helped to eliminate many errors while typing the final draft. John H. Collins, Professor Emeritus of History, and Professor Kiffin Rockwell, both of Northern Illinois University, gave valuable help with classical references and kindred matters.

Our thanks for kind permission to use the portrait of Ernest Duvergier de Hauranne are due to the Bibliothèque Nationale, Paris. Robert, comte de

Montalivet, a descendant of the author's elder brother Emmanuel, has generously supplied information about the history and the traditions of the family. Thanks are also due to the libraries and collections which have allowed the use of illustrative materials belonging to them; appropriate credit is given in the picture captions themselves.

The editor is indebted to M. Albert Krebs for information and documents relating to General Régis de Trobriand, our author's host during his visit to the Army of the Potomac, and in particular would like to mention three published articles by M. Krebs: (1) "Un épisode des relations littéraires franco-américaines: Régis de Trobriand et la *Revue du Nouveau Monde* (1849–1850)," in *Revue de Littérature comparée* (Paris, Jan.-March, 1953) pp. 76–92; (2) "Le comte Philippe-Régis de Kérédern de Trobriand (1816–1897)," *Les Cahiers de l'Iroise*, revue éditée par la Société d'Etudes de Brest et de Léon, Oct.-Dec., 1967, pp. 202–206; (3) "Régis de Trobriand et le *Courrier des Etats-Unis*, journal français de New-York (1841–1865)," *Revue d'histoire moderne et contemporaine* (Paris, Oct.-Dec., 1971) pp. 574–588.

Finally, it is a pleasure to acknowledge the expert assistance given by Elizabeth Hadas and by Rachel Hadas Kondylis in making the index to this and the first volume of this work.

The editor is also grateful for the opportunity to be associated in this project with *The Lakeside Press*, R. R. Donnelley and Sons Company, whose tradition of fine printing and bookmaking cannot be too highly recognized.

Route of
Ernest Duvergier de Hauranne
1864-65

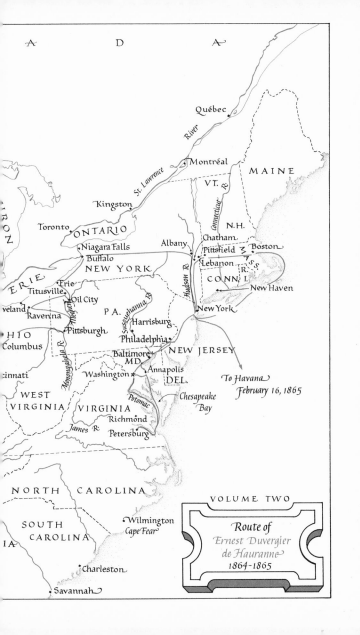

CANADA

Québec

St. Lawrence River

Montréal

MAINE

VT. R.

Connecticut R.

Kingston

N.H.

Toronto

ONTARIO

Niagara Falls

Albany

Chatham

Pittsfield

Boston

Buffalo

NEW YORK

Lebanon

R.I.

CONN.

ERIE

Erie

Oil City

Titusville

Hudson R.

New Haven

Allegheny R.

leveland

Ravenna

P.A.

Susquehanna R.

New York

HIO

Columbus

Pittsburgh

Harrisburg

Monongahela R.

Philadelphia

NEW JERSEY

Baltimore

MD.

Annapolis

DEL.

cinnati

Washington

To Havana
February 16, 1865

WEST
VIRGINIA

VIRGINIA

Potomac

Chesapeake
Bay

Richmond

James R.

Petersburg

NORTH   CAROLINA

SOUTH
CAROLINA

Wilmington

Cape Fear

IA

Charleston

Savannah

VOLUME TWO

Route of
Ernest Duvergier
de Hauranne
1864-1865

A Frenchman in Lincoln's America

1

The Presidential Election

Chicago
November 5, 1864

THE election campaign has finally reached its
climax. The day before yesterday a brass band
marched by just outside my window, followed by a
triumphal chariot full of women draped in banners.
I made my way behind the procession to the Court
House under whose portico I found several widely
spaced knots of people listening to the shouts of
various orators. Two men at an upper window were
showering them with leaflets. Everyone rushed to
pick them up, and I had some difficulty in getting
one for myself.

It was one of those amazing appeals to the voters
that is half circus poster and half sermon, written in
short sentences interspersed with single words occupying a whole line and all heavily spiced with
capital letters and exclamation points—the sort of
thing that shows how the Americans excel in catering to the lowest levels of public taste. It carried
this portentous title in large black type: "THE
TRUTH!" There followed a long list of the dire
consequences that will be sure to follow the election of McClellan. "Twenty million people under
the heel of 300,000 slave-owners!"—"A Confederacy of the Northwest!"—"A Democratic insurrection
(see the threats in the *World* and the Chicago

Times)!"—"McClellan leading the revolt (see the speeches at the Chicago Convention)!"—"The theater of war shifted from Atlanta and Richmond to New York, Cincinnati, Philadelphia and Chicago (see the Richmond papers supporting the Copperheads)!"—"Barricades; civil war!"—"Our streets drenched with blood—Our countryside laid waste—Our country's credit ruined—Gold at 2,000 and the price of necessities in proportion (see the history of the French Revolution and the Reign of Terror in Paris)!" Do you doubt any of this? Here is a table comparing "Republican Prices," "Democratic Prices," "McClellan Prices (those that would result from his compromise with Jefferson Davis—that is, guaranteeing the Rebel debt and paying the Southern states for their war costs," —and finally, "Rebel Prices," such as will be seen "if Belmont* succeeds in raising a Democratic insurrection." Tea, which now costs one dollar a pound, will cost 200 dollars; sugar will cost 50, and similarly for coffee, tobacco, spices, linen, cotton cloth, woolens, coal, iron and copper—lead alone, alas, "will be only too abundant." If this table appeals to you, "vote for the Rebel list."

But if, on the contrary, you want the Union's flag to "float gloriously from the Great Lakes to the Gulf, from the Atlantic to the Pacific, over a hundred free states without a single despot, over fifty million—soon to be a hundred million—people without a single slave, then sweep the country

* Mr. August Belmont is one of the leaders of the Democratic party. [He was, in fact, the chairman of the party's National Committee.]

Photograph Taken about 1865   Courtesy of the Chicago Historical Society

Chicago Court House

clean, once and for all, of the party that is so greedy (Floyd), pro-secessionist (Buchanan), hypocritical (Seymour), rabid (Vallandigham), traitorous (the Sons of Liberty), infamous (Fernando Wood),[1]—this gang of slave-merchants and perpetrators of rebellion, debts and taxes that calls itself the Democratic party! . . . Vote for Abraham Lincoln!"

Despite all these incendiary flares the crowd remained cool and phlegmatic, barely responding with a few automatic hurrahs because they seemed to feel these were expected of them. People came and went or exchanged listless comments in whispers, seemingly bored and not knowing what to do

[1] John B. Floyd, a Virginian, had been Secretary of War in Buchanan's cabinet; it was widely but probably wrongly believed at the time that he had supplied the South with large amounts of arms and munitions on the eve of secession, whether for cash or not, but his bad administration left the Federal military machine in weakened condition at the outbreak of war. James Buchanan was Lincoln's immediate predecessor as President; his policy of Union *and* conciliation drew unwarranted accusations of sympathy with the Confederacy. Horatio Seymour was Democratic governor of New York during the war years and was much attacked by Republicans for his Copperhead sympathies. Clement L. Vallandigham of Ohio, another Democratic politician, was arrested in May, 1863, for allegedly attacking the Lincoln government and its policies in a speech; he was tried and convicted by a military commission, but rather than make him a martyr Lincoln ordered that he be led outside the Federal lines and set free. Fernando Wood was a New York Copperhead who, with his brother Benjamin, published the New York *Daily News*; Fernando was a member of Congress and a leading figure in the Chicago Democratic Convention of 1864. [Notes by the editor will be indicated throughout this book by Arabic numbers; those by Ernest Duvergier de Hauranne will be shown by asterisks.]

with themselves. A passerby elbowed his way into one of the groups and shouted "Three cheers for McClellan!" Everyone burst out laughing. The next day the Chicago *Tribune* described the parade and the meeting in enthusiastic language, rivalling the accounts we read in our newspapers about the "indescribable enthusiasm" with which princes are always greeted. "Copperheads were seen," so says the *Tribune*, "taking to their heels, pale and terrified, as if overcome in advance by the fate that awaits them on November 8." One must distrust all such accounts of triumphal demonstrations, of "gigantic mass-meetings," that fill the newspapers of the two parties at this time. People lie as shamelessly in America as in Europe, with the sole difference that since here everyone has the right to lie, no one has the privilege of being believed.

In the evening I was present at a more impressive event. There was a meeting at Bryan Hall, a large auditorium built in the form of a theater and holding an audience of several thousand, the kind of hall that is a necessity of American life. The first and principal speech was by the governor of Illinois, Richard Yates, a former Democrat and a delegate to the Chicago Convention who since that time has deserted to the Republican camp in the hope (according to certain malicious gossip) of obtaining one of the two Illinois seats in the United States Senate at the end of his present term of office. He is a robust man and was wearing a blue suit with yellow buttons; though he tried to give an impression of gravity, he succeeded only in seeming slightly raffish and uncertain. He has a high forehead, long hair and a wide, humorous mouth; his face is drawn and lined, owing, I am told, to his immoderate use of strong liquor, a defect that is fairly common among men of the West. Except for a few "hangs" and "damns" and other inevitable vulgarities, his speech was lacking neither in force nor in wit. He began by speaking of his recent conversion, deliberately making fun of himself and painting a most unflattering portrait of his former supporters at the convention as a man who well knows whereof he speaks—*quorum pars magna fuit* [who played an important role]. As he grew more heated, his arms and legs began to execute a kind of dance; he bayed like a bloodhound as he hammered out his words with remarkable vigor; when he came to the end he was hopping up and down, striking his heels together to lend emphasis to his points—a trick quite frequently used by American orators.

After him came an incredibly energetic fellow with a beard, shining eyes and a nervous, vibrant voice; he shook his mane and ran up and down the platform while pouring forth in some foreign accent an exotic flood of richly figurative language that delighted the audience. The crowd, however, missed its favorite orator. "Coy! Coy!" they began to shout on all sides. Then amid cries of joy there arose a strange figure, thin and sad, bristling with a great black beard and long, thick hair, hollow eyes and a somber expression, who might have been a German Jewish peddler. "Sirs," he began in a booming, hollow voice, "I did not want to speak tonight because I did not see in the hall the flag of the United States. I never speak without having before my eyes the glorious emblem of our country." Then, with a proud, tragic seriousness, he delivered himself of a succession of inimitable buffooneries that made the whole room shake with laughter. He hung the Copperheads, cut off their heads, chopped them into mincemeat, roasted them over a slow fire and then, making a visit to "His Excellency the Devil, a gentleman of very good social standing," he amused himself further by portraying the Copperheads impaled upon glowing forks as they burned in the lowest depths of hell. The audience shivered with pleasure. Such are the sweetmeats that delight the common folk here in the West. As for the orator who delivered this fine speech, he is not a German Jew at all; he is Professor [Amasa] McCoy, a man famous throughout the whole West for his irresistible eloquence, one of the foremost in the battalion of speakers enrolled for the duration of this campaign in the Republican ranks.

At last old John Wentworth rose to his feet— "Long John," as he is called—a heavy drinker, a former mayor of Chicago and a member of Congress for the past fifteen years. He is the boss of the city government and still lives on the remnants of his former popularity. A real colossus, he has a long, heavy torso, a sort of hogshead perched on long legs; his head is small, bald and deep red in color; he has small, piercing gray eyes, a thick, square-cut jaw, a harsh voice made hoarse by drink—in short, the very prototype of the demagogue. He is said to be a talented speaker, but on this occasion I did not have the chance to admire his celebrated loquacity. He had come simply to throw down the gauntlet to those who hope to remove him from Congress, for here in Chicago it is against him that all the efforts of the Democrats are directed.

Long John, though he has strong supporters, has implacable enemies even in the ranks of his fellow-Republicans; he is said to be brutal, violent, and overbearing. He is accused of being both too eager to obtain and too miserly to spend public money. The Chicago police live in poverty; I have seen policemen in ragged uniforms and with holes in their boots; but Long John obstinately refuses to raise their pay. The Catholics, nearly all of whom belong to the Democratic party, are his special enemies. When the Sisters of Charity wanted to set up an establishment in this city, he subjected them to the crudest kind of persecution. The Chicago Democrats have exploited all these grievances; they have printed lists of candidates for the use of Republican voters—called "anti-Long John lists"—from which his name alone has been omitted. For the Democrats it is a matter above and beyond partisan politics: if they lose the general elections, they will still be satisfied if only Long John goes down to defeat.

The next day there were more big doings. Mr. Chase,[2] a former Cabinet member and the inventor of paper money, was to be in the city and speak to the Republicans in Sherman Hall. Two hours ahead of time the hall was full; the crowd even filled the

[2] Salmon P. Chase of Ohio, a leader of the Republicans' radical wing, who resigned as Secretary of the Treasury June 30, 1864, over the refusal of Congress to accept all of his financial policies. Lincoln later appointed him Chief Justice of the Supreme Court.

street outside, and an immense number pressed against the closed doors. Guided by an obliging friend I wormed my way through corridors jammed with people and climbed by a hidden staircase right onto the speakers' platform. The crowd there was also closely packed and I was almost suffocated. Suddenly I heard a rising murmur: "Look! There's Chase!" The crowd parted and I saw approaching a blond, clean-shaven man buttoned into a black frock-coat; he has an upright, military bearing and his manner was one of modest simplicity. A tall, strongly built man, he has an enormous head, though it is in good proportion to his athletic body. His fearless blue eyes, his strong, forceful features and indeed his whole bearing seemed to reveal a firm and powerful personality.

His eloquence is greatly praised, but I must admit that I didn't find it exceptional. It is true he had given a speech that morning and had travelled all day on the train. Popular speakers in America lead a hard life during election campaigns, one so demanding that party leaders are unequal to the strain and are obliged to take on as assistants a whole legion of professional orators who do the bulk of the work for them; they reserve for themselves the large cities and the most conspicuous occasions. In any event, the Chicago audience is not difficult to please; it goes into ecstasies over the flattest ideas, the most extreme and unsuccessful attempts to rescue a floundering figure of speech.

In Mr. Chase's whole speech there was only one passage that was at all interesting or noteworthy. After having tickled nationalistic prejudices by speaking of the army which, once the war is over, will liberate the American continent from the yoke of foreign despots, and of the navy, "the finest in the world"—which, if ever England and France should join together against the United States, would teach them both a lesson—he began to claim the credit for having bestowed on the nation the gift of paper money. Truly, one would have said, on observing his naive vanity, that the *assignat*[3] was a new and original discovery of his and that in a time of national distress it had taken supreme genius to hit upon the expedient of printing unlimited quantities of paper money which the public is obliged willy nilly to accept.

As for the ignorant and unthinking crowd, assembled only to look at a well-known person, in their joy at having satisfied their curiosity they acclaimed the very thing they complain of every day. "I promise you," said Mr. Chase, "that if you will put down this rebellion, within six months every greenback in your pockets will be as good as gold!" This statement was greeted by frenzied applause, by delirious cries of joy, as if the magic words of this new Law had in fact changed the contents of all their purses into gold. "Three cheers for the father of greenbacks!" And the three cheers duly shook the hall.

[3]The term *assignat* had come to be synonymous with rapidly depreciating paper money. The original *assignats* were issued during the French Revolution of 1789; by 1797, when they were repudiated, they had fallen to about two percent of their face value. John Law, alluded to below, was a Scottish financier whose bank and stock company, chartered in France, crashed in 1719 with the bursting of the "Mississippi Bubble."

Crowds are the same everywhere, so that when in Europe we speak of the superior enlightenment that allows America to maintain a liberty which we are unable to preserve, we do ourselves an injury we do not deserve.

These Americans, who look down on us from the height of their moral grandeur, are actually nothing but overgrown children. To be sure, they claim to tower head and shoulders over all the other peoples of the earth. Having easily seized the fortune that was ready-made for them in advance, they have the vanity and the lack of foresight of all lucky adventurers. Separated by nature from the European world and protected by three thousand miles of ocean, they believe they owe to their own strength alone the safety which is due above all to their remoteness. They believe themselves to be the giants of Brobdingnag and talk loftily of us poor Lilliputians of Europe.[4] During the Crimean War [1854-56] Senator Reverdy Johnson,* viewing with pity such a battle of pygmies, said with laughable fatuousness, "With our small army and General Scott, we could finish it off in a week."

Americans are offended when told that their country is subject to the same general conditions as the rest of humanity. This imperturbable assurance, this bold insolence of theirs, is in some ways a vir-

---

[4] References to *Gulliver's Travels*, by Jonathan Swift. The Lilliputians were six inches tall.

* Mr. Reverdy Johnson, Democratic senator from the state of Maryland, is not to be confused with Andrew Johnson, former senator from Tennessee and today [1866] President of the United States.

tue, for it permits them to run with confidence on ground that is crumbling underfoot and to prosper in circumstances where we would think only of locking our doors and windows and hiding in the cellar. Nevertheless, they must not, out of sheer bravado, let this pride push them to the edge of a precipice. Today they are undergoing the trial of their manhood. If they lose their footing, they will never again mount their stilts; but if they remain erect they will come out of this test stronger and wiser than before.

November 6, 1864

LAST NIGHT it was the Democrats' turn. They held a large meeting in Bryan Hall which I conscientiously attended. I even let myself be decorated, for twenty-five cents, with a McClellan badge that bears photographs of both McClellan and Pendleton, but the speeches were quite soporific. The first speaker—some "Honorable" or other—having worked himself up from a ponderous drone to the emotional heights of a steady scream, my attention began to wander and my ear to take in less and less. A small incident aroused me: the speaker, in one of his denunciatory passages, asked what Lincoln had done with the immense resources that have passed through his hands. "Done good for his country!" answered a voice from the back of the hall. The meeting was thrown into an uproar; many people were angry and indignant and threatening shouts were heard; the speaker had to extend his personal protection to the indiscreet heckler who had broken the rule of silence usually observed by opponents who attend meetings of the other party. After that I again closed my eyes, so I can't say what else may or may not have happened there that evening.

Certainly it was nothing very remarkable. These meetings are all alike, like the clubs whose torchlight processions disturb the streets of the city every night. When two opposing clubs meet, they confront one another, exchange insults, try to outdo one another with groans, whistles and catcalls, and finally separate after a brief scuffle in which a few heads are broken. Last night everything was quiet when a loud burst of music from wind instruments echoed through the streets. It was the "Norwegian Union Club" coming to serenade Long John Wentworth at the Hotel Tremont where that worthy citizen is in the habit of playing billiards until a late hour of the night. The long line of men carrying torches and lanterns remained for some time under our windows, shouting in chorus "Hip! Hip! Hurrah!" in honor of Long John. Democrats gathering on sidewalks and in the nearby streets responded with hisses and with cheers for McClellan. A band of young boys charged into the procession, but a few kicks and some burns inflicted by the flaming torches dispersed them. Great events like this occur every day in Chicago.

Sometimes the clashes are a bit more serious. At Clinton [Iowa] a Democratic meeting was broken up by stone-throwing. Elsewhere General [John A.] Logan, a Republican, having twice been assaulted by Democrats, was obliged to surround himself with a troop of armed friends and make his speech holding a loaded pistol in his hand. As a rule, though, the crowds are well-behaved, and the two parties manage to get along well enough in private. The Americans, who kill one another sometimes as readily as they would a dog, are not boisterous or quarrelsome by nature. It is only that they use stronger language than we do, and that where we would be content with an oath or an insult they use a knife or a pistol.

The Baltimore vote-stealers[5] have all been sentenced to life imprisonment, notwithstanding the fact that [Moses J.] Ferry has clearly been hand-in-glove with the police; no doubt some way will be found to keep him out of jail. However, the trial of Colonel [Samuel] North is still going on. The guilt of this other New York State electoral official, also denounced by Ferry, is far from being as fully proven as that of Donohue. Governor Seymour has tried several times to rescue Colonel North by having the case sidetracked; but the Secretary of War, [Edwin M.] Stanton, has obstinately refused to grant him his wish. The Democrats see in this trial an infamous Republican scheme to ruin them, while the latter are attempting, as in the case of the "American Knights," to exaggerate the importance of the trial. Fraud has certainly been committed, but isn't there also spying, provocation and scandal-mongering being set on foot by the government itself?

[5] In his first volume Duvergier de Hauranne had given an account of the discovery of these large-scale frauds involving the ballots of soldiers from New York state. One Edward Donohue, appointed as registrar by Governor Horatio Seymour, a Democrat, had engaged in or connived at wholesale falsification of records and other abuses. Colonel North and Ferry were among his accomplices.

The *Herald*, which holds aloof from both parties like Diogenes in his tub, sometimes expresses opinions that are full of justice and common sense; it points out that political machinations of this kind have been in use for a long time and that one should view them as nothing more than mutual warnings for each party to be on its guard. In a free country fraud will always be denounced by the injured opponent who will be on the watch for it. Don't forget that professional gamblers regularly cheat one another, but their tricks balance off in the long run and result in perfect equality.

November 7, 1864

THIS MORNING on awakening the city learned with amazement that it had just escaped a terrible calamity. A vast conspiracy had been exposed, a plot organized by the Democrats and the Rebels that was to have been carried out tomorrow. According to the posters outside the offices of Republican newspapers, there was a plan to free the ten thousand prisoners-of-war at Camp Douglas and to furnish them with arms for looting and burning the city. The crime was engineered by the "Sons of Liberty" and the conspirators have accomplices in Chicago. Two or three colonels, a captain and a judge—titles that abound in America: one finds colonels who are bartenders and majors who drive cabs—and a number of city employees and militia officers have been clapped into prison. Sixty guerrillas sent from the South were captured while they were awaiting the signal. The authorities have seized two wagons loaded with arms and munitions of war. All this, at any rate, is proclaimed by the laconic, mystifying and seemingly panic-stricken posters around which people crowd together as if in a state of shock. At the office of the *Evening Journal* the goggle-eyed crowd can see formidable samples of the arsenal with which the ten thousand Rebel prisoners were to have been equipped: one large horse pistol, one army revolver, one small pocket pistol in its case, a little powder flask and a box of cartridges the size of a watch. The conspirators' entire armament could be packed in a candy-box.

I almost forgot to mention the most terrifying weapon of all, the one most certain to spread panic—a large, rusty knife that looks like the stub of a broken cavalry saber—"found" (followed by three exclamation marks on the poster mounted in the window) "found under the shirt of a man who answered, when questioned as to the knife's purpose: 'It's to cut the abolitionists' throats!' " You see what kind of stage effects are used to arouse the indignation of the most enlightened people in the world! The Republicans pretend to be filled with righteous indignation; the Democrats, taken by surprise or at least pretending to be, claim that they are the victims of an atrocious hoax. They say the whole thing is just a crude trick, a pretext for intimidating arrests and threatening troop movements; the accused are called spies and accomplices of the authorities, and the alleged guerrillas are said to be hirelings of the police. Thereupon a new poster appears and the Republican papers run new articles giving more details of the conspiracy; they tell how the guerrillas got drunk in a tavern and how, when the "wiskey" [*sic*] had loosened their tongues, the Republic was saved. This whole story is unconvincing, and I can see in this business only monstrous fraud. The Democrats would certainly like to match it with a similar piece of trickery borrowed from Barnum's bag of tricks, but as the opposition party, with the governor, the city government, the army and the police against them, they are reduced to playing the martyr's role: they complain, they accuse, they reproach; but their position is a sorry and unenviable one because the mob always sides with those who furnish them the best entertainment.

Fraud, falsehood and violence—these three things play a large part in any American election campaign, as indeed they do elsewhere. I would say a little more than elsewhere if I didn't want to keep the place of honor for ourselves. We have the great advantage that with us all the official influence is on one side. Here the odds tend to average out, so that the advantage enjoyed by "right-thinking people" is neutralized. In our country we subtract votes, we "rectify" them, we maintain a paternalistic surveillance over the voter; his free choice is subjected to a salutary discipline. Here, by contrast, he is only too free to use or abuse his suffrage—even, on occasion, to multiply it. I am told that it is a common practice to send bands of mobile voters from one polling place to another. The fraud is so blatant that the press even dares to encourage it and to give, in so many words, this strange advice: "Vote early and often!" Thus it is not always numbers that give a party the majority, but the energy, activity and cleverness it can put into play. Sometimes it is just plain force, as when an armed gang takes control of a polling place, occupies it and allows no one but its own voters to enter—a custom, incidentally, that is more familiar to Southern "chivalry" than to the "vile populace" of the North.

An eyewitness of the last presidential election in Baltimore told me about an incident that cannot fail to give one an edifying view of the political customs of the South. In that city, then completely Southern in its sympathies—it was preserved for the Union only by the decisive action of General McClellan and Colonel, later General [Benjamin F.] Butler—the Republicans had to work hard to avoid being swamped by the Democrats. The party leaders had gathered near a polling place to encourage and rally their followers. The Democrats decided to dislodge them. They armed themselves with tiny daggers as fine as needles which they hid in their sleeves, and whenever an opponent turned his back he was struck from left and right and tormented by continual pinpricks. In the end they were forced to give up the fight and go away. Elsewhere a Democrat seeking to frighten voters away drew his pistol and pointed it at a citizen who was so bold as not to share his opinion. The latter took to his heels, but the Democrat ran after him and shot him down at close range. No one seemed at all upset; the police who were present did nothing, and the killer continued to pass out ballots for Breckinridge with his bloody hands. You will find this hard to believe and will ask if such a thing is possible. Don't forget that this man belonged to the governmental party in Maryland, the party that controlled every public office. In Baltimore people have seen the cannon aimed at the polling places, threatening to mow voters down with grape-shot as if they were prisoners or galley-slaves. There are some who call this sort of thing an "excess of liberty."

The Northerners are more peaceable. In general they prefer entertainment to fighting. Sometimes the Democrats set off fireworks; at another time the Republicans announce a huge parade with a "Union Car" and a "Monitor" and a naval engagement by torchlight on the lake. Enthusiasm is measured by the length of the parade. I am told that some have taken as long as three hours to march past. Minstrels in theaters and preachers in churches lend their aid to the contestants; mediums cause the dead to speak; not a single chance is overlooked. The story is told of an unfortunate candidate to whom a bear trainer was giving strong competition. He had an ingenious idea: he hired the fellow, added him to his entourage and presented the act free of charge to his audiences. After that, large crowds gathered to hear him and he was elected by a handsome margin.

This morning I saw marching through the streets a lot of people who care very little about who wins the election. There were about nine hundred European immigrants, men as well as women, Germans for the most part, shepherded by recruiting agents of the Mormon government. Several hundred of them pass through here every month; you can be sure that they are neither fanatics nor even converts; they are only poor folk fleeing the grinding poverty of their native land; they have been attracted here by the promise of good wages and an easy life.

The Mormons have made strenuous efforts for a number of years to increase their population. They already number a hundred thousand and they realize that the United States will soon overrun their territory if they do not make haste to fill it with a large population. All I hear about their wealth, their prosperity and the flourishing state of business in their city is truly marvelous. A farming and manufacturing people, they are well in advance of the rough adventurers and miners the United States sends out to the western mountains. They have become the suppliers of all their neighbors and keep them, so to speak, in a state of dependence upon their industry. Mule teams setting out from Salt Lake City supply the territories of Montana, Arizona, Idaho and even parts of Colorado and New Mexico with all sorts of produce and equipment.

The Mormons no longer have very much hope of surviving as an independent nation surrounded by the Federal Union. They are said to be ready to give up some of God's ways in order to adopt the ways of their contemporaries. Their method of recruiting new settlers does not tend to increase the number of believers. There is nothing, not even the sacred dogma of polygamy, that is not losing ground. Indeed, one may hope that before many years this strange society will conform to the prevailing laws and customs rather than risk its own destruction.*

* In the month of May, 1865, Mr. Schuyler Colfax, formerly Speaker of the House of Representatives, and some other leading politicians paid a visit to the Mormon territory, coming, it appears, more as ambassadors than as simple

November 8, 1864

THE VOTING has finally begun. I have just been walking for five hours from one ward to another without seeing the slightest sign of disorder anywhere. I had expected at least to find noisy, excited crowds surrounding the polling places, ready to draw their knives. How astonished I was in the first ward I visited to see a calm, quiet group of three or four hundred persons who were strolling up and down near the polling place talking in low voices! The arrangements for voting are not elaborate: there is a window from which a pane has been removed where an official receives and scrutinizes the ballots. A board fence rails off a narrow passage along the wall in such a way as to force the citizens to walk in single file past the window. The latter are patient and good-humored and wait for two or even three hours in a queue until their turn comes. Party workers stand about in little groups; those whose job is to hand out ballots offer them silently and without trying to force them on anyone; often men of opposite party allegiance will be seen talking to one another in a friendly way, calmly discussing the merits of their respective candidates. Here and there you may see one or two bewildered Ger-

---

tourists. They were received with open arms and Mr. Colfax, speaking at a large meeting held in his honor in Salt Lake City, was so bold as to refer to polygamy as a barbaric custom which civilized neighbors could not long tolerate; he urged his listeners to give it up, assuring them at the same time of the good will of the United States, which would be happy to regard them as friends and brothers. There was a time when the Mormons would have stoned him to death for saying such a thing. Times must have changed.

mans being guided to the polls like Panurge's sheep.[6] One hears quips, profanity and the whole charming collection of epithets and exclamations with which the Americans embellish their thoughts; sometimes two opponents will give one another a shove or a belligerent glare, but these quarrels are soon pacified by a handshake. Now you know just what these dreadful American elections are like.

It is true that the rain has done its part by cooling some over-heated heads; it is true that the city government rigorously enforces the law that keeps the saloons closed on election day; and it is also true that fear of the Federal troops stationed at Camp Douglas, and the effect of the arrests announced yesterday, have kept the Democratic minority in check.

Furthermore, the Americans are not in the habit of blurting out all their thoughts or of noisily provoking fights just for the fun of it. They exchange civilities like "God damn you!" in a cool, mocking tone with a smile showing on their lips. Every nation has its own ways—in our country we love arguments and go out of our way to start them; we indulge in a great deal of loud talk in which there is not the slightest trace of real animosity. Here, when it comes to a serious quarrel, they go directly

[6] The author makes reference to an episode in Rabelais's *Gargantua and Pantagruel*, Book IV, Chapters 5-8. Panurge, the jester, quarrels with a sheep-trader named Dingdong on board ship. To punish the latter for his arrogance Panurge first buys his biggest ram at an exorbitant price, then throws the ram overboard; the rest of the flock follow their leader, carrying Dingdong and his henchmen with them to a watery death.

and without any transition from calm, ironic conversation to pistol shots fired at point-blank range.

This is why people would rather avoid arguments. Betting is preferred to fighting. Public meetings are the people's favorite entertainment and elections are the great game of chance, the American national lottery. Men bet on the elections as on a horse-race or a cock-fight, and this is one of the most characteristic features of this country's political customs. The mania is not limited to rich capitalists like Mr. Belmont, who wagers large sums in order to create confidence;[7] it is a game that everyone plays and around each polling place there is a sort of open-air gambling house where bets are offered and taken. "Six shillings there'll be a majority of at least 600!" "Ten dollars on a majority of 500!" "One to twenty!" "Two to ten!" All the odds are worked out and posted for each candidate. I am sure there are speculators or professional bookmakers who take bets as they do at racetracks such as Ascot or Chantilly.[8] Meanwhile, large decorated wagons drawn by four horses and filled with hired musicians drive about the city in the rain, stopping

[7] General Benjamin F. Butler describes in his *Autobiography and Personal Reminiscences* (Boston, 1892, p. 761) how on the Thursday evening before Election Day, between the acts at the opera in New York, August Belmont offered to bet $1,000 that McClellan would win but declined to close with the general when he accepted the bet. Butler also notes that on Election Day Belmont's vote was challenged on the ground that he made election bets, "and under that challenge he declined to vote." (*Ibid*, p. 770)

[8] Ascot was and is Britain's most famous and fashionable race-course, while Chantilly, north of Paris, was its French equivalent.

in each ward opposite the "polls" where they encourage party members by playing patriotic tunes. Some wear gray uniforms, others blue. Wounded soldiers do voluntary sentry duty opposite each polling place to impress the voters. This is, after all, a harmless charade, but don't imagine that they came to be there just by chance. Here, on the home grounds of up-to-date sharp practice, everything is calculated and prepared in advance, and one must not be taken in by all the theatrical effects contrived by the parties for staging these elections.

Everywhere I went I acted as though I were a voter, taking a ballot from one party and refusing the others, doing the opposite in another place, elbowing my way into this group and that, listening to the oratorical contests among local party leaders. Everywhere I found evidence of strong feelings held in check, along with much good-humored joking. When, on approaching a polling place, I saw two ward leaders conversing in a friendly way as they handed out ballots for opposing candidates, I felt quite certain that their good manners were not very sincere and that their main purpose was to keep a close watch on each other. When I accepted a ballot from one of them, his rival—seeing that he had no hope of winning me over—stood aside and let me pass without a word, but he certainly had a scornful and disappointed expression on his face.

Wandering from precinct to precinct and pretending to vote everywhere, I must have seemed like one of those itinerant voters who are paid to run all day from one part of the city to another, joining all the queues in order to cast their votes in as many districts as possible. Several times I thought I was being looked at askance. At the polling place in the tenth ward a young man wearing the gray-blue uniform of a wounded soldier muttered to a companion out of the corner of his mouth—but loud enough for me to hear—"That fellow has a lot of gall, confound him! I've run into him at all the polls; he has already voted four times." I was tempted to put his theory to the test: I should have cast a vote for McClellan here, a ballot for Lincoln there, keeping my conscience quiet by balancing my votes for Republicans with as many for Democrats.

The informality of these elections, it seems, is so great that an unknown foreigner can present himself at the polls, mumble a false name to the official who asks for it and then proceed to vote as though he were a citizen; indeed, the experiment has actually been made. In fact, considering that so many people here move from place to place or have just arrived from abroad, no one can be very sure who is a foreigner and who a citizen. If the Federal law were to be scrupulously observed, perhaps half the voters of Chicago and perhaps as many of the other residents of the state of Illinois would be disenfranchised. Of all the Germans and Irishmen who come each year to scrabble for a living in the West, there is perhaps not a single one who dreams of fulfilling the strict requirements and waiting for the expiration of the long period of residence prescribed by law for those who seek to become citizens of the United States. They pay attention only to the laws of Illinois which, like most of the western states, gives the vote to foreigners after only six months of legal residence. Furthermore, the Federal law also states (in rather self-contradictory fashion) that any citizen of any state of the Union is at the same time a citizen of the United States. To tell the truth, the exercise of political rights is not regulated by any definite provisions of law; the vote belongs to anyone who demands it, sometimes even to anyone who simply helps himself to it. And if I were willing to change my nationality, I should not despair of being included this very day among those who are voting for Mr. Lincoln.

The American elections have preserved many of the uncertainties and irregularities of the British system. The other day a Democratic paper denounced a Republican plot to bring to some city in Ohio a whole army of fraudulent voters who would then be returned by railroad to vote in their own town. The law prescribes a secret ballot, but without providing for any effective means of enforcement. Furthermore, custom is generally opposed to secrecy, with the result that voting is, to all intents and purposes, public. All citizens have the right and duty to be on the watch for abuses; they can stand behind the wooden partition as the voters file past, listening to the questions of the official and the answers of the voter. One can see how alert they are, leaning over the railing, studying faces, counting votes, sometimes interrupting with the traditional formula: "I challenge that vote!" No one could be more brazen than the guilty person caught red-handed; he knows what a great risk he is running, the severe penalties the law provides for. He tries to bluff, but in the end he takes back his ballot and that is an end to the matter. This is the best method of supervision, but when fifteen to eighteen hundred people vote one after another at the same place, not much attention can be given to each one. The election judge himself is the agent of a party, and even if he doesn't use his power to alter votes, at least he will never use it to question the votes of his friends. The right to appoint these judges belongs to the ward leaders who form what is known as the "ward committee," which is itself directly elected by universal [manhood] suffrage. It is to be feared that he acts less as a disinterested arbiter, obliged to be impartial even against his own party, than as a Democrat or a Republican anxious to serve its interests.

There is one thing that makes up for all these evils: it is the spirit of order and legality that is manifest after the battle. This is the great merit of American democracy. It demonstrates the utility even of their casual attitude toward justice that so often astonishes those who are accustomed always to consider absolute values. The Americans are a practical people, wise enough to accept accomplished and irrevocable facts. As soon as the election is over, all complaints cease. People no longer care to know if, submerged in the flood of the popular vote, there were a few fraudulent ones. They are more concerned to consider whether it is more prudent or more advantageous to recognize the new authority or to combat it. Each one, while straining to seize the prize of this rather tumultuous battle from his adversary, is resigned in advance to hand it over to him when the end of the jousting-match has

arrived. So, at the very hour when you would expect the flames to break out, the fire is extinguished
as if by a miracle, and all the threats of the two
parties are appeased by the performance of a great
national duty.

November 9, 1864

PRESIDENT LINCOLN has been elected by a large majority. Since yesterday it has been evident that the
Republicans would carry Chicago. This morning
we learned that they have won in all states except
New York and a few others where the vote, when
counted, is likely to go to the Democrats. All night
long, people have been crowding into the newspaper offices and even into the lobby of my hotel,
avidly reading the hourly dispatches brought from
the telegraph company and posted up in big letters
on the walls. The Democratic papers, which yesterday were spouting fire and flames, have a hang-dog
look this morning and try to console themselves for
their defeat by emphasizing local victories.

The most amazing thing is the profound calm in
which the great event has taken place. The newspapers bring us no reports of rioting, no tales of violence or disorder. Over the whole territory of the
Union, from Boston to St. Louis and from Washington to Chicago, Election Day was a day of truce,
and all parties laid down their arms with astonishing unanimity. Never, so long as the Republic has
existed, has anyone seen so peaceful an election; yet
never was an election held under more dismal por-
tents. The most optimistic expected some blood to
be spilled. Some went so far as to predict that the

re-election of President Lincoln would be the signal for general insurrection and anarchy. But after the rowdy carnival of the election campaign, when all sorts of passions were unleashed and the hour of danger seemed to have struck, the people sensed the solemnity of the occasion and voted quietly. This turbulent democracy, which had seemed on the point of tearing itself to pieces, spontaneously felt the need to impose self-discipline and to invest the choice of a new government with gravity and order. One must not hesitate to proclaim it from the housetops: this is an event that does the greatest honor to the good sense and patriotism of America.

What, then, is the guardian angel that protects democracy? To what does she owe this spirit of order, perseverance and wisdom which her friends themselves have never counted among her virtues? She owes it to her "party organizations." These despised words contain the whole secret of American liberty. These slapdash conventions that are convened in the name of the people to nominate candidates and draw up the party's program, are obeyed with a unanimity that proves the political intelligence of the country. In America there is no issue so local, so private, that it is not connected with the great political and constitutional questions which divide the nation; the questions of war and peace, of Lincoln or McClellan, are linked with the choice of a police chief or a street-cleaner.

It is true that they do not have our admirable centralized administration which, according to the time-honored phrase, "the whole world envies us." Nor do they have the no less complete political centralization that places the opinions of a whole nation under one management. Political centralization does come spontaneously to exist here nonetheless, directly encouraged by liberty, but this unity arises within two or three large parties that share public support. These powerful associations, which alternately govern and are governed, conquer and are conquered, resisting or attacking one another simultaneously in every part of the country, always have as a rallying point some important question of national interest and develop among the citizens who belong to them a unanimity more complete than under the most absolute despot.

On this day of the presidential election, which one might call the culminating point of American political life, the parties contest not only the choice of a president, but also fight for control of all the local offices which, because of their common origin, are of the same complexion as the central power. Each party therefore makes up what is called a "ticket"; the ballots carry not only the name of the presidential candidate and the party's presidential electors, but also those of the governor, lieutenant-governor, the governor's cabinet officers, members of Congress, members of the two branches of the state legislature, and even judges in the states where judicial office is elective. Thus the election that has named Abraham Lincoln and Andrew Johnson President and Vice-President of the United States, has at the same time made Richard Oglesby governor of Illinois, William Bross lieutenant-governor, S[amuel W.] Moulton representative-at-large for the state, John Wentworth representative for the First

District, and so on. Once the candidates are nominated, they are all elected or rejected together, and the "ticket" of the winning party is always elected in its entirety.

In point of fact, each party has organized in advance a complete alternative government, even including a swarm of minor politicians ready to fill the lesser offices. Every four years the whole administration can be turned out of office. If the President changes, so do all other officials from top to bottom—that is, wherever the new administration has obtained a majority. This vast network of party organizations doubtless has its drawbacks. It puts everything in question at the same time and makes everything continually dependent on the passions of the day. Moreover, by making public employments into resting-places where no one stays very long, the party system gives power to greedy adventurers rather than conscientious administrators. These temporary rulers consider public office a prize of which they want to carry off at least a morsel; but the same spoils system gives to the parties a discipline that makes voting prompt and predictable. Every citizen enrolled in one army or the other presents himself during the campaign at his assigned rank and post. Except, perhaps, in New York and in cities with a large Irish population, one almost never sees in America the thoughtless voter who comes to the polls without knowing why, who votes without knowing for whom, and who is easily won over by the first offer of a "ticket" accompanied by a glass of brandy. Here all the voters have received their marching orders in advance, and if most of them have nothing but a hazy notion of the consequences of their votes, they nevertheless agree without exception that—depending on which party they belong to—McClellan is a coward or Lincoln is an "s. of a b." [*sic*].

You are aware that the Constitution of the United States provides that the election of a president shall take place in two stages. This formula has become a pure legal fiction. The voter in the first stages imposes a binding mandate on the second-stage elector, who is committed in advance to support a certain candidate. The sovereignty of the people is publicly recognized to the degree that the ballots carry the names of the presidential candidates above the list of electors pledged to them. Of what use, then, is this complicated but empty formality, this apparent continuation of a principle of which hardly a shadow remains? The Americans would be very reluctant to change it. They think this system has the advantage of forcing the parties to be disciplined, of tightening their organization and obliging them to give united support to their chosen candidates. The more democratic their institutions are, the more indispensable the two-stage election [the Electoral College] seems to them. It is not, as our own democrats imagine, an underhanded way of nullifying the popular will; on the contrary, it is the only way of saving democracy from impotence and confusion.

Finally, it is the party organizations which, in American democracy, generate and preserve national unity. A legal enactment is not sufficient to create a nation. And in spite of the supreme authority of the Constitution of the United States, the Federal Union could not maintain its authority over separate and sovereign [state] governments if the latter were absorbed in parochial quarrels. If the Americans are to be a united people, it is essential for all the passions and all the interests of local factions to be linked with a set of principles common to all, and that is precisely the service rendered by the parties. It matters little that the United States Constitution leaves to a state such as Illinois or Missouri a great part of its sovereign independence, that it even grants (for the sake of argument) the absurd right of secession, if the same ideas and feelings inspire the Republicans of Iowa and those of Maine, if the Democrats of Ohio follow the same political leadership as the Democrats of New York. Nothing gives people a conservative bent like the practice of having the government present itself frequently to the public [to have its mandate renewed].

Democracy carries within itself its own antidote. While a strict system of external order often merely gives rise to a false sense of security by hiding from a complacent society the fire that is consuming it from within, this system, which brings political conflicts into the open air where they seem to represent a continual danger, is in reality the most powerful source of unity and the surest guarantee of political order. If daily life is less calm, at least there are fewer of the sudden explosions that paralyze a nation with surprise and shock so that it becomes the half-dazed captive of the first [dictator] who comes along. There is less danger in having an opposition and parties than in a government upheld only by the habitual docility of the people. That is the evil against which American democracy is protected. It may sometimes be found weak and unprepared in the face of some unexpected peril; it may squander or leave unused material resources which an absolute ruler would have been better able to manage; but it can never lack moral strength, for this strength is drawn not from its administration and army but from the very heart of a nation through the arteries of the great parties that govern it.

November 10, 1864

THIS MORNING I went to Camp Douglas. On a bare, sandy plain there is a large enclosure or palisade surrounding a kind of city of wooden buildings. There isn't a tree nor a blade of grass; everywhere the ground is trampled hard. The prisoners are quartered three to a room in wooden barracks neatly aligned along the streets. Since the scare of November 7, and for several days afterward, visitors' passes have been refused to all outsiders, so I was not able to see the prisoners themselves in their quarters; but I have seen with my own eyes the proof of the fantastic plot which I outlined to you the other day with so little belief in it. Major[9] W.,

[9] No high-ranking officer whose surname began with "W" was in command or second-in-command of Camp Douglas at the time. The camp was commanded by Gen. B. J. Sweet throughout the war. It seems probable that Duvergier de Hauranne was conducted on a tour of the camp by an officer whose name or rank he did not clearly understand; in any event, "Major W." has proven impossible to identify, though he may possibly be Aquilla Wiley of the 8th Regiment, Veterans' Reserve Corps.

Photograph Taken about 1864

Confederate Prisoners at Camp Douglas, Chicago

who commands the camp, has shown me the loaded rifles, the cases full of loaded revolvers, the supplies of cartridges, powder and detonating caps that were seized in a hotel near the camp gate. The weapons are of such a nature as to leave no doubt concerning the use to which they were to have been put, and the abundance of the supplies, the haste with which they seem to have been prepared, the innocent appearance of the trunks that held them— all this convinced me that the Republicans have invented nothing but the theatrical touches and the ridiculous details that have only had the effect of casting doubt on the truth. People often make these miscalculations in this fine country of America where lies pour down so hard that truth itself cannot go unclothed.

Camp Douglas serves as a prison for ten thousand Confederates guarded only by a single regiment of ill or convalescent soldiers. The Major himself, a young man of twenty-five, crippled for life, hobbles about on his crutch with an agility that is painful to watch. The only physical defense is a frail wooden fence with a guards' platform running around the top. Sentinels are posted here and there, but it could easily be breached by one or two blows of an axe. It is understandable that sixty resolute men could plan on gaining access at night to the prisoners' quarters, arming them and then setting them free to loot the city.

I have been given a most gracious welcome by M. Ravin d'Elpeux, the French consul, an excellent man of great ability, who gave me a great deal of valuable information. The first time I called at his house a play was given in French. I saw gathered together there the whole of the small French colony of Chicago. It is composed for the most part of rather recent immigrants, some of whom have still not given up hope of returning home some day. In the West, and especially along the Mississippi River, there are, moreover, some completely French settlements. These have been in continuous existence since we gave up our colonies and they have lost none of their national character. In Detroit, a city whose very name betrays its origin, French is still spoken in many families.

M. d'Elpeux has visited some villages in Illinois which have remained entirely apart from American society, where the Picard and Norman dialects are still spoken. The Americans are so thoroughly detested in these settlements that they cannot live there, and in one of these towns, a place of several hundred inhabitants, the only person who understands English well is a Yankee merchant who used to go there every year to trade and has finally decided to stay for good. Seeing these places which time has passed by is like being transported back to the eighteenth century. One of the Chicago libraries has an old map, handed down from our first colonists; it is covered with French names, most of which have since disappeared. On this map all of North America is shown as part of the French Empire. This mute witness and a few poor hamlets are all that remain, in the midst of the American flood, of those times that almost seem antediluvian. But there is something touching in the remarkable persistence of the old French culture. While the Germans, for example, grow new skins in a few years' time, we keep our identity everywhere we go. We would rather be snuffed out by a conquering nation than adopt its language and customs.

Richmond, Indiana
November 11, 1864

HERE I am once again a victim of the railroads' negligence. This time I didn't lose my baggage; it is I myself who got stranded in mid-journey along with a whole trainload of other travelers. I left Chicago last night, hoping to reach Cincinnati by this morning; but this morning we aren't even halfway there. Finally they simply dropped us off here beside the tracks, twelve hours behind schedule, to wait for the next train. The line, it seems, is blocked by military traffic and the company makes up for its lost civilian business by letting the customers take their chances. Nothing could be more boring than the countryside where we now are; Sologne or the Beauce are not more monotonous. From Chicago to Cincinnati stretches a limitless plain, without hills, without variety, where one has no sense of the distances; there are vast, age-old forests; there are depressing, poorly tended fields that lie in a narrow strip along the railroad track; the villages are all alike, with their wooden shacks and dried-up corn-fields; then the forest begins again. This country has surely been overrated because of the imagination or mendacity of travelers.

Richmond, where I have been strolling about to kill time, is a pretty little town near the border between Indiana and Ohio. Judging from a hasty inspection, the population must be between six and seven thousand. No traveler has seen all America if he has only gazed to his heart's content at the majesty of her forests and the filth of her great cities. He must also see these new small "cities," still hardly more than villages, which represent the transition from an agricultural to an industrial way of life. A stone's throw away from the main streets are tilled fields and meadows still surrounded by houses; beyond, some hundred yards away, looms the edge of the untouched forest. There are a few large houses, then cottages of wood or brick, all neat and well fenced, some even tastefully embellished, the brand-new churches, a schoolhouse from which comes a chorus of children's voices reciting their lessons like a psalm, long avenues lined with gas lamps. Along the main street are a few large buildings, as in a large city, which rise as though by enchantment in the midst of a cluster of little gardens that are green and full of flowers. Everything testifies to ease and well-being. Ohio is a state of relatively old settlements, where wealth has had time to spread and establish itself.

It is not the same in all the states of the West, not even in those that seem to have the most brilliant prospects. There, in addition to the great fortunes acquired recently and risked continually in industry and commerce, one can find many people still struggling to overcome the poverty they brought with them. In Wisconsin there are whole communities of Germans and Swedes who are almost starving to death, driven to the wall by the competition of the Illinois farmers. This is true even on the prai-

ries, where the topsoil is fourteen feet deep and all
that one needs to bring new land under cultivation
are a few sulphur matches, a plow and two horses—
even here the farming families that have recently
arrived from Europe subsist only by waging a bitter
daily battle with poverty. This, I am told, is due to
several causes. First, the Illinois Central [Railroad]
Company puts a high price on the lands originally
given to it when it sells these same lands in small
parcels to the immigrants. In the second place, the
roads are very poor and there are never-ending difficulties in getting the year's harvest to market. The
company, having no competition to fear, can control freight rates and keeps them at an exorbitant
level. Often the unlucky farmers cannot market
their crops for lack of a little ready cash to pay the
cost of shipment. Nor is this all; there are no real
roads, so that a distance of five miles to the nearest
railroad station through woods and swamps is the
equivalent of sixty miles on our highways. During
the rainy season it is impossible to do any hauling.
If, by good luck, the winter snow is deep and hard,
everyone hastens to hitch up his sled and carry his
harvest to the railroad; but then the market is glut-
ted and the crop doesn't even sell for what it cost to
produce. In short, this existence is so harsh and precarious that many settlers, burdened with debts,
have decided to make certain at least that they and
their families have enough to eat by making a deal
with an agent who undertakes to supply them with
enough necessities to keep them alive in return for
the whole produce of their land. In this way they
are able to survive, but you can imagine in what a

state of penury and dependence. Even then the taxes must be paid, and the interest on their debt with a payment on the principal is due to the company that sold them the land. The latter is very stingy in granting them credit, so that they must borrow in advance on the wheat they are harvesting and thus they depend for their daily bread on a stranger who never pays them in cash. It was poverty that drove them here from Europe, but they find life almost as hard and humiliating here.

The fault lies with the railroad companies. If, instead of keeping their debtors always at the very brink of insolvency and pressing their claims to the last penny, they would instead moderate their demands a little, perhaps these poor people would repay their forebearance a hundred fold. It is assuredly their right—the absolute right of everyone—to attach whatever conditions he pleases to his services. Monopoly is always an evil; but free competition is not a sovereign panacea either. There are natural monopolies that cannot be destroyed, and their consequences ought at least to be mitigated. These companies had to obtain charters and concessions from the government; I don't see why in exchange the state could not insist on moderate rates and effective operating rules.

Columbus
November 13, 1864

I DIDN'T stay long in Cincinnati. Everyone I wanted to see there was out of town. So I hurried on to Columbus where I am now enfolded in the quiet of Sunday. Columbus is the capital of Ohio, located in the exact center of a big quadrilateral bounded by "the beautiful Ohio" River, Indiana, Pennsylvania and Lake Erie. All around the city lies the immense, monotonous plateau of the [Old] Northwest. There is scarcely a dip in the terrain within a radius of sixty miles. The city itself is attractive and is laid out on a large scale. Across from my hotel, on a large square planted with trees, rises the gigantic mass of Ohio's famous State House, which rivals the Capitol in Washington. This ugly building, with long colonnades, peristyles copied from some Greek temple and a truncated spire—a sort of thick, squat tower which looks unfinished—has nothing remarkable about it except for the vast scale on which it is built.

It's Sunday, and that one word tells the whole story—silence, immobility, solitude. The hotel seems to be asleep. For company I have only a provincial newspaper, and a rather poor specimen at that. The Republicans have definitely carried all the states except New Jersey, Kentucky and Delaware. The Democrats still contest the outcome in New York state and the [New York] *World* claims that Governor Seymour has been re-elected. The city itself, despite the presence of General Butler, who had been sent there to maintain order, gave a majority of 37,000 to McClellan. A few timid complaints are being made by the losers; they attribute their defeat to the army vote. Even if that should turn out to be true, I am not inclined to feel much sympathy for a party that has set new records for dishonesty. I am quite willing to believe that armed force had a significant influence on the election in the border states; I admit that in Louisiana, for example, and in Tennessee, where Nashville, a Rebel city, contributed only twenty-five votes to McClellan, farces were played out under the threat of the cannon and cavalry saber. General [Eleazer A.] Paine, the "Butcher of Kentucky," who was so dramatically relieved of his duties there not long ago, has now been given a command in Tennessee and has put into practice the theory of government he once outlined to the leading citizens of Paducah, who had been arrested and imprisoned at his orders. "You are a bunch of rascals," he said, "and I'm going to take everything you've got and leave you naked; I'll shoot you or hang you if I have to. I will do whatever I must to make every man and woman in this place say, 'I belong to the United States'." With such courtesies and the law of the "test oath," backed up from time to time by a military execution, people are kept in a state of salutary fear and elections are carried out in military fashion and under strict discipline.

Nevertheless, if you set aside Tennessee, Louisiana, West Virginia, even Missouri where, in spite of everything, the Republican party has a large following, and Maryland, where the new constitution abolishing slavery in the state was voted by only a bare majority—a few hundred votes at most—and if you even set aside the vote of Nevada, which was admitted to statehood just before the election, President Lincoln still has an imposing majority. In 1860, he received 168 electoral votes against 49, although the popular vote taken as a whole gave 139,000 more votes to the Democrats. This time he is assured, it is said, of 213 votes against 21 in the Electoral College, and in the popular vote he has beaten his rival by 400,000 votes.

The Richmond press pretends to rejoice. "The Republicans," they say, "cannot flatter themselves that they will ever lead us back to the Union and, since they cannot force us to come back, they will soon be obliged to agree to our independence." Is this uncompromising view really sincere? I doubt it very much, or rather, I have no doubt at all about it. The Confederates are making the best of a bad situation and are trying to turn a brave face to the enemy. They know very well that the Republicans will never recognize them and that the only way of denying them their victory is to keep on fighting to the last man. They can decide the future of the Union; but the people of the North, for their part, will determine whether they live or die. Will they be mad enough to refuse to live?

In any event, slavery's last hour has struck. It is true that the liberation of the black race is being accompanied by a great massacre of emancipated slaves. Both sides have freed them from their chains only to use them as cannon fodder, as obedient gladiators in the butchery of the battlefield. This is not precisely the kind of emancipation a philanthropist would desire, but it is the American way. From the moment they cease to be owners of human livestock they discover how much they dislike the competition [of the blacks]. In Illinois, which just gave a 20,000-vote majority to the policy of the abolitionist manifesto "To Whom It May Concern," there is a law forbidding blacks to enter the state. Those who have lived there for a long time have still not been given the right to own property. Even the boldest innovators, the ones who are accused of sacrificing the whites to the blacks, of starving the families of citizen-soldiers for the benefit of ex-slaves hired as mercenaries, still do not advocate either political rights or civil equality for their protégés; they demand only the freedom to produce and to sell, which are the inherent rights of all human beings. According to the old "black code" of Illinois, which was not abolished until 1853, any Negro who dared to cross the state's borders was considered to be a fugitive slave from a neighboring state. He was sold by authority of the courts and awarded for a year to the highest bidder so as to give his former master time to reclaim him. Any white man finding a Negro on his land had the right to chase the trespasser off with a whip and to confiscate the product of his labor. The present laws are more humane: before dealing severely with the black, the law generously allows him ten days of grace; but if he stays longer than that he is put in prison, fined, sold to a temporary master to pay the fine; when he regains his freedom, he is sold and resold again and again as long as he remains in the state.* Yet Illinois is a "free state!" There is in this same state a law that strictly forbids intermarriage between whites and non-whites. Those found guilty are punished by fines, thirty-six lashes and not less

* This shameful legislation, now fallen into disuse and attacked by the abolitionists, has recently been reformed, but the part relating to marriage has not been changed. Racial intermarriage is strictly prohibited.

than a year in prison. The minister, judge or town clerk who performed the marriage is likewise liable to a heavy fine, and the marriage itself is declared null and void. Such is the concern of Western reformers for their dear brother with a black skin!

The Northerners' opposition to slavery is not so much more disinterested. The banner [of emancipation] is nevertheless unfurled; it must now be followed, and the principle will triumph in spite of private feelings. You will recall that to amend the Constitution of the United States there must be a two-thirds majority in both houses of Congress. A constitutional amendment abolishing slavery has already been voted by the Senate, but it failed to get the necessary majority in the House of Representatives. Today the great majority the Republicans have won in the presidential election makes it certain that there will be an almost unanimous vote for the amendment in the new Congress. Abolition, decreed at first as a war measure, will soon receive legal sanction. Whether the South consents or resists, slavery is a thing of the past.

People are speaking of peace overtures; already they are talking about who the negotiators will be. The truth is that the North has never been able to speak to the South with more force and authority. If it were not out of its mind, the South would listen and, since it is prepared—in order to continue the war—to strike down slavery with its own hands, it should agree to give it up voluntarily in order to obtain peace. Abolition of slavery is said to be the only condition the North would impose and, this sacrifice being already half made, how much would it really cost them to rejoin the Union? Nothing but the humbling of their pride—but that is just what costs the most. These four years of war have changed civil discord into a kind of hatred of one nation for another. Furthermore, the rivalry between North and South goes back a long way into the past; they have considered themselves hostile brothers for a very long time. When the abolitionist Republicans want to refer to the years when there were Democratic majorities in Congress, they speak of "the period when the South oppressed us," without realizing that they are almost justifying the South's criminal rebellion. Instances come to mind of the Abolitionists' resistance to the ruling party, of their unavowed desire for independence and separation, of the time when Horace Greeley, speaking of the national flag, cried: "Tear down the flaunting lie!" They are fighting now for the flag they once insulted, just as in the old days the South would have fought to defend the Federal banner if the North had attacked it. Their cause [abolition] is the right one, whether one judges on grounds of morality, of patriotism or of liberty. They bring to their struggle, however, a bitterness that is the result of their long humiliation.

Don't think that I'm excusing the Rebels, but a civil war, when it has lasted as long as this one has, is the fiercest and most merciless of all wars. If people easily forgive foreigners, they vow eternal hatred for the enemy in their own family, in their own home. Think of the behavior of both sides in this war, of the murders and pillaging on both sides, of the terrible practice of shooting prisoners, of the

even more terrible custom of killing dozens of innocent prisoners in reprisal for each new outrage by
the enemy. Even when, in judging these atrocities,
you make allowance for the Americans' normal brutality, you can appreciate how deeply the two sides
have come to detest one another. I doubt that more
corpses can ever fill in the river of blood that separates them. The salvation of America depends upon
the voluntary submission of the South, for the war
can only end by forcing the South to surrender.

2

A Visit to the Oil Fields

Pittsburgh
November 15, 1864

I'VE just got here from Columbus and it took seventeen hours to travel about 250 miles. We moved at the speed of a tortoise, stopping in open country every two miles or so. At every station the train was shunted about; it jerked back and forth; then it stood still, waiting for I know not what. There are sections where the rails are so flattened, split or eaten by rust that the wheels can hardly cling to them. Another train had just plunged a hundred feet into the Ohio River because it had been going too fast around a rather sharp curve, and we saw the wreckage. Farther along there was a wooden bridge which crossed at a great height over one of the Ohio's tributaries, a bridge so flimsy and shaky that the engineer had to pick his way across with extreme caution, moving no faster than a caterpillar, a fraction of an inch at a time. It took ten minutes to make the crossing because the engineers were afraid each time they advanced the throttle of starting vibrations that would shake the whole structure to pieces. Nevertheless, twenty trains use this bridge every day and will go on using it as long as it doesn't decide to collapse. The whole idea is to save money: they risk human lives for the same reasons that some people refuse to throw away old, tattered clothes until they are completely worn out.

The railroads are rather like the government. In any nation everything is related to everything else; private organizations, like public institutions, reflect the national character and customs. We Frenchmen are noted for carrying caution to the extreme of formality, for being punctual to the point of fussiness. We like to create unneeded jobs; we want public services to function with perfect regularity, and we tolerate large profits, sinecures and laziness at the top. Here one finds low salaries, great energy and intelligence at the top, but disorder and negligence below.

If you go to New York, Boston or Chicago and visit the offices of any large railway company you will climb a dark staircase in a crowded building which contains the offices of fifteen or twenty traders or bankers. You knock at a small door, you go through two or three smoke-blackened rooms. A busy man, the manager or superintendent, is seated at a plain pine table, leafing through big, thick ledgers arranged on a shelf in front of him; four or five hard-working clerks are diligently scribbling away, bent over their desks behind a sort of barrier where members of the public come to stand at attention as if they had been called before the bar of justice.

This is the whole central administration of a large industrial enterprise. On the other hand, no one is much concerned about details; the lesser employees do pretty much as they please; there are regulations, but no one pays any attention to them. It is understood that they must always yield to the whim or the convenience of the moment. In France we have comfortable seats, we are warm, and so forth; a strong government looks out for us and a legitimate complaint made by a single individual to that paternal authority would, at least in theory, receive satisfaction. Here you are thrown into a democratic crowd where you can move neither arms nor legs without bringing your elbows and perhaps even your fists into play. If you try to make a complaint, you are inaudible amidst the general uproar; besides, one voice alone is never listened to. You may have justice on your side, yet you will be helpless unless you also have force behind you because, in spite of all our preconceived ideas about the benefits of *laissez-faire*, in small matters the individual is just as completely crushed under this regime as under our omnipresent bureaucracy. One can't deny the immense advantage of a democratic system for the good of the greatest number, nor ignore the speedier progress it makes possible for that impersonal being called a nation. But our political philosophers should not praise it too much in the name of rigorous abstract principles and stern justice! Democracy in practice—and in Europe we know it only by name and in theory—is a perpetual mêlée in which a lone individual can't raise his head without making himself a target for someone to shoot at. He must follow the herd or else the popular masses will trample him underfoot.

I have wandered far from the Columbus-to-Pittsburgh railroad. The Ohio countryside was still beautiful in spite of winter's mournful hues. After the broad plains of the West, I took a great deal of pleasure in the fields and villages, the numerous

farms and the pretty Norman[1] valleys. As we came
north we climbed higher and the terrain became
more broken; we were approaching the Alleghenies. Soon we saw deep valleys, with mountains in
the distance, and at last we saw the Ohio, which is
still deep and wide—it doesn't seem to have grown
smaller since Louisville—and its smooth ribbon
flows calmly between two ranges of high hills. The
ground, however, was covered with snow. The forests, so beautiful a month ago, have lost their last
leaves; the trees looked like brooms made of twigs.
Here the river bends sharply to the north and bars
our way. They are building a new railroad line that
will go straight from here to Pittsburgh through
West Virginia, and the piles of the enormous bridge
that will cross the river are already finished. Meanwhile the train stays in the valley; the roadbed follows a shelf along the hillside, sometimes overhung
by steep slopes, sometimes running among lower
hills where pretty villages nestle in the hollows.
One of these, Steubenville, whose population is almost entirely German, is built on the shoulder of a
hill across from a bluff, at a place where the river
flows through a narrow gap; the surroundings are
agreeably rural. The skies were blue, the bare
slopes in the distance took on velvety purple tones,
the gilded surface of the river was still flecked with
a delicate blue. I was enchanted by the glimpses I
was able to get by peering past the shoulders and
hats of my neighbors in the crowded car. Night

[1] Duvergier de Hauranne is comparing the Ohio landscape
to that of the French province of Normandy with its many
small rivers, wooded areas and hedgerows.

came, and my seat-mate, a young farmhand in a red shirt, fell asleep, pinning me down with his long legs and tenderly resting his head on my shoulder.

The weather here in Pittsburgh is bleak, rainy and foggy—just like London. I soon got tired of the roofs and smoking chimneys which was all I could see from my windows, so I ventured out for a walk in the mud. Pittsburgh is one of the strangest cities not only in America but in the whole world. It already has 111,000 inhabitants—more than 200,000 if you include the suburbs. Standing on the spot where the French built Fort Duquesne, at the confluence of two large rivers, the Allegheny and the Monongahela, which join to form the Ohio, it occupies the tongue of land between the two rivers and a hill covered with private dwellings. To the West the Allegheny, 500 yards wide, flows between two lines of hills which widen out a little toward its mouth. To the south the Monongahela is confined between steep banks that continue in the distance along the Ohio. The site is extremely picturesque. Let me add that Pittsburgh is in the middle of the Pennsylvania coal-mining region, that there are mines and smelters everywhere, that the narrow river-bank opposite the city is covered with factories whose furnaces have filled the valley with people, that large boats plying the Ohio stop here, that the smaller-scale river traffic begins here, that the docks are crowded with steamboats and that the three rivers are alive with shipping of all kinds.

I followed the shore as far as the great suspension bridge over the Allegheny, one of those daring but solid feats of engineering that are done so well here in America. There are only two piers, nearly 500 yards apart, both of open iron-work. Cables converge there from all directions like the radii of a circle or, if you prefer, like the ribs of a fan; they serve to stabilize the massive deck which is supported by two thick cables. The railings and the cross-beams are of solid iron. Strings of large horse-cars cross it on iron rails. There are no abutments on the two banks, but the cables are anchored at ground level where the bridge rests on its foundations. It is one of those fragile structures which, like the bridge at Niagara [Falls], seem likely to last forever; but the engineers are already calculating how long it will be before the Niagara bridge lets an overloaded train plunge into the Whirlpool. It is probable that this bridge, too, has its last day inscribed in the book of the Fates. Night was falling, so I returned to the city. It was as smoky as Newcastle or St.-Etienne;[2] the houses were as black as those in London. For the rest, Pittsburgh is a composite of New York, Cincinnati and Philadelphia, with the same wide streets and the same mud. Its only claim to distinction consists of some beautiful churches in the Gothic style whose tall steeples seen from a distance give a deceptive appearance of European antiquity.

There is nothing new since the election. The political horizon, though not much clearer than it was, is profoundly calm. The war drags on as usual and

[2]Newcastle-on-Tyne in northeastern England was the center of a coal-mining and manufacturing region, as was the city of St.-Etienne in the south-central part of France. Both were noted for the thick pall of smoke that poured from their factory chimneys.

will continue to do so until cold weather freezes it solid like the rivers. General [William T.] Sherman is marching on Charleston, it is announced with a line of exclamation marks. For a whole year he has done nothing else, and nothing indicates that he will not make another long stop like that he made in Atlanta.

I am leaving tomorrow, not for New York, but for Oil City and the land of petroleum. I have been warned that the snow and rain of the past few days have made travel almost impossible in that primitive part of the world where oil gushes forth from the lower depths of the infernal regions.

Ravenna, Ohio
November 16, 1864

THIS MORNING the weather was frosty and bright, which brought joy to my heart. Yesterday I made the acquaintance of a dealer in kerosene who was so obliging as to offer to be my guide. He showed me the principal factories of the city, but these gave me only a rather poor opinion of American industry. The glass works of Pittsburgh produce nothing but trash. On the other hand, I saw two or three fine mills—a steel mill where the methods were out of date but the equipment seemed to be first-class, a nail factory using enormous machines, a factory where horseshoes were shaped by a steam-powered press whose driving wheel has a diameter of over thirty feet.

Finally, I visited the cannon foundry that produces the world's largest monsters of destruction. I saw one of these, the most terrifying of all, whose twin brother has already been used on land at the siege of Atlanta; this one is to be placed all by itself on one of the biggest warships of the Federal navy. Set crosswise, it will cover the full width of the deck. This prodigious weapon fires a forty-inch [*sic*] cannonball and it has been calculated that each shot will cost in all about a thousand dollars.[3] What fantastic devices men invent to kill each other!

I left Pittsburgh in the direction of Cleveland, following the delightful valley of the Ohio for quite a distance. I have never seen anything more cheerful, more lively or more varied. There is an unbroken series of villages, islands, churning steamboats, and the railroad is built along a narrow terrace above the winding river. It was already dark when I got off at Ravenna, a small Ohio town at the junction with the Atlantic and Great Western line which was to take me to the oil country. But there was no train that night, so I had to look for lodgings there. My baggage was not at the station; no doubt it had been put off at the point where the two lines come together. "Go over there," I was told, "It's only a quarter of a mile." So off I went cross-country through snow and mud. I walked one mile, then two; the village was already far behind me and I still hadn't come to the junction. So I returned to the village covered with mud; but the hotels were no longer open. I had to pound on the door and beg to be let in. As for supper, I mustn't even dream of it; innkeepers have their rules, and this one informed me that in his house no one gets anything to eat after nine o'clock.

[3] This was probably a 20-inch Rodman gun.

Titusville, Pennsylvania
November 17, 1864

WELL, here I am in the Land of Oil. It isn't exactly
the spot one would choose for a honeymoon. But I
consider myself fortunate to have seen this new and
fascinating aspect of American society. Rain, snow,
mud and all the ugliness of the season lend a still
more outlandish quality to this counterpart of the
California gold-rush. Picture to yourself a sea of
mud criss-crossed by a few rough, broken sidewalks
made of insecurely fastened boards; imagine a few
dozen small wooden houses filled to overflowing
with people for whom there has been no time to
build shelter; one or two so-called streets lined with
hotels and stores but inundated like the rest of the
town with the ever-present mire. There one finds
brightly lighted show windows, music and dance
halls where brass instruments accompany the
screeching of harsh, tuneless voices—and everywhere barrels of oil, the air everywhere polluted by
the stench of oil—this is the Eldorado[4] in which I
have just arrived in the company of three or four
hundred other travelers in a train as crowded as
though it were going to a festival or pleasure resort.
This city of oil and mud is called Titusville. It
didn't exist seven years ago; today it is the center of
this whole region and the terminus of a railroad
which will soon be continued to Oil City, the very
heart of "Petrolia."

No one can imagine without having seen it the

[4] Eldorado was a hidden valley in the Andes visited by the
hero of Voltaire's *Candide.* The ground was covered with
gold nuggets, and the sheep grew fleeces of gold.

eagerness with which this greedy mob plunges into the mad scramble for wealth. Oil has dethroned gold. Workers who are looking for a well-paid job, ruined financiers who have come here to try their luck once more, adventurers of all sorts, from all countries and wearing all kinds of clothes, run a free-for-all cross-country race to find out who will be the first to dig himself into the muck and bar the way to late-comers.

It was raining, the night was black; the train came to a halt; everyone rushed pell-mell to the nearest hotel in whose already-jammed lobby there was no room for this new embattled horde. So we all set forth again, straggling along in single file, with some people carrying lanterns, across vacant lots, along a narrow wooden sidewalk where one was continually stepping into holes that were impossible to see in the darkness. At every cross-street the column hesitated, some crept ahead to test the footing; then the boldest spirits decided to press forward, picking their way among the mud-holes by trial and error, with some of those most in a hurry plunging in up to their knees. Never mind, we keep on going, clutching our bundles or toting our suitcases on our shoulders, the women as well as the men sprinting like long-distance runners. The first ones to burst into a rooming-house got the rooms, beds, sofas and chairs; the slower ones were left out in the rain and the muddy streets. I ran like a madman, leaving my baggage at the station and shivering in anticipation of the prospect of spending a night out of doors in the mud-bath, but I stumbled in the mire, I lost my way, I fell behind and finally arrived with my legs sheathed in mud up to the calf, only to find closed faces wherever I went—there was not a mattress, not even a blanket to be had. No one could even promise me a chair. Fortunately I had some companions in misfortune who were more persuasive than I; the hotel-keeper, telling us to follow him, set out to make the rounds of the village, leading his little army through the drenching rain, placing one person in this house, another in that, at last dropping me off at the end of a dark, out-of-the-way alley in a "boarding house" whose tiny vestibule was so crammed with people that I once again despaired of having a roof over my head that night. But I was allowed to write my name in the register. Then I remembered my baggage left at the railroad station—this meant another expedition in which I almost lost my way, came near foundering in the mud-holes and nearly broke my legs stepping through gaps in the sidewalks. As I was making my way back plastered with mud, I was envious of the high boots that allow the natives to make their way about in this morass.

When I asked for some dinner I was shown into a small room where all the guests had to line up to await their turns, hastily bolting their food to make way for the next batch. It would be hard to imagine a more motley swarm than the one that is buzzing about our over-crowded beehive. You find samples of all the levels of American society intermingled here, very different in appearance, yet fundamentally very much alike—I don't say "class" because the Americans boast of not having any, and the fact is that if hopes and attitudes differentiate people more than their clothes, this equality is not an illusion. Here one finds a hodgepodge of all types of people who make up the great American family, ranging from the country bumpkin with his nasal speech to the expensively dressed speculator from the city, rather similar in his bad manners and showy clothes to a Parisian sales clerk; one meets with every professional type from the bearded adventurer with a predatory face and dishonest, shifty eyes, whose hand seems never to be far away from the "bowie knife" hidden under his coat collar, to the calm, level-headed merchant who comes to camp here for a season with his wife, children and baggage.

One sees a lot of former soldiers in this crowd; their bedraggled uniform trousers and jackets are everywhere. Or, to take another example, there is the newly-minted "gentleman," a species that is so numerous and so typical in America, wearing a new frock coat, flashy jewelry and a thick goatee, his jovial contentment shining through his coarse, crude ways. One can tell from his smug expression that Oil Creek has been a bonanza for him and has filled his pockets with gold at the same time that it has filled his barrels with petroleum. Besides, his good humor goes well with his plump, ruddy face; but his wife, a doughty old battleaxe whose features are stamped with that indescribable vulgarity which often clings to those who have come up from the lowly occupations of life, holds herself stiff and aloof in her ridiculously elaborate finery which she seems to have had copied from a reliquary. She looks like some harridan of the market-stalls who, by a stroke of luck, has acquired a lot of gold ingots and now, her head held high, comes to triumph over her old friends, the fishwives, showing off her silk dresses. She, too, is an authentically American type, and you well know that I have no liking for these "ladies" with their manly ways and bold speech; they would be perfectly capable of traveling alone to the ends of the earth, but one always expects to hear them swear like a drill-sergeant and drink "wiskey" [*sic*] like a teamster.

Thanks to my honest face I have obtained a bed in the parlor, where I am now writing to you with no room to move my elbows while the ladies sit around the table gossiping and a black servant sets up our extra cots in closely-spaced rows. The master of the house, seeing that I am a foreigner, has overwhelmed me with politeness; he tells me in a tone of triumph that I shall have a "single bed"—by this expression he means me to understand that I shall be able to luxuriate all by myself in the comfort of a cot six feet long and two feet wide. You can see that I am being treated like a great lord.

November 19, 1864

YESTERDAY MORNING at six o'clock I made my way through the streets of Titusville to the station, satchel in hand. This time daylight made it possible to avoid the mud-holes. The train took me to Schaefer's Farm in a car so full of people that it seemed as if the floor might actually collapse under its burden. Shaking and groaning, it labored on as though about to break in two. One may behold here another choice bouquet of American ugliness in this stuffy box where people are smoking and spitting while the windows remain tightly closed. Young and old, large and small speculators—everyone jostles his neighbor here with the most perfect equality, except for four or five New Yorkers gotten up in the latest Paris fashions who seem to maintain an air of reserve and superiority. A few distinguished, intelligent or sympathetic faces are conspicuous in this crowd, where they seem out of place, doubtless thrust into the torrent of business by the force of prevailing example and by their mercantile culture, which offers no other career to a man of means. They talk, they argue, they buy or they sell: "dollar" and "oil" are almost the only words one hears. Even making due allowance for the democratic customs of the country, is there not a natural bond of brotherhood among gamblers that effaces all distinctions? When they join the fraternity, do they not dedicate themselves to the same cult of money-making, renouncing in advance every sort of esteem save that which can be gained by luck or by successful chicanery? A gambler leaves his moral sense at the door of the casino. He is no longer worth more than the value of his fortune, and if one reflects that this may flourish today only to collapse tomorrow, that it may tower like a mountain this evening only to vanish by tomorrow, leaving a bottomless pit of debts—and when you realize that in America the rich man and the beggar can exchange places in one day—you can understand why there is such full equality between the "rowdy," who is just beginning to make his pile, and the yellow-gloved adventurer who can so quickly fall to his level.

But here I am at Schaefer's Farm, a miserable

hamlet about to sink into the swamp. There was the usual steeplechase to get lunch, another to hire a horse. I wanted to get to Oil City that same day and leave in the morning for Buffalo, but the river was in flood, the ford was impassable and all who tried to get across came back discouraged. I was told there was a steamboat about to leave that would descend Oil Creek rapidly thanks to the rain-swollen current. Very good, but when would it make a trip upstream? There was also said to be a mountain trail, but a stranger would run the risk of losing his way. Could I have a guide? What an idea! I must go alone and take my chances or else give up the trip. My decision was soon made: someone pointed out the far-away path I must take and I set off on horseback at a brisk clip.

First I climbed a hill by an almost invisible track, then I entered a maze of muddy or partly submerged trails where big stones were treacherously hidden under the liquid mud, but the local horses are used to this. I must have traversed ten valleys and forded ten swift streams or swollen brooks, inquiring the way at each of the isolated cabins along the way. An old Irish farmer all but threw his arms around my neck on learning that I was a Frenchman and, as such, a natural enemy of perfidious England. A seedy French expatriate who no longer knows how to speak his own language asked me if I wanted to buy some oil. All these small property-owners seemed to me to be well-off, almost rich; in the past five years their land has gained enormously in value. Those farmers who do not dare to run the risks of the enterprise themselves sell off pieces of their land to companies organized by speculators who sink the wells and buy the machinery, often going bankrupt but sometimes making fabulous profits. It is strictly a game of chance. Here and there, at the far end of some deserted valley, one can see the worm-eaten scaffolding of an abandoned well; in another spot there is the thin spiral of smoke that shows where a steam engine is at work; a little farther away a herd of cattle is grazing in a meadow; only man himself is absent or at least almost invisible. The countryside is partly wooded, partly in cleared fields; it seems fertile, although it looks a little forbidding in the drab colors of autumn. Abundant streams water the valleys, springs seem to gush from every crevice.

From the high plateau which my road was crossing I was able to look down the valleys of Oil Creek's tributaries and catch some truly magnificent glimpses of the river itself. Large pine forests cover the upper slopes and mingle their dark foliage with the bright purple of the oaks, whose leaves do not fall with the first frosts. All these colors blended into a mass of dark violet, softened by the light blue haze that bathed the distant horizon. The great trees in the foreground had lost all their leaves; but the brush, which is more hardy, had kept its blood-red color, at once brilliant and dark, which lent contrast and served to frame the picture. The sky was gray, enlivened here and there by traces of blue and by bright spots on the clear, pale background which seemed impregnated with the cold of winter.

Such was the general aspect of the region in that lingering fall season. An occasional house was to be seen and the countryside was criss-crossed by dirt roads which seemed to owe their existence only to continual use without ever having known the shovel, the pick or the roller. A sense of great loneliness brooded over the landscape, taking possession of the traveler, especially one afraid of losing his way. This vast region, thinly populated though not actually deserted, incompletely cleared rather than uncultivated, gives one a good notion of what our countryside must have looked like a few centuries ago at the time when, according to our novelists, their heroes traveled on foot or on horseback; but the piercing whistle of the locomotive, the hoarse note of the steamboat, which broke the silence from time to time, reminded me that this is another age. Finally, after three long hours in the saddle, I rode down through a narrow ravine to the floor of the valley where I found the river and the strange little town that carries the fitting name of Oil City.

This place is a striking example of the remarkable brutality with which industry destroys nature. Here is a valley that was wild, quiet and beautiful; but in just a few years it has been transformed into a foul cesspool, strewn with loathsome barrack-like buildings from which the tumult and smoke of a large city are already pouring forth. This certainly is the capital city of the land of mud. I have seen nothing like the road that clings to a shelf of land along the river, serving the innumerable wells that are scattered through the valley. Tired of being continually splashed, I ventured into a field where the ground seemed firm; I forced my reluctant horse to leave the road in spite of his protests and suddenly there he was, belly-deep in the mire, rolling from side to side under my weight as he tried to find a solid footing in the morass.

That put an end to my voyage of discovery; I had seen enough to give me an idea of the prodigious activity that goes on in this God-forsaken little hole. For some fifteen or twenty miles the valley is filled with smoking engine-houses and scaffolds shaped like sawhorses on which a wheel and a pump are mounted; apparently the latter is very powerful because the average depth of the wells is about five hundred feet. The rate of exploitation is so rapid that in some places the oil-bearing strata are exhausted, and between Oil City and Titusville there are already a thousand idle pumps. Formerly the oil spurted to a great height like water from an artesian well. Then it was only necessary to collect it, and some wells yielded two or three thousand barrels a day; the supply had to be controlled for fear of glutting the market. Oil then had a high price and some wells could produce as much as 10,000 dollars' worth in twenty-four hours. Such immense wealth was too good to last, and the average yield per well at present is twenty dollars a day. There are heavy oils which need no further preparation before being burned; but some of the lighter grades are distilled and concentrated.

All these industries, mainly mills and refineries, are jammed together along the narrow riverbank; some even encroach on the bed of the river itself. There is an uninterrupted procession of large boats piled high with barrels and borne away downstream by the rapid current. The wilderness of the pine

Photograph Taken in 1864

Oil Barges in Western Pennsylvania

Courtesy of the New York Public Library

forests lie close at hand. While waiting for the completion of the railroad, the two ends of which are already under construction and will meet here on this very spot, nothing but the natural highway offered by the river has been provided for carrying on this large-scale movement of goods. This ability to improvise an entire industry and this eagerness to pursue profit despite all obstacles are authentic traits of the American character. In the heat of competition the very conditions needed for a rational exploitation of resources are neglected. It is here that one becomes aware of the need for a far-sighted regulatory authority, one that would itself provide those works of public utility which will not be undertaken by the jealous, greedy individual in a hurry to make money. Though we have seen far too much intervention by the public administration in our business affairs, let us take care not to judge *ab irato* [in anger] and thus swing to the opposite extreme where one asserts that to make *certain* everything needful is done it is enough to *permit* those things to be done. Nothing is better than the spontaneous enterprise of private individuals when their ventures are actually carried into effect. But there must be a power charged with providing for social needs as a matter of course whenever individual initiative is not up to the task.

What seems bad to me in our French centralization is not so much the duty the state takes upon itself to do certain things, nor the right it arrogates to itself to demand from the taxpayer the means of accomplishing those tasks, but the monopoly it maintains in some fields and its refusal to allow

anyone else to encroach on its preserves. It would
be better for the central authority not to interfere in
the affairs of others, not to impose its plans, its engineers, its ways of doing things on the local authorities; but when the latter fail to do things necessary
to the public welfare, then let Paris have the right to
see to it that those needs are attended to.

On my return trip I was taken by surprise halfway along my route by nightfall, by that abrupt
coming of darkness without any twilight which is
typical of the American sky. The night soon got so
black that I had to guess, rather than follow, the
way. One has reason to be in low spirits when he is
obliged to make a trip like this in an unfamiliar
region on a dark night if there is a good chance of
your going astray and all the dogs of the neighborhood for miles around greet your approach with
furious barking. Every now and then a light would
appear in the distance ahead, but it would soon
flicker out. My weary horse lurched whenever he
stepped into a mud-hole and stumbled over rolling
stones; he seemed uneasy and bewildered. Once at a
fork in the trail we were not in agreement: I urged
him to the left, but he turned to the right. I stopped
him exactly at the turn and left the choice to him.
He thought about it, then thought some more, but
couldn't seem to make up his mind. What a dilem-
ma! I opened my eyes wide, trying to see through
the darkness. Straight ahead I thought I could see a
black shape which I believed to be a lone tree I had
noted as a possible landmark in the morning.

I rode toward it and suddenly discovered that I
was already on the final slope: below me I could see

the lights of the village twinkling. Just a few more steps and I would reach my goal; but how was I to get back onto the trail through the forest? Every path seemed to fade away and disappear in the undergrowth. Three times my confused horse lost his way in the thickets; three times we had to grope our way back. Guided by the sound of dogs barking, I made my way through the woods to a cottage where a feeble light was flickering. I knocked. A woman's voice told me to be on my way. I departed with a pack of watchdogs at my heels. I walked a long time, dragging my limping horse behind me. I came to another cottage, knocked loudly, waked up the farmer and frightened his family. At last he lit his lantern and set me once more on the right road. I scarcely noticed that my feet got soaking wet when I waded through a swamp at the bottom of the hill. However glorious the stars were that moonless night, the prospect of sleeping in the woods until daybreak, exposed to the frost of a November night and the bite of the north wind, was not romantic enough to tempt me, and I was happy to find myself at last in a real bed.

In the morning on awakening I had to clean my shoes myself, dry my clothing and wash some of my dirty linen. At Titusville they had absolutely refused to polish my boots; this time the innkeeper, trying to be ingratiating, allowed me to borrow the brush and the polish. A strange country and even stranger people! This incident, better than anything else, lets you put your finger on the mainspring of this society, lets you really understand how completely the profit motive dominates their feelings and their inclinations, even all their pleasures, making them sacrifice the very thing that ought to be dearest to them, that physical well-being which is, after all, the object of all their hard work. Anywhere else in the world a sink-hole like this would be a hideout for desperadoes or tough, hardened adventurers ready for any job, a band of robbers of the kind that each new industry, like every army on campaign, carries along in its train. Here, on the contrary, it is the casino where capitalists come to risk their fortunes, the Baden-Baden[5] where the newly rich come to seek the thrills of the gaming table. They are drawn by the risk itself, by the uncertainty of a bet that can ruin them tomorrow. They are drawn, that is, by the oil exchange which is now established at the actual point of sale of the oil. When I board a railroad car, there they are gambling; when I go into a hotel, the lobby and dining room are miniature stock exchanges where deals are worked out between the grog and the coffee. If I meet two men on horseback splashing through a swamp, you may be sure that they are talking about some risky proposition like buying a piece of land or sinking a well, about what the prices will be next week or at the end of the month. Betting, always betting on something or other—that is the whole meaning of life to these barbarians in muddy boots who, in order to get a closer look at the cards, rob themselves of all the comforts and pleasures of life.

[5] Baden-Baden was a fashionable German spa and resort at this period. Its principal attractions were its luxury hotels and its gambling casino.

In Europe indulgence in this vice is accompanied by all sorts of subsidiary attractions. Here the passion itself is so strong, so compelling, that nothing more is needed. The greed of the typical American is of heroic proportions and he doesn't know the meaning of fear. He goes down like Schiller's diver into the depths of Charybdis[6] to retrieve a golden goblet; but he will also (if you will excuse the figure of speech) crawl down and dig out a copper penny from the bottom of a sewer.

Erie
November 19, 1864

NOW THAT I have made my visit to the court of "King Oil," let me tell you his history in a few words. King Oil is of recent origin, although he is already the rival of "King Cotton." His first subjects were the Indians, who used this mineral oil in their religious ceremonies and applied it to their wounds as a salve. He was then concealed in the bowels of the earth, appearing to the outer world only in the form of a few springs which ran into the rivers and spread their oily substance over the surface. The French were the first to try to release him from his prison. The excavations they made to reach his subterranean dwelling-place are still shown to tourists. In 1845, miners were able to open a well at Taren-

---

[6] Friedrich Schiller, in his ballad, "Der Taucher" [The Diver], has a young hero dive down to great depths to retrieve a golden goblet at great risk to his life. Charybdis, in classical times, was the name given to the Straits of Messina, which was considered very dangerous to ships passing between the rock, Scylla, and the strong currents offshore.

tum, near Pittsburgh. It was not until twelve years later that large-scale pumping began at Titusville.[7] In 1860, there were already some 2,000 wells in operation. In 1862, they produced 300,000 barrels per week, and in 1863, the value of oil exports to Europe rose to six million dollars. Meanwhile, other sources were discovered in Ohio, [West] Virginia, Canada, the Western states and Utah, on the main route to the Pacific coast. New wells in West Virginia and in Marietta, Ohio, are already in full production. Bituminous oil, which yields petroleum, is found in only eight states, but the total area containing petroleum deposits is estimated at 62,000 square miles. The value of this oil is incalculable. In spite of the exhaustion of a large number of the most productive wells, the oil industry is developing at an amazing rate. It gives work to thousands of men; everyone is bewitched by it; and I have already told you what a speculative fever it has caused in the regions where discoveries are being made.

There are two classes in America: those who work with their hands and those who speculate on the labor of others. Whereas the number of workers is always too small for the needs of the country, and immigration barely adds enough to keep up with the demand, the class of speculators proliferates and is always too large in relation to the true needs of

[7] This was the first successful attempt to drill an oil well. It was done by "Colonel" E. L. Drake, engaged as supervisor by the Seneca Oil Company. The well attained a depth of 69.5 feet on August 28, 1859—Duvergier de Hauranne's "twelve years later" is too short by two years—and delivered about 25 barrels a day at first, producing some 2,000 barrels before the end of the year.

commerce. Try to picture to yourself this common type of itinerant trader; he is a dry, thin, bony man with a deeply lined face and an unhealthy appearance who always seems to be absorbed in financial calculations. This is your true Yankee. Do not ask him to do any other kind of work; he is busy rather than hard-working. He knows how to get around and talk with all sorts of people, how to keep his finger on twenty different pieces of business at the same time, how to sort out the tangled threads of some baffling, many-faceted business problem; but he leaves hard manual work to foreigners—the Irish, the Germans or the French Canadians. He himself takes pride in doing nothing but brain work and in having the power to set huge machines in motion without lifting his little finger. I had already observed in Canada the unequal division of labor between the two nationalities. The Yankee, back at home after making his commercial rounds, sits down in his office or shop, a cud of tobacco in his mouth, a newspaper in his hand and his feet on the desk, waiting for a customer[8] with regal nonchalance and talking politics with the neighborhood statesmen. At night he goes to a tavern to play a game of pool and drink a glass of punch. For every serious trader, how many of these parasitic middlemen must there be who bring to the business world the sleazy atmosphere of a gambling-den? They form a worthy counterpart to our coupon-clipping bourgeoisie, for both classes consume wealth without

---

[8] Duvergier de Hauranne uses the French phrase, *"attendant le chaland,"* which literally means "waiting for the skiff" or "waiting for the ferry"—that is, an opportunity for profit.

creating any in return. Still, they are not entirely useless; they stimulate business activity and help to increase the mobility of capital. And nature is not yet tired of producing fresh fuel every day to stoke these insatiable furnaces; indeed, this is the real reason for their success. One benefit of democracy in this country is said to be the great ease with which enterprising people are able to get rich. It is true that by making education equally available to everyone, democracy puts all those competing for fortune on the same starting-line, and it lowers the psychological barriers which in France still make it impossible or at least very difficult to gain access to a desirable career. But the main reason for the general well-being in America is the natural abundance that attracts everyone to the contest. Suppose that all the land in America were occupied, all the mines exploited, all the rural districts as densely populated as ours; imagine, for an instant, what America will be like in the year 2,000—and then tell me if you believe it will still be as rich and full of energy as at present.

In the last analysis, the character of a people depends on the circumstances in which nature and their own past have placed them. I don't blame the American people for being speculators, nor the French people for dozing comfortably on the income they draw from permanently invested capital. How could the Americans be anything but eager to get rich? How could the spirit of their society be anything but the love of gain? This is their very reason for existing. America is no longer, as it once was, a refuge for the persecuted and the proscribed, the promised land of those who sought liberty though they had to go to the far ends of the earth. For a long time now, New England has no longer received many families with acquired fortunes, the elements of a mature society that needed merely to take root in new soil. The age of the Pilgrims and the Quakers has ended; they have put their stamp only upon the general form of American society and upon the political institutions they have bequeathed to it. The human building material of America now is drawn from the cast-offs of Europe. America owes its tireless activity and its prodigious growth precisely to the profit motive, often sharpened by poverty. In a word, American society is a society of paupers who have gotten rich, are in the process of getting rich or have come to America hoping to get rich. They throw themselves on their prey like famished hunters; it will be some time before they will have had enough.

Even when they succeed in satisfying their original voracity it will be many generations before their thirst for gold is quenched; some spectacular failures will be needed, as well as the realization that business yields less profit than in the past. Do we often see our financial nabobs retire in their old age and become immune to the lure of high profits? And yet we are a people with aristocratic prejudices, looking down on wealth that is gained in this way, preferring stability and permanence. We often flatter the possessors of new fortunes, but we are without pity for those who lose them, thus revealing the contempt that had been masked by our previous adulation. Nothing like this exists in America, nothing to discourage the speculator or make him even consider the merits of another way of life.

The laws, which in France make leisure attractive, cooperate here with the national mode of life to stimulate the spirit of adventure. A father is not obliged to leave his property to his children;[9] often he distributes it far and wide, prompted either by a taste for ostentation or by genuinely philanthropic motives, and pushes them out into the world where they are thrown on their own resources and obliged to make their own way. Fortunes are made by one generation, lost by another—if, indeed, this doesn't happen several times in one lifetime. Hence it is necessary to return to the maelstrom of business just at the moment when one would like to steer his ship into a safe harbor. There are no rich legacies, no glittering sinecures like those which aristocratic societies keep in reserve for their disinherited children, no liberal occupations which the public patronage can make into a career and a livelihood; but instead, within the grasp of everyone, there is the dream of California, the great pile of gold to be won by the lucky speculator.

Is it so surprising that everybody throws himself into the fray and that in this democracy even the rewards of politics are scorned by speculators? They consider office-holding a last resource for the

[9] The legal reforms of the French Revolution, perpetuated by the Napoleonic Codes, forbade parents to disinherit their children and required that all children must share equally in all bequests. Primogeniture was thus abolished, but some authorities believe that excessive subdivision of family farms resulted in some regions, thus placing a premium on late marriages and the two-child family.

incompetent or a roundabout means of gaining a fortune. When you have nothing to start with, you become all the more grasping with success. Tradition, custom, example, [social] origin and even the spur of poverty all combine to make speculation the queen of American society. Here her rule is absolute, uncontested, inevitable. You are asked if you speculate as you would be asked if you like to eat; the two things are considered equally inseparable from human nature. You must put aside your refined tastes, your over-civilized aversions and your exaggerated politeness, or you will be written off by the Americans as an aristocratic snob.

As I write this letter I am standing up in a barroom full of noise and people. We have just learned from the railroad agent that we are going to have to spend the night here because of a delay in train service. This sort of thing occurs so frequently when one is traveling on the railroads of America that it would wear out the patience of a saint. I left Schaefer's Farm at noon, expecting to arrive in Buffalo at about ten o'clock—that's what the timetable says—but at Corry we were given notice that we would not get to Buffalo until tomorrow morning. For four hours we marked time beside the tracks, chilled by the fog and the cold night wind. Corry is an important junction where three or four railway lines come together, but the munificence of the companies has extended only as far as the building of two wooden shelters where tickets are sold to the crowds that shove and jostle to buy them. At this moment I am in Erie, beside the lake of the same name, ready to board the train for Buffalo.

Buffalo
November 20, 1864

I GOT HERE at daybreak; I was unable to sleep a wink. All these exertions have begun to wear me down. I have decided to return directly to New York, where I shall spend a few days greasing the wheels of my machine before resuming my tour.

I have just returned from a stroll through Buffalo. It is a very large city with very large houses on very wide streets, located on a very large lake; in addition to all this, it gives me a depressing sense of bareness, banality and monotony. The main streets, lined with brick buildings covered with signs of all sorts, testify to the intensity of business activity on weekdays, though everything is sound asleep today in a glacial Sunday hibernation that is like public mourning. The horsecars, which run continually, are the only signs of life to be seen. I do not count as living creatures the automatons who march along swinging their arms with a stiff, measured step, staring straight ahead.

I walked as far as the harbor, which extends many finger-like branches into the city in the form of several canals; here, even on Sunday, a fair amount of activity is going on. All along the wharves, and on a tongue of land or sand-bar that serves as a breakwater for the port, there rise, as in Chicago, thirty or forty immense grain warehouses or "elevators" as high as church steeples. Their number and their colossal proportions clearly reveal the city's principal business. Buffalo, which was nothing thirty years ago and now has more than a hundred thousand people, is the chief port at this end of the

Great Lakes and holds in the East the same place Chicago holds in the West. All the products of the West make their way here and are collected in the city's warehouses, whence they are sent out into the hinterland or shipped by canal to the New York market. Wherever you look along the horizon of Lake Erie you always see it dotted with gray sails and columns of black smoke.

When it comes to public morals Buffalo is one of the strictest cities in the United States. The religious fervor of its citizens is proverbial, and so is the acrimony of the numerous sects that compete for souls. Methodists, Congregationalists, Episcopalians, Unitarians, Presbyterians, Baptists, Catholics and many more wage war on one another with sermons and pamphlets, with screeching and self-mortification.

Every Sunday the congregations meet all day long; half the population is to be found in the churches; that is why the streets are deserted. By contrast, what a witches' sabbath goes on inside the "temple!" All day long I have heard screams, shouts, a clatter of words, then some hymns, followed by incoherent cries—all coming through the roof of a building underneath my windows. What could it be? A cock-fight? A boxing-match? A political meeting? A fencing academy? But how could any such thing be taking place on Sunday?

Finally, thanks to the evening quiet and to the increased volume of the speaker's inspired roaring, the meaning of some of this hullaballoo finally dawned on me, reaching my ears through the windows and closed blinds. The building is the house of prayer of a pious congregation and the harsh, hysterical voice, like that of a raging madman, was that of a saintly minister or of some layman moved by divine inspiration in a fit of "enthusiasm" who was addressing supplications to the Lord. I heard the words "Oh, Lord!" being repeated in every possible tone of tearful entreaty or screaming frenzy. The man sounded as if he were standing barefoot on a bed of live coals. I also heard the shudders, the sighs and the stifled cries of the audience. Evidently this shepherd is greatly admired by his faithful flock, and tomorrow they will all be telling each other how edifying his words of the day before had been. Then a hymn was sung with all the possible false notes known and unknown. Finally another voice was raised, a woman's voice this time; though it was muffled by the walls of the building, I heard enough to realize that she was successfully imitating the lamentations and frenzies of the prophet. The latter once more shook the heavenly vault, and another hymn has just brought the meeting to a close as I sit writing these words. I don't know to what sect these possessed people belong, whether they are Anabaptists, Mormons or Shakers. Beyond all possible doubt they are either great lunatics or great impostors, perhaps both at the same time, so complex is our nature! Americans enjoy such nervous crises; in religion, as in politics, delirium is for them the height of eloquence. Do you remember the Neapolitan preachers of San Gaetano?[10] They have enough fury and lung-power to bring down the walls of Jericho; but the howls

[10] Noted for their ability to command vast audiences.

they make when they have the toothache stand in the same ratio to these superhuman convulsions as a comic opera ditty bears to one of Verdi's greatest dramatic arias.

New York
November 22, 1864

YESTERDAY on the train I witnessed a little drama of private life. Six or eight Democratic soldiers had boarded the car and were soon trading smutty stories. This kind of low-life behavior must be fairly common in a country where respect for good manners, as well as respect for the law, is left to the discretion of the individual. In fact, I am surprised to find so many sober, well-behaved soldiers when there is no discipline that forces them to mind their manners, so that they could play the bully with ease. My agreeable companions began to talk about politics and to blaspheme, "damning" each other at every second word and "damning" the blacks especially for having been the cause of Civil War. A respectable citizen traveling with his daughter finally reached the end of his patience and said to them politely, "Gentlemen, may I remind you that there are regulations against offensive language?" The result was general indignation; these "gentlemen" do not allow anyone to teach them good manners nor take a superior tone with them. "He is a damned black Republican!"*—"I'll be God-damned if we've said a damned word that might offend a woman's ears! Are you a preacher, old man?" To this they

* "Black Republican" is the epithet usually applied by Democrats to the abolitionists.

added all the insults soldiers know how to dispense so freely. Still, in spite of themselves, they were a little overawed; after several minutes they got up and moved on, still swearing, into the next car. Only one remained, a very young man, slightly drunk, who began to threaten each one of us in turn, mumbling "I'll kill the man who won't say 'Hurrah for McClellan!' " The first man he tackled was an elderly farmer with white hair who helped him back to his seat in a good-humored way, leaning over towards me to grumble about "these damned soldiers." I was the second victim; our young man suddenly sat down beside me and, shaking his fist in my face, asked if I was a Republican. My obstinate silence discouraged him. He continued his antics farther down the aisle until the conductor, with a cheerful and placating manner, came along and read him a paternal lecture. No one dared to throw him out.

The reason is that the uniform is beginning to be feared in America. Here, in the state of New York, the soldiers are content with making a little noise, but elsewhere—in Tennessee, in Louisiana and, in general, in all the states where martial law is in effect—they often kill people and when they do, it is only a venial offense. The military governor of Tennessee, now Vice President Andrew Johnson, recently addressed a gathering of colored people. "Two people," the newspaper calmly reported, "lost their lives during the meeting." One of them, a soldier, very foolishly shouted "Hurrah for McClellan!" He was immediately surrounded and "shot," as the English language puts it with such

forceful conciseness. The other victim threw some
stones at the speakers and the guard felled him with
a single rifle shot as he was running away. The reporter adds that a mulatto was killed in reprisal by
the comrades of the soldier who had shouted "Hurrah for McClellan!" Meanwhile the orators continued their harangues. Such acts, encouraged by the
impunity they enjoy, have a grim meaning. Were
there not complaints just the other day because the
President had pardoned a Confederate officer who
was to have died in retaliation for crimes committed
by the Rebels? "Justice," it was said, demanded that
this prisoner should die. What a strange idea of justice for a Christian nation to hold!

People are also debating the arbitrary arrest of
Lieutenant-Governor [Richard T.] Jacob of Kentucky and his banishment to Rebel territory. I
believe he has long been engaged in traitorous dealings with the enemy.[11] The Democrats complain of this
summary punishment without benefit of trial, which,
even when considering the emergency suspension of
habeas corpus,[12] is not enough to justify. They see

[11] This incident was an episode in the heavy-handed repression by the military authorities in Kentucky of writings
and speeches attacking the Lincoln administration, even by
Unionists like Jacob, who on Nov. 11, 1864, was ordered to
be held incommunicado and banished to the Confederacy.
The U.S. Senate ordered an investigation and President
Lincoln promptly pardoned Jacob and Frank L. Wolford,
another Union Democrat arrested with him.

[12] Attorney-General Edward F. Bates asserted the President's power to suspend *habeas corpus* on July 15, 1861;
suspension by Executive action was made general on Sept.
24, 1862. The Habeas Corpus Act, passed after much debate in Congress on March 3, 1863, provided that "during

this as a criminal infringement of the Constitution and of civil liberties. Such measures are inevitable, however, in a country where the laws leave the government powerless.

This is precisely the defect—though some would call it the merit—of American democracy. The authority of the government is, so to speak, elastic, and provided that public opinion supports it, acts of arbitrary authority can come to be accepted on the plea that the defense of liberty requires them. The law has not foreseen this situation. License and high-handed behavior join hands to subvert the law and help each other to trespass on the domain which the law is unable to defend. Lack of foresight, it must be said, is the American failing *par excellence*, and it is evident in this unsystematic body of law they have improvised to answer the most pressing needs of a new society, like the log cabins the pioneers use for temporary shelter. It is also in the nature of popular government to give to the law a violent, capricious cast, an instability that robs it of respect. In addition, the diversity of state laws—oftentimes their flagrant contradictions—and

the present rebellion, the President of the United States, whenever, in his judgment, the public safety may require it, is authorized to suspend the writ of *habeas corpus* in any case throughout the United States, or any part thereof." Despite a small number of arbitrary arrests and imprisonments, these powers were not, in general, abused—a modern authority has concluded that "in the suppression of anti-governmental activity the government under Lincoln was milder than that of Wilson, though facing greater provocation." (J. G. Randall and David Donald, *The Civil War and Reconstruction*, 2 rev. ed., Lexington, Mass., 1969). *Habeas corpus* was also suspended in the Confederacy.

the perennial conflict between state and Federal law, make the use of the police power illusory and in troubled times actually make impossible the use of this complicated instrument. Each case must then be treated as an exception. There are neither fixed principles nor generally enforced regulations, nor consistency in the use of force; society lives by expedients from day to day.

Is that really our ideal? Are we not confusing the theory of democratic government American style and the so-called constitutional theory of the governments of Europe? The latter requires that national representatives govern by means of laws they have made, laws whose supreme authority controls the executive power, which is only an instrument. What do we discover here? Confronting the elected law-making bodies, there arises a second power, also deriving from popular suffrage, also authorized to call itself the people's representative, whose powers can expand until they amount to a dictatorship. The French Republic gave itself a president directly elected by the people, and we know how that republic came to grief.[13] In spite of the fiction of

[13] Prince Louis-Napoleon Bonaparte, overwhelmingly elected by universal manhood suffrage to the presidency of the Second French Republic in 1848, mounted a *coup d'état* on December 2, 1851 as his four-year term was about to expire and proceeded to rule as Emperor of the French until his overthrow on September 4, 1870, after he was defeated and captured by the Prussians. Like his illustrious uncle, Napoleon I, he ruled dictatorially for most of his reign, submitting his actions from time to time to popular plebiscites that were all more or less manipulated. Duvergier de Hauranne's point is that popular elections and universal suffrage are in themselves no barrier to an authoritarian regime.

election in two stages, the President of the United States is also chosen, in effect, by direct popular vote. In each of the states there is a governor who is directly elected by the people. The United States Constitution does indeed give Congress the power to depose the President, but when has this terrible right been used? He is responsible, not to Congress, but to the people, and only on Election Day. The members of the Cabinet are merely his agents, responsible to him alone, and can be replaced only by him. There are even some states where the voters choose the members of the governor's cabinet at the same time as the governor and this endows them with the same prestige as the chief magistrate himself. The theory of democracy calls for an executive power that is the people's own servant, immediately dependent on them alone, a potential instrument of revolution that can, if necessary, fly in the face of the law. Such a servant can become a master when democratic instincts are not restrained and effectively balanced, as they are in America, by long-standing traditions of individual liberty.

3

Boston: The Literary World

New York
November 23, 1864

EVERYTHING has been going well since the election, and day by day the ridiculous threat of a Democratic revolt seems less and less real. On the other side, the good grace of the losers is matched by the moderation of the winners. Honest Democrats are at heart pleased to see the Union so strongly supported by the people. Those who are still smarting from their defeat are nonetheless willing to accept the people's sovereign decision as final. They are taking a more moderate tone in order to conciliate majority opinion, and they restrict themselves to giving advice to the government on how to make peace. Some of them—the course of events having so sharply curbed their prejudices— even begin to put forward practical proposals for solving the slavery issue by some scheme providing for gradual emancipation of the blacks.

I have no idea what Mr. Lincoln will do. He is now at the zenith of his career, at that supreme height which the political sun of an American statesman can never again attain once it has been passed. Everyone is already thinking about the election of 1868 the way schoolboys on the opening day of school start to dream of the distant day when they will again be free. Everyone wonders who will be the next President of the United States—Butler, Banks, Seward, Grant or Sherman? This is all empty speculation because it represents an attempt to solve a problem that one doesn't even know how to formulate. Who knows what the state of affairs in each of the two halves of America will be in four years' time!

The *Herald,* that whimsical newspaper which wound up supporting Lincoln, placing McClellan in the ranks of those irrevocably dead candidates whom not even the trumpets of an electoral Last Judgment could resurrect, proposes an unexpected solution by offering itself as a candidate for the people to vote for. It demonstrates in a humorous article that if the war were to end, nobody but itself or General Grant could lay the nation's quarrels to rest. Its reasoning boils down to this: soldiers know how to make use of force, so they make good presidents; "lawyers" only know how to create a clamor and stir up disputes just for the pleasure of arguing their cases interminably before the tribunal of public opinion; but a newspaper like this one knows how to dance on a tight-rope above all parties and, just as it attracts subscribers everywhere, so will it be able to attract voters and govern the country.

General Grant, in spite of all that is said about his modesty, his integrity and his respect for civil authority, is already beginning to put on princely airs. For a long time he has been very firmly slamming his door in the faces of Cabinet members who have tried to look a little too closely into the affairs of his army. Today he sent Mr. Lincoln a message expressing satisfaction with his performance and con-

veying kind congratulations in the tone the Tsar of
Russia might use when writing to his dear cousin
the Emperor of Austria. "I beg you," he wrote to
the Secretary of War, "to give my compliments to
the President." These condescending ways seem
rather incongruous on the part of a general who is
addressing himself to his Commander-in-Chief who
gave him his command and can take it away, but the
fortunes of the "Illinois Tanner" are at present
even more inflated than those of Lincoln, the "Rail
Splitter." There have been Presidents of the United
States in quantity, but the rank of Lieutenant-General has been vacant since the War of Independence.[1] Grant is thus the immediate successor to
Washington, an enormous piece of luck of the kind
that democracy confers today only to snatch it away
tomorrow without the slightest warning.

America is at present honoring one of those
ephemeral heroes who change from week to week.
Grant has a rival for the applause of the masses in
the person of Captain [John A.] Winslow. This naval officer, who defeated the privateer *Alabama*, has
been literally borne in triumph from one end of the
United States to the other. Boston has just given
him a splendid welcome, New York is clamoring
for him and the national propensity for imitation—
which reminds one of Panurge's sheep—will surely

[1] A special act of Congress was needed to restore the rank
of Lieutenant-General of the Army; this measure became
law on February 26, 1864. Grant's nomination to the grade
was approved by the Senate March 2, and on March 9 his
commission was handed to him at the White House by President Lincoln. This placed him in supreme command of all
the armies of the Union.

bring him many more ovations. Prominent men like Mr. [Edward] Everett do not hesitate to harness themselves to his triumphal chariot. You would almost think that the fight between the *Alabama* and the *Kearsarge* was the most glorious feat of arms in this century. The hero, puffed up by his unexpected fame, goes from banquet to banquet telling the tale of his great deeds. If you believed all he says, you would think that all by himself on his little boat he held the envious powers of Europe at bay, paralyzed with terror, that he thumbed his nose at the French navy, slapped a British admiral in the face and defied Lord Russell by sailing right up the Thames—indeed, that he has made the name of America shine like a fiery sword in the eyes of a terrified Europe. But at the same time, he seems to have let his glory go a little to his head. "The defeat of the *Alabama*," he says, "is only a small part of what I have done for my country. If I am worthy of all these honors for this one deed, I deserve a great deal more for my service on the Mississippi and on blockade duty outside the ports of the South." Who still remembers these actions today? Who will recall next year the glorious exploits of the *Kearsarge*? The American public soon gets enough of its idols. Clever men never let themselves be exploited in this way; they prefer to be the impressario who sponsors one of these seven-day wonders; in this way they avoid inflating for themselves the dangerous balloon of popularity that rises so high and so swiftly, but will just as suddenly let fall those it has lifted up.

Boston
November 25, 1864

I TOOK THE BOAT from New York to Boston the day
before yesterday. I was driving down the wide avenue called Broadway in a great hurry, cursing the
many carriages that continually got in my way. I
won't give a lengthy description of the hopeless
traffic jam I ran into on the docks nor the difficulty
I had getting on board. When my cab got stalled in
the tangle of horses and wagons, I leaped out and
made my way on foot, followed by a porter with my
trunk. Nor shall I weary you with an inventory of
the densely-packed throng of passengers on the big,
luxurious boat which runs on a regular schedule
between New York and Boston.

One must actually come to America to get even a
notion of how heavy the traffic is. The crossing
from Paris to London is not at all comparable to the
travel that takes place daily between these two rivals for the title of chief metropolis of the United
States. Three railroads and three shipping lines,
whose enormous boats are capable of carrying 800
to 900 passengers, are scarcely able to accommodate
the vast number of travelers who present themselves
at their ticket-windows.

It is true that I made my trip on the day before
Thanksgiving, a day of prayer and good works proclaimed by the President, and half the population
seemed to be going somewhere. It is an old custom
to spend this patriotic holiday with ones family. As
on Christmas in England or New Year's Day in
France, the traditional goose or turkey is eaten under the paternal roof. Nowhere is this custom more

faithfully observed than in New England, the land of strong traditions and long-standing customs. The church bells are rung as on Sunday, the people put on their most sober formal clothes and go to church to hear a political sermon—for although human concerns invade the pulpit even on days consecrated to religion, they are in full control on this day of national rejoicing. In every parish church a platform for political speakers is set up; in one town the war may be debated, somewhere else the question of slavery, and the Constitution in yet another place; but everywhere the discussion is dominated by the national questions of the day. Republican preachers are inspired by the President's proclamation; the Democrats use the proclamation of Governor [Horatio] Seymour [of New York], who joins in the call to public prayer but uses ambiguous language. He prays for the chastisement of the wicked, the return of justice and the safety of the country, leaving everyone free to interpret justice and patriotism in his own way. However, the normal activities of life go on; people do not feel obliged, as on a Sunday, to behave in a solemn, mournful way. The public parks and residential streets present a picture that is lively without being boisterous. It is truly a festive occasion, a day when people dare to raise their heads and speak out loud, free of the funereal constraints of the Sabbath.

Otherwise there is nothing new, and there were no newspapers this morning. This evening the press carries a rumor that the three states of Georgia, Alabama and Mississippi are ready to sue for peace in the hope of preserving slavery, which is more

Engraving, 1859

Heavy Traffic on Lower Broadway

From *Harper's Weekly*, Courtesy of the New York Public Library

gravely threatened today by Jefferson Davis than by
Mr. Lincoln. Caught between two fires, the poor
slaveowners do not know which devil they should
look to for salvation. If this news is true, there can
be no doubt that it is all up with the rebellion.

The question of drafting blacks into the [Confed-
erate] army has turned the Confederacy upside
down. There is a moderate group in the South that
recoils from heroic measures. This party, frequently
accused of leaning toward treason, recently renewed its vows of loyalty to the lost cause, but with
just a hint that it is time to throw in the sponge.
The leader of this party, as you know, is Governor
[Joseph E.] Brown of Georgia, the opponent—one
might almost say, the personal foe—of Jefferson Davis, the same Governor Brown who is said to have
entered into negotiations with General Sherman
which he was obliged to disavow when news of the
talks leaked out. Although he continues to speak
loudly and firmly against the North and has even
signed the resolution giving President Davis full
control over the slaves of Virginia, the Carolinas,
Alabama and Mississippi, he is known to be secretly
opposed to a measure that would bring about his
own ruin. The question of slavery is bound up with
the old antagonism between Georgia and its rival
state [Virginia]. At the beginning of the rebellion,
when conventions in South Carolina and Georgia
voted the famous ordinances of secession, Virginia
still hesitated to follow their lead. Later she took
over the conduct of the war and Georgia slipped
back to second place. So when President Davis outlined to the Confederate Congress his proposal—

unthinkable in that body—to free all blacks who would join the army, violent disputes arose between the representatives of Virginia and those of the "cotton states," dissension that seemed to foreshadow an imminent rupture. Virginia, which has nothing more to lose, ardently supports this desperate expedient; but Georgia, Alabama and Mississippi, much of whose wealth is still tied up in Negro slaves and who look forward, in addition, to making a great deal of money from the sale of their cotton [when the war ends], are strongly tempted to ask the Union for protection from the ruthless extremism now being advocated by the chief spokesmen for the desperate pro-slavery faction.

The poor secessionists! They precipitated a civil war; they set up a government to defend and propagate slavery; and now this government takes them by the throat, saying to them in its turn: "Give up your slaves!" Then they look for help to their old enemy; the Federal government becomes the only remaining hope of the supporters of slavery, the last resort of those who hope at the very least to see slavery continue until it dies a natural death. In the meantime, the debates go on in the congress at Richmond, the members coming at times, it is said, to "fisticuffs." The most determined speakers denounce the proposed measure as confiscatory. The South would dishonor herself, they say, by lowering the banner of slavery; she would betray her creed and her pledged word. To enlist the Negro by offering him his freedom would amount to the recognition that he is not unworthy of freedom and that slavery is not the highest social status which the

Creator has decreed for him. It would also mean abandoning as a threadbare lie the basic principle of the Southern social structure. If you also note that the champions of slavery are still owners of slaves and that their opponents no longer own any, you will have detected the secret behind those noble passions which, on one side as on the other, serve to call forth such chivalrous devotion.

The government party answers that this is not the time for conscientious scruples nor humanitarian theories, that the war has devoured the white population, that it is necessary to fill the ranks with blacks or else admit defeat. But the Georgians don't consider themselves beaten; they reply that the reserves are not yet depleted, that the blacks would not make good soldiers and that the claims put forward by a rapacious government must be resisted. The government points to [the successful use of black troops by] the armies of the North. Then they fall back on their final, unassailable argument: "You have taken all the white farm laborers; now only the Negroes are left to work in the fields; it is their labor that feeds us. If you put guns in their hands in place of hoes and sickles, we shall soon starve to death. The institution of slavery has been, up to the present time, the South's chief source of strength, for it has enabled her for four years to wage a war that required the mobilization of all her free men. By ending slavery you will cut your food supplies and thereby put an end to our resistance." But what can be done? Where can new resources be found? Men are needed on the battlefield, men are needed in the cornfields. As even the British admit,

Lee has no more than the shadow of an army. The choice now lies between peace and famine. Jefferson Davis is sure that one more vigorous effort will suffice to end the war, after which the South can make good its losses at leisure: this is the government's position. But even as they proclaim their confidence, the Confederates must have fear and despair in their hearts. Even if, by emancipating and recruiting black troops, they find enough men to go on resisting for a short time, they know full well that after one more campaign famine will put them at the mercy of the North, reduced to begging the enemy for a crust of bread. Then and only then, clemency, moderation and brotherly forgiveness will be possible. But until then, considering how obstinately these men are determined on their own ruin, the word "peace" seems to me a snare and a delusion.

November 28, 1864

I HAVE already described to you the city of Boston; it is now time for me to show you some of its people. Everyone here has welcomed me with open arms. I have already been showered with invitations to dinner and evening parties, quite apart from my having received a host of callers—for it is the hospitable custom of the Bostonians to come to meet a visitor, thus taking the first step toward the establishment of an acquaintanceship.

For my début I dined yesterday at the Atlantic Club with the flower of Boston's literary and political society. There were a good number of men who are well known on both sides of the ocean. The famous naturalist [Louis] Agassiz, the philosopher

and poet [Ralph Waldo] Emerson, Mr. [Charles]
Sumner, who introduced me as his guest, Senator
[Henry] Wilson of Massachusetts, Mr. Richard
Dana, a distinguished jurist and writer, Mr. [Oliver]
Wendell Holmes, the well-known poet who is the
author of an ode that has almost become a national
hymn,[2] and many other more or less celebrated persons. I sat at table between Emerson and Agassiz.
The latter is solid and robust with large hands, a
powerful voice and a simple, serious cast of mind
that makes his rather heavy, slow speech pleasant to
listen to; he is a striking figure because of the remarkable impression he gives of intellectual power.
Mr. Emerson, in contrast, is thin and frail with a
cheerful, ironic expression; he looks a little like a
poet and very much like a philosopher; he is also
very decidedly endowed with originality and a
sense of humor, a little like [Jean-Jacques] Ampère[3]
but more abstract, more profound and less sparkling in his conversational manner.

[2] The poem, "Old Ironsides," prompted by Holmes's indignation on learning that the Navy intended to scrap the
U.S.S. Constitution, was published in 1830 and aroused na-
tion-wide efforts to save and preserve the ship, first at Annapolis (where it was rescued from Confederate seizure by
General Benjamin F. Butler early in 1861) and then at the
Boston Navy Yard to which it was taken on Butler's initiative. It is now a National Monument.

[3] A French traveler who visited the United States in 1851.
Duvergier de Hauranne had read his book, *Récit de voyages
dans différentes parties de l'Amérique du Nord* along with
other writings by European visitors to America. The reference may be to his father, André-Marie Ampère, the French
physicist for whom the electrical unit, the ampere, was
named.

Seated opposite me was Senator Wilson, a man of great ability who has risen, it seems, from the ranks of the common people and has kept in his speech a certain trace of his country origin—good-natured, modest, with a face that shines with honesty, but rather shy, as I imagine must be the case with our Ballanche[4] and with other naturally superior persons who have found their own level with difficulty. The Atlantic Club is a small academy, closed to the uninitiated, to which one can be admitted only by satisfying the double requirement of literary reputation and friendship. The prevailing atmosphere is one of simple cordiality and pleasant good fellowship combined with an air of distinction. It is a hundred leagues removed from the mercantile tumult of New York.

I spent Sunday in the country in one of those Massachusetts villages where not a single peasant is to be seen. Nothing could be cleaner, more peaceful or more countrified than this kind of suburban town which could almost be called a city. The general well-being that seems to prevail here is a pleasure to see. Yet the soil is poor, consisting mainly of rough, granite hills covered with scrub pines and grayish juniper. Between the rocky outcroppings there are fields surrounded by dry stone walls where little wooden buildings are used as stables.

---

[4] Pierre-Simon Ballanche (1776-1847) was a French writer whose religio-sentimental poems and novels helped to prepare the way for French Romanticism. He was a friend of Madame Récamier and of the Duvergier de Hauranne family. He was a member of the French Academy and was apparently known for his shyness.

Everywhere the bare rock emerges from the stony soil. In the distance the sea stretches out in long, silvery strips between misty promontories. It is divided into thousands of tiny channels, forming an archipelago of islands and land-locked basins. Boston's harbor, its peninsula and its ships, so completely fills the foreground of the view that the observer cannot believe he is on the shore of the ocean. The landscape has an austere and delicate charm, colored by gentle, serene melancholy. It recalls by contrast the rich valleys of the West, watered by muddy, fertilizing rivers whose banks are enriched by the decayed remains of a thousand generations of plants, while domes of dark foliage tower above the tall columns of the forest trees. What a difference there is between these two types of natural environment! Yet visible signs of wealth are to be found everywhere along these forbidding shores, while the lush forests of Indiana contain nothing but a few poor log cabins whose chinks are filled with river mud. What a magician, then, is man, who can make so much from so little!

November 29, 1864

I HAVE MADE two new acquaintances: Mr. Wendell Phillips, the famous abolitionist orator, and Mr. [Edmund] Quincy, the grandson of a man famous in the history of America[5] and himself one of the leaders of the abolitionist party. Both were eager to in-

[5] Josiah Quincy (1744-1775), patriot and leader of the American Revolution in Massachusetts. With John Adams he defended the British soldiers placed on trial for their part in the Boston Massacre and helped secure their acquittal.

troduce me to their native city. Mr. Quincy, a dis-
tinguished-looking man with sensitive features,
slightly aloof but an agreeable talker, is known in
Boston for his scholarship and his knowledge of local antiquities. He showed me all the little historical curiosities from the colonial period: the costume
worn by [Benjamin] Franklin when he signed the
treaty of alliance with France, Washington's epaulettes, the location of the old house, now destroyed,
where Franklin was born, the Bunker Hill battlefield and the granite obelisk that has been erected
on the spot where the famous [Joseph] Warren died.

Just for the record I shall also mention the cannons of the arsenal, the "Monitors," those floating
batteries of artillery, the steel-plated blockade-runners captured from the Confederates and the huge
unfinished men-of-war, now abandoned as obsolete,
which have been left to rot in the shipyards. The
new ships that are to replace them have very
strange, awkward shapes, some rising only a few
inches above the waterline, others long and slender,
with hardly any superstructure, bulging in the middle and tapering away to flattened ends that slope
down to below the water level. To the same degree
that the old sailing ships were picturesque, spacious
and graceful, these low, armored gun-emplacements
are like hideous prisons. The most noteworthy discovery I made at the Navy Yard[6] was the workers
themselves. When you see three hundred men file

[6] Duvergier de Hauranne uses the term *arsénal*, and the
presumption is that he meant the Boston Navy Yard in as
much as his discussion has principally to do with ships and
naval matters.

past on their way back to work after lunch, all wearing good, respectable clothes, some of them completely middle-class in appearance, you find it hard
to believe they are just ordinary workmen. Our city
workers, of whose intelligence and education we
boast while deploring their vices in the same breath,
are nothing but a pack of ragamuffins in comparison
with these gentlemen.

What we call "the common people" [*le peuple*]—
that is, the class of ignorant persons who have no
hope of rising in the social scale, does not exist in
Massachusetts; and the secret of this marvel, the
magic wand that raises everyone to the ranks of the
middle classes, is education.

Do you want convincing evidence of what I say?
Come and examine the three levels of free schools
in which the city of Boston teaches all its children,
advancing them from the elementary school as far as
they wish to go: to the study of history, literature,
ancient and modern languages (Latin, French and
Spanish), mathematics, physics, chemistry, natural
science—even, if they want to go that far, to Greek
and astronomy. Come and see the large libraries
that are open to one and all, founded for the most
part by private individuals, where every resident
has the right to borrow books on the strength of his
signature alone. The principal library circulates
two hundred thousand volumes just in the city of
Boston. You think, perhaps, that this free circulation of books gives rise to continual thefts? Well,
the librarians tell me it rarely happens that a book
is not returned. Furthermore, nothing could be
more honest or likely to inspire confidence than the

Engraving, about 1864

U. S. S. Constitution *at Boston Navy Yard*

(Seen from East Boston)

readers' faces. I couldn't watch them go by without feeling something akin to respect, so novel was it to see common folk reading and studying not only the novels of Wilkie Collins or Alexandre Dumas but even big, thick tomes that would have discouraged me. I observed the same studious, well-behaved, respectable conduct in the schools I visited this morning with Mr. Phillips as my guide. I saw no sign that the children are ever punished. When the teacher had to leave the classroom, she left the children unsupervised with an assigned task to complete and went out, locking the door behind her. Not a single child moved from its seat or from its little table. When it came time for the oral recitation, they were so attentive, so docile and eager to learn that I was astonished. These people truly have resources of serious-mindedness and sober decency that are worth fully as much as the flighty wit of which we are too fond of boasting.

The Boston schools are administered by a board whose members are directly elected by the people; it is presided over by the mayor or, in his absence, by the president of the city council, both of whom are *ex-officio* members. Each ward or neighborhood is entitled to six members; one third of these are replaced each year. This board has complete control over all matters pertaining to the public schools, the building of schoolhouses, the ranking of students by classes, the recruitment and remuneration of teachers and the organization of the curriculum. A Superintendent, appointed by them for a year at a time, functions as inspector and as administrator of this little assembly. The board is sub-

divided into elected committees, each one dealing
with one of the special branches of education: the
latter submit their detailed reports every year to the
main board which, in its turn, publishes a general
report for the information of the public. There are
three types of schools graded in ascending order
according to the level of instruction and the pupils
must pass examinations in order to be promoted
from one level to the next. In the "primary"
schools, of which there are about two hundred and
fifty, the children learn to read, write and do arithmetic. In the "grammar" schools they learn grammar, geography, bookkeeping, elementary science
and American history. Finally, in the upper
schools, or "high schools," they study modern languages, drawing, higher mathematics, world history
and literature. There is also an institution specializ-
ing in the humanities, the Latin School, also free of
tuition, where children of the wealthier families are
often prepared for their University studies alongside the children of working men. As for the High
and Normal School for Girls,[7] students are accepted
in order of merit and leave with diplomas that attest
to their qualification for teaching. They learn
French, Latin, drawing, music and science—everything a schoolteacher needs to know; this is the
training school for the new teachers who are needed
every year.

At the Normal School I saw grown-up girls,
dressed like young ladies, taking a French lesson
given by a professor who is an unfortunate political

[7] Like its counterpart in Philadelphia (see below, pp. 499,
501-2), this school led the way in raising standards.

refugee. They were daughters of artisans and small shopkeepers in the city. Most of them were more knowledgeable than many of our rich young ladies, women's education being no less thorough here than that of men. Furthermore, in their manners, in their appearance, even in their speech, they are completely ladylike, and it is jokingly reported that in the city council the establishment of this school was opposed by [rich] fathers who were afraid their sons might lose their hearts to these girls and marry them. In the boys' school I watched while lads only fifteen years old solved problems in trigonometry or fluently recited the meaning of lines from Virgil. How should one then be surprised to learn that after such an education they often keep up for a whole lifetime the strong interest they acquire in all the classes of this school in literary and scientific matters, that in the evening as relaxation from business shopkeepers go to hear Agassiz speak about glaciers or to listen patiently while Emerson gives one of his lectures—no doubt with great wit and even with some profundity, but in a monotonous and hesitant voice—on his perennially favorite subject of education?

I was one member of his audience, and I must admit that I found the evening rather long. But the public seemed delighted and crowded around the lecturer after his speech as though to express silent congratulations. The women came in large numbers to this talk, though the subject was not the least bit frivolous. This is because here in Boston they play a role that is well above the one we allow them in France. Teaching is their special domain; most tasks involving books and papers are reserved for them. Of the approximately six hundred teachers employed by the city schools, more than five hundred are women. In the public libraries, apart from the bearded directors, the various departments are staffed by young women. In government offices, in courthouses, in the public archives, they are employed as clerks and copyists. Nothing seems odder to a European than to see their cheerful little faces in such solemn places. In the anteroom of the district attorney serving the Federal court in Boston I found, not a sergeant-at-arms nor a male civil servant seated at the desk, but a very young woman who ushered me into the magistrate's office. Frankly, this sort of thing would scarcely be conceivable in France; it would seem shocking to us—at the very least, it would make people laugh. So much the worse for us! Nobody here sees anything wrong in this way of managing things.

But let us return to the public schools. The city of Boston is justly proud of them, and it is said that only those of Philadelphia can be compared with them. They cost the taxpayers $800,000 a year. The average annual expense per child ten years ago was only about $12.00; now it is $15.76. Nor is this great public institution the only one the city has established; to it must be added the special schools, which are partly supported by private charity: "reform" schools (houses of correction for unruly or homeless children), asylums for the blind and for the deaf and dumb; and finally, prisons where wayward girls are morally rehabilitated and educated. When one sees the results of these efforts, one begins to understand the power of local initiative and the advantages of liberty.

The Americans have long since solved the problems over which we Europeans are still wringing our hands. Free schooling, that revolutionary novelty, the bogeyman of so many timid souls, has existed here for two hundred years. At the founding of the colony, the Puritans made it obligatory, subject to a fine for noncompliance, to maintain a school in each township: this was the origin of the admirable system of universal popular education. But of course I am in error in calling it a system, for in the United States there is no systematic body of law governing public education. Each locality has its own laws, and each school has its own rules. There are schools of all kinds: some are run by the state governments, others by the cities, and still others are private establishments. The only thing they all have in common is the spirit that guides them all. The very same educational opportunities cannot be offered everywhere; only the very large cities have established high schools which give, so to speak, an aristocratic education. Sometimes in smaller towns generous private persons have founded "academies" to provide the same course of study. The state often contributes money to these academies; thus the state of Massachusetts spends, year in and year out, some ten million dollars, half for schools, and half for charitable institutions, hospitals or reformatories. Its role is to encourage, to stimulate and to support, but not to administer.

The Americans rightly say that their system of public education is the keystone of their republican institutions. They are not afraid that the people may be less law-abiding or well-behaved as they grow more self-reliant and better educated. They think, on the contrary, that it would be madness to entrust political power to an ignorant populace and that in a democracy one can never do too much to promote the education of the citizens. We like to spin fine theories to define the reasonable limits of popular education and measure out the infinitessimal dose of book learning the working man needs. We like to believe that one drop more would poison him by raising his aspirations too high, that he would then despise his humble condition, scorn manual labor and die of hunger because he would be too proud to work. We also reject free education as contrary to the individualistic principles of political economy, the doctrine that says everyone must earn what he gets and sees in social existence nothing but the calculating exchange of services that are precisely equal in value.

I recognize that in theory this doctrine is perfectly logical and I will go so far as to concede that the right to free education represents a burden imposed on the rich by the poor, a classic example of redistributory taxation. I would even call it "socialism"—that dreadful word that arouses such horror, that name so terrible that in France it suffices to discredit even the most useful reforms.

But what of it? Is it more important in politics to go by theories or by results? What importance is to be attached to an abstract system of ideas when the general well-being, the morality and the freedom of a whole country can be bought at the heavy cost of sacrificing a syllogism or an equation? In this instance we aren't talking of the schemes of utopian dreamers, which we can easily refute with the irresistible argument that they are impossible in practice. On the contrary, it is on practice, on long and successful experience that the Americans base their claim that free education is not only a boon to the people, but is, in addition, a prime necessity for any real democracy.

I am ashamed when I think of the intellectual poverty of my country. I am no longer surprised by our strange method of applying the principle of universal suffrage. We must do one of two things: either give political rights only to the rich and well-educated, which would be an impossibility today, or else take our stand squarely in support of the cause of equality and give a royal education to the new rulers of our society. It has often been said that the essence of France is her middle class, and that was true as long as they alone had a part in governing the country; but since the sluice-gates have been thrown open to popular rule, the middle classes, if they are not to fall to the level of the common people, have no choice but to raise the people to their own level. Some may ask what use working men will make of their knowledge—they will busy themselves with the affairs of their country. Some ask what reason they would then have to accept their lowly position in life, but it will not seem so humble when education has enabled them to improve their lot, so that a carpenter is the intellectual equal of a bourgeois. Certainly education becomes useless, and even dangerous, if you deprive the people of their political rights, or if you do not take education seriously; but it is indispensable if democracy is not to degenerate into disorder or let itself be lulled to sleep by some despot.

I do not leave out of account the obstacles which stand in the way of adopting these reforms in our country: first, there is our administrative centralization, an apparatus that is too complicated and cumbersome to set in motion; then there is the immense financial burden such a task would impose on the state; finally, there is the need to combine the idea of duty to that of rights and to join the principle of obligatory attendance with that of free tuition. Local governments cannot be expected to make great efforts immediately after their liberation from the tutelage of the central administration. They are now simply sponges that an all-powerful hand squeezes and then refills. They need to be emancipated, yet at the same time they need some guidance. I know very well that we are caught in a vicious circle because we lack the moral impetus that comes from progress. The Irish immigrants who arrive in Boston in the condition of uneducated backwardness that prevails in their native land are all eager to send their children to school. They swim with the current and let it carry them along; they are under strong incentives to bring themselves up to the average level. With us it would be necessary to provide powerful legal constraints to achieve the same result.

The ways of despotism are, I admit, much more convenient: you need only a small number of educated men to lead the great flock of the common people with the aid of a few shepherd dogs who obey without knowing what they are doing. But in a democracy the flock must lead itself and the shepherd as well. The founders of the [Massachusetts Bay] colony understood this two hundred years ago when they laid down the principle of free public education. The day when every French city of two hundred thousand people will, like Boston, provide four million [francs] a year to pay for its schools, we shall have achieved an enormous political advance as well as a very great moral benefit.

As I finish this account of my visit to the schools, I should like to acquaint you a little with my kind and capable guide, Mr. Wendell Phillips. The first thing that strikes one is his gentle good nature; it is difficult to imagine that this man, who is so simple and so charming, could be the powerful speaker and dedicated reformer whom everyone agrees in placing among the very greatest living American orators. He is a tall man with an aquiline nose, a prominent chin, a high forehead, reddish hair that is turning gray and light brown eyes in which one reads good humor and serenity. He always wears a wide-brimmed gray hat which gives him something of the appearance of an elderly botanist. He is said to possess a large fortune which he devotes entirely to the cause of Abolition. Looking at him, one wonders where he keeps the reserves of energy on which he has drawn in many perilous encounters, and the passionate conviction that has earned him the hatred of the pro-slavery forces.

Such are the men I see every day in Boston, men whose manners are as simple as their minds are

Photograph, about 1865   Courtesy of the New York Public Library

Wendell Phillips Entering His Home
at 26 Essex Street, Boston

superior. Spend some time in the libraries or the museums and you will find everywhere this type of scholarly gentleman dressed in black, his facial expression kindly and open, his manner courteous, his conversation marked by the quiet charm conferred by advanced studies. A nation assured of an unfailing supply of such men will never need to fear for its survival. When I remember that only a few years ago they were insulted, mistreated and even beaten, that to be enlisted in the ranks of Abolitionism and national reform was to be condemned by public opinion to inevitable ostracism; when I remember that they persevered nonetheless and that today their cause has triumphed, I am filled with confidence in the future of America.

It was not so long ago that in Boston, the very capital of egalitarian abolitionism, Mr. Phillips was threatened in his own home by an angry crowd—all his friends had to arm themselves and rush to his defense. Once in the West, speaking to a gathering of Democrats, he stood his ground on the platform for an hour, exposed to a hailstorm of stones, eggs and apples, which rained down upon him from all parts of the hall. He went on speaking nevertheless with unruffled courage until the chairman of the meeting came forward and begged him to retire in order not to exasperate the crowd any further. When I went to call on him in his modest little house, he showed me a marble bust with noble, masculine features expressive of the most striking grandeur—it was the head of the heroic John Brown, the unschooled Connecticut farmer, the armed missionary of human liberty, who declared his own personal war on slavery and paid on the gallows for his glorious apostleship. I also saw the crude spear with which this warrior out of the Old Testament fought in the Virginia mountains at the head of a little army of fugitive slaves when their persecutors came to track them down. The blood of John Brown has been as fruitful as that of other martyrs. His tall figure is already a legend enshrined in the American memory; when black regiments go into battle they march to the warlike strains of *John Brown's Body.*[8]

November 30, 1864

YESTERDAY I visited the poet [Henry Wadsworth] Longfellow, whose name at least is probably familiar to you. Mr. Longfellow lives in Cambridge, one of the more rural suburbs of Boston, in a large, plain, wooden house which nevertheless has an atmosphere of ancient simplicity. The high mansard roof, the ornate lightening rods, the heavy pilasters of the façade, the sections of pruned hedges and the geometrically shaped trees planted in a zig-zag pattern, together with the strict formality of its French-style flower-beds—in all these ways it contrasts strongly with the comic-opera cottages that line the avenue and, as architects say, serve to situate it in a

---

[8] It is impossible to be sure whether the earlier song, *John Brown's Body* or Julia Ward Howe's *Battle Hymn of the Republic* is meant here. The tune was the same and both used the refrain beginning "Glory, glory, hallelujah"; Union troops both black and white undoubtedly sang both songs. In addition, there was a third set of words sung to the same music, the March of the 4th Arkansas [Black] Volunteers, which was also a favorite in the Federal armies.

time-period. In fact, this house is a sort of historical landmark: it served as General Washington's headquarters during the War of Independence. The first time I entered its doors was two months ago, in the company of Mr. Charles Sumner. We didn't bother to use the iron knocker on the oaken front door, but walked right in, passed through the empty rooms, left our calling-cards in a parlor furnished simply but in good taste, and then slipped out like a pair of burglars, having seen neither a servant nor a dog nor the master of the house. Still, the books, the paintings, the art objects, the studious and inviting atmosphere of the library decorated with bouquets of flowers, everything showing the good taste that had obviously inspired all these modest arrangements—everything in keeping with the choice of a secluded way of life in the country, though actually not far distant from the literary society of Boston. The domestic tranquility, the unlocked and welcoming front door which we had so unceremoniously opened—all this had predisposed me in favor of the occupants of this house even before I made their acquaintance.

Yesterday I returned, escorted by a close relative of the poet. For the last three years Mr. Longfellow, whose life has been shadowed by a great and irreparable sorrow,[9] has hardly left his house and has been willing to see only a few of his old friends. These all told me, "You will see how good he is, how kind and gracious." Some even added, "He is an angel!"

[9] The tragedy referred to was the death of the poet's second wife, Frances Appleton Longfellow, of severe burns in 1861.

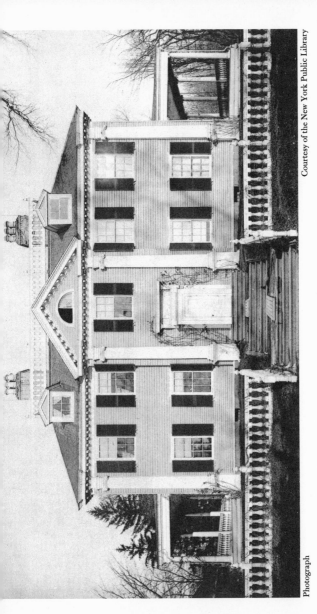

Photograph

Courtesy of the New York Public Library

Longfellow's Home, Cambridge, Massachusetts

And surely, if ever moral goodness and beauty were imprinted with visible lines on a human face, they are conspicuous in the mild but noble features, in the open and friendly expression of the man who rose to offer me his hand. He is, to be sure, no longer the fashionable poet whose portrait I have seen in the print-sellers' shops, for in the last three years he has aged so terribly that one scarcely recognizes him. His long gray hair and his broad, bushy gray beard make him look like an aging Homer; his ever-charming smile is now almost always obscured by an indescribable sadness, but his grave, strong face still radiates an almost-feminine sweetness. Above all, what a difference there is between this serene father of a family, who oversees the education of his children as well as the management of his household, and our flashy, show-off poets who are always striking heroic attitudes on the pretentious pedestal of their utter fatuousness! That difference alone prejudiced me in his favor to the same degree that I am disgusted in advance by the fraudulent self-dramatization of certain self-styled geniuses and by the petty arrogance that goes along with it.

I do not know his works well as yet, but in leafing through his poetry I found, alongside some things that are perhaps a little ordinary and uninspired, a number of passages that are very fine, marked as they are by the restraint and the exquisite delicacy that are always present in his work. He excels chiefly in his choice of words and images, in the fresh, early-morning purity of his colors. The form, always rich and full of beautiful touches, has at the same time a naïve and, one might say, a Homeric quality. It is this that is the mark of the true poet. He continually finds similes that are captivating, almost childlike, but have also a simple, serene grandeur. What could be more beautiful, for example, than the grave but swiftly-evoked image of "the benediction that falls from the priest's hands as the seed falls from the hands of the sower?" What could be more delightful than the two lines: "These words fell on the heart of Evangeline as the snows of winter fall on an empty nest from whence the birds have flown?" His whole poem *Evangeline*,[10] an experiment and perhaps a risky one with an unfortunate metrical scheme, is nonetheless a jewel comparable to Goethe's *Hermann and Dorothea*. In his *Hiawatha* the inspiration, usually tender and melancholy, rises with ease to epic heights. In *The Golden Legend* he has borrowed his inspiration from the philosophical symbolism of German poetry. His odes are recited everywhere and compete with the lachrymose verses of [Alfred Lord] Tennyson for the favor of female English readers. I have met

[10] These two quotations from *Evangeline* read as follows in the original:

> But when the service was done,
>   and the benediction had fallen
> Forth from the hands of the priest
>   like seed from the hands of the sower."
>
> (Part II, lines 510-11)

and:

> But on Evangeline's heart fell his words
>   as in winter the snowflakes
> Fall into some lone nest
>   from which the birds have departed
>
> (Part II, lines 525-6)

Americans who find fault with his poetic style for being too full of romantic reveries and prefer to Longfellow's calm sensibility the lyrical and ardent [James Cullen] Bryant. He is a genius of the second rank, I will admit, a demigod who rules the flowery lower slopes of the poetic Olympus, inferior perhaps to the great gods enthroned on its peaks amidst clouds and tempests, but a man of great talent and charm. His conversation is simple, without vanity or ostentation, turning by preference to literary subjects, but ready to show interest in anything under the sun. He questions more often than he gives his own opinions and seems to have an admiring and enthusiastic interest in European intellectual movements, especially those of Paris. This is the attitude I am accustomed to finding among most of the really distinguished people in America who have any experience of Europe. Such persons do not speak disparagingly of France and do not have for themselves that naïve and conceited admiration of which I sometimes complain. On the contrary, they have an awestruck and exaggerated worship for Europeans, for their ideas, for their manners and for their traditions. They regard Paris especially as the center from which all intelligence radiates, the school of all refinement, the home of a gifted and cultivated people whom younger nations ought to take as a model. Alas! We no longer have a very good claim to exercise this kind of fascination, though it still holds sway over all those [in other countries] who think or write.

A victory won by General [George H.] Thomas in Tennessee was announced today. Yesterday it was a set-back for Sherman and the emergency measures taken by Governor Brown of Georgia to introduce universal and compulsory military service. The governor has responded to [Sherman's] invasion by proclaiming that the public safety is in danger. He has called to the colors all males between fifteen and sixty without exception. Those who have some claim to deferment lose the benefit of their exemption if they do not immediately declare the grounds for it on the spot; anyone who tries to evade military service will be sent immediately "to the front." If a railroad refuses to carry soldiers its directors will be arrested and sent to the army. However, the [New York] *World*, a newspaper that is not given to maligning the Rebels, gives a detailed and heartrending account of their horrible sufferings, of living conditions worse than those of pigs in a sty, of wanton cruelties inflicted by the Confederates on helpless Union prisoners. Finally, those good patriots who are disgruntled by Lincoln's election are trying to work off their anger by setting fires in the big cities of the North. The Secretary of War learned just the other day from his spies that an arsonists' plot was being mounted in New York, Washington and Baltimore; the same day, fires were set in all the hotels and public buildings and on board a number of ships in New York harbor. The day before, a band of disguised Rebels had taken up their posts in all parts of the city with carpet-bags full of phosphorus, kerosene and other inflammable materials. Some of them were captured, but the rest got away and the city suffered nothing more serious than a good scare. The *World* and the *Daily News*, both Copperhead newspapers, tried to make a joke of the whole incident and professed to see in it nothing but a clumsy piece of provocation staged by the abolitionists; but everyone knows very well what it was all about and I leave it to you to imagine the indignation this escapade has aroused here against an enemy who is not ashamed to employ such tactics.

December 2, 1864

THE DAY before yesterday, I was invited to dine at the home of Mr. Loring,[11] a noted lawyer and jurist, an outstanding citizen, respectable and respected by everyone, an American of the old school who drinks his first glass of wine to the health of the President of the United States and discourses on the legendary exploits of the frigate *Constitution*, whose prow, mounted on a column, at present decorates the Navy Yard.[12] Afterwards I was introduced by Mr. Quincy to a weekly gathering attended by a certain number of distinguished Bostonians at the home of Chief Justice [George Tyler] Bigelow. I met there the leader of the Democratic party of Boston, Mr. [Robert Charles] Winthrop, formerly Speaker of the House of Representatives, who proudly bears the name of one of the oldest families of Massachusetts. He is a learned man, kindly, with simple man-

[11] Probably Charles Loring, who is mentioned in Chapter 5 as the presiding officer of a meeting held to raise money for the United States Sanitary Commission. He was a prominent Bostonian of the period and a man of some legal as well as literary reputation.

[12] See footnote 6, page 105.

ners and a mild disposition, whose upright, generous character is recognized even by his opponents.

The next day, I went to see him at his home, where he has a large collection of family mementoes, many dating from the original Puritan colony of which his celebrated forbears were governors, and others from the still more distant time when the family had not yet left England. He showed them to me, not without pride, and then accompanied me to the Athenaeum, an art gallery that in no way gave me an unfavorable idea of American art. Some old English and Italian works, a few French canvases, a strong Spagnoletto, a pale Ary Scheffer and a superb Rembrandt lend the collection, so to speak, its tone and style.

Without seeming to be so, Boston is rich in art objects; although it has no large museum, there is hardly a single wealthy home whose owners do not enjoy being surrounded by beautiful things. Those who have no masterpieces are still likely to have some fairly good pictures, and they have such a high regard for them that one is aware of the esteem in which they hold such things. Among their native painters, they claim one named Stewart [Gilbert Stuart (1755-1828)] a brilliant and colorful portraitist of the last century, and another one named [John Singleton] Copley [1738?-1815] who is serious, correct, a little thin, but a rather effective organizer of scenes and costumes. He really belongs to the good, solid line of representatives of the English school which has left no descendant in the crowd of conscientious mediocrities who are so much admired today in London.

Mr. Winthrop also presented me to Mr. [George] Ticknor, one of Boston's leading lights, but more a political than a literary luminary. Everything in his house recalls the interiors of English houses—it is spacious and comfortable, decorated and furnished with simple, unostentatious luxury. He himself is a still-vigorous old man, elegant and fastidious, with his beard dyed in the English style; he is the very image of a British statesman. All in all, he strikes me as interesting and extremely distinguished, although perhaps less likable than Mr. Winthrop. They both belong, Mr. Ticknor especially, to what is called the Copperhead party. They are supporters of slavery here in the heartland of Abolition; both are somewhat aristocratic in the most egalitarian region in the world. When they express their views freely, they predict the downfall of liberal institutions and the dismemberment of the Republic; they are political anachronisms who do not willingly accept their fate. Mr. Ticknor especially, with an obstinacy to which his seventy-three years no doubt entitle him, has always resisted the movement that is regenerating America at the present time. I see in him a man of the past who has refused to alter or even moderate his opinions and who, although curbing his tongue out of consideration for the irrational attitudes of his contemporaries, remains nonetheless at the bottom of his heart a convinced friend of slavery. Reserved by nature, supercilious by instinct and reticent by necessity, he speaks only with great reluctance about current events. All I could draw from him on the subject of America was a scornful comment on the men who

are ruling the country, his belief that American institutions have degenerated and after that a gloomy
silence more eloquent than many words. His drawing-room, which, incidentally, is the meeting-place
of a circle of very eminent literary people, a refuge
for believers in slavery, where a visitor who does
not wish to offend anyone dares not speak very freely. I made the acquaintance there of a certain Mr.
H., whom everyone has pointed out to me as one of
the chief spokesmen of the party and who, while
claiming to be more opposed to slavery than anyone else, has worked out a complete theoretical argument for it, omitting only the logical conclusion.
It is remarkable to observe how those who profess
such unsavory views assume a shamefaced expression in spite of themselves when giving voice to
their beliefs. When an idea exercises such power, it
clearly has the force of an invincible conviction and
it would be as useless to argue against it as to try to
sail straight into the wind.

This morning, Mr. E., a kindly and learned old
gentleman, drove me to Cambridge, the home of
the university. Cambridge is predominantly a city
of students and professors; there one finds Harvard
College, a large, flourishing and distinguished private institution that America proudly upholds as a
worthy rival to the state-supported universities of
Europe. All the rich families send their sons to
study there as in England they send them to Oxford
and Cambridge. Harvard College in the North, the
University of Virginia in the South, have long educated America's most distinguished men. Supported
by generous donations, it counts among its former

rectors (or presidents) some of the most eminent citizens of Boston.

The university buildings are surrounded by extensive landscaped enclosures and are widely separated by meadows that are still shaded by groves of oaks and elms. The professors live in attractive small houses only a few steps away from their laboratories and lecture halls, just as a parsonage adjoins its church. I saw the spacious library reserved for the students, admirably housed in a large building of brick and iron, built especially for this purpose and supplied with all the latest European publications. My guide took me to visit Professor Asa Gray, whose name is well known to all botanists. He is a gentle, serious man, kindly and alert, who watches over his greenhouses and collections of plants with a thoroughly paternal affection. He is still young, moreover, and does not give at all the impression of an elderly scholar.

Finally, we went to call on Mr. Agassiz in his museum. I had already heard him lecture on several occasions. He had at the most thirty listeners who had come from outside because his talk was not part of the official curriculum of the university; it was simply a course for amateurs to whom the illustrious scientist is trying to demonstrate the positive practical benefits of studying elementary zoology. At the lecture's end, new lessons were voted upon. The attentiveness of his small audience of Cambridge gardeners and artisans was certainly no less remarkable than the accommodating attitude of the professor who, eager above all to teach, deferred with such good grace to the wishes of the public.

4

Boston Lawyers and Politicians

[Boston]
December 4, 1864

I PAID a visit yesterday to the Court House to see
how justice takes its course. I entered by the in-
conspicuous little door through which, ten years
ago, the two runaway slaves Sims and Burns made
their exit guarded by two files of soldiers.[1] They
had just been restored to their masters by an order
of the court, which acted in accordance with the law
then in force but in defiance of the anger of the
people of Boston who threatened open resistance to
this act of legal violence. An immense crowd was
besieging the Court House and filled the streets
through which the mournful procession must pass.

[1]Thomas M. Sims and Anthony Burns. The two cases
were actually separate, the Sims case occurring in 1851 and
the Burns case in 1854. The circumstances described by the
author are essentially the same as in the Burns case, though
extraordinary measures had to be taken in both instances in
view of the intense popular indignation, the gathering of
large crowds and the denunciations by Boston's leading abolitionists of the Fugitive Slave law of 1850 under which the
two black men were arrested and returned by reluctant judges to their owners. Anthony Burns was later sold by a well-
disposed master to individuals in Boston who gave him his
freedom; he attended Oberlin College, became a minister
and—after being forced to leave his church in Indianapolis
by racist harassment—went to Canada where he was a successful pastor.

The city was full of troops, loaded cannon were placed so as to command street-crossings. The prisoners slowly crossed the city, accompanied by a silent but angry crowd, and were led on board the ship that was to take them back to slavery. That day is still fresh in the memory of Bostonians. The hateful fugitive slave law, which played so great a part in bringing on the Civil War, will always remain a humiliating and bitter memory.

The South during that time was in control of the government. It ruled at the White House with Presidents [James K.] Polk, [Franklin] Pierce and [James] Buchanan; it reigned in the Senate with [John C.] Calhoun; and it dominated the House of Representatives by means of an artificial majority which it enjoyed, thanks to the existence of slavery.[2] The South even presided over the Supreme Court in the person of Chief Justice [Roger B.] Taney, the author of the infamous Dred Scott decision [1857] which extended the institution of slavery into states[3] where it had been forbidden by acts of Congress. At that time, if Northerners dared to speak against slavery, if they protested against the iniquitous privilege that turned it into a source of politi-

[2] The original text of Article I, Section 2, of the United States Constitution contained these words, of which the bracketed portions were later superseded by the Fourteenth Amendment: "Representatives . . . shall be apportioned among the several States . . . according to their respective Numbers, [which shall be determined by adding to the whole Number of free Persons, including those bound to Service for a Term of Years, and excluding Indians not taxed, three fifths of all other Persons.] . . ."

[3] The Dred Scott decision applied to the *territories*.

cal power,* if they tried to keep the territories free of slavery, or if they wished to protect against slave-hunters those blacks who had become their fellow-citizens,† the South could not find enough hard words and insults to hurl at its critics, calling them trouble-makers, fanatics and enemies of the Union. The more they felt public opinion turning away from them, the more they added to the barbarous legislation protecting slavery.

Once the fugitives had settled in the North, their pursuit and extradition became difficult. Judges,

---

* The representation of the Southern states in Congress was based, not on the number of voters nor on the total white population, but on the total number of inhabitants both black and white, with the slaves counting for only three-fifths of their actual number. In this way the white population, which alone was granted rights of citizenship, found in slavery a source of augmented political power. This shocking inequality is now [1866] being called into question in the reconstruction of the Southern states. The Democrats, some Republicans and President Johnson himself are of the opinion that this established custom must be allowed to continue, at least temporarily. The Radicals, on the contrary, believe that the privilege was part of the slave system and that blacks ought no longer to be counted when calculating the number of representatives to be elected by the Southern states until they obtain the right to vote under the same conditions as whites.

† In the state of New York colored men have the right to vote if they have an annual income of $250 from real property. In Massachusetts they enjoy the benefits of the common law, that is, the poll tax for them, as for any citizen, is only $1.50 a year. They must, in addition, be able to read the state constitution in English, for universal [manhood] suffrage is not in effect, as one can readily understand, in all the states of the Union. Most states still require that political rights be subject to certain types of qualification.

who were often unable to ascertain an individual's true identity, preferred in doubtful cases to let the guilty go free rather than run the risk of condemning the innocent. Southerners, angered by what they called a denial of justice, finally got Congress to pass a law that removed cases concerning fugitive slaves from the ordinary courts and gave jurisdiction to special commissions created for that purpose. From then on, acquittals became rare and hunting fugitive slaves became a regular occupation. Real slavers, "slave-catchers," were to be seen overrunning the free states like conquerors, carrying off great numbers of people. Artisans, farmers, law-abiding citizens, long-time residents of their localities, were seized in their homes, taken in chains to Southern ports and auctioned off like cattle. The South had revived the slave trade in a new form and had done it in a civilized country in the name of the law. Such, however, were the many outrages and indignities which the Northern states patiently suffered! And there are some who dare to say that they were oppressing the South!

But let us return to the Court House. You are aware that judges are elected in most of the western states. The voters, when they change their government each year, also change their magistrates, either directly by an explicit vote or indirectly by electing a governor who fills judgeships with his own men. In either case, justice is no more free of the powerful influence of the political parties than the administration or the legislature, and it is only due to the universality of the jury system that such bad institutions can be made tolerable. It is not like this in

From *Harper's History of the Great Rebellion*

Senator Charles Sumner of Massachusetts
Engraving, from a Photograph

Massachusetts. Justice here is not subject to the vagaries of popular emotions nor considered a prize to be taken in tow by the victorious party. Unknown here is the absurd and even scandalous requirement that judges stand for re-election every five years, every two years or even, as sometimes happens, every year by those very same persons whom they themselves will have to judge. Instead, judges are named by the governor, who cannot subsequently remove them from office. However, it is not impossible to remove them, and the democratic principle also plays its part in this ingenious system. First, the legislature must approve the governor's choice, and the two chambers retain the right, after due deliberation, to disqualify a judge for misconduct.

Though it lacks the symmetry and uniformity of the French system, the [Massachusetts] state judiciary has four hierarchical levels: the justices of the peace; municipal or police courts, which often act as debtors' courts, sitting without a jury and rendering immediate decisions in minor cases where the disputed claim is less than twenty dollars; the superior court of the county, consisting of a judge and a jury, which sits at least twice a year in each county, hears all important cases and has the same function as our court of appeals; and lastly, the state supreme court, one of whose judges sits in turn in the various counties with the assistance of an associate county judge who prepares and outlines the case for him. The supreme court plays much the same role as our court of cassation, pronouncing only on questions of law, though its decisions are not considered generally applicable nor as creating binding precedents

for the future. Criminal cases go directly to the state
supreme court, where they are tried before a jury.*

I first attended a police court: the case being tried
was that of a poor Irish servant girl with red eyes,
lowered head and a terrified look. Her mistress, a
"lady" wearing a hat and shawl, accused her of having stolen the purchase price of a piece of cloth.
The judge, sitting alone (the superior court is the
only one where two judges preside), conducted the
trial from his bench, which was raised barely a foot
above the rest of the room; he was dressed simply in
a black frock coat like an ordinary citizen. He
didn't behave in a portentous manner nor put on
any majestic airs either in his behavior or in his
speech. He did not have the bad taste to take satisfaction in his easy triumph over a poor, humiliated
sinner. He spoke to her in a friendly, kind-hearted
way, doing his best to forestall the flood of tears and
sobs that continually threatened to burst forth.
Then he turned to her accuser and quickly took her
testimony as well as that of a shopkeeper who confirmed her version of the affair—for in Massachusetts the accuser's word alone is not, as in Illinois, a
sufficient proof.

Next came a businessman demanding payment of
a large debt amounting to several thousand dollars.
The judge questioned him, and took note of his

* This court also has concurrent jurisdiction with the superior court in all civil cases where the sum in litigation is
greater than $4,000 in Suffolk county [including Boston] or
$1,000 in other counties. From these details one can form an
opinion of the remarkable diversity that still exists in administrative and judicial institutions at the state and local
levels.

complaint; then, since the sum in dispute exceeded the limit of his competence, sent the case to be tried before a jury which sits in the county superior court. In half an hour the judge had disposed of four or five cases. From one minute to the next policemen led in additional defendants and brought forward more witnesses. There is no preliminary investigation conducted in secrecy. What we call the judicial *instruction* took place in open court before the judge of the tribunal who interrogated, not the accused, but the witnesses or the plaintiffs. The attorney for the defense replied on behalf of his client by conducting a "cross-examination," and then summarized his case. Finally the judge announced his decision. If the case is one that must be tried before a jury, he refers it to the superior court. If an accusation is clearly unfounded, he dismisses the case without appeal or any other recourse. This hearing must be held within twenty-four hours, or else the accused must be allowed to offer bail and be freed from detention pending his trial.

When a case has passed through these three jurisdictional levels, state law is satisfied, but justice has not yet said its final word. Alongside the state courts, or rather, over against them, sits the Federal court, which hears appeals under the laws of the United States. Finally, above the Federal courts is the highest judicial authority, the Supreme Court of the United States. Here we go from purely judicial matters into the political realm. The Supreme Court of the United States does not, any more than the state supreme courts, possess the power to render general or legislative decisions, but, since its decisions are sovereign and without appeal, it has in reality enormous power to interpret the law. A series of Supreme Court decisions pointing consistently in one direction is really equivalent to a final determination of law. You know, of course, its powers [under the Constitution]. Not only does it interpret the laws of the United States as a court of last resort, overriding the decisions of all lower courts and law-making bodies, but it also hears directly certain cases that could not be submitted to a lower court. It hears all cases that arise between residents of different states. Finally, it hears cases to which the states themselves are parties.* It interprets acts of Congress, as well as the Constitution itself, of which it is the guardian. This enormous power brings before the Supreme Court all those momentous debates concerning state or national sovereignty, the supremacy of state or Federal law and the division of powers that inevitably give rise to disputes in a federal republic. For this reason the Supreme Court in Washington is compelled to take an active part in politics and is obliged to adopt a position on all the burning questions of the day. In short, it is the official arbiter of the great quarrel over "states' rights" for which the Civil War is being fought.

It is very difficult for us [Frenchmen] to appreciate what vast importance the judiciary power has in

* Originally it judged cases brought against a state by residents of another state, but the Eleventh Amendment to the Constitution, adopted under Democratic auspices, stipulates that the states as such can no longer be sued before the Supreme Court.

the operation of American institutions, a role that is at the same time conservative and liberal, which, while preserving the balance and the subordination of the various powers in relation to one another, offers by far the strongest guarantees of individual liberty to be found anywhere. A federal form of government was the necessary condition for giving such importance to the judicial power, an importance that is almost incomprehensible in our unified societies and centralized governments.

With us, all laws spring from one single power, though it may be hidden under diverse names, and they form a homogeneous whole in which it is difficult to change any single part. There certainly are some general principles in our constitution that do not always seem to agree with everyday practice, but these are nothing but window-dressing, as when the principles of 1789 serve to embellish our Imperial constitutions just like the classical bas-reliefs on the façade of the Bourse [stock exchange] or of the Opera. The inscription stays above the portals; no one thinks of removing it; but neither does anyone dream of taking its deceptive promises seriously. Just try, in a hearing before a justice of the peace, to invoke the principles of 1789 that are written into the constitution; try to protest, in the name of the constitution, the decision of a prefect; try, if you live in Paris or Lyon, to refuse to pay, on the strength of the principles of 1789, a tax not voted for by your elected representatives; try, indeed, to deny the validity of an article of the civil or criminal code because it is contrary to the constitution! The judges will laugh in your face. In practice a particular provision of law has more force than a general law, and even the highest courts, which ought to interpret the law in its broadest sense, prefer to base their decisions on the most trivial regulations of a police chief or mayor rather than on the abstract principles of the constitution.

Things are not done this way in America. The Constitution of the United States is truly the supreme law, overriding all other laws. It is not wrapped in the aura of a remote divinity inaccessible to human concerns. Placed at the summit of the legal pyramid, above all state and local legislation as it is above all the many state and local courts, it is not an impotent idol to whom vain homage is paid, but a sovereign authority which demands and obtains obedience. It rises above other sources of law by virtue of its all-inclusive jurisdiction and by virtue of its role as mediator among all other authorities. The repository of this sovereign power is the Supreme Court of the United States. Nor is that all. The Constitution is not only the final recourse whose remote authority is invoked as a last resort, but in addition it is an established principle in American law that it is always controlling, and that it may be appealed to even before the lower courts. One must not believe, for example, that a judge in Massachusetts heeds only the law of Massachusetts. He is bound first and foremost to follow the laws and the Constitution of the United States. The Constitution is, in short, a law that governs everyday practice, a law that actually works rather than a mere collection of sterile precepts. Its general principles are at the service and within the reach of all.

In this way the judicial power intervenes every day in public affairs. When a citizen finds he has reason to complain of an abuse of power, he brings a charge, not against the government, but against the official who represents it and is held by the law to be personally responsible for all his acts. In France we think we have done wonders by making the administrative machine a unified and impersonal entity, by clothing the officials who run it with a kind of inviolability. The Americans, on the contrary, were determined not to place power in the hands of agents who could act with impunity in the certainty that they would never be called to account. They also believed that it would be dangerous to make the government itself responsible for abuses committed in its name. Every office holder knows when he takes up his duties that he must be ready to answer to the courts for the proper execution of the law; he is even obliged to pay into the state treasury a bond which guarantees the payment of damages he might be ordered to pay. Wherever one looks one finds this judicial power which is the true control, the real counterweight, the indispensable mechanism that makes democracy work.

Here especially lies the great difference between American institutions and ours. In France the judiciary is a great administrative machine, disciplined like an army. It would be pointless to authorize the prosecution of a bureaucrat guilty of breaking the laws of his country. What weight would be given to the voice of a single citizen demanding the enforcement of a law that is a dead letter? When we want more freedom we lay hands on the heads of the executive branch; by imposing strict accountability, we force them to carry out our wishes. In short, we put liberty at the center of our public life so that it may be felt at the extremities. The Americans, who have diffused freedom uniformly throughout the body politic, have no need to exercise such strict supervision over the head. Their Congress is not, as in England, an "imperial parliament," a body that holds the reins of government in its own hands; instead, the power of the President, already held in check by popular election, is further limited by the Supreme Court.

Cabinet members are merely docile agents of the President, but the fact that all government officials, great and small, are responsible to the courts more than makes up for the fact that heads of administrative departments are not responsible to the legislature. American liberty has a character all its own which we cannot understand unless we put aside all the accepted ideas that are current in our country. It is no wiser to apply our experience to America than to wish to model ourselves on her.

December 5, 1864

YESTERDAY, Sunday, Judge Russel [*sic*—probably Charles T. Russell] took me to see a "school ship," which is simultaneously a naval school, a correctional center for delinquent boys and a refuge for homeless children. After a short religious service led by the captain in the ship's main saloon, several trustees of the school addressed the youngsters, making speeches that were half religious and half humorous; some of their expressions might have offended the taste of a more refined audience, but their liveliness, sympathetic frankness and friendly exhortation had a better effect than all the fine phrases a Frenchman would have felt obliged to deliver. The art of adapting ones ideas to all minds, of speaking to all sorts of audiences and of putting oneself on a level with the uneducated without descending to vulgarity, is just as easily learned in the school of democratic customs as is the coarse demagogy that I have often described to you. The school itself is not a bad one: the trouble is that those who learn its lessons are very often bad men. In America there are plenty of rabble-rousers who can do nothing but speak to a crowd of drunken Irishmen; but there are others who are able to make themselves understood by people of the most limited intelligence without in any way debasing their character or sacrificing any of their dignity.

This morning it was the turn of Mr. Hale, a judge of the municipal court, to escort me along with a large group of other visitors to Deer Island, where there is a prison, a house of correction, an asylum for the poor and a disciplinary school. There I saw on a smaller scale nearly the same thing as in the large institutions of the city of New York. However, the two systems do not follow the same rules: New York City opens its asylums to everyone; Boston admits only poor people who have lived at least two years in the city. As in New York, it is a heartrending spectacle to see the women imprisoned for prostitution wearing their rough, shapeless dresses and smocks of coarse, gray denim. They are treated with a mixture of extreme concern and strict severity.

Massachusetts treats as serious offenses not only vagrancy but also fornication and drunkenness. The
old Puritan harshness has left its imprint on the
laws. I have also been told of a house of correction
or "reform school" for very young girls where they
are taken in and rehabilitated in private families,
but the school is located twenty miles from Boston
and I did not have the time to go so far to see it.

December 7, 1864

I HAVEN'T YET spoken of Mr. [Edward] Everett.
I recently paid him a visit. An old man of
medium height, dressed all in black, his back somewhat bent, he rose from his chair and came forward
to greet me with the simple, courteous manner of a
perfect gentleman. The room in which he received
me is one of those large English-style libraries
which serve both as a living room and as a study. It
is forty years since Mr. Everett has been in France,
and yet he speaks perfectly correct French. Naturally, I was hoping to cut short the usual polite small
talk, to have a meeting of minds, to talk with him
about his country and mine, to find out a little
about his opinions, to discover ideas or sympathies
we might have in common. However, Mr. Everett
combines his benevolent politeness and cordiality with a diplomatic reserve that is not easy to
overcome. Instead of answering me, he showed me
some books which had been sent to him to be sold
at a Sailor's Fair, a charitable and patriotic enterprise in which he has been much interested of late.
He showed me photographs and etchings that had
just arrived from Paris. That was not exactly what I

had been looking forward to, but he seemed to have had more than enough of politics so that he wishes to think about it as little as possible in his private life. Nor does he have one of those restless, probing minds that are eager to extract the juice from every new intelligence they encounter and avidly sort through the bundle of information and new ideas that foreign visitors are likely to bring with them. He told me he had lost touch with European affairs and had virtually ceased to be concerned with those events or problems.

He gave me the impression of a man who is idly strolling in a beautiful garden; he is unhappy when someone throws unfamiliar stones onto his neatly gravelled paths. This attitude is often found among professional literary men and a visitor soon realizes that Mr. Everett, by nature and training, is above all a scholar. He belongs to that small group of learned people for whom there is no place in America, with the result that they are forced to disguise their true identity under a politician's frock coat or a clergyman's collar. At the time when ecclesiastical garb was so much in style that a number of men took holy orders because it was the fashionable thing to do, only to give up their clerical careers after a short time, Mr. Everett was a famous preacher in the Unitarian Church where his flowery style was particularly appreciated by women. Later on, all the chief literary lights of Boston exchanged the service of God for the service of mankind and Mr. Everett, no longer an ornament of the pulpit, became a lecturer and political orator.

This new career and the notable talent that he

Photograph from *Boston Illustrated*, about 1865

View at the Head of State Street, Boston

displayed in all his undertakings, carried him to the Senate, to the Embassy in London and finally to the Cabinet after the death of Daniel Webster, whose disciple and friend he had been. During the last presidential election four years ago he was not among the leaders of the Republican party, nor was he a supporter of Breckinridge, a Southern sympathizer. He was an Old Whig allied to the moderate Democrats, being himself a candidate for the vice-presidency on the middle-of-the-road third-party ticket headed by [John] Bell. Events have shown the futility of these ill-starred attempts at conciliation: while Mr. Bell went over to the South the day after Mr. Lincoln's election and played an active part in the rebellion,[4] Mr. Everett, faithful to a lifetime of honor and patriotism, took his stand among the most ardent defenders of the Union cause.

Since that time he has accepted the abolition of slavery without reservations and has consistently interpreted "states' rights" in as narrow a sense as any Republican could wish. During the election of last month he was one of the most decided supporters of President Lincoln. He has been able to separate himself resolutely from those with whom he was long allied in public life, from the men among whom he had formed his closest friendships. He has

[4] John Bell of Tennessee was the presidential candidate of the Constitutional Union party in 1860, receiving the vote of the border states Tennessee, Virginia and Kentucky. Though a defender of slavery, he placed the Union first and it was owing to him that Tennessee remained in the Union until after the firing on Fort Sumter. He advised resistance to Federal troops entering the state, but took no further part in the Civil War.

done it without bitterness but without indulgence, speaking his mind candidly to all parties, but always abstaining from the painful personal attacks that seem in America to be considered a normal part of the give-and-take of politics. As free from ambition as he is from rancor, he thinks in his old age only of using his gifts as an orator to serve the national cause and of putting his shoulder to the wheel on the bad stretches. Yet like all men of integrity he has been the object of unrelenting hate and hostility on the part of his former allies against whom he has decided to fight, perhaps without finding among those whose cause he has adopted the gratitude and sympathy he had a right to expect. Of all his former friends only Mr. Winthrop judges him fairly and has remained faithful to him. All the others cannot forgive him for what they call his treachery. And I know some Republicans who condemn him even more harshly than the Democrats. He is nonetheless one of the most worthy citizens and most highly respected men in America.

But to tell the truth, Mr. Everett is not exactly popular. The average American democrat prefers men of his own sort, men nearer his own level, to those who have great intellectual refinement. If you will but glance at a list of the Presidents of the United States in the last thirty years, those who held office between Jackson and Lincoln, you will find only mediocrities.

You will not find [Henry] Clay, nor [Daniel] Webster, nor even [Stephen A.] Douglas (a much-overrated figure, but one who has left a deep impression on political life), nor Mr. Everett himself, although he once aspired to the Presidency. His eloquence is not the kind that pleases the crowd. His fine orations, always composed and written out beforehand, are smoothed, polished and embellished by painstaking effort.

I seem to see him (though I have actually never heard him make anything more than a few commonplace remarks) rolling nicely-constructed phrases from his tongue with as much pleasure as a famous actor, sometimes speaking in an urgent, rapid, seductive rhythm, though always measured and harmonious, sometimes pausing to emphasize some thought—and finally, at the end of his peroration, waving his thanks to a delighted audience with a gesture midway between a salute and a graceful bow. There would not be a word, an intonation nor a gesture that had not been carefully studied and rehearsed. Mr. Everett leaves me with the same impression as many famous preachers: he is an admirable speaker, but he has not converted me.

What a contrast between his style and that of Wendell Phillips! I have just been to hear him at a large meeting which, following custom, he had held at the Music Hall[5] to give his views "on the situation." This man does not have a polished literary style; his speeches are not written with a view to how they will look in print. He speaks everywhere, to anyone that will listen; he is always ready when a call comes. He himself says of his speeches, "They are nothing but ordinary talk." He aims at achieving a purpose but not at making an effect. He said to me the other day on his return from a speaking

[5] The author may be referring to the Academy of Music.

tour in Maine, "For those of us who are active as propagandists it is not essential to write beautiful passages but to convince and arouse those who listen to us." His speeches are effective, elevated in tone when his meaning is elevated, simple when he is dealing with ordinary ideas; and his words are always suited to the mental level of the group he is addressing. His manner is generally calm, though with strong undertones of intense emotions and with occasional thrusts of sharp, biting wit. Sometimes his tone is conversational and informal; at other times he rises to great oratorical heights; but his most striking quality is his perfect serenity, which is intimately bound up with his confidence in the goodness of mankind. All these qualities taken together make him one of the most remarkable and most appealing speakers I have ever heard. He is America's greatest orator. I know that Mr. Phillips is a revolutionary, a fanatic, an agitator, a radical—indeed the very incarnation of radicalism. He is one of those thinkers who hold themselves aloof from practical matters, who perhaps would be incapable of governing the country himself; and in any event his nature is such that he lacks the ambition to do so. He is, as the English say, an "eccentric," one of those passionate, uncompromising spirits whose role is to be a perpetual gadfly to the sleeping conscience of the people. "An idea!" he was exclaiming a short while ago, "A single idea! There is the source of power in an individual and of greatness in a nation." You can find fault, if you like, with these dedicated, stubborn souls who lack that moderating admixture of skepticism and indifference which

conventional opinion calls common sense. But it is
these singleminded men who redeem America from
the crime of slavery. Faith, bold energy, the devotion of a whole lifetime to a noble cause—these are
perhaps no longer French virtues, but they can still
arouse admiration in the heart of at least one
Frenchman.

December 8, 1864

Now the American winter is really beginning. After
an "Indian Summer"—a spell of mild, calm, sunny
weather such as we often have in November—which
lasted longer than usual, the north wind has suddenly begun to blow. It is time for me to leave this
Siberian climate and head for the south. Were it not
for the war, it would be the right time to go to
Alabama or Florida, to St. Augustine, the Nice of
the United States, to those warmer climes which the
rebellion has put beyond the reach of Northern suf-
ferers from chest ailments.

But I have become acclimatized to Boston. Every
morning in the club where I have been given membership privileges I sit and read my newspaper like
an habitué, or I watch the cheerful play of sunlight
on the white façade of the State House and on the
green lawn of the park. In the evening I enjoy the
pleasures of society, especially that of literary people and politicians. I am received by the leading
families of Boston, a distinguished if not exactly
fashionable group, who go to a ball dressed in frock
coats and plain high-necked dresses. Still, they have
all the real qualities, if not always the superficial
signs of good breeding. One of the houses where I
have been given the warmest of welcomes and

where I go with pleasure, is that of Dr. [Samuel Gridley] Howe, a former supporter of Greek independence, a friend and comrade-in-arms of Lord Byron, and a man of forceful and chivalrous character. Mrs. [Julia Ward] Howe, besides being one of the muses of Boston,[6] is (to borrow the words of a competent judge) "a near-genius," and is in addition to all her other qualities a woman with a gentle manner and a keen mind.

She took me once to her club where I was witness to a very strange performance: strange in that here the women have their clubs just like the men. Don't jump to conclusions, though—it was not a gathering of egregious bloomer-girls or of militant feminists (*Vésuviennes*).[7] It was simply a literary club made up of society women who gather every week at the home of one or another of the members. Men are in principle strictly excluded, but each lady has the right to bring with her one and only one male guest to each of the weekly meetings, and she must

[6] Julia Ward Howe wrote and lectured for the abolition of slavery, for women's suffrage and for other liberal causes, preached as a Unitarian and helped found an organization to work for world peace, besides helping her husband edit the Boston *Commonwealth*. Her most famous work is *The Battle Hymn of the Republic*, written to a tune ascribed to William Steffe, a Southern writer of Sunday-school songs; she wrote new stanzas in December, 1861, after watching McClellan's army march into battle near Washington singing *John Brown's Body*, with its chorus of "Glory, glory, hallelujah!"

[7] The "Vésuviennes" were young working women in Paris during the Revolution of 1848, mostly between the ages of 15 and 30. They shared their wages and lived communally; their name suggests the fiery enthusiasm with which they demanded to bear arms in defense of the Republic.

choose him from among those most worthy to be
introduced into this learned assembly. It was a great
honor for me to be admitted on such short acquaintance. The meeting had an entirely academic
flavor. We sat in a circle around the discussion leaders. The first one, comfortably seated on an otto-
man, read in a low voice and let fall, so to speak,
from her lips a long physiologico-mystical discussion of the effects of opium and hashish on the
mind and character in a style permeated with the
languorous qualities of both. Another read an ode
and some light verse. The audience maintained
throughout an imperturbable seriousness, showing
its pleasure only by the restrained smiles and dis-
creet applause allowed by conventional politeness.

They relaxed this control only after the program
had come to an end and everyone had gone into
another room where supper was being served. Then
the general chatter, the clinking of glasses, the music of happy voices—all this unexpected exuberance
seemed like the boisterous outbursts of a roomful of
children released from school. Suddenly silence was
called for. One of the male guests, putting on a
tragic expression, presented a dramatic monologue
full of broad humor, this time amidst resounding
laughter and lengthy applause. The locale was a
courtroom and the performer was imitating (I was
told) a well-known Boston lawyer with all the
howling, stamping, shaking and capering which I
myself, with wonder and amazement, have often
found to be the stock in trade of popular orators. It
was the dessert of the occasion and the menu of this
literary feast recalled to mind those Chinese din-

ners that begin with sweets and candies only to end with highly flavored chunks of meat and stews.

Today, December 8, the electoral colleges of the various states meet in their capital cities to name the President of the United States, and the election of Abraham Lincoln becomes official. This is also the day when the President will deliver his message to Congress. In spite of rumors of a change of policy, the American people do not show any of the feverish anxiety with which we await the speech from the throne at the opening of our legislative chambers.

Genuine democratic institutions have this result, that the voters choose not only a man but also a policy and a political philosophy. It was on the Republican "platform" that Mr. Lincoln was elected President of the United States, and it is on the Republican platform that he must make war or peace. As for the remarks he is about to make, they will not fall like a thunderbolt from the dark clouds of executive majesty. They will simply give expression to the policy that has once again received the approval of the nation.

December 9, 1864

TODAY once again I had to take my daily dose of philanthropic establishments, vowing solemnly to myself that this time would be the last. Now, after a day spent walking about among prisoners, children and indigent old people, I've dined with the members of the electoral college of Massachusetts at the home of their president, Mr. Everett. It was an official convocation of the most formal and solemn character, though not all the guests were in evening dress. There were speeches, a number of rather pompous toasts were proposed, a reverend clergyman, his eyes raised to heaven, extemporized two patriotic prayers, one before and one after the meal in the guise of grace and benediction, while the diners sat with heads bowed. The company broke up at an early hour and I went on to the club to finish my evening with President Lincoln's son.[8]

The meeting of the Electoral College is nothing but an empty formality. The electors are no longer chosen district by district as was formerly the case; they are elected on a single list for the whole state. While they are still described either as electors-at-large representing the whole state or as electors for particular districts, they are actually all chosen in the same way. This reform—or rather, revolution— has come about imperceptibly as customs have changed. Certain states which have never named their electors in any other way were exercising an influence disproportionate to their true importance. While other states often neutralized their own votes because they allowed their Electoral College to be divided, the former threw their whole weight to one side only and thus greatly influenced the outcome. Equity demanded a uniform system. All the states

[8] Robert Todd Lincoln, who graduated from Harvard in 1864. He received an army commission and served on Grant's staff in the final months of the war. Later he practiced law in Chicago and was Secretary of War in the cabinets of Presidents Garfield and Arthur. President Benjamin Harrison appointed him as ambassador to Great Britain. Duvergier de Hauranne mentions that he met him again in Washington (see Chapter 10, p. 344).

then began to cast their votes in single blocs with the democratic unity of ancient republics or of the French people naming an emperor. The consequence has been to annul the influence of the minority in each state.

You can understand how useful this system was to the secessionists. In the rebel states the law of the majority became so powerful that it needed to take no account of the Unionist minority who wished to remain faithful to the government of the United States. An individual was no longer a citizen of the United States, but a citizen of Massachusetts or of Virginia. The right to rule the Union was a prize won by the various states in turn, an instrument of domination by the strongest states leagued together to oppress the states that were weaker. While apparently losing none of its sovereign attributes, the Federal authority was reduced to impotence by the excessive power of the state majorities.

The inconveniences of this arrangement are now beginning to be seen, but is it possible to reverse the natural tendency of democracy? It would be easier to overturn all divisions between the states and to merge ten million voters into a single national electorate. This radical solution has in its favor the spirit of the times and it is not impossible that Congress will think of it one day or another. Administrative unity would be, it must be said, the natural consequence. America would see the opening of a new era of progressive centralization that would be fatal to its liberty. She counts on the judicial power as a defense and the fact is that in the United States this power does play a moderating role which seems hardly compatible with the spirit of democracy. We must go back to our ancient *parlements* [9] and imagine their prerogatives to have been uncontested in order to understand the force of this "veto" exercised by the Supreme Court and the authority of its interpretations—which are sovereign, although they do not emanate from the legislature—when these dictate to the President the commands of the law. But if for several presidencies the political tides continue to sweep the country along in the same direction, the Supreme Court itself will see its authority impaired and overwhelmed. Hasn't Mr. Chase just been named Chief Justice to replace the pro-Southern Judge Taney precisely because of his Radical opinions, and haven't the Republican papers said that this choice was necessary to obtain from the Court severe judgments against the Rebels? It is to be feared that the judicial power may one day become the docile handmaiden of political power.

The remedy, in my opinion, is not in greater national unity. On the contrary, what is needed is an even greater delegation of power to local governments. The problem lies not in the Union's lack of strength, but in the fact that in a number of ways the states are too powerful.

[9] The French "*parlements*" of the Old Regime were high courts of law that claimed and frequently exercised powers of "judicial review." They maintained that royal edicts did not have the force of law until "registered" by the *Parlement* of Paris or one of the twelve provincial *parlements*; the Crown, however, could override their objections and command the registration of new laws in a special proceeding called a *lit de justice*.

5

Boston: Religion and Public Spirit

TODAY is Sunday, a dismal day in this former Puritan colony. It is said that a stranger, arriving in Boston on a Sunday, noticing the lugubrious atmosphere of the city, asked if some great public disaster had taken place. The streets are deserted, the houses are silent, all doors are closed. The whole city seems to be congealed, together with its inhabitants. At the time for church services families walk silently, heads lowered, dressed in black, like a funeral procession. Meanwhile the church bells toll slowly and mournfully as though they were announcing someone's death.

This morning, obeying their call, I went to a Presbyterian church to hear a renowned preacher. I entered a large square hall with balconies and broad pews where a meager audience was sitting comfortably. Hymns were sung. Soon the minister, a man with a large mustache, dressed in ordinary clothes, opened a large notebook placed in front of him and, half reading, half reciting from memory, pronounced a florid sermon. I have rarely heard even among our conceited Parisian preachers such empty rhetoric and affectation. Thunder, waves, tempests—the whole stock of banal metaphors echoed in each sentence and, so to speak, marked the

rhythm of each passage. Nothing could be less edifying or less solemn. The style of the speaker,
which might have taken on some solemnity under a
sacerdotal robe and with other priestly accoutre-
ments, was merely ridiculous on the part of a man
dressed in an everyday suit. Superficial display can
sometimes be a mask, but nothing is more dangerous than simplicity. One must at least be sincere
when appearing on the stage in ordinary clothing.

A large city is always a poor place in which to
measure the depth of a country's religious sentiment. Here inspirational leaders charge so much
per ticket for their meetings and place advertise-
ments in the newspapers announcing, "Reverend
Dr. X. will speak tomorrow at Tremont Temple at
two o'clock; his knowledge and talent are well
known; he will speak on the ways to be happy; admission 50 cents." These enlightened creatures who
sell divine grace could not be great apostles. Many
men embrace the holy ministry as they would
choose any honorable and remunerative profession.
This lawyer became a "clergyman;" that "clergyman" became a merchant. A congregation is treated
like a business establishment, like the clientele of a
lawyer, a notary or a broker, whose revenue varies
according to the talent of the incumbent. Its size
increases or disappears like that of a lawyer or doctor. Sometimes the pastor himself owns the church;
then he manages it like a theatre, renting or selling
places to the faithful.

Usually he lives on an annual income provided
by his parishioners, which he is able to demand for
himself when necessary without false claims to a

supposed disinterestedness. When he wants to set his son up in business, give his daughter a dowry, build himself a house, even travel in Europe, he announces it from the pulpit and asks for the assistance of his congregation. If donations are not made quickly enough, he knows how to set matters in motion. Mr. X., a famous Brooklyn preacher, obtained from his flock ten thousand dollars for travel in Europe. The following Sunday, he deigned to thank them. "For fifteen years," he said, "I have devoted my life to the well-being of your souls; it is only just that you provide for my temporal needs," and he ended by asking for ten thousand dollars more for his family, who would otherwise remain without resources during his absence. The sum was pledged on the spot.

I hear your cries of disbelief. Do not be too indignant. Are you really sure that under other pretexts and perhaps with less frankness, the same thing is not done in France? What is so extraordinary about being paid for ones trouble?—Would you call that trafficking in holy things?—Does the priest earning a salary commit simony? The Reverend Mr. X. and his fellows do not sell amulets nor indulgences, nor elixirs of life, nor favors from the celestial throne. They sell their advice, their sermons, their time, the work of their minds, spiritual merchandise which they cannot give you for nothing. Americans are practical men who understand the necessities of life, and prefer admitting them clearly rather than trying to disguise them. They do not take literally the words of the Scripture when it says that God will feed his saints like the birds in the skies and clothe them like the lilies of the fields. If the form of these arrangements shows a certain commercial brutality, at least no hypocrisy enters into it nor any sacrilegious hand. What shocks us so strongly seems quite simple to the Americans. They do not feel that the minister's dignity is violated by receiving directly from them the salary he has earned; but they would believe him in danger of being gravely compromised if he had to beg favors from a government official or bureaucrat. It is all a question of custom and convention!

Perhaps you are wondering why I speak so rarely of religion. There is a very simple reason. In spite of the large number of churches, religion is not very important in America. They are not concerned with concordats, nor temporal power, nor the continuing controversy over the relationship between Church and State. The question is not hanging fire, as with us; it was settled long ago to the satisfaction of everybody by establishing complete freedom of worship. In France even the supporters of that radical solution do not understand the practice of this liberty for which they call. They wish to make religious liberty an inherent right or privilege of the human conscience, around which an immovable barrier should be placed. They refuse to allow politics to have any influence on religion, or religion any influence on politics. That is the condition of its independence. They are willing to leave ministers free within their churches and sacristies, but if they ever try to leave, our liberals are the first to fear usurpation. Religion and politics, they feel, should live side by side without ever meeting.

This is not what Americans mean by religious freedom. They feel that to separate religion from human affairs would condemn it, so to speak, to suffocate in a vacuum. Their religious ideal is not a cloister, a graveyard where souls go to die before their time; it is rather a school of active morality associated with all aspects of life. Their religious freedom takes shelter, not in private privilege, but in the whole great edifice of public freedom. They open a church as they publish a paper; they establish a religion as easily as a political association; for all these things are equally permissible in the name of the same principle. Also, when the preacher speaks from his pulpit, he is not limited to discussing a moral commonplace or commenting on fine points of doctrine. He frankly discusses practical matters of every-day life. He preaches about a citizen's duty, about slavery, about the presidential election. He makes the pulpit into a rostrum, and sometimes he turns the care of souls into a real exercise of intellectual and moral authority.

The Catholic population, especially—for the most part ignorant and credulous—are absolutely directed by the priests, even in their material interests, and it often happens that the government calls on the authority of the bishops. Last year, the German and Irish population of Boston was shaken by financial panic, and wanted to take their money out of the savings banks because the latter had placed their funds in national bonds. The bank directors then consulted the bishop, and the next Sunday, in all the churches in the city, Catholics received, between the Evangel and the Credo, the advice not to withdraw their money. That example of temporal influence would be envied by clergy everywhere; it is the result, however, of religious liberty.*

In order to comprehend the full extent of this freedom, you must first understand the active and, so to speak, *Protestant* quality of the religious spirit in America. Americans do not make religion an impenetrable sanctuary. They never separate it from reason and morality. *"Credo quia absurdum"*[1] would be only an absurdity to them. Their faith is not an abdication of thought, but a reasoned assent of the

---

* Here is an incident that shows how close is the alliance in the United States between religious freedom and political freedom. When the Civil War broke out, all the churches and sects were divided on the question of slavery and secession. In the South, the Anglican church or (as it is called in America) the Episcopal church, separated completely from that of the North, forming a new organization. It has persisted for some time in maintaining its separate hierarchy, remaining as a reminder of the war; it obstinately refused to reëstablish in its liturgy the customary prayers for the President of the United States. In Washington two members of the Cabinet, [James] Harlan [Secretary of the Interior in 1865-1866] and [Edwin F.] Stanton, wanted to force the use of these prayers, but President Johnson stamped his foot in anger. "Was this war fought," he asked, "to save the Union or to oppress the churches?" It should be noted that last November [1865] delegates of the Southern Episcopal Church, assembled in a national convention in Augusta, Georgia, renewed their old ties with the dioceses of the North.

[1] "I believe because it is absurd"—attributed to St. Tertullian, one of the Latin Fathers of the Christian Church, who argued that one can gain no merit in God's eyes by believing only that which is clear, reasonable and consistent, but only by an act of faith that accepts *all* divine revelation, no matter how seemingly illogical, improbable or contradictory.

mind. A man who is accustomed to direct himself in all matters does not want to be led blindly. He wants no intermediary between God and his conscience. The pastor to whom he willingly listens is not, in his eyes, a miraculous being, divine, initiated into secret mysteries, a favorite of the celestial court, but simply a wise and pious counselor whom he has chosen for himself and whom he will abandon for another when he believes he ought to change. Also, anyone can preach the word of God; there is no need of a title or diploma to have the right to give religious instruction. Not only is it not forbidden by law, but it does not offend public opinion. Religion in America is for everyone; it is not a book open only to a few. It is, if I dare say so, as democratic as her other institutions and customs.

Only Catholicism, although profoundly modified by this political and social climate, remains strongly centralized with a powerful hierarchy and, so to speak, an aristocratic organization. However, American Catholics are the first to praise the regime of Protestant freedom against which they battle. They will tell you that only here, thanks to American freedom, are they able to establish the powerful associations and exercise the political influence which would be regarded elsewhere as a public danger. Antipathy exists between Catholics and Protestants, but there is no profound hatred because no one has special privileges and everyone breathes equally the free air of liberty. As to Presbyterians, Episcopalians, Unitarians and the others, in spite of their sharp doctrinal differences, they all resemble each other. If sometimes a dispute arises between two

Protestant sects it is more likely to be rivalry for local influence than a religious quarrel. The sects attack each other, slander each other and accuse each other of damnable heresy and diabolical error. What does it matter to the public at large? They let these groups indulge in mutual recrimination while they themselves are drawn to a broader Christianity, holding the Constitution to be the foundation of all laws; in matters of faith, they accept and honor the Scriptures as their religious charter. Furthermore, it must never be forgotten that their religion is not imposed from above in the imperious and threatening manner that repels an independent mind. On the contrary, it appeals to their consciences as a friend, and when they submit it leaves them the illusion of their independence. What good would come from doubting their religion? The Americans do not have time for such doubts.

They accept the yoke of public opinion, an invisible power, always present, which is obeyed more willingly than an authoritarian force. It bends us all, shapes us, persuades us unawares. A great deal has been said about the religious tyranny created and enforced by public opinion in the United States. Opinion is certainly the great power in democracies and it tramples anyone who tries to bar its way. Also, although there already are unbelievers in America, nobody dares to be openly irreligious. At present, that is the limit allowed by the fearsome tyranny of public opinion. All it demands is that religion should be respected and that it should not be openly attacked. Beyond that it permits a great deal of latitude to non-conformists.

Among these eccentric Christians there are some who clearly go beyond the permitted limits. One of them, speaking to me about Renan's *Life of Jesus*, said it was strange that the best explanation of Unitarian doctrine had been written in France. This book, which so many Frenchmen would like to burn, is read here a great deal and is highly praised. That proves that there still exists in America considerable freedom of opinion. Ideas of modern philosophy mingle with the currents of religious thought, refuted by some, adopted by others, discussed peaceably everywhere. Perhaps, in the eyes of devout believers this is the most dangerous form of error, a hidden trap, *"insidiae diaboli"* [wiles of the devil]; but to a moralist, it is the most innocent philosophy, even the most beneficial if it satisfies the doubts of a few troubled thinkers without destroying their religious feelings, if it halts them on the slope of disbelief without throwing them into a violent and hostile denial of religion. It is possible they are no longer Christians; but since they call themselves Christians, they believe they are, and that is halfway to being Christians.

If you ask me my conclusion, I will tell you in two words. One should not be horrified at what has too often been called religious anarchy in America. It is not true that public opinion causes an unbearable tyranny in religious matters. Neither is it true that there is no serious religion in America. A nation that includes prayer in all parts of its public and private life is certainly a religious nation. Finally, if we admire religious liberty, we must not believe that we can establish it in France merely by passing a law. We cannot stand with one foot in liberty and the other in administrative rule. We shall not be able to imitate American religious liberty without first imitating all its other liberties.

December 12, 1864

I HEARD the philosopher [Ralph Waldo] Emerson speak last night, heard him this time and understood him because I was sitting only a few feet away, and I want to do him justice now. The awkwardness of his manner and the monotony of his voice both cease to matter when you can follow the precise but capricious thread of his thought. I would be embarrassed to have to repeat what he said, for it seemed to me that his lecture had neither beginning, nor middle, nor conclusion. However it was full of such original intuitions, expressed in language so full of a personal flavor, with touches of imagination so unexpected and so charming that I understand the great fame of this original and profound thinker. He has a curious and inquiring mind, more like Montaigne[2] than anyone else. Like him, he is skeptical and good-humored, destructive and optimistic, satisfying his mind with doubts which leave others hungry, recognizing neither discouragement nor illusion and happy just to exercise his powers of thought. Is it really true, however, that Mr. Emerson is a skeptic? That accusation is easily made against independent thinkers who are not chained to any system or prejudice. Emerson, on

[2]Michel Eyquem de Montaigne (1533-1592), the great French essayist whose constant refrain is "What do I know?"

the contrary is a believer; he has faith in the search for truth, faith in moral and material progress in the world, faith above all in the infinite possibilities of human nature. What he refuses to accept are the conventions, the worn-out rules, the useless baggage, all the burdens of the past which stifle the mind. In his book *Nature* he emphasizes especially the idea that nothing is worn out, that nature is as new as on the first day. "Be yourself," is his favorite precept; learn how to walk without following a trodden path, and you will feel in yourself the force of the heroic ages. Speak to Nature without an interpreter, make an effort to stammer her language, and she will answer you as she did your ancestors. This doctrine suits a young, bold, lively race of people by whom the traditions of the Old World are disdained, for whom the future has no limits. America already has independent seekers in whose eyes doubt is a reason for hope and obscurity is a road to light. But as yet she knows neither Epicurean skepticism which leads to indifference, nor the hopeless skepticism which breeds despair.

December 13, 1864

THE Constitution of the United States, which opens the presidency to party competition every four years, does not provide for all the branches to change at the same time. It prolongs the term of the incumbent President and of the Congress for six months after the election. In this way the old administration is supported, during its half-year of grace, by national representatives elected during its reign. This conservative arrangement can at some times mean delays and obstructions. When an election has confirmed the incumbent President in office but supported a more forceful policy than in previous years, it can be an embarrassment for him to have to deal with a legislative body imbued with the prejudices of the old term for, in spite of the lesson of events, the latter can still maintain resistance for a long time to reforms which are inevitable.

At the moment President Lincoln stands in this position in relation to Congress. For two years Congress has agreed with him on all points with one exception, and its notorious docility was exasperating to the Democrats. The great unsettled problem, the fundamental question of present policy, is the abolition of slavery. Congress has sanctioned all war measures by a simple majority, but has always lacked the two-thirds majority necessary to transform the President's proclamation emancipating the slaves belonging to the Rebels into a constitutional amendment abolishing slavery. It is certain in advance that the new Congress will vote for it unanimously. Will the present Congress do it first? Will it be carried along by the current of public opinion? That is the question posed by the President in his message to Congress, the question which the present session is going to consider.

Otherwise, the Congress has never met in a more peaceable frame of mind. The losers in the November election are remarkable for their good grace and resignation. Mr. [George H.] Pendleton, [Democratic] candidate for Vice President, who saw his own constituency turn against him, is said to have given a very warm welcome to Thaddeus Stevens, the leader of the Republican Party in the House. The President was the first to set an example of generous moderation. "I do not blame those who have fought against me," he said. "I am convinced they have acted according to their consciences." He has advised the winners to be magnanimous and the losers to be obedient. Soon nothing will trouble the calm of the assemblies except the customary harangues of the incorrigible Senator [Garret] Davis of Kentucky demanding peace and [Northern acceptance of] secession with epic perseverance.

A financial proposition, however, came close to setting the House of Representatives afire. Thaddeus Stevens of Pennsylvania has discovered a way to give paper money the value of gold. The secret, very simple and not so new, consists solely of declaring by law that the paper dollar is worth exactly a dollar in gold, and of reinforcing this flourish of the magic wand by punishing with imprisonment and a fine all those of little faith who might doubt its power. The ingenious economist thinks the value of paper money depends solely on men's opinion of it and that all one needs to do to maintain it at the official level would be to constrain that rebellious opinion. I am astonished that, profiting by his discovery and pushing his theory to the limit, he did not consider the possibility of raising the value of paper *above* that of gold. Others have suggested a remedy even more simple and radical: let Congress pass a law ordering anyone who has gold to sell it at par for paper to the first bidder. Such are the financial theories in fashion on this side of the Atlantic. In this enlightened country you can find people mad enough to tell you, "That would really be an excellent measure." Mr. Stephens, a worthy man, is Chairman of the Ways and Means Committee; he is accustomed to impose his will on the House. This time, however, the absurdity was too evident, and his proposition was ceremoniously tabled by an almost unanimous vote.

Actually, the idea is not new, and it greatly resembles the financial doctrines of the Confederate government. A month ago (November, 1864), a Richmond newspaper very close to the government, sketched out a quick and infallible remedy for their financial troubles. "Our people," it said, "are infatuated with 'hard cash.' Since nothing can cure them of this ridiculous and stubborn belief, let us make a concession to public prejudice. Let the government procure some gold by selling surplus bales of cotton to the English, and let it fix once and for all the ratio of gold to paper money. For example, let it offer one dollar in gold against three paper dollars and let that be the unchanging and obligatory level of all transactions. Anyone who resisted would be sent to the front lines. The proposal is extreme; but great ills demand great remedies!" Here in the North the madness is merely ridiculous; but in the South, as you can see, it is tragic and bloody. Since Lincoln's election, the price of gold has risen in Richmond too; at one time it reached $6,000.[3] Still, this incredible rate is illusory, unreal, artificial, upheld by speculation alone, and one finds people

[3] That is, one gold dollar was worth $6,000 in paper money. The result was to drive food prices so high that bread riots occurred in Richmond at the beginning of April, 1863.

willing to exchange paper for gold at any price. All coinage that has escaped the appeals of the government is hidden no one knows where. Legal [paper] money is so mistrusted that in spite of severe laws ordering its obligatory circulation, the most necessary goods are not available to purchasers. They are hidden to avoid selling them for paper money. I saw a refugee from the South, a former trader in Mobile who had fled to avoid conscription which threatened him in spite of his sixty years of age. A meeting was held one evening at the Union [League] Club to hear him speak. He related that it was impossible to find salt pork for his family at any price. The people of the South live like anchorites[4] on the immediately available products of the earth and, although it is said that the land is so fertile that with the slightest amount of cultivation it is impossible to lack corn and sweet potatoes, I cannot believe that courage so poorly nourished can last forever.

In the Richmond congress there is a peace party which is growing every day. Mr. Foote, of Tennessee,[5] having proposed, with strong reservations and protests of loyalty to the Southern cause, that peace

---

[4] Anchorites in early Christianity were usually hermits; they carried the practice of self-denial to an extreme, including the wearing of rags, living in caves or desert places and fasting for long periods of time.

[5] This is a confusion on the part of the author; he is referring to Senator Henry Stuart Foote, United States Senator and then Confederate Senator from Mississippi. His criticism of Jefferson Davis grew more and more severe and in January, 1865, he and his wife attempted to cross over into Federal territory; she was successful in reaching Washington, but he was captured. (See Chapter 10, p. 328.)

overtures should be considered favorably and should even be encouraged, was able to find 20 supporting votes. It is true that his proposal was tabled by a large majority; but you must remember the recent diatribes of President Davis against anyone who even speaks the word peace. In the obstinacy of the Rebels there is something forced and violent which betrays the weakness hidden behind their stoical declarations. They are in the grip of fear and a shared sense of guilt which pushes them like cattle to the slaughter. They are creating tyranny out of the false patriotism they themselves invented. In the South loyalty is the indispensable virtue and an accusation of lukewarm enmity for the Yankees could lead a man to the gallows, that is (because the South makes use of condemned criminals in its army), to the front lines and the trenches. It is a curious and sad sight to see these people pushed in spite of themselves, as the fatal consequence of their mistakes, to voluntary ruin, undeserving of pity. They are like a man who has thrown himself from a precipice and yet, while falling, clings vainly to rocks and bushes. The length of this resistance and its desperate character have delivered the Rebels over to a military dictatorship which today is dragging and grinding them to the last man under its millstone. This is the strength and the danger of military despotism—it sinks its claws so deeply into the body of a country that nothing can make it relax its hold nor prevent it from drinking the last drop of the nation's blood. If all the citizens joined together to find a way to destroy this tyranny, it would be in vain; each one is chained with the iron

links of discipline and is forced to serve as the
means of oppressing his neighbor. A whole nation
then marches to its ruin with the desperate energy
of an army that is forced to fight at gun point.

The Southerners have boasted of their lack of interest in the outcome of the presidential elections.
"It matters little to us," they said, "whether Lincoln
or McClellan is elected. Perhaps it would be better
to have Lincoln with whom we could be sure of
all-out warfare and not have to fear the shame of a
cowardly peace." On the other hand, Vice President Stephens, on the eve of the elections, wrote a
letter in which he explained with unusual frankness his reasons for hoping McClellan would be
elected. "The neutrality of European nations,"
he said, "was due to their ridiculous enthusiasm
to end slavery. If McClellan is elected President
of the United States and offers them union *with*
slavery, then immediately the European powers,
released from their inconvenient humanitarianism,
would hasten to recognize his government and give
him their support."

What sincere patriot can retreat now? What
American, devoted to his country, can renounce the
abolition of slavery when the enemy himself states
that it is the power of this idea which aids the
Northern cause while gaining the respect of Europe? If you want to know the secret of the rapid
growth of abolitionist opinion, you have only to
listen to the Southerners. For four years all their
deeds, all their words have resulted in the success of
the doctrine they have been fighting. I understand
Mr. Wendell Phillips and other single-minded

men who hope that the partisans of Davis will defeat the Brown supporters in Richmond,[6] and that diehards will keep control. Without realizing it, the pro-slavery extremists help extreme abolitionists.

News from Europe brings us echoes of the anger aroused in the English press by the capture last fall, of the Confederate blockade-runner *Florida*, the ship that was just rammed and sunk by a Federal transport ship as it dropped anchor in the harbor of Hampton Roads. On October 6, 1864, Captain Collins, commanding the ship *Wachusett*, arranged with Mr. Wilson, United States consul, to seize the *Florida* by force in the neutral waters of the Brazilian port of Bahia.[7] The angered inhabitants, it is reported, would have killed the consul without the protection of the Brazilian government, which, however, has demanded reparation for the outrage. The Federal government would have granted it; but national arrogance, as before in the *Trent* affair,[8] was aroused beyond all reason. The

[6] That is, the peace party led by Governor Joseph E. Brown of Georgia.

[7] The capture took place on October 7, 1864. The *Florida* was actually a commerce raider rather than a blockade-runner. The Federal sloop *Wachusett* was commanded by Commodore Napoleon Collins. The *Florida* surrendered after being rammed and fired upon and was taken north by her captors. Though Northern public opinion was enthusiastic, Secretary of State Seward condemned the seizure as unauthorized and unlawful. The *Florida* sank on November 28 following a collision with an army transport.

[8] On November 8, 1861, two Confederate commissioners bound for London and Paris were forcibly removed from the British mail packet *Trent* on the high seas. (See Volume I, p. 74 note.)

press condemned in advance all the conciliatory steps that had not yet been taken; the Copperheads insinuated, not without secret pleasure, that the loss of the *Florida* might well turn out to be to the advantage of the Confederates. It was difficult for Mr. [William H.] Seward [Secretary of State] to offer Brazil anything more than verbal excuses. As matters stood, restitution of the prize to the Confederates would have been humiliating and impossible. At that moment, the miraculous intervention of Providence solved the problem by the opportune destruction of the *corpus delicti*; the *Florida* was sunk at its mooring, and the Washington government could without embarrassment send its excuses and regrets to Rio de Janeiro.

In this affair there are two separate questions, that of legality and that of justice. Educated Americans themselves admit that it was no more legal to take possession of the *Florida* in the port of Bahia than to seize Rebel envoys on board the *Trent*. I admit that the aggressive action, the complicity of the consul and also the rather shameful manner of escaping embarrassment by invoking the *deus ex machina* of a shipwreck,[9] does not do any great honor to the United States, but this should be the end of the matter.

[9] The use of the phrase "*deus ex machina*," an allusion to the descent of a god from an overhead machine contrived in some ancient plays to resolve difficulties in the plot, suggests that the sinking of the *Florida* was deliberate; this was not the case. It did, however, allow the crisis to be settled more readily because Union public opinion would scarcely have tolerated the return of the vessel itself, but did permit amends to be made to Brazil.

It has pleased European governments, and some governments in America, following their example, to recognize the Rebels as belligerents. They have their reasons, but in the eyes of the United States the Confederates cannot be regarded as a nation against whom war is being waged according to the rules of international law. They are rebels and traitors to be pursued by law. The seizure of one of their boats is not at all an act of piracy; on the contrary, it is an act of justice. Brazil, whose neutrality was violated, certainly has the right to complain, but when England makes a pretence of taking up the challenge in the name of outraged justice, she ought to keep in mind her own behavior. The action for which she reproaches the United States she has herself committed perhaps a hundred times in the course of the last hundred years. A statesman well versed in maritime and diplomatic history, involved in the administration of foreign affairs, has made a collection of numerous acts of violence which the power of England has cloaked with the appearance of lawfulness. And today still, under the cover of her neutrality, hasn't she furnished vessels and arms to the Rebel privateers? The *Florida* was built, armed and equipped in an English port; she has never dropped anchor in a Confederate port. Two months ago, five hundred thousand Englishmen insulted the Americans in a public address, under the pretext of preaching peace; a little later, they organized donations and sales to benefit the Confederates and held a fair in Liverpool which had as its avowed goal the support of the rebellion. Today they are asking to be allowed to send agents

to carry consolation and alms and—who knows?—
perhaps to foment revolt among the Rebel prisoners. Truly, they are going too far, and these English,
while they insult the pride of the Americans, ought
to remember that in matters of arrogance they are
the elders and the masters.

December 14, 1864

THE OTHER DAY I met Judge R. who said to me,
"Are you leaving before Tuesday?" He told me
there would be an important meeting of the Sanitary Commission that day which would be attended
by all the distinguished men of Boston, including
Mr. [Edward] Everett. Governor [John A.] Andrew
was to preside. Attracted by this promise, I went
last night to Tremont Temple, uncertain of finding
a seat. At first, the large hall was nearly empty;
later, I found eight or nine hundred people present
at the most. The organist gave us the obligatory
introduction to all meetings, the chorus from *Judas
Maccabeus* [by Handel]—Boston is an artistic city
where music is held in honor. Soon the dignitaries
appeared on the empty platform, about twenty
bored, chilly gentlemen, wrapped in their coats,
who had just been occupying the front row of seats.
No Everett, no Andrew. Mr. Quincy presented the
presiding officer, Mr. Charles Loring, who opened
the session with a proper, pleasant, facile speech.
After him, Mr. [Richard Henry] Dana rose and gave
more or less the same address in a colder fashion.
To vary the theme a bit, he undertook to prove in
learned fashion that institutions do more good than
governments are able to do, and spent a half-hour

answering objections no one had made. Then a small young man came up to the lectern, notebook in hand, to explain the report of the administrative board of which he is the agent. I was satisfied that I had heard enough and left, having learned that the Sanitary Commission furnished necessities, shelter and food for ill and wounded soldiers, that it sent provisions to the camps and kept regularly large books of statistical accounts where the medical and administrative staff could find precious information. I heard too that it is due to the genius of American institutions that these good deeds are generously undertaken in full independence of the government and that it is the glory of the American people to have conceived and organized these useful works so spontaneously. I knew this lesson already and could have recited it for myself.

For a long time I have not written to you about the war. Sherman was recently near Savannah after having captured Augusta, Macon and Milledgeville and finished a bold campaign totally unlike the slow movements customary in American strategy. The Richmond papers announce that he is near the sea (they are unwilling to say where), facing a Confederate army and about to engage it in combat. This means the Confederacy is cut in two. In spite of the uncertainty of the rumors one hears, I feel they augur well for this campaign, and here are my reasons. Sherman has an army of seasoned veterans and the army opposing him is made up of militia raised in haste and recruited, to adopt the melodramatic expression of General Grant, "by robbing the cradle and the grave."

Nashville, on the other hand, is under siege, but no one finds this upsetting in a country where war has become a chronic malady. The newspapers carry curious descriptions of the capital of Tennessee. Never, it seems, have there been larger crowds of strangers and speculators. The streets are busy, trade is regular and peaceful, the hotels are crammed full of people. Boardinghouse keepers are showered with gold and hope the Civil War will last forever, while only three miles away the two armies exchange cannon shots. It is a curious example in our time of the uncertain existence of the republics of antiquity and of the cities in the Middle Ages—always threatened, always on the eve of pillage and ruin but accustomed to danger and immune to the fearful terrors that do more harm even than war!

Congress remains very calm. In the Senate, Mr. [Henry] Wilson [of Massachusetts] proposed to free the wives and children of black soldiers in the states that have remained loyal to the Union. Mr. Sherman's bill passed, calling for construction of five "revenue-cutters," actually five small warships, to protect the Great Lakes frontier as much against piracy as against smuggling.

Lastly, something more important, the House of Representatives passed with a twenty-vote majority a Federal bankruptcy law which will now be studied in the Senate.

The serious event of the day is the acquittal of the St. Albans raiders by the criminal court of Montreal. You recall the strange hesitation of the Canadian authorities in bringing the perpetrators to trial.

This judicial matter was at the same time an affair of state. M. [Georges] Cartier, Minister of Justice, came to Montreal himself to confer with the court and give it the instructions of the Cabinet. The trial opened after a month of delays.

At the first session, without even hearing the plaintiffs, Judge Coursol[10] upheld the defendants' lawyer. Under the pretext that the affair implied an international question and that in a matter of extradition the arrest warrant, in order to be valid, ought to carry the signature of the Governor-General, he declared himself incompetent and ordered the release of the prisoners.

The lawyers protested in vain, the Queen's Counsel himself remarked that doubtless the decision of the judge had been misunderstood and that he could not under this pretext pronounce a general acquittal on all six points of the accusation when the court had only one point presently under consideration. The judge flared up, angry that his decision should be contested, and ordered its immediate execution, whereupon the brigands took their leave to the applause of the crowd.

Then the plaintiffs went before another judge and obtained a new warrant. They looked for the High Constable, but were unable to find him. The Chief of Police, twice summoned to re-arrest the fugitives, asked for time to consider the matter. The money itself, the money stolen from the bank, was

[10] Judge Charles-Joseph Coursol of the Montreal Criminal Court may have been influenced by Canadian public opinion, which at this time was strongly in sympathy with the Confederates.

returned to the outlaws by the judge's order and when the High Constable finally appeared, all trace of the fugitives had been lost. A fine example of how justice can be bamboozled!

This is a bit of folly for which the Canadians may have to pay before long. Washington government would indeed be almost unconceivably easy-going if it didn't rattle the saber a little bit now. Nationalist sentiment is rising with unexpected and threatening vigor, accusing England of making its colonies the headquarters of Rebel outlaws. Piracy on the high seas as well as on Lake Erie, the construction of Confederate blockade-runners in British ports, and the outfitting of raiders on British soil—all these things point in the same direction. It is often said that the time has come to administer a decisive lesson to little Canada, who has just given a donkey's kick to the wounded eagle, and also that the great, hypocritical British lion who encourages such insolence also needs a shot or two from the American Ironsides.[11]

If Lord Monck [the Governor-General] and his patron [Lord] Palmerston [the British Prime Minister] do not make full and prompt reparation for this outrage, their failure to do so will seem like a declaration of war on America. They may be counting on her preoccupation with her internal problems, but let them beware! The bull caught by the horns

[11] It is not clear whether the author is referring to the armored warships of the *Monitor* type, called Ironclads, or whether he means Oliver Cromwell's cavalry, know as "Old Ironsides." The *U.S.S. Constitution* was also called "Old Ironsides."

is still capable of a kick that could break up the Canadian union and shatter its fragile, lacy structure.

December 15, 1864

WE ARE HAVING a lot of snow. Boston has a mantle of frost; the city, filled with innumerable sleighs and the sound of tiny sleigh-bells, does not take on a mournful look in winter. The pure, gripping cold of this climate bites the ears, nose and lips and turns the face red and blue, but it doesn't have the grim, foggy, unpleasant dirtiness of our European winter. I can understand how this constant cold could be preferred to our continually changing weather. Besides, I am about to travel southward and have only one more day left here. I leave Saturday for the country of the "shaking Quakers," dancing dervishes who also, by the law of their religion, own everything in common, drink only water and do not marry. I shall observe the Sabbath in their company and be in New York on Monday.

I had often been warned about the dreary Puritanism of life in Boston. New Yorkers, who detest the very shadow of their rival city, predicted that I would quickly get bored here. But up to the present, I haven't found myself at a loss for a minute. Except that there is no opera here, the American Athens offers amenities very different from the mob of immigrants and speculators who proudly call themselves the metropolis. Here in Boston one is at the true center of American civilization; it is from here that intelligence radiates to shine upon this unfinished nation. I know the Bostonians hold it an honor to be called "Yankees" and I am quite sincere when I tell them that I divide America into zones, with intelligence and morality varying in inverse ratio to the distance from New England. A lengthier and more careful study of their society hasn't changed my first impression. This small corner of the globe is a model for all mankind and if the customs, the institutions and the enlightenment of Massachusetts were in the course of time to permeate the more recent strata of the New World's population, it would augur well both for democracy and for America.

In general, two things are lacking in American institutions because these two elements are inimical to popular power: stability and authority. Popular suffrage, with all its hazards and caprices, is the sole source of power before which all others are reduced to nothing. The very laws it has made can be bent to its will and if, in certain large national concerns, the people show a truly impressive discipline, it is because the popular will has organized itself, renouncing for a time the anarchy which is its usual state. To achieve this, though, it is necessary that the masses' inertia be overcome by some great patriotic sentiment. In business details and in the day-to-day affairs of government they again lapse into disorder, the usual state of things. One can expect from them those irresistible movements which imprint a general direction on the nation's policies, but it is useless to expect to find in this country any workable system of order except where old traditions and long habit have built into the laws a salutary principle of authority.

It is in this that New England's superiority can be

found. A heritage of respected principles, transmitted from generation to generation, has become the body and strength of their polity. Public law, so vague and uncertain in the fluid, incompletely unified states of the West, has here been fixed by two centuries of tradition. The government, by turns so bold and so weak, is always poorly regulated in those hastily formed commonwealths, where its absolute dependence on the popular vote is its only brake. Here its powers are well established and its limits are clearly known. Administrative practices are uniform and above reproach. In each "township" the "aldermen"[12] draw up and publish their printed budgets; the minutes of town meetings and other public assemblies are exact, detailed and carefully kept. The city of Boston publishes as many pages of documents as one of our ministries. Vital statistics, so badly neglected elsewhere, are kept in duplicate here, as they are in France, and each clergyman or magistrate sends to the county seat a copy of the papers he has executed. Even property transfers, wills, deeds of gift and contracts of sale are collated with extreme care and are copied into a huge register that is kept in Boston in a building of steel and granite erected for that express purpose by the state. The members of the state government are not all elected individually as in the West. One man, the governor, is elected annually and he himself chooses the members of his cabinet, sharing executive responsibility with them. The governor is not ineligible after one or two years in office; he can be re-elected seven or even ten times. I have told

[12] The author presumably meant "selectmen."

you how the judiciary is organized in Massachusetts and how its unusual authority gives it the double character, so rare in a democracy, of independence and stability. In a word, this democracy is fully as conservative as it is liberal and should be seen and studied by all those admirers of republican institutions who may need to renew their enthusiasm.

You can see how much the origin of societies, like that of governments, affects their future. How many young branches have been grafted in the course of two centuries onto the worm-eaten trunk of the old Puritan colony! How many new and corrupt elements are now incorporated with it! Yet in its original constitution there is something indelible which has outlived the men who wrote it and which, like a seed of morality, continues to increase in the foreign earth of new generations. It is a hearth onto which is thrown all sorts of strange fuel, but from which the same flame continues to rise. The barbarians passed over the Roman world without destroying it; the invasion of modern races has not killed the seed deposited on this barren coast by the hundred pilgrims of Plymouth.

If you want to understand the society that has developed here, simply think of its origin. Neither hunger for profit nor misery formed it, but the need for moral independence which still infuses the atmosphere today. The first citizens of the original commonwealth were not people who had narrowly escaped from famine or been emancipated only the day before. They did not come by chance, guided by their emotions rather than their reason, to put democracy to a stormy test. They were propertied people, enlightened and austere, who had gone into exile in order to be free, men whose first care—even before stepping onto the land where in imagination they were already building the America of the future—was to proclaim those principles which are still the law of their descendants. They arrived as equals, but equals in education and self-sufficiency, not in ignorance and poverty. Nothing could have drawn them to this sandy shore except a need for solitude, far away from other men, where nothing could trouble their liberty.

While today waves of people spread over the fertile western plains which can be brought under cultivation in a day, the colonists of New England had a long struggle against a less fertile soil and this lengthy effort made necessary by their laborious beginnings had its effect upon the solidity of their work. Their descendants, in the midst of the newcomers who now surround them, still maintain the double superiority of education and wealth. For them the West is not a rival: it is a clearing in the forest whose products they can exploit and it is also an easy outlet for their surplus population. The Germans and the Irish doubtless modify the character of western society profoundly, but the bulk of the population of the West, or at least the element that dominates that confused mixture, still belongs to New England by its origins and ideas. This province is the nursery whose young shoots are being planted over the whole of America.

For in truth the states of the West are only colonies; it is New England that founded them. They in turn create her wealth; the wholesale migration westward of her younger generation is the principal reason for her marvelous prosperity. There is no reason for that division of family wealth and property which is a cause of impoverishment among us. Land is not parcelled out among the heirs; custom leaves it to the eldest. The younger sons, as in England, seek their fortunes in distant places, most often by pitching their tents in the forests [*sic*] of Nebraska or on the plains of Kansas. Instead of crowding together, as in Europe, until no space is left and the surplus is forced to emigrate, they go forth, leaving the fruits of their work to those who remain and never allowing resources to be overtaken by needs.

These hardy adventurers soon become men of the West; once they have left their native region, once away from the network of tradition and habit that surrounded them here, they lose the spirit of order and legality that seems a part of the old soil. The day will certainly come when the Westerners, more permanently installed on their new and finally conquered lands, will complete what is now unfinished and imperfect in their moral culture and in their makeshift political institutions. Meanwhile, and for a long time to come, the Northeast will maintain its superiority. In the huge, agitated body of American culture, the western states are like robust arms that nourish the body by their labor; New York is the stomach that rejects or digests what it takes in from the two worlds. As for New England, she is the head, the seat of intelligence and thought.

6

A Protestant Monastery

Pittsfield, Massachusetts
December 18, 1864

I DID NOT see the "Shaking Quakers." This is a
new trick of the imp who seems to seek out and
persecute every form of idle curiosity on my part. I
arrived here last evening from Boston and hired a
sleigh this morning to drive to Lebanon (New
York) before the hour of the "meeting," the name
the Shakers give to their religious service. All the
countryside for ten miles around here belongs to
them. We saw some of their villages along the way,
recognizable by the large houses of three or four
storeys, by the gloomy silence and by the strange
absence of everyday activity. [New] Lebanon, the
largest village, is their main center. We drove down
a wooded mountain into a valley still pleasant to
look at, even under a cold, white blanket of Siberian snow. A tidy new village full of signs of recent
activity extended along the road on either side.
There were large buildings of brick or of wood,
with foundations of dressed stone, vast barns, huge
farm buildings, but not one cottage, not one summer house, not one flower-garden to brighten the
grim monotony. Rows of white curtains were hung
in the long, regular lines of window openings.
Nothing could be less alluring than the resulting
picture of uniform comfort and irreproachable

cleanliness. One new house, rising to a height of five
storeys, seemed more like a hotel than a rural
dwelling. There was no room here for ornament or
pleasure, nor for any of the pleasant whims of individual taste. Communal life had placed its mean
and depressing imprint everywhere. Even the
church was only a large, plain barracks capped by a
low, squat dome like a bowler hat. That morning,
its door was locked. Because of the extremely cold
weather, each of the different sections of the community was privately observing the strange ritual
which had attracted me there. I knocked at a door
where the word "Office" indicated the dwelling of
one of the "headmen." The latter, who are at the
same time the temporal and the spiritual leaders of
the congregation, are entrusted with the administration of its worldy interests as well as with the care
of souls. A grave and simple person, clad in a
French-style coat buttoned all the way up the
throat, with a white flowing tie ironed in regular
pleats with its two ends drooping on either side, a
pale, clean shaven face, with smooth hair cut evenly
around his head, came to open the door and welcome me. "It is cold," he said. "I regret that we
don't have a fire. You have doubtless come to attend a meeting?" "Yes, that's true." "I am sorry.
We are not meeting in the church today. We have
just finished the service in this house. Go a little
farther along to that white house you see from the
window. Perhaps you will be admitted there."

I thanked him and re-entered the carriage, struck
by his gentle, respectable appearance and his simple, cordial welcome. I was a stranger, an intruder,

Shaker Village, Mount Lebanon, New York

evidently a curiosity-seeker and an unbeliever who had come in order to be amused by these people and to laugh at their expense, but every human creature, it seems, has a right to their benevolence and hospitality. They say, in effect, "You come with a smile on your lips and with mockery in your heart. You come to look at us as if we were animals in a zoo or inmates of a lunatic asylum. Sit there, my brother, warm yourself by our fire, nourish yourself at our table." At least, my guide told me, that is how they show hospitality during the week. On Sunday, doors are shut and houses closed, and their souls, absorbed in the ecstasy of holy rites, do not descend to worldly cares. The church nonetheless is open to all comers, and doubtless the sublime spectacle of choreographic leaps heavenward by the whole pious community may have converted more than one soul disgusted with earthly life.

From time to time, when the holy spirit inspires them, these poor people interrupt their shouting and dancing to deliver impromptu sermons, prayers or exhortations to the unbelieving public. It must be a curious thing to see them jumping, with their hands in the air like trained dogs, their eyes raised to heaven, sobbing and trembling as they utter all manner of inarticulate cries of supplication, the men on one side, the women on the other, dressed in their somber uniform of rough gray wool, until their leg muscles become fatigued, until sweat pours from their bodies, or the weight of their carnal envelope drags down to the level of the ground their souls which were ready to take flight upward to the heavenly regions. To wear down that vile flesh, to mortify it by celibacy, to subdue it by obedience, to shake off the burden of corporeal life, to free the generations to come by preventing their birth—this is their moral teaching, which, you can see, has more than one similarity to Catholic monasticism and also to the fakirs of India. Convinced that existence is an evil, they dream of the extinction of the human race and consider that the day they fulfill the divine law of total destruction will be the beginning of the eternal reign of the "saints" awaited by all visionaries. Until that time, they own fields, farms and factories; they trade, they buy land, they invest money, they seek converts through active propaganda that is not always innocent. They take in orphans and foundlings; often they even buy or steal them. If I am not mistaken, among the small sad faces which watched me curiously from the windows of those prisons, there is more than one little "Mortara"[1] carried off by force under the aegis of the faith.

When I arrived at the door of the white house, I knocked discreetly and listened. Vague sounds, more like shouting than singing, were to be heard from time to time. Another gray figure with a pale, clean-shaven face opened the door and asked what I wanted. His expression was also grave, simple and solemn; he looked more like a Catholic priest than a Protestant minister, and even more like a monk

[1] Edgar Mortara was a little Jewish boy of Bologna who was abducted from his parents by a fanatical serving girl on the pretext that in this way the child might be brought up in the Catholic faith; she refused to surrender him. The incident occurred in 1858.

than a priest. In spite of his perfect manners, it was clear that this man was less obliging and less hospitable than the first had been. He asked me what country I came from and went back into the building. When he returned, it was to say that the meeting was about to end, and that he was very sorry he couldn't let me come in. "Is it curiosity that brings you here?" he asked, "or perhaps . . ." He did not dare to finish the question.

"Oh," I replied, "I don't believe I have been touched by grace." And thereupon, already impatient with this questioning, disgusted with the masquerade I would have had to play in order to be admitted, and not wanting to offend these good people, I thanked him and left. I felt the embarrassment of a man who peeks through a keyhole, or who insinuates himself by sone kind of trickery into a Carthusian monastery.[2]

During the return trip I tried to question my guide, but he knew very little about his Lebanon neighbors. He couldn't tell me whether the Shakers had voted in the presidential election or for whom, nor whether they had with good grace paid their tribute to conscription. I was left with my personal impressions, which are truly quite different from what I expected them to be. Aside from the extravagances of behavior they have borrowed from the early Quakers, the Shakers are not the crazy clowns I was led to expect. Their community is nothing but one large monastery, and they themselves are

[2]The Carthusians followed a particularly strict monastic rule and were very insistent on the injunction not to admit laymen to their houses.

the monks and nuns of American society. A visitor arrives with the intention of laughing at their folly, but when he has spoken with these gentle, grave men, when he has seen these pale, downcast women, when he thinks how much virtue and obedience is necessary for a society to exist and prosper under such laws, he almost respects these irrational but pious folk. He realizes that it is a question of something genuine, of a need, or if you will, of an illness, and not just some grotesque deformity of human nature, and that, to say the least, laughter is not called for. Perhaps however, if I had seen them at their gymnastics, I would have found it less easy to keep a straight face.

Perhaps you are wondering exactly where I am. Pittsfield is in western Massachusetts, near the New York state border. It is a small country town, cheerful and busy, and it boasts about ten thousand inhabitants. The surrounding region, like the rest of Massachusetts, is hilly and wooded, with many lakes and rivers. It has fine scenery and resembles the Alps, though on a much smaller scale. Yesterday on the train I traveled through extensive forests which made me think of Pennsylvania and Ohio. The inhabited areas hereabouts are very thinly settled, and the wilder parts of Massachusetts contain an abundance of delightful summer retreats. One of them, Lebanon Springs, where a fountain of mineral water gushes forth, is situated on a hill two miles from the Shaker village overlooking a valley with a distant view of a range of low, wooded mountains. It remains delightful even in winter, when it is wrapped in a funeral shroud of white spotted with black which will not be lifted from the land until spring. At the moment, the north winds are glacial, and when a man is busy keeping the blood circulating in his nose, his hands and his ears, he has little attention to spare for the sparkling snow lit up by the winter sun, nor the somber contrast between the dark shapes of evergreens against a landscape otherwise colorless.

Just between ourselves, my wardrobe is beginning to disintegrate. This serves to remind me that the winter season is advancing, and that the same army cannot make two campaigns in a year without reinforcements. I must resign myself to encouraging the industry of native workmen by paying double for objects worth only half their price. I know of no country where the basic cost of living is lower [than in America], but neither do I know of one where the accessories are more costly. In the best big-city hotels you can get your room and board, everything included, for one dollar a day in paper money. On the other hand, the usual price of an overcoat is $125. All moderately fashionable articles are so expensive I wonder how the [social] "lions" of New York can manage to live when their income is often so meager. In the lower-class sections disdained by socialites, an apartment twenty-five feet by one hundred, adequate for one family, rents for $5,000 to $6,000 [sic].[3] High prices have not yet affected the necessities of life, though people here complain that

[3] These figures are impossibly high, even on the assumption that Duvergier de Hauranne is speaking of a single-family dwelling on a yearly basis. Even if we strike off a zero from each figure, and assume a rental of $40-50 per month

these prices have tripled in the last three years. Nevertheless, carriages continue to drive every day through Central Park, crowds continue to eat and drink every night at Delmonico's or the Maison Dorée.[4] The Americans say the superfluous has become for them a necessity.

New York
December 19, 1864

HERE I AM, back in New York, the big city. Back to the perpetual clanging of fire-engines on their way to one of the city's innumerable fires; back to the rain which (eventually) cleans the streets but begins by filling them with lakes of slush that has nowhere to drain away. As I return now to this American Babylon, I feel the same affectionate disgust that I have felt, after a night of travel, at the sight of [the outskirts of] Paris, sordid and muddy in the morning light. So quickly does one become accustomed to places and things that I can easily imagine I am returning home.

I was telling you yesterday about the Shakers, and of how much I regretted having been unable to be present at their prayers. But I have had an encounter that is worth all the meetings and all the dancing in the world, because it gave me a more exact idea of that singular society. I was on the train going from Pittsfield to Chatham, when I saw an old

for an apartment in a block of lower-class tenements, the estimate still seems excessive for the period even at the height of the wartime inflationary curve.

[4] These were both very high-priced restaurants catering to high society and the rich. Their prosperity at this time reflects, of course, the large profits being made out of the war by speculators, army contractors and profiteers of all kinds.

[farmer], strangely clad, to whom I paid no attention at first. I saw him again at Chatham in the tiny waiting room of the station, where he was warming himself by the stove. I noticed then that he was wearing the costume of the "Shaking Quakers": a gray frock-coat, a white collar, brown kneebreeches and gaiters. Add a broad, gray, wide-brimmed hat, a true Quaker hat, and you see the whole picture.

I was examining him while reading a novel by Hawthorne, when this unusual person spoke to me in French. "How," I asked, "did you get the idea I might be French?"

"I saw immediately by your appearance that you were neither American nor English."

I then learned that this roughly dressed farmer had lived for a long time in Paris, that he had been rich, that he had belonged to Parisian high society, that he was very knowledgeable, if not about our current affairs, of which he had only a vague idea, at least about those of our past. His manners were those of a man of the world; he had a refined sense of social nuances; all this, in addition to the variety in his conversation, quickly won my interest. He told me that he had children living in New York, that he was going to visit them, that as far as he was concerned, he did not regret at all his lost fortune, and that the simplest, most retired life was what suited him best for the few years he had left to live.

I thought he was going to talk to me about his strange religion and the part it had played in his decision to renounce the world. However, he left all that for me to guess at without attempting to discuss it directly; and, as for myself, I did not dare ask

Photograph

Courtesy of the Newberry Library, Chicago

Shakers Wearing Traditional Costumes

indiscreet questions. We sat together in the train. His extreme simplicity of dress, his countrified air and his Quaker mannerisms seemed to have disappeared. We talked about everything, politics present and past, American as well as French, and even about literature, and I was more and more astonished at the good sense of this man.

I had thought of the Shakers as gloomy fanatics bowed down under an iron rule, pious lunatics lost in apocalyptic notions and grimly dedicated to the destruction of the human race. I had thought they saw their follies not only as a means of personal sanctification but as a universal law to which they hoped to convert all mankind. This father going to see his children did not rail against unbelievers and was deeply interested in the earthly welfare of the human race whose extinction his religion proclaimed to be the highest good. He was still concerned about all the worldly questions which ought to have left him disdainful or indifferent, and even remained a patriot deeply moved by the dangers and sufferings of his adopted country. He resembled so little the notion I had formed of the sect that I sometimes wondered if I had not perhaps made some mistake.

But there was no mistake: his costume betrayed the man as surely as if he had worn a sign on his chest. I realized that he was a Radical Republican and (as was to be expected of someone wearing a Quaker hat) an ardent abolitionist. Far from predicting the end of the world, he counted on the future to right both the injustices and the disasters of the past. I have seen few men who had a more active faith than this voluntary adherent to a doctrine of immobility and annihilation. He was like a monk who, having left his cell, is recalled to life through contact with men and who, forgetting that he had been resolved upon his own destruction, once again concerns himself with human thoughts and hopes.

Do you now understand the true character of this bizarre community? It is neither an unprecedented form of craziness nor a uniquely American phenomenon. It is, quite simply, a monastic order, the refuge of all those who feel ill-at-ease in the world and who seek a retreat in order to prepare for death. People espouse the religion of the Shakers just as they would enter a convent. Unhappy, disappointed people disgusted with life go there to find rest, and the strenuous ceremony of Sunday gymnastics does not prevent them from finding a deep tranquility, an anticipation of the death which they desire. Furthermore, they are free to leave if they should recover their taste for life. I was told about a young woman from Albany, disappointed in love, who adopted the woolen gown and flat bonnet of a Shaker woman and brought a dowry of several million [francs] to the divine Spouse. Common ownership of property, communal living, celibacy and obedience are found in all religious orders. To complete the resemblance, just as there are dupes and intriguers in monasteries, [so there are here] those who make profitable conversions and those who give all they have to the congregation; thus the generosity of Shaker neophytes is said to benefit those responsible for their conversion.

7

The Campaign in Georgia

YESTERDAY the *Tribune* appeared with a single word as a banner-headline: "THUNDER!" Below was an astonishing piece of news—the taking of Savannah with 11,000 prisoners. The more or less truthful dispatch received by the Secretary of War only claimed 1,100. But the *Tribune*, citing a Baltimore paper as its source, felt authorized to add a harmless zero to the tally of victory. Today's later news has cooled the thunderbolt. [General William T.] Sherman has not taken Savannah; he has only laid siege to it; and its garrison of 12,000 men "cannot fail" to surrender. At the same time the Confederate General [John B.] Hood has been repulsed from Nashville and, although he claims the honors of victory, he retreated after five or six of his generals had been killed or wounded. It is also said that [Confederate General Nathan B.] Forrest has been killed by [the Federal troops of General Lovell H.] Rousseau at Murfreesboro [Tennessee]. From all sides good news arrives, and only Grant, the sphinx of Richmond, remains silent and motionless.

Meanwhile the President has just called up 300,000 more men. Most of the states had evaded the last "draft" of 500,000 men by counting the volunteer units already supplied by them outside their quotas. Thus the city of New York, having proved that it had freely given to the army and navy 30,000 more men than had been required of it up to that time, found that it had furnished three-fourths of its quota in advance. The gigantic call-up of 500,000 men was thus more a regularisation of past obligations than the creation of new sources of manpower. It is to make up for the insufficiency of this earlier levy that the President is now calling up 300,000 men.

The buying of exemptions—a fiscal expedient included in the early, makeshift draft laws—left regimental rosters short of men or filled them only at the expense of the poor and has now been abolished.* Every citizen, when his name is drawn, must henceforth serve in person or else provide a substitute. At the same time, all soldiers on leave who are fit for service are being ordered to rejoin their regiments. You can see that the war is being waged in earnest and that the Union forces have no intention of letting themselves be outclassed by the Confederates who threaten to gain numerical superiority by enlisting their black population and by drafting 150,000 young men who, according to their statistics, will reach the age of military service in the coming year.

Financial measures are no less energetic. Congress is preparing to enact a new tax of 25 percent which will be added to the fares on all railroads, omnibuses, steamboats and hired carriages in the United States. At the same time, there is a proposal to impose an additional sales tax of one cent on all

*See Volume I, Chapter 4, pp. 119-22.

transactions whatsoever. Not only must all checks, bank drafts, receipts and commercial documents carry the Federal stamp, but every little thing one buys is subject to a stamp tax nearly equal to its value. You can't buy a sheet of paper, a box of lozenges, a bottle of Eau de Cologne or even a picture postcard that doesn't need a revenue stamp as its passport. In this country, which claims to have taught the world the doctrine of "free trade," the smallest transaction, the shortest journey, is so heavily burdened with taxes today that it almost seems as though the government had its heart set on bringing all economic life to a halt. I don't condemn these unavoidable measures, any more than the enforced resort, *in extremis*, to an income tax. How else would it be possible to carry on a war the cost of which, on the average, amounts to at least two million dollars a day? I only want to show you how tight the strings are stretched and how profound a transformation has taken place in the last few years in the economic life of this nation, formerly free from restraints, but today bridled and hobbled by every sort of restriction.

Meantime, the debt is growing every day and new currency continues to roll off the printing press. To raise the rate of exchange for paper money the authorities have had the idea of issuing notes that bear interest at five or six percent, but far from lending any buoyancy to the dead weight of previous issues, the new ones have been dragged down to the same low level. They are circulating at the same rate as ordinary "greenbacks." Why, indeed, should they be worth more? They will be redeemed on their due date in "greenbacks" previously issued, and the promised interest payment will serve to raise their price only on the eve of redemption.

Furthermore, the "national banks" are a poorly disguised way of increasing the issue of paper money. Up to the present time, even though Congress has in theory reserved to itself the power of regulating the monetary system, the most complete anarchy has in fact reigned. Banks were founded by the thousands and issued notes that were practically worthless, being backed only by a specie reserve, by land or by some other type of real asset, reserves that were often ridiculously small (or, indeed, nonexistent) in relation to their note-issue. One could find banks whose notes were backed by wheat, cotton or potatoes. There was scarcely a village that didn't have several banks, and they flooded the country with paper money that would have found no takers in a society less active, less enterprising, less desperate for means of exchange or having less faith in the natural resources that in time would make all these dreams come true. However, the force of habit served to maintain all these innumerable banknotes at their face value. There was no obligation on anyone to accept them. People were free to refuse them or to take them only at a discount, and in this financial chaos more than one shipwreck has taken place.

Mr. [Salmon P.] Chase, taking advantage of the Civil War [financial crisis] and the [consequent] issue of paper money, conceived a bold revolutionary stroke and made use of the very dangers that threatened the financial structure in order to establish

order and uniformity in that sphere. Profiting by
the temporary popularity of Republican principles
and by the movement towards centralization impressed on public opinion by the need to defend
the authority of the United States, he undertook to
bring the banking system back under the control of
the Federal government. He did not try abruptly to
re-establish the Bank of the United States that had
previously been brusquely suppressed by President
Jackson to the applause of the democratic element.
Instead, amidst the general disorder of the old monetary system caused by the new resort to paper currency, he induced the banks to submit voluntarily
to the yoke of Federal authority and obey uniform
national laws enacted by Congress. From the day
when Treasury paper became legal money, bank
notes fell to the same fluctuating level as the
"greenbacks," thenceforth following their ups and
downs. However, since the banks kept their former
assets, including their reserves of precious metals,
and since the suspension of gold payments lessened
the real value of their note circulation, the relation
of their note issue to its backing in real values has
become more reasonable, and their operations have
gained in security what they have lost in volume.
But they still constituted a source of dangerous
competition for the Treasury, whose unsupported
promises could not equal the real security offered
by the state banks.

It was then that Mr. Chase organized the national
banks and persuaded Congress to enact (on February 25, 1863) the law entitled "Act providing for
the issue, circulation and redemption of national

currency backed by securities of the United States."
Private banks were offered the opportunity of trans-
forming their gold and silver reserves into paper
reserves, thus pocketing the entire difference between the rates for gold and "greenbacks." The new
backing was to be deposited in the Federal Treasury in the form of United States government bonds
in an amount equal to at least one-third of the
bank's capital. In return, the Federal Treasury
would deliver to them its own banknotes up to a
limit of nine-tenths of the value of the bonds deposited. These notes carry the endorsement [and hence
the guarantee] of the Treasury, which thus stands
behind the bank's note issue.

To persuade the old banks to join the new system, ruinous taxes were imposed on them. They
were made liable to a tax of one-half of one percent
of all their deposits as well as to another tax of one
percent of their total circulation in excess of nine-
tenths of their capital. Finally, they were persuaded
to put their funds into United States bonds by a tax
of one-half of one percent on all funds otherwise
placed. In contrast, all the national banks that con-
formed to the requirements of the new law were, as
a special concession and by Federal fiat, exempted
from paying certain state taxes. Those were great
temptations, especially for banks that had over-ex-
tended themselves. Without calling in a penny's
worth of their own banknotes, without depreciating
in any way the current value of their notes—indeed,
while gaining the backing of the government and
the protection of forced circulation for their notes—
they were able to pay their debts, get free of their

difficulties and in addition even realize a profit. The poorest banks set the example, which was soon followed everywhere, and today more than 300 banks have become national banks.* The number will continue to increase until their total issue reaches 300 million dollars, the limit fixed by law.

These are the principal points of Mr. Chase's great financial reform, now being hailed as a victory and a benefit of the war.† The strongest banks are still holding back and prefer their own modest solidity to the ostentatious patronage of the State. They do not wish to become machines for the manufacture of money, mere branches of the Washington Treasury. The others, after having distributed to their shareholders a dividend in gold, the remnant of their old reserves, can still increase the face value of the paper reserve which has replaced it and can increase their note issue by a corresponding amount. They help the Treasury float its loans by buying government bonds which they transform into legal tender. They have become new printing presses for turning out paper money, auxiliaries to the one in Washington, which is by now somewhat worn out.

This process acts as a centralizing force of the first magnitude. It tends to substitute for the credit of many private enterprises that of a single entity—

---

* One of the Philadelphia banks was able in this way to distribute a dividend of 110 percent to its shareholders.

† The number of national banks has greatly increased in the two years since 1863. No less than 1,600 have been chartered in that time, and Mr. Chase's reform is now an accomplished fact.

the Federal government. I admit that order is a good thing, but it is necessary to understand what it conceals and at what price it has been bought. No one can honestly dispute its present usefulness; considering the danger, all means of finding money are good. All the same, the large additional amounts of paper money being issued, the increase of public obligations, this financial unity which so closely ties the national prosperity to the management of the public treasury with the result that, if the government's credit collapses, all is lost and America will have lost the vitality of private initiative that has been its strength and glory—all this, I repeat, seems dangerous and revolutionary to the Democrats and disturbs even the Republicans. Prosperity in the United States has been able to subsist—and still is able today to go on flourishing—independently of the government. A few years from now, it will have become inseparable from government and the embarrassments of the public treasury will be the nation's woes.

It is said on the other side that private interest is the most powerful bond of patriotism, and that national unity, high standards of public honesty and the authority of agreements made in the name of the State will grow stronger as a larger part of each citizen's private life is involved with the nation's destiny. Though I see nothing but empty charlatanism in the frequently repeated assertion that the American people, in borrowing from themselves the millions they spend, can neither impoverish themselves nor sink under a load of debts, I cannot help acknowledging that public integrity is more secure the more it is identified with everyone's self-interest. Had the United States done its borrowing abroad, I would fear that the day after the end of the war the people would be tempted to repudiate the debt. It is because the debt is a national one that bankruptcy becomes more difficult in proportion as the debt is more widely held. In the large cities, there are few artisans or common workmen who do not have a personal interest in seeing that the government fulfills its obligations.

It is precisely the smallest investors who would suffer the most from bankruptcy. In all cities there are savings banks which accept small deposits and put them to work, paying annual interest at a fixed rate of five percent besides paying dividends from their profits every five years. Without exception, all these banks have placed their funds in government bonds so as to obtain high rates of interest. Guardians and trust officers, to spare themselves the worries and difficulties of administering the funds in their care, which would expose them to continual criticism, have gotten into the easy habit of putting the assets of their wards into United States bonds, and the courts, which in this country exercise the powers of our family councils, are always happy to approve of so patriotic an investment. It is for these reasons that small property owners are the most interested in public probity and that repudiation is coming day by day to seem more unlikely. Only landowners, farmers who have no capital or who have invested all their capital in their land support such a high-handed policy of throwing overboard both taxes and the national debt.

Thanks to the difference in value between gold and paper, the acknowledged total figure of debts contracted during the war exceeds by far the sum actually advanced by the lenders. A number of loans were floated at a premium of 150 percent of their face value. Nevertheless, they have remained above par: the reason is that, with industry in trouble, with the banks paralysed by taxes and not offering as much interest as [government] bonds, the nation's savings have been diverted on a huge scale into the Federal Treasury. But how long can the latter count on enjoying this temporary advantage which it owes to the deplorable state of the nation's finances? Will the Treasury pay back in gold what it received in paper? There will be no lack of voices to declaim against the injustice of that. It is said that, to avoid redemption [in gold], a part of the debt will be consolidated, replacing bonds bearing interest at six or even seven and one-half percent by others bearing only five percent.

Even supposing that all the war loans are repaid one after another as they fall due, how can one get rid of paper money? You know that "greenbacks" are neither payable on demand nor due on a certain date. They are an anticipation without interest of the proceeds of future loans; the government, having used up its existing credit, is discounting its future borrowing power. The guarantee of the value of the "greenbacks" is contained in these words printed on the reverse side: "receivable in payment of all loans made to the United States." Unless the Treasury is rich enough to resume specie payments and destroy all the "greenbacks" that flow back into its coffers, it will be necessary to float new loans in order to buy them up.* There are those who go so

* It is now [1866] known that a resumption of specie payments has become certain, though it cannot take place at once. It redounds to the honor of the Republican administration and its Secretary of the Treasury, Mr. [Hugh] McCulloch, that they wish to live up to every last one of the Treasury's promises. The Democrats want only to establish a reserve fund to guarantee the value of paper money and then vote an annual appropriation for the amortization of the debt. They hope in this way to avoid the heavy taxes that would be necessary for the rapid reimbursement desired by the Republicans. They form the "expansionist" party whose present leader is Mr. John Van Buren. The "contractionists" believe with Mr. McCulloch that it is essential to withdraw paper money from circulation, maintain heavy taxes and retire each year as much as possible of the public debt. In his latest report to Congress Mr. McCulloch has called for the eventual repeal of the Legal Tender Act under which paper money was introduced. He has urged Congress to retire first of all the so-called "compound-interest" notes as they fall due; this is a type of interest-bearing obligation which is merely a disguised form of paper money. At the same time he is asking for discretionary authority to issue a six-percent loan, the proceeds of which will be used to redeem the "compound-interest" notes as they mature. He advocates, as a general policy, the gradual extinction of the debt as it falls due. The two Houses have also passed a concurrent resolution condemning in advance any proposal tending to repudiate the debt, which today amounts to more than $2,700,000,000. As for revenue, it is estimated at 396 million dollars [per year], more than two billion francs. Yet the American people who, in addition, pay at least as much again in state and local taxes, do not seem to feel crushed. They are determined to give the lie to all predictions of national bankruptcy. If they persist in their courageous resolve, they will have given an example of probity that is all too rare and revealed a sense of honor that one is not used to attributing to democratic nations.

far as to say that a permanent debt is the necessary condition for a firm national union and that the burden must be borne continuously so that the nation may remain accustomed to it. Thus America would, in a short space of time become a convert to the financial methods of the principal European nations. She would have a debt like France and, also like France, she would have everything except our centralized administration. Although many signs indicate that for a long time the wind will be blowing in this direction, I doubt that the fundamental, essential character of a country can ever be significantly transformed.

I fear only one kind of centralization in America, one to which democracy is always inclined because it levels individual, traditional and local influences, drowning them in the anonymous flood of the political parties. A victory for political centralization is only to be feared when the current has flowed too long in the same direction and has cut itself a channel through the resistance of free institutions. As for [America's acquiring] a really centralized administration, the impulse of public opinion can at times make all the separate wheels turn together and give the appearance and even the real effect of unity; but the machine does not derive this power from its own nature, and those who predict that America will shortly have a centralized government are taking fright at an imaginary specter.

December 21, 1864

CONGRESS has just taken a notable step toward ministerial responsibility. A member has proposed that from now on Cabinet members be subject to call to explain their actions on the floor of the House. The committee report, as drawn up by Mr. [Thaddeus] Stevens, will recommend adoption, and it is probable that the active resistance of Mr. Seward will not prevent its passage.[1] Thus, even in a republic where the executive power is subject to periodic renewal by popular election, where its action is limited by the power of the judiciary—the sole interpreter, without appeal, of the sovereign Constitution—the need is still felt to tie the hands of government more tightly and to put the agents of the executive power more directly under the control of the nation's elected representatives. What response will be made by those of our political philosophers who do not believe executive irresponsibility is incompatible with liberty?

Mr. Seward seems to be very unpopular with Congress just now. The reproach of weakness is brought against his foreign policy not only in relation to Mexico and England but also with respect to Brazil. The famous Monroe Doctrine, which symbolizes the national pride and aggressive spirit of the American nation, is thrown in his face. It is even rumored that his disagreements with Congress will force him to resign. A lively skirmish is expected over the admission of Mr. [R. King] Cutler and Mr. [Charles] Smith, would-be senators from Louisiana.[2]

[1] This was merely an incident in the political in-fighting between Radicals and moderate Republicans like Secretary Seward and nothing came of Stevens's proposal.

[2] In April, 1864, a constitutional convention in Louisiana, which had been under Federal occupation since the spring

You know that senators are elected, not by direct popular vote, but by the state legislatures, with each sending two senators to Congress, whatever the size of the state's population. But since last July Louisiana has a new state constitution, a semi-military document produced by General [Nathaniel P.] Banks and a Mexican-type *junta* chosen exclusively by known friends of the Federal government. Thus Louisiana's rights of statehood have been restored, at least on paper; the reorganized state government exercises its full sovereign rights; but officials are elected, under the protection of the military authorities, by a twentieth, at most, of its citizens. That is called "reconstruction" of the state of Louisiana, though it serves only to give an appearance of legality to a state of martial law. Louisiana could have been made a "territory" for the time being; that is, the policies of the Washington government could have been imposed on her without giving her representation in Congress. She could have been left for a while longer under the undisguised rule of a military commandant and this arbitrary exercise of power would at least have had the merit of honesty. It was thought preferable to give her the fictitious

---

of 1862, adopted a constitution abolishing slavery; the popular vote in favor of this constitution was more than ten percent of the number of voters in 1860 and the state thus met the requirements of Lincoln's tentative plan for reconstruction, so he proceeded to act as though it had been fully restored to the Union. Elections to state and Federal offices were held, but their validity was challenged, the two senators mentioned were not seated, and Louisiana had to comply with the Reconstruction process which was laid down after Lincoln's death by Congress.

status of a sovereign state in order to wield in her name in the halls of Congress the power of which she has been despoiled.

Congress is considering whether or not to take this fiction seriously. Both parties are seemingly of mixed minds, Republicans against Republicans and Democrats against Democrats. Some Republicans are taking their stand on the Radical policy and support the Sumner-Wade plan to reorganize the conquered states as territories;* others give their unreserved approval to all the dictatorial measures of General Banks. As for the Democrats, some are moved by their well-justified dislike for the General himself and for the military rule he personifies. Others are wedded to the poorly understood idea they have of the imperishable rights of the states, holding that the latter cannot legally be excluded from the Union and that their internal affairs ought to be immune to intervention by Congress. Finally, the dictator of Louisiana has come to Washington in person to support his protégés, and no one doubts that the two senators will be seated.

More than ever one hears talk about the abolition

* The Radicals still support the same policy today [1866] against the less harsh Reconstruction policy adopted by President Johnson. The Radicals want to use military force to impose on the Southern states all the reforms they think are required by national honor and public safety, the one they consider most important being black suffrage. The President, without rejecting their entire program, thinks the Southern states must be allowed to accomplish for themselves the reforms demanded of them. The Radicals demand action; Mr. Johnson is content to speak the language of authority, dictating to the Southern states the indispensable conditions of their return to the Union.

of slavery. Mr. Sumner yesterday asked favorable consideration of a petition by the Reverend Mr. Beecher* and 3,000 citizens of New York who demand complete and immediate emancipation. A considerable fraction of the Democratic party is rallying to this great reform for the good reason that they see public opinion determined on this course of action and they want at least to get a share of the credit. Jefferson Davis, for his part, has not given up his plan of freeing blacks to serve in the army. One of his newspapers expresses indignation against the outmoded institution of slavery which stands as a barrier to the independence of the South. "Let us deprive our enemies," the paper says, "of the pretext of abolition. We will no longer make war to retain slavery, but only to maintain freedom for the whites." As you can see, the great question now is whether the society of the South can be brought back into the American family; as for slavery, it has received its death-blow, and the war now can serve only to make its funeral a bloody one.

The abolitionist spirit has reached Havana. Whites and blacks, but especially the whites, convinced that the system of slave labor is harmful to their public and private prosperity, have joined together, we are told, to obtain an act of emancipation from Spain. The resistance of the mother country does not discourage them. A plantation owner who has 2,000 slaves is reported to be in the forefront of the abolitionist agitation. Thus the American Civil

* Mr. Henry Ward Beecher, preacher and abolitionist orator, brother of Mrs. [Harriet] Beecher Stowe, author of the famous novel, *Uncle Tom's Cabin.*

War, in which it was said that slavery played no part, will have been the signal for its collapse all over the world. The tiny abolitionist sect, which was for so long the butt of general scorn and persecution, will have been the spark that was successful in touching off the invisible explosive force of human conscience and reason.

Congress is still preoccupied with the Canadian question. The [Canadian] government is suspected of connivance with the judge who so chivalrously acquitted the St. Albans raiders.[3] Jurists say that the alleged grounds for acquittal were too thin to have satisfied an honest mind. The extradition process, which the court placed under the sole authority of the British government, was explicitly defined in an amendment to the statutes passed by the Canadian legislature and approved three years ago by the Queen. The arguments given by the judge are not even empty pretexts, and several American and Canadian newspapers are asking if some of the money stolen from St. Albans, in passing through his hands, did not stop there. The Canadians are beginning to be alarmed at the possible consequences of their error and, except for some wild Yankee-eaters who extoll the judge's decision as an assertion of

[3] During the night of October 19-21, 1864, a band of about 25 armed Confederates operating from Canada attacked the town of St. Albans in northwestern Vermont, killing one citizen, wounding several others, looting some $200,000 from three local banks and setting fire to a number of houses before making good their escape with a number of captured horses over the border into Quebec. Thirteen raiders were later arrested in Canada with funds amounting to about $75,000 in their possession.

patriotic pride, the leading organs of public opinion are clamoring for his resignation from the bench. The chief of police has anticipated a similar demand by resigning his office.

The international railroads are getting ready to suspend their service and are already putting their equipment in a safe place. Canada is inundated by rumors of new schemes being hatched by the Confederate bandits. It is reported that they have bought ship and arms, that they are going to burn Buffalo, Cleveland and Detroit. Three regiments of volunteers are said to have been formed and it is announced that 200,000 men will soon be ready to take the field.

In the United States there is a strange organization, the Fenian Brotherhood, a large Irish association, half open and half secret like freemasonry in France; its program is hatred of England and freedom for Ireland. For the movement the Fenians limit themselves to meetings, to patriotic ranting, to comic-opera rituals imitating religious ceremonies and to the encouragement of immigration from Ireland. Though they don't have much money, they claim to have hundreds of thousands of men ready to fight. They hope to push the United States into a European war that will encompass the downfall of Britain, that loathsome foe for whom the sons of the Irish "paddies" nurse an implacable hatred.*

* Since the latest troubles in Ireland, the Fenians have stripped the veil of secrecy from their doings. They have set up a representative republic on the model of the United States. They have elected a "congress" which met recently in Philadelphia and a president, Colonel [John Joseph]

All the same, they are a real nightmare for the Canadians who fear a Fenian invasion and see in the large Irish population to which they have given asylum a monster ready to devour them. If there were to be another raid by the Confederates, war would

---

O'Mahoney. They have issued bonds to be redeemed after the establishment of the Republic of Ireland, have organized an army and have even bought a "capitol building" in New York where they have installed their government with all the pomp and circumstance of a stage principality. They speak every day of landing an army in Ireland where they have many sympathizers and of sweeping the country clean of "the myrmidons of British tyranny." The *Herald*, now their "official" paper, prophesies that within a year England will have become a republic. There matters stand, and considering that the proceeds of the loan are being wasted in advance on extravagant preparations, the poor people, who are being told that it is their patriotic duty to invest their savings in this cause, run the risk of never seeing their money again. The American government is accused of secret complicity with the Fenians. This reproach is unjust. It is true that at their request President Johnson has freed the famous John Mitchell, one of the leaders of the Irish rebellion of 1848, later compromised in the secession of the Southern states. But the government has continually tried to discourage them and has repeatedly denied the rumors of an alliance so eagerly spread by their leaders. The United States has no desire to pick a quarrel with England and it would no doubt have called these trouble-makers to order long before this if it were not necessary to consider public opinion. Remember, too, that in America everyone enjoys an unlimited right of association. In this country, where everyone carries a loaded revolver in his pocket, it is not a crime to put on a uniform and parade in the streets with a rifle on your shoulder. The President has no right to hinder citizens in the exercise of their natural liberty as long as they do not seriously disturb the public peace, and it would do too much honor to the Fenians to consider them dangerous.

break out and the Celtic hordes would be let loose on the colonists of British America! In a first reaction of anger General [John B.] Dix, commanding the military department of the North, issued a war-like proclamation authorizing anyone who might be the victim of such attack to take reprisals on his neighbors. Congress discussed the creation of a fleet on the Great Lakes and the immediate abrogation of the Treaty of Reciprocity which, by extending to British subjects all the commercial privileges of American citizens, undercuts the Canadian party that supports annexation to the United States.

Everything was tending towards war, but the government has prudently called a halt. The President, guided by his own good sense or accepting the wise advice of his Secretary of State, disavowed the manifesto of General Dix by forcing him to retract his statement. Mr. Sumner, with a wisdom and moderation that do him great credit, fought energetically in the Senate against taking any warlike measures, insisting that the commercial treaty not be broken without giving Canada the required six months' warning and that the question of arming the frontier be sent to the Committee on Foreign Relations before going to the Military Affairs Committee. "The Rebels," he said in substance, "are pursuing a further aim in these raids besides robbing a few banks and killing a few citizens. They want to force us to declare war on Great Britain by causing the cup of our complaints and her injustices, already full, to overflow. Do not fall into the trap, do not compromise the success of the other war, but if you put down the insurrection, in one blow you will have carried off the victory for both causes."

America has too often been accused of provoking other countries and trampling on [international] law. If we consult the history of the last few years, we shall see that she knows quite as well as her European elders how to be moderate in the face of force or to bow before the right. When it is recalled that there were no American privateers flying the Russian flag during the Crimean War, we should be less inclined to award a trophy for good faith to English neutrality [during the Civil War].

Doubtless we shall never see an Austrian, French or Russian newspaper make a vain and ridiculous threat to land in Ireland and dismember the British Empire, but rhetorical flourishes of this kind do not indicate any impairment of the nation's solid good sense. It would perhaps be desirable for some of our know-it-all monarchies to borrow from American democracy the wise policy of its founders: do not seek for distant spheres of influence nor ruinous adventures beyond the seas.

December 23, 1864

NOW CHRISTMAS and New Year's Day are about to arrive with their festivities. Having come to New York to see people, I ought to jump into the whirl-pool of the pleasure-loving society that has gathered here for the winter, for as a distinguished foreigner I would find all doors open to me. So far in my travels I have missed this personal experience of learning to pass judgment on the infinitely delicate and elusive subject of social mores. These things are not discussed in books nor written into constitutions, and I should profit from the opportunity to study them. I have a great dislike of purely formal occasions. I do not like to solicit the good will of people for whom I care nothing; I do not like to be obligated to people who care nothing for me. Therefore I have gone to only one evening reception.

It was one of those balls that are called "dancing classes," but are really clubs for young girls who come with their mothers as well as a male escort if they like. In New York there are many of these merry little groups, and they meet every week at the home of one of their members. Each girl usually arrives in the company of two young gentlemen, one of whom—the one she likes the most, no doubt—escorts her home after the ball. Since I knew no one there, I was left entirely to myself. I had already noticed, however, even among those who were wearing white ties and evening dress, something of those democratic customs which seem to have got into people's blood. A total stranger speaks to you in a familiar manner, asks for information or asks you to introduce him to Miss So-and-so. Those who made this request of me, I must admit, were out of luck.

America is the land of informality. You have read in M. [Jean-Jacques] Ampère's account[4] the amusing anecdote of the coachman who asked where the *man* was who had hired his carriage, calling himself the *gentleman* who was to drive him. Each day spent in America brings new proof of the truth of this story. When I first arrived in New York, this

[4] Jean-Jacques Ampère visited the United States in 1851 and wrote a two-volume book about his travels.

highly civilized place, I got into a carriage and paid the driver, who turned his head and cried out: "Where's this fellow's baggage?" In Pittsfield I took my place in the sleigh waiting to drive me to the hotel; it was cold enough to split rocks, so I snuggled down into the depths of the cab; the coachman stuck his nose out the door on his side and cried, "Where *is* the fellow?" I asked the small shoe-shine boy for my shoes; he affectionately threw his arm around my neck and patted me familiarly on the shoulder. Another time, on a steamer, someone swore at me because I got in the path of his broom. Even here, on the horsecars, you see the conductor chatting on equal terms with his passengers. When a lady enters, the conductor puts his hand on her shoulder and shoves her along by tapping her gently on the back with his fist. We call him "Sir," while for the most part he dispenses with this formality. Once in Boston, a Frenchman who was peaceably seated in a streetcar felt a cane brush against his legs and in the interval between jabs heard a voice say, "Move over!" The person speaking in this discourteous way was standing there in front of him, a well-dressed man of good appearance who seemed to have no notion of how rude he was being.

An American wears his hat glued to his head; he gives you a careless greeting, has the same casual handshake for everyone; sometimes he acknowledges your existence with an imperceptible nod; he has a way of leaving abruptly without saying goodbye—these are the usual forms of behavior among cultivated people. In them one sees the manners of a

people who have no time to lose nor any imagination to waste on useless compliments. This simplicity is really very convenient, and even those it
shocks the most hasten to adopt the prevailing
style. I am afraid that some day I shall have to re-
learn my forgotten French etiquette, the lack of
which would offend no one here. On the contrary,
Americans seem embarrassed when someone's manners are too formal. "Oh," said a New Yorker,
speaking of a well-bred Englishman who had lived
for a long time in the Spanish colonies where he
had picked up a too-flowery style of deportment,
"he is a very fine gentleman, but painfully polite."[5]

But may Heaven keep me from slandering America and from making its inhabitants seem hateful or
ridiculous to you! They deserve neither of those
judgments, and the absence of fine manners here is
balanced by sincere cordiality and kindness. If I
keep coming back to the subject of American manners, it is only to show you how thoroughly democratic equality permeates the customs of this nation.
Perhaps also I return to this theme only out of national vanity, politeness being, to tell the truth, the
only trait of national character on which we French
can still lay claim to an incontestable superiority.

Well-bred Americans who travel in France are
charmed by the universal courtesy they meet with
there. In England, society is divided into two
classes, the arrogant and the servile; we alone have
the privilege of being at the same time a democratic
and a polite people. In England the common man
removes his hat when he speaks to a rich or titled

[5] This remark is given in English in the original text.

gentleman who, in reply, calls him "My good man" or "Fellow." But in America everybody feels free to treat you like an old chum. Only we Frenchmen, whether of high or low estate, have learned how to keep a sense of proportion in our etiquette. To give praise where praise is due, we are one of the most polite people in the world; we don't have so many virtues that we can afford to give any away.

I was telling you yesterday about the probable success of the constitutional amendment;[6] its passage now seems certain. The Democratic party is finally yielding to the inevitable and is trying to fill its sails with the very same wind into which it would like to steer. Its position has accordingly undergone a decided change. The New York *World*, a Copperhead newspaper, ran a great abolitionist manifesto the other day in which emancipation was perhaps not exactly praised, but—what amounts to the same thing—was accepted as a necessity, almost as a *fait accompli*. The reasons given are very simple and even rather shameless in their rough common sense. "It is clear," they say, "that the Democratic party will never be able to rally the country in support of its [present] platform and become a majority party. We must therefore abandon it and write a new one containing an 'abolition' plank. Everyone is free to think as he pleases in private, but slavery has to be struck out of the party's official program."

[6] The Thirteenth Amendment, adopted in Congress January 31, 1865, and ratified December 6, 1865. The abolition of slavery is explicit in the text: "Neither slavery nor involuntary servitude . . . shall exist within the United States, or any place subject to their jurisdiction."

In France cries of "turn-coat" and "traitor" would have been raised; it would have been stated as a principle that political beliefs ought to be held as sacred as those of religion and that parties should never touch a single stone in the changeless temple of their doctrines lest they set an example of disloyalty for individuals to follow by being the first to desert a defeated cause. Here, on the contrary, political parties know how to change their course when they see that they are about to be driven onto a rocky coast, and it is by virtue of these timely maneuvers that they save their whole crew. Does this policy of concession shock your strict ethical standards? All the same, it is the only way to avoid becoming a political corpse, a lifeless torso without arms or legs, a blind deaf-mute retaining in its impotence only the empty consolation that its secret thoughts are its own. There is nothing shameful in giving up a part in order not to lose the whole, in throwing overboard some of the cargo in order to save the rest. There is no future for a party which allows itself, stoically and silently, to be sent to the bottom nor for one which, in order to avoid extinction, takes refuge in dishonorable surrender; there *is* a future for a party that can keep itself afloat. For better or for worse, there are times when one must bow to an accomplished fact because it is a waste of time to struggle against the inevitable. Here in America it is the abolition of slavery; in France it is universal suffrage. The force of circumstances, which forces pro-slavery politicians here to vote for abolition makes it necessary for our conservatives to become democrats if they want to revive liberty.

December 24, 1864

THE QUARREL with Canada is dying down and the vote on the bill to abrogate the treaty of reciprocity has been postponed until after the Christmas recess so that it may be given more thoughtful consideration. The Governor-General, Lord Monck, has seen his duty and has done it by ordering the pursuit of the fugitives. One has been recaptured and it is hoped that the others will soon be caught. At the same time he issued a proclamation urging his country to maintain a scrupulous neutrality. On its side, Congress is calming down; its great concern at the moment is the Radicals' crusade against the "reactionary" Seward.

It has been said that Lincoln is only a straw man, a puppet whose strings are pulled by Seward. On the contrary, it appears that, under his rough exterior and naïve good humor, Mr. Lincoln is a true statesman, more supple and more adept at political intrigue than many a veteran of behind-the-scenes political warfare. He has been able, without ever departing from his own principles, to keep his balance between the two hostile factions of the Republican party.

As long as public opinion demanded temporising and half-way measures, Mr. Seward remained absolute master of the Cabinet. Now that the tide of public opinion is receding from him, he is in danger of being stranded on a lonely shore, marooned in the Department of State.

Ministerial responsibility, although not provided for by the American Constitution, is nonetheless a natural law which no government can escape. The concealed working of this machinery is of course slower and more difficult [here] than in monarchies. A minister, instead of resigning (as in England) at the first hint of stormy weather, can withstand a number of heavy volleys at close range before he is forced to strike his colors. Still, the time eventually comes when, after he has been buffeted again and again by a hostile majority, he must either bow to the opposition or beat a retreat.

This is what Mr. Seward will have to do if ever the time comes when his enemies decide to get rid of him or if ever the President discreetly passes the word to them to train all their guns on him. It is not by any means a foregone conclusion that "Honest Abe" must be clumsy just because he is honest. His policy is to be like an intelligent weathervane, able to predict future winds, turning neither too late nor too soon in their direction and remaining always in accord with them.

The House of Representatives has just delivered what looks like a rebuke to the President by voting after a noisy debate to reaffirm the Monroe Doctrine, but in reality it was a rebuff to Mr. Seward. When Mr. [Henry] Winter Davis read the resolution he was submitting to the House, the text of which held that, as a general rule, the foreign policy of the President ought to follow closely the wishes expressed by Congress, it was noted that there had been a significant change: the word "President" had been replaced by the term "executive department." Moreover, the dominant opinion in both Houses is pushing the President more and more toward a Radical position.

This cannot fail to run counter to the natural moderation—I won't say "the lukewarm liberalism"—of the Secretary of State. Mr. Seward no doubt admired the adroitness of a gifted disciple when Senator [Henry] Wilson [of Massachusetts] attached to the resolution calling for an inquiry into the arbitrary arrest and abduction of Lieutenant-Governor [Richard T.] Jacob of Kentucky[7] an amendment—"provided that the inquiry be compatible with the public interest"—that implicitly cancelled it. But when the Senate's attention was afterwards called to the doubtful loyalty of a large number of government employees in Washington, and when that body voted to impose an oath of allegiance on all the inhabitants of the District of Columbia, without exception, and forbade anyone who had not taken this oath to carry on any kind of business, the debonair Secretary of State—who, it is said, allows himself to be arbitrary in small affairs that remain secret and does not like spectacular, sweeping measures of an extra-legal character— must have bitten his lips with a pitying smile. Mr. Seward, in fact, likes absolute power only when it is exercised in silence, when it is wielded behind closed doors or at police headquarters where compromising words are whispered quietly among fellow-conspirators while the protesting cries of the victims are muffled behind heavy doors. The Radicals, on the contrary, are backwoodsmen, political executioners who can cut a tree at its base or knock an enemy on the head without thinking twice about the commotion the fall will make.

[7] See Chapter 2, footnote 11, p. 86.

December 27, 1864

YESTERDAY I made a second trip to New Jersey to visit General [George B.] McClellan for, although here in America I support the winning party, that is no reason for me to forget the losers. Again the general was absent and I was unable to see him. Nevertheless, I was struck by the first words I heard in his house: "Good news this morning!" The good news was the taking of Savannah. I know of some families in which this victory of a Federal army would be greeted by barely-suppressed cries of consternation. But in the home of the general, who might well be thinking about his broken career, about the fame others have stolen from him, the family still finds it "Good news!"

And indeed it is a great piece of news. Not that the victory was as complete as one might have hoped. A dispatch received yesterday spoke of 13,000 prisoners, but the official report has reduced this to 800. General [William J.] Hardee escaped with his garrison. Yet no matter how the Rebel papers try to disguise the fact, this undramatic and not very costly campaign is bound to have incalculable results. Georgia, that wealthy state from which the Richmond government has drawn such great resources, has been ruined from one end to the other by Sherman's march to the sea. His army is composed of veterans long accustomed to the misery and reprisals of war who have little pity for the sufferings of the enemy. For a long time now, the exhausted South has used boldness to create an illusion of strength. Hardly six months ago, when the Rebels were close to Philadelphia and Baltimore and were about to lay siege to the national capital for a second time, who could have guessed that their seemingly invincible power was nothing but an empty shell?

Two months ago, when General Sherman conceived his daring plan—foolhardy in appearance but in reality easy—of piercing the heart of the Confederacy and clearing a path through it to the sea, there arose a multitude of prophets who predicted that he was about to dig his own grave: [General John B.] Hood would block his retreat; his army would be cut to pieces and annihilated piecemeal in the mountains of Georgia; he was putting his head in the lion's mouth. Skeptics shook their heads and smiled pityingly. Many were unwilling to believe that he was giving out his real intentions, and the Richmond papers ironically counted the 300 miles that separate Atlanta from the seacoast. Well, he set out anyway, breaking his communications and supply lines and destroying everything as he marched, leaving Hood's army nothing but a devastated countryside on which to subsist. For six weeks his army's risky advance was reported only in the form of vague rumors or enemy reports.

Suddenly the great news burst upon the world: Sherman had reached the coast, he had joined up with the fleet, he had taken Fort McAllister and was besieging Savannah. During this new Anabasis,[8] comparable—at least it is being compared—to the

---

[8] The reference is to Xenophon's account of how a Greek army of 10,000 men surmounted great hardships in its march from Mesopotamia back to the Mediterranean by way of the Tigris valley and Armenia in 402–401 B.C.

exploits of the Ten Thousand, the new Xenophon has encountered no serious resistance nor lost more than a few hundred of his 60,000 veterans. It is true that Georgia, very different from Asia Minor, offered great hospitality to the conquerors. Instead of impassable trails, snow-capped mountains and frozen wilderness through which the Ten Thousand fought their way, Sherman found a still-rich agricultural region with railroads, turnpikes paved with planks and a clear sky smiling on fields of rice and corn. Instead of savage, inhospitable tribes that harassed the [Greeks'] famished and dwindling column, he dealt with a defenseless population from which all the able-bodied males had been conscripted save for a handful of feeble militia to which the Richmond government could send no aid but the name and sword of [General P. G. T.] Beauregard. True, there was the army of General Hood, who had thought he could draw Sherman in his pursuit by threatening Tennessee. Sherman, in fact, at first made as if to follow him, but then left him engaged with [General George H.] Thomas in a battle that drew in all his forces. Semi-victorious at Franklin, but crushed at Charleville by Thomas, Hood lost sixty cannon and 8,000 prisoners—half of his forces. Railroads have been cut, rivers are in flood in his rear and, while his cavalry was being beaten in Kentucky, that of the enemy was harassing his fleeing and scattered troops. Hood has suffered a real disaster.

Meanwhile Sherman continued his triumphal march, laying the country waste as he went. Not one plantation was spared, not a village, not a herd of cattle or sheep. Cotton was burned, horses were seized, animals in stables and barnyards were massacred to provide an endless supply of loot. Thus Sherman's army lived, as they say in the American language, "splendidly," leaving behind it nothing but fire and famine. Only a few poorly organized bands of militia and a few troops of cavalry attacked them. Only one fortified place, Savannah, encircled by flooded rice paddies which form a sort of lake around the city, and only one army, that of Hardee, about 13,000 strong, was able to put up any resistance to him. A few cannon balls and artillery shells were exchanged, but after only three days of siege, when the Yankees had pushed a number of crude trenches up nearly to the walls, Hardee set fire to the arsenal and powder-works, destroyed the little flotilla anchored in the port and retreated across the river with 12,000 men under the protection of some heavy guns on boats which he blew up afterwards. Eight hundred men posted here and there to cover the withdrawal were taken prisoner. Twelve locomotives, three steamboats and thirty-two thousand bales of cotton were seized and saved from the fire. At last the members of the city government went to surrender to Sherman, appealing to the generosity of the "magnanimous enemy" whom they had called a vile Yankee the day before. At the same time, General Gillem,[9] with a corps of light cavalry, invaded Mississippi and Alabama and cut the Ohio and Mobile Railroad, brushing aside all resistance. Then a "monster-expedition" prepared in advance

[9] General Alvin C. Gillem, whose corps was attached to the Army of the Tennessee.

set out to take Wilmington, the last large port in Confederate hands, and the entrepôt of its clandestine trade with the British island of Nassau.

The Richmond papers consoled themselves with vain bravado. "Savannah is taken—but it's no great loss! Savannah is not the whole Confederacy, nor even all of Georgia. It is only Savannah, a den of Jews and Yankees, which Hardee ought to have burned to the ground as he left, and we should almost congratulate ourselves on being rid of it." The Confederacy, they say, has lost none of its inexhaustible resources; the more it shortens its lines of defense, the more invincible it becomes!

But soon Charleston will fall to Sherman and Wilmington, too, will be taken. Although the Rebel press may try to console itself in advance for the expected fall of Richmond by saying that after all, Richmond is only Richmond, a city whose loss will not in any way endanger the future of the country, that on the contrary the armies will be even stronger when they no longer have the tedious task of defending cities, I wonder what will remain of the Southern Confederacy after Virginia, Georgia, the Carolinas and Alabama have all surrendered unless it is the wilderness of marshy forests that covers Florida. There the Rebels would indeed be safe from all attack; they could carry on their resistance until yellow fever cut them down, turning them into food for the alligators. Much better to follow Senator Foote's example and give up before it is too late to save something from the débâcle.

In this connection, behold the fine dissension that is now beginning to appear in the Richmond

Congress and administration! Mr. Foote,[10] formerly a fire-eating secessionist and a vehement critic of Mr. Seward in the United States Congress, submitted his resignation [from the Senate of the Confederacy] after making a speech, a very daring one in the circumstances, in which he boldly attacked the "despotic"—calling the thing by its name—ways of the Confederate President. He complained about the suspension of laws, the impotence of Congress and the universal servility that encourages dictatorship. "I do not want," he said, "to be a legislator in chains," and took his departure, predicting that there will soon be a military *coup d'état* that will destroy even the few remaining vestiges of the former civil liberties.

Governor Brown, for his part, fell back on the rights of Georgia, complaining—with some justice—that the men who could have driven Sherman out of his state were being used instead to defend Richmond. From all sides peace proposals are being put forward in the [Southern] state legislatures and although these are invariably "tabled" by a majority that is fearful and docile rather than confident, they point to the rapid growth of a peace party. Having rebelled in the name of "states' rights," the Southerners are now destroying their supposedly imperishable nation in the name of those same rights.

As always with troubles for which there is no remedy, people put the whole blame for disaster on the government. President Davis is so threatened that even the Richmond newspapers—those devoted servants whose ranks he has so often purged and

[10] See Chapter 5, footnote 5, p. 173.

whose leaders he has chosen—are divided and have partly turned against him. The poor dictator must have his salary raised: $25,000 in Confederate paper is not enough to keep the wolf from the door in a country where just one turkey costs $100. *The Examiner* and *The Whig* have angrily denounced him for this in terms so outspoken that the government may close them down. The press is becoming more refractory in direct ratio to the attempts made to gag it. [In France] the absolutism of the Ancien Régime stifled thought and believed itself to be strong in proportion to the absence of public discussion. Modern civilization has changed that: journalism has become the king-pin of authoritarian governments. The Confederate President, who is a friend of science and progress, would like to borrow from us the regime which the whole world envies and have all the newspapers run as governmental agencies. It was no fault of his that the Congress did not vote to establish a militant patriotic press whose task it would be to manage public opinion, with journalists accorded privileges such as exemption from the draft like judges or clergymen—in other words, receiving officially from his hand their desks, pens and paper. But I feel certain that there is in the American temperament some innate primitiveness that rejects discipline. In vain does Mr. Davis seize the presses and send recalcitrant writers off to the army. The opposition always springs up again, the weeds always crowd out the good grain he has sown, so much so that today it is said that he is ready to hand over his field for a final harvesting by the warlike scythe of General Lee.

That seems the only way out of the present chaos, which is the final crisis of [the Confederacy's] grim death-throes. When war pushes a nation onto the downward slope of dictatorship, there is no choice open but to go all the way to the bottom. The most timid then become the most violent and, not having been able to pull back in time, they rush forward into blind and desperate fanaticism. The very ones who are most eloquent in denouncing the consequences of the evil do not dare open their eyes to its true cause or to its remedy. If their territory is cut in two, their armies destroyed, their finances ruined twenty times over, it is not because they have persisted in an insane war; it is because "Hood replaced Johnston in Tennessee," because Davis insisted on running the campaign personally, because "he lets the troops go hungry" while he makes Congress give him a few barrels of meat for his table and a few bales of hay for his horses.

Even the farsighted Senator Foote, who is getting out of the house before it collapses, denounces Davis's misgovernment in his farewell speech. While cursing tyranny he calls for more of it, prolonging the rebellion and giving it a new lease on life. Those who proclaim in advance what the future will bring are useful because they impart the force of their ideas to the course of events, but they are the wrong people to hold in their determined, inflexible hands the frail rudder of executive leadership. As for President Lincoln, he goes on with his old game. This can be seen from the fact that he is being referred to in more indulgent terms by the most uncompromising abolitionists whose leading spokesman is Wendell Phillips—a militant group that on principle stays aloof from the government.

A month ago, Mr. Phillips was still speaking of President Lincoln only as a beaten opponent, forced against his will to serve the good cause. Today he gave a major speech at Cooper Institute attacking General Banks's proposal for emancipation (an ingenious system which retains slavery in all but name by making all black men, even those who were already free before the President's Emancipation Proclamation, into serfs and beasts of burden of the United States government). He [Phillips] opened his talk by paying a splendid tribute to Abraham Lincoln, "the most honest man in the country," only to refer to him later in a casual manner tinged with irony, showing that a professional politician can expect only a few disdainful concessions from this proud, unyielding spirit. But among the abolitionists Wendell Phillips plays only the part of the look-out stationed atop the mast to cry out when land is sighted, and those who do the steering take a more conciliatory course. The accord between them and the President is so complete that General [John C.] Frémont is spoken of as the most likely successor to Mr. [William L.] Dayton [as U.S. Ambassador] in Paris. The general says to anyone who will listen that he has been offered the post twice and that he has refused it twice, which leads one to think that he had wanted the post but had finally realized that it was not going to be given to him. Still, he is not the only one to be obliged in spite of himself to proclaim his own disinterestedness and to fall back proudly on the pose of being above the battle. I know someone else who is burning with a desire to obtain that same post but consoles himself by saying he is too good a democrat to allow himself to be seduced by the favors of a corrupt government.

However this may be, the Radicals already have some embassies to pass out. If, as expected, they reward Mr. [William P.] Fessenden or Mr. [Edward] Everett with this vacancy, it is because their leaders did not want the cake for themselves. While I do not exactly consider them paragons of wisdom, I think they can render a great service to the country by [staying in Congress and] passing laws rather than by running after jobs in the administration. Their revolutionary vigor cannot fail to enhance the importance and the authority of the legislature. If ever Congress achieves the uncontested supremacy to which it aspires, the leadership of a parliamentary party will become the royal road to power, and the Cabinet will be nothing more than an executive committee of the two chambers. It is often said that the old machinery of government is incompatible with this new [Congressional] power, and that local independence, the sovereignty of the Constitution and judicial review will all have to give way before the ascendancy of the legislature branch. For my part, I see no reason why this should be so. It seems logical to me that the executive branch, having acquired power over more areas of policy, should be made less independent—in other words, now that its hobbles have been removed, a double bit should be put in its mouth.

December 31, 1864

THE GREAT EXPEDITION sent to take Wilmington was a total failure. [Admiral David D.] Porter command-ed the fleet, [General Benjamin F.] Butler the forces to be put ashore. Neither one had the supreme com-mand, so dissension began as soon as they set sail. When they reached Fort Fisher, they bombarded it for twenty-four hours, expending, I believe, twenty thousand cannon balls. General [Godfrey] Weitzel landed with 3,000 men and advanced to make a reconnaissance up to the walls of the fortress while a hail of Federal cannon balls kept the fort silent and hermetically sealed like a tortoise in its shell. A few soldiers then climbed up on the parapet; one of them even got inside the fort, killing an aide-de-camp and making off with his horse. That was the moment for a bold stroke or else the whole under-taking was meaningless. General Weitzel wanted to launch the attack, but the two commanders were jealous of each other. In the end, Butler proved to be lacking in audacity; without even leaving his ship, he ordered his troops to re-embark and then returned unashamed to his camp on the James Riv-er. Meanwhile Porter, left alone, vented his rage in a furious but ineffectual bombardment. He wrote Butler a letter that was all but insulting—still, what good did that do? Whose orders had Butler failed to obey? The navy insists on burning up its pow-der: the Lord only knows how many millions of dollars have gone up in smoke! One might think that the experience of the last few years would have taught the Americans that at least in war it is vital to have discipline and a single commander. It seems

Engraving

The Attack on Fort Fisher

From *Harper's History of the Great Rebellion*

that in this affair General Grant has shown no more foresight or initiative than a doorpost. He has been called "Butcher" Grant; now, after an expedition like this one—more costly in powder than in men— he might well be called "Head of the Fireworks Department."[11]

Last night I met Admiral [David G.] Farragut at the home of Mr. [George] Bancroft, the famous historian of the American Revolution. Mr. Bancroft is an erect old man, thin, sallow, white-haired and abrupt in his manner. His general appearance can be described only by the English word "tough." He may not have an exceedingly brilliant mind, but those who know him tell me that they have rarely encountered a mind so active or so industrious, a memory so capacious or an intellect so sound. Despite his seventy-odd years, he is seen every night in society, gay, talkative and still young in spirit. Every day he dictates long passages without referring to notes and reads everything published in the old world or the new.

Science, literature, history, philology, ethnology—one can talk with him about anything under

[11] General Butler, in his *Autobiography and Personal Reminiscences* (Boston, 1892) pp. 774-824, claimed in his own defense that his decision to withdraw his troops was justified by the exhaustion of the Navy's ammunition and consequent inability to maintain supporting fire. He also feared that Confederate troops approaching from the north would attack his assault force in the rear and that a threatening storm would make it impossible either to supply or to re-embark his men if the fort did not surrender almost immediately. It is generally agreed that coordination of land and sea forces in this operation left much to be desired.

Photograph, about 1864   Courtesy of The National Archives

Admiral David G. Farragut

the sun; he is always up-to-date and familiar with the latest ideas.

As for Admiral Farragut, he is a man of few words. He is a simple man with a very attractive face: a broad, square forehead, a frank, piercing glance and a modest, benevolent expression. He says that Wilmington is almost impregnable by sea because of the shallow water which prevents heavily-armed warships from entering the Cape Fear River. Only the small, light blockade-runners can pass easily. It is not even possible to block all the mouths of the river. During the climax of the bombardment, four blockade-runners were able to enter the estuary by way of side channels. All the same, the admiral believes that Wilmington, too, will fall, but only when Sherman marches north along the coast, sweeping the enemy before him, taking Charleston and joining up with Grant to close the iron circle in which Richmond is imprisoned. Then the last Rebel army will be crushed. As for the states of the deep South, branches that are already separated from the main trunk, they will fall like a body when the head is cut off.

The Richmond papers proclaim that Lee's army is prepared for a great event, and that he is about to strike a blow that will astonish the world. In fact, his army does seem to be stretching its limbs and hunching its shoulders like a wrestler who is preparing for some great feat of strength. But the poor Southern journalists have been concocting so much spurious news lately that I believe this mountain, too, will give birth to nothing but a mouse. There is a suspicion that the great strategic movement may be the evacuation of Richmond, where food and supplies are unobtainable. The Rebel high command—the army, the president, the government departments and the official gazette—would move to Danville, in a part of Virginia that is richer and less exhausted by war. One can only liken this to the flight of a wounded hare that drags itself from one hiding-place to another until the dogs close in and tear it to pieces.

One final comment: the passport system exasperates everyone on both sides of the frontier. The Americans enforce it with the pitiless rigor to be expected of any people that has turned its back on free institutions. Those who must cross every day—the local farmers, railway employees and even a child who was caught unawares on the Canadian side—have had to buy passports. American consuls unjustly require payment in gold and profit from the exchange. The man accustomed to liberty is the most terrible of all possible agents of tyranny. I try to imagine what America would be like under French laws, and I shudder at the oppressive uses to which she would put them. A nation needs to have had a long history of despotism in order to learn how to lengthen its chains a little.

8

New Year's Day in New York

THE END of the year invariably brings a flood of statistics. The newspapers claim that 1864 has broken the record for railroad accidents. A tally kept by the *Herald* shows about 500 killed and at least 2,000 injured. The total seems enormous and I for one will not say that the American railroads are blameless. Still, if you consider the great numbers of passengers and the great distances they travel, you will find that the casualty lists are not yet excessively long.

Do you want to know the total population of the United States or that of each large city? You are asking for more than the Americans know themselves. Do you think that statistics are as uniformly and as scientifically compiled in the United States as in France? But where (in this country) will you find those officials that a centralized administration has in abundance? Where will you find exact, conscientious census figures? Where in America will you even find public registers of vital statistics?*

---

*The records of births and deaths are supposed to be kept by the ministers of the various churches and then put in order by the justices of the peace. The latter also deliver official certificates based on the statements of witnesses. This imperfect system often causes great confusion.

You can easily imagine the vagaries of local officials, their negligence, their lack of uniformity. Bear in mind also the astonishing ebb and flow of the human tide that washes over the New World. Do not expect the keeping of records to be one of the benefits of "self-government," for that is an eminently bureaucratic science and can flourish only in the hothouse atmosphere of a perfectly centralized government. Go to China or France if you want all the columns to add up to 100 per cent or if you like nice round numbers. In America, from time to time,* in order to get some idea of the progress that has been made, they take a census by guess and by approximation as one might throw a sounding-line into quicksand or try to measure the speed of a ship hastening under full sail over a wind-tossed sea. Long before the separate items can be added up or the totals made public, the figures are out of date. Now and for a number of years to come, one has to depend on the census of 1860, but four or five years in America equals a half-century in France. It is really more than a half-century because, although the total population may not have changed greatly, large numbers will surely have moved and new cities, perhaps even whole regions, will have been carved out of the wilderness.

Sunday
January 1, 1865

ALL THE GREAT FESTIVITIES will take place tomorrow because Sunday is always consecrated to immobility

---

* A general census is taken every ten years in the United States by the Federal government.

and boredom. Tomorrow all the women will stay at home, decked out in their most beautiful finery and the men will run to and fro like cab horses, bringing candy, flowers, jewelry or merely their own presence—it depends on how well they know one another—and the traditional greeting, "A Happy New Year!" just as at Christmas time one wishes everyone "Merry Christmas!" Everywhere refreshments or "luncheons" await the scurrying visitors who from ten in the morning until seven in the evening are not allowed to rest until they have delivered the three hundred New Year's greetings that may be required of them. The women are seated like queens on their thrones, covered like holy relics with all the jewels they own. And no one is exempted from the obligation of kneeling before them. The feeble grandfather drags himself to visit everyone not excluding his grand-daughter; the head of a household goes out to drink innumerable glasses of wine in the course of his rounds; meanwhile, a thousand strangers come in procession to sit at his hearth. You can see that New Year's Day is not, as it is in France, or as Christmas Day is in England, a family holiday; in America that place belongs to "Thanksgiving Day." Instead, New Year's Day here is the time when people work off all at once the obligations they have accumulated during the past year due to lack of time or inclination. It is typical of the utilitarian Americans to devote a whole day in this way to social functions, to regard them as a job to be done, as a plain and inescapable duty to be gotten out of the way so that the rest of their time may be free for their business or pleasure.

As for me, a newcomer in New York society, I shall need to make only about twenty-five visits and accept some twenty-five glasses of sherry, which I shall of course cleverly arrange not to drink. Whoever said of Americans that they are a sober people has only seen the surface. If they drink so much ice-water on trains it is only for lack of anything better, and because "whiskey," "bitters," "punch," "cocktails," and "drinks" of all sorts have lit in them an insatiable and inextinguishable fire. Every man, great or obscure, from [Daniel] Webster to [Stephen A.] Douglas, feels the need of that ingredient to keep the spark of life burning.

General Grant, before his rise to fame, was known in Illinois as a whiskey drinker of extraordinary proficiency, while Douglas, the "Little Giant" of the West, was for years more or less under the influence of alcohol. Westerners have attained to such a level of manly strength that strong drink, like poison to Mithridates,[1] no longer does them any harm, and their mental processes borrow from the alcoholic element nothing but its violence and never reveal any weakness or lack of clarity under its influence. This ability, like all our moral or physical faculties, only grows stronger with exercise, so much so that a man who drank only moderately in his youth, becomes an outstanding tippler in middle life and can hope to scale the highest peaks of inebriety in old age. Mr. Webster, who seems, by the way, to have acquired a long list of vices, went

[1] King Mithridates, an enemy of Rome, is said to have tried to acquire immunity to common poisons by gradually taking larger and larger doses.

through two distinct periods in his life, one in which he drank only wine and a later one after he had switched to brandy. People still refer to Mr. Webster "before he lost his taste for wine," as one might speak of "Raphael before he painted *La Fornarina*,"[2] and even those who revere his memory don't feel that they dishonor it by mentioning these little foibles.

It is also said—and I am only reporting what I have heard—that many women have a decided taste for what promises to be the poor man's drink and that, when given a choice, they prefer the famous "Bourbon whiskey" to the fine wines of France or Spain. They say, by the way, that a worthy Yankee once asked a French prince to send him a case of "Bourbon," no doubt thinking that the Bourbon family had gained fame and fortune by its manufacture. The other day on a train, in first class, I actually saw an Irish "gentleman" pull a bottle of brandy from his pocket and offer it to the woman seated next to him; she took several generous swigs, after which they proceeded to chew tobacco together like old friends—but these, thank God, are not the manners of the drawing-room. Such rustic blemishes as I detect are hidden or disguised by an overlay of European manners, for there are swarms of cosmopolitan Americans who have acquired French or British ways and these people set the tone for the others who have lived their whole lives in the shadow of

[2]Reference to the famous portrait of a beautiful Roman woman, a baker's daughter—hence the title *La Fornarina*—with whom the painter was in love during the later (Roman) period of his career.

the City Exchange or in some smoky office on Wall, Beaver or Pearl Street.

Just the same, it is a society with only moderate appeal for a man who likes peace and quiet, who enjoys small gatherings and conversation by the fireside. It is more like a whirlwind than a social milieu, and the lessening of activity caused by the Civil War, by private family mourning and by the shrinking of some fortunes has not made these gatherings less frivolous nor more intellectual. The people you meet there are thoughtless, noisy, full of snobbery and vanity, eager to fawn upon those who boast of their worth but very disdainful of anyone who doesn't advertise such ridiculous pretensions. It is an article of faith that New York is the pleasantest place in the world and so you must always be passing out compliments if you don't want to be looked at askance. Let us consider for a moment who belongs to this "high society" that is so pleased with itself.

The men, for the most part, are completely immersed in business from their childhood on. The world of finance swallows them up before they reach their fourteenth birthdays and those who have received what is called a "collegiate education"[3] are pointed out with admiration, as rare exceptions to the rule. Women, left to their own devices from childhood, begin at an early age to hunt for a husband; this pursuit makes use of all their energies and—especially in a society like this—calls for frivolity, furbelows and false pretenses rather than culture and genuine merit. They are by no means

[3] These words are in English in the original text.

sensitive creatures, poetical dreamers, misty-eyed moralists or carefree coquettes. Rather they are calculating business people who absorb from the society in which they live a matter-of-fact, mercenary outlook. These rational little scatterbrains, whose extravagant costumes resemble those of our reigning hostesses, cast their baited hooks upon the water not so much for the pleasure of fishing as for pecuniary profit. If a girl is in the marriage market, a crowd of suitors will automatically swirl around her. If, on the other hand, she seems aloof and difficult to approach, nobody will go near her.

All these young ladies—and you will meet none but *young* ladies because the rest of the feminine world seems already to be shut up in the tomb of domestic life—each of these young ladies has two or three beaux on her string and has no wish to exchange one in the hand for two in the bush. No one is admitted into her intimate circle unless he is willing to take an active part in the game. If you want to enjoy New York society, if you don't want to remain a lonely stranger in the merry crowd, you must take care to attach yourself to someone's triumphal chariot—or, to use a more homely figure of speech, to some girl's petticoats. From that moment you and she are inseparable: you go together to the park, you accompany her to an evening party and see her home, you are always at her service like some necessary piece of furniture—a slippery game that will leave you in the end, depending on your cleverness and your scruples, either a cheat or the victim of one.

Throw in fatigue, the serious discomfort of not

being able to sit down when the women themselves remain standing, the hullabaloo of conversation carried on—not in the ordinary, moderated tones we are accustomed to—but at full lung-power, with vocal bursts more appropriate to a public meeting than a fashionable evening party, and you will understand why I find American balls so disagreeable. The physical exertion, the shouting to make oneself understood, the reverberation in a small room of two hundred loud voices—all this would shatter nerves hardened by volleys of musketry or by the uninterrupted roar of the cannon that vainly fired a hundred and seventy-five shells a minute on Fort Fisher the other day.

Nor does this tumultuous society find me very much to its taste. I prefer to visit only a small number of friendly houses and a few distinguished but rather solemn people who favor me with a kindness I wish I could meet with more often. Miss *** is one of the *belles* of New York and an intelligent, charming person besides; she told me that gossip says I am "very wise"[4] and have an old head on my young shoulders. A "sage" like me would not know how to take part in the amusements of these happy featherbrains who think it the greatest and most exquisite pleasure to go "sleigh-riding," that is, to go off with a crowd of merry companions on a horse-drawn sled, coming back in the evening at top speed, their shouts echoing up and down Fifth Avenue. Nevertheless, at this moment I am the most dissipated of men; I can hardly keep an evening free

[4] These words, as well as the others in quotation marks in this paragraph are in English in the original text.

From a Lithograph in Color by John Bien after John Bachmann, about 1865   Courtesy of the New York Public Library

Winter Sports in Central Park

to see *Hamlet* with the famous actor [John Wilkes]
Booth about whom one hears so much talk.

January 3, 1865

I PAID nearly forty calls yesterday. Judge R., a gentleman of the old school belonging to the colonial
Dutch aristocracy, has been kind enough to introduce me in person to a large number of additional
homes. When night fell I was still trudging along
and was beginning to get enough of this twelve-
hour steeple-chase. I have, however, learned to tell
who is who in those two very different groups that
make up New York society. One, not very numerous and sometimes a little too proud, lives in a style
that is decorous, severe and more or less old-fash-
ioned. It consists of original "Knickerbocker" families, descendants of the first Dutch burghers, who
have allied themselves with old English families
established in New York state before the Revolution and War of Independence, together with a
certain number of more recent families whose vast
landholdings or securely based great fortunes make
up for their lack of ancient lineage. This "landed
aristocracy" still possesses, especially in the regions
that lie along the Hudson River, old manor houses
and estates of an almost princely size—but these are
decreasing in number day by day. The members of
this class live in New York in huge, English-style
mansions furnished with luxurious simplicity and
almost always including a collection of paintings,
some good, some bad, as in the palaces of Italy.
They have retained a certain pride of ancestry. One
day, at the home of a lady who is a friend of mine,

an Englishman of good family took it into his head to say to me, not without some condescension: "You know, in America people don't have ancestors." Everyone immediately took the impertinent fellow to task, "No ancestors, you say! We have as many as you do!" And I assure you that this was not merely offended plebeian dignity. These same people put on a disdainful expression when speaking to me of a notorious *parvenu*—one, however, that they deign to receive in their homes.

The other segment of high society, much more numerous and often mingling with the other, is that of financiers and businessmen. In their houses you see luxury without good taste. While they like things that are big and solid, they also admire everything that glitters. There is a certain Mrs. *** who persists in addressing me as "Count" in spite of being shown my very bourgeois visiting card. In a historic mansion on Fifth Avenue lives Mrs. X., a Scotswoman of rather humble origins, wife of the owner and editor[5] of one of the great New York newspapers who is also one of the political and financial powers-that-be in the country; there she holds court, enthroned and bedizened at one end of a sumptuous chamber with great banks of gorgeous

[5] Probably James Gordon Bennett the elder, founder, editor and publisher of the New York *Herald*, a newspaper of which Duvergier de Hauranne had a rather poor opinion. (See *A Frenchman in Lincoln's America*, Vol. I, pp. 397-402.) Mrs. Bennett was of Irish rather than Scottish origin. The Bennetts had an estate in Washington Heights in addition to their mansion on Fifth Avenue. (Don C. Seitz, *The James Gordon Bennetts, Father and Son, Proprietors of the New York Herald*, Indianapolis, c. 1928.)

flowers at her right and a sideboard heaped high with crystal, gilded silver and truffled dishes at her left. The abundance of fine wines and choice delicacies, the profusion of gilded cornices and mouldings, the lurid paintings and the whole decorative scheme of these over-ornate, tasteless reception rooms was in harmony with the ostentatiously expensive *toilette* of this strange woman with her domineering look, her tireless flow of vulgar talk and her bejeweled arms and throat. All the same, she was reviewing a parade of politicians and military leaders who had come to pay their not altogether disinterested respects to the guiding spirit of the newspaper and to lay their tribute of flattery before the infatuated Moloch of the American press.

The lady of the house caused to be repeated in loud tones the names of her friends, General D., Admiral F. and I don't know how many others who had no compunctions about investing their moral capital with no return of the principal but with huge interest payments in the form of printed praise. There are some gods to whom the world offers incense from fear of the pain they can inflict. Mr. X., though not without principles, is not without genius. He has thought up his own version of our *Figaro-programme*, a theatrical chronicle filled with all the latest gossip about local celebrities; he makes use of this as a kind of pass-key for opening the doors of high society to his wife. But, as always happens, people find fault; many shrug their shoulders as soon as backs are turned.

Another recently founded dynasty is that of Mr. Z., originally an inn-keeper, the former manager of

a large New York hotel which still bears his name.
One evening I entered a house furnished in rich but
simple style whose harmony was not spoiled by the
great luxury that was in evidence. I found there two
very elegant ladies, gracious in manner and charming in conversation. One of them presently sang to
us; her voice was not very strong and she didn't sing
with much feeling; yet she was mistress of all the art
that the lessons of the best teachers could give her.
Both these ladies spoke French and have lived a
long time in Europe. The door opened and in came
an old gentleman tottering a little on his gouty legs
and leaning on a cane. He wore black formal
clothes, a wig of the latest style and dyed whiskers
like those of Lord Palmerston. All in all, with his
grave, courteous and somewhat vacant air, he made
me think of an elderly English nobleman bent by
the weight of years. Later I learned that this nabob
got his start in life as the keeper of a middle-class
boarding-house. The family went to the watering-
places of Europe to wash off the blemish of their
origin, and no doubt they will go back again to rid
themselves of the bothersome memory of their
humble beginnings. Another such lady, who shines
today in the aristocratic drawing-rooms of Parisian
society, used to do her own cooking and wash her
babies' diapers. Such fortunes are made and such
metamorphoses occur more frequently in America
than anywhere else. Thanks to universal education
and to the general feeling of equality that prevails
here, a person can rise in the world without a painful struggle; he can move with ease from one sphere
to another. Between those born rich and those who

have just become rich there is no unbreachable barrier, no obstacle deriving from their earliest education. The women (and this is an advantage they enjoy in all countries) have a prodigious adaptability. Take a farm girl and push her into the upper-class world; you will be able to make a lady of her in a few months.

Among the men, on the other hand, there are instances of obdurate boorishness that one finds all the more objectionable in that no one takes offense. A fellow of this stamp slouches into polite society as though it were a stable, wearing clodhoppers, his hat on his head and his hands in his pockets. It is said that the newest gold is the shiniest. But most of the time there is nothing the poor lout can do: he will never be anything but a heavy chunk of base lead wrapped in gold or silver foil. This sort of fellow makes a good enough impression when you see him at a distance in his box at the opera or riding in his carriage through the park, holding in his hand the whip that went with his original profession and the reins of four lively horses. But when you see him close up, he is nothing but a farm-hand who will never wash off all the barnyard dirt and will always look as though he had just got down from the driver's seat of the horse-car on which he started his ride to fortune. You meet him, you greet him politely, but you soon turn away, weary of wasting the smallest bit of courtesy on such poor and ungrateful soil.

Take a close look at how he is dressed and you will quickly see what he is like. He wears rough, badly made clothes and carries himself awkwardly like a laborer. After all, good clothes are a branch of good manners and a person's posture and language are always those that correspond to his true nature. The man I've been describing is Mr. Y., who made his money by the most shameless kind of speculation. He appears to be on very friendly terms with a number of highly polished gentlemen whose ways are charming and gracious. Mr. Y. seems to be infatuated with himself and, although there are some scrupulous people—who are generally regarded as snobbish and out-of-date—who refuse to have anything to do with him, most people take him at his own valuation. And yet, look how prejudiced people are (for American society is no more exempt from such attitudes than any other) against Mr. Z., who is a man of honor and a man of the world, but whose old profession of inn-keeper is still held against him. The other fellow, having enriched himself in gambling houses, has won his patent of nobility and, although a complete blockhead, is a member in good standing of the aristocracy of speculators. What a shame they don't create barons in America![8]

January 4, 1865

LAST EVENING, at a lavish ball where we both felt a little like outsiders, my friend Mr. *** was talking

[8] In France, especially under the two Bonapartist regimes of Napoleon I and Napoleon III, the rank of baron was freely conferred on newly-rich citizens who had ingratiated themselves with officialdom. These "barons of the Empire" were often resented and looked down upon by the older landholding nobility.

to me about his forthcoming departure for China as coolly as though it were merely a question of going from New York to Philadelphia or Boston. Ten years ago, Mr. ***, who belongs to a rich and distinguished family of this city, was sent while still very young to represent an important trading firm in Hong Kong. Last year he came home on a six-month leave to renew acquaintance with his half-forgotten country and to see again the changed faces of his family and friends. He is now about to return to his post and does not know for sure whether he will ever come back. There are few families in New York that don't have one of their members abroad— not just wandering about as a traveler in a distant part of the world—but permanently transplanted into another hemisphere where he is rapidly becoming a stranger to his own country. Such trials are accepted with incredible resignation and sense of duty. You have perhaps heard the story of the American father whose son arrives from Australia and knocks unexpectedly at his door; he receives him politely, asks after his health, offers him a chair and finally invites him to stay for dinner.

The American family rather resembles a nestful of sparrows. The fledglings escape as soon as they have enough feathers to fly and claws to defend themselves. They forget the maternal nest and often the parents themselves no longer recognize their offspring. They took the trouble of caring for them when they were small and weak, but once this task was accomplished, their rights and their duties lapsed at the same time. This is the law of nature in all its cruel simplicity; the family bond endures only so long as it is indispensable to all the members involved in that bond.

It must be said, however, that if parents give very little to their children, they demand even less. Paternal authority has never been a rule that was strictly observed in the American family, nor has filial obedience been one of its greatest virtues. Nor do parents exert themselves to retain the authority they are losing or make any effort to prevent the chick from breaking out of its shell. On the contrary, they take pleasure in developing the child's precocious instinct for freedom; they hasten to let him stand on his own feet, whether because they want to be free as soon as possible of a troublesome duty or because they don't like to prolong a sort of domestic sovereignty owing to an excessive respect for the spirit of independence that is deeply ingrained in them. The fact is that nowhere are children so free, so bold, such *enfants terribles*, as in America. In public places, on trains, for example, you can see them running about, shrieking loud enough to split your ear-drums, climbing on your knees, playing with your shoe laces, spelling out the words in the book you are holding in your hand or speaking familiarly to you without being scolded by anyone. They are not overwhelmed either by the speeches, precepts and fine moral lessons with which we are so prodigal, good advice that slides off as easily as water runs off glass. That does not mean, though, that children often undergo the violent means of persuasion known as "the reason of the strongest;" Americans have always reserved that for their blacks, [whom they consider] a refractory breed of animal that understands nothing but the rod or the whip. As for children and horses, they have always treated them with kindness, believing them to be intelligent, reasonable beings in whom one must take care not to arouse the instinct of rebellion. To awaken the child's reason they depend on experience rather than punishment; instead of binding children hand and foot until they reach adulthood, they let them learn by hard knocks beginning at a very early age. It is this unfettered education that allows Americans to mature and to develop practical sense at an age when with us this faculty is still slumbering, wrapped up in the dreams and illusions of adolescence. With us education of the mind preceded the development of character; but it is just the opposite here.

The moral education of American girls, you will be interested to know, is considered complete by the age of twelve years. They come and go freely, often alone; their notions of conduct seem to be completely formed and it is taken for granted that they have already been made acquainted with all the facts of life. They are not led by the hand as if they were blind, with injunctions to keep their eyes always lowered, until suddenly one day the full reality of life is revealed to them. Nothing American girls need to know is kept from them because they are to be the sole mistresses of their destiny. So they make their own decisions without illusions and without being swept off their feet; and when they meet with disappointments or difficulties, they must accept them without complaint since they can blame no one else for their mistakes and failures.

This rough school of experience and freedom is no less salutary for young men. No sooner do they reach the age of reason than they must come to grips with the practical obligations of life. They are absorbed by business, by concern for their personal advancement and by the hard work demanded of them in the profession they have chosen; they are moulded by these concerns, which leave upon them an imprint that is perhaps somewhat crude; but it does have the merit of preserving them from the unwholesome restlessness that takes hold of unoccupied minds, that saps the character and makes the intelligence sterile. Before he is twenty years old, at an age when our young men are still seeking their path, tormenting a reluctant muse or else floundering amidst insubstantial visions of utopian change, the young American is already thinking of occupying his place in the world, of marrying, of founding a bank or business firm and of leaving the temporary shelter of his father's roof.

As for the family tie, it lasts as long as the members live together around the same fireside, but it dissolves as soon as they scatter because there exists no bond of inheritance or of common interest that can keep it intact. It is well known that in America one's freedom to bequeath one's property is unlimited; the only restriction placed on it is in favor, not of children, but of wives. In the state of New York, where unless it is stipulated otherwise in the marriage contract all property except real estate is held in common, widows inherit by law one-third of their husbands' real estate. In some other states—in Illinois, it is said—wives retain independent ownership and the control of their property. The wife's claim always comes before those of the children; but except for the share reserved for his wife, a father can dispose of his fortune as he pleases; he can disinherit his children and they have no right to complain; sometimes he leaves them only a very small part of his wealth. More often he favors one to the detriment of the others. For example, he may leave the bulk of his fortune either to the eldest son or to one of the others. In Massachusetts landed properties are almost never divided; the eldest son takes the land while the younger ones go into trade, industry or finance; or they may go west to carve out fortunes for themselves. The father of a family can even settle his estate on his eldest male descendants in succeeding generations, though this entail is limited, it is true, to two generations and is legally binding only on the immediate heir. Thus American law is the exact opposite of French law, providing for testamentary freedom, unequal inheritances for children and even for entail up to a certain point. Everything that our French democracy condemns as hateful remnants of feudal oppression American democracy allows in the name of liberty. Here again we see that in this matter of wills and inheritances the same question arises: Which is true democracy—that in which the love of freedom dominates, or that which sacrifices freedom to an insatiable love of equality?

We like to boast in France of being one of the most democratic peoples in the world, if not the very model of a perfect democracy. And yet, if we look closely, in spite of the Civil Code, the princi-

ples of 1789, "the career open to talent"—in spite
even of universal suffrage—we have hardly repudiated except in words the moral traditions of the old
monarchy. Instead of a noble caste, already largely
breached by the middle classes in the last century,
we now have a privileged class of administrators
and bourgeois. This class believes that thanks to the
equal division of inheritances we have destroyed
forever the aristocratic spirit of the Old Régime.
But in reality we have only broadened it; we have
spread it, so to speak, through the whole body of
citizens. What is the great fault we have found with
(for example) the English aristocracy? It is that they
have raised up a class predestined to wealth, a class
that has no reason to work; it is that they have fos-
tered in this class a spirit of idleness, pride and
selfishness. But, to speak frankly, aren't all our sons
of bourgeois families who inherit annual incomes of
three thousand francs or so—aren't they really little
would-be aristocrats? And what about the idleness
of our provincial bourgeois who moulder in their
small towns knowing no other use to make of their
lives than to squeeze their tenant-farmers or to go
and gamble away their families' subsistence in a
café—isn't this wretched idleness an aristocratic
vice? And when our young men, whom we send to
the city to learn a profession, think they need do
nothing at all on the pretext that they have a right
to dissipate in advance their share of the family's
wealth—don't you think that they are, in their own
way, giving themselves the airs of aristocrats and
playing the young Marquis?

Will it be argued that there is a much more tender

relationship between father and son when [as in France] the law imposes mutual rights and duties? Even that is doubtful; I see them walking side by side, united and inseparable in the eyes of the law; but they are more like two prisoners shackled to a common chain than two friends lending each other a hand. Even supposing that self-interest is at bottom the true source of human affections, do you believe that a son respects his father more if he thinks of him as a man saddled with an unwanted debt or if he has no reason to expect anything and may at the most hope that his father will give him out of tenderness that which the law does not oblige him to give? In a French family, the father is all too often, in the son's eyes, the temporary guardian of the wealth that is really his, the business agent who, for the moment, keeps his accounts and will soon have to hand them over. I prefer the American family, where the son expects nothing from his father except what he has deserved.

In England the system of primogeniture produces, for every aristocrat, as many as twenty hardworking and enterprising [younger sons] who will enrich their country. The eldest sons themselves are the natural protectors of their families; and though they occupy an exalted station, public opinion obliges them to make an unselfish use of their wealth and leisure, so that one can certainly not say that they are useless to their country. In France, we have in their stead twenty impoverished aristocrats who eke out an existence from their income and would think it a disgrace to earn their own living. They clutter the anterooms of public officials, begging for alms in the form of a little government job. One can truthfully say that public administrators form the aristocracy of France. At least it is in the bureaucracy that one learns to take on all the disagreeable formality and all the supercilious ways of the aristocrat. Furthermore, for a long, long time now the pride of what was called the aristocracy in our country has been founded not upon a feeling of individual authority and independence, but upon the arts of the courtier, that is, upon the spirit of the antechamber. The French nobility was, if I may be forgiven my bluntness, no longer anything but a class that had been reduced to an elegant and privileged domestication. Everything depended on enjoying "favor"—and this is still true. Our nobility was proud of its livery and its idle life. Just watch how a bureaucrat takes the measure of a simple mortal, showing the same superb disdain with which the watchdog of the fable—the *honnête homme* of the seventeenth century, whom we still have with us—lectured his cousin, the poor, wild, famished wolf.[9]

Just as in olden times no one could imagine any greater happiness than ministering to the person of the king, we today know no greater honor than to be underlings of authority. We like to bow to it, to obtain privileges from it, to mark ourselves off from

[9] The wolf envied the dog his fine food and lodging until he learned that these could only be had by wearing a collar and chain. (La Fontaine, *Fables*, I, 5) "*Honnête homme*" is an untranslatable expression referring to the later seventeenth-century ideal of a well-read, accomplished, well-behaved person, neither boorish nor pedantic, but devoted to moderation and something of a conformist.

the powerless and identify ourselves with those who wield power—in a word, to become one of the elect. And considering that the number of the elect is immense today, that everyone aspires to be among their number and that the division (and hence the modest size) of fortunes makes it a necessity, it comes to pass that the bureaucracy, its would-be members and its veterans compose nearly the whole population. Many people who have just enough money to get along, to live off their incomes without having to work, nevertheless feel a great need for an official stipend that will enable them to live in comfort. Those who have once lived upon the heights fear they will lower themselves by working. What, then, has really changed in our customs? Nothing but the stage on which we display our pettiness. We boast that we have done away with the pomp and circumstance of aristocracy, but we have merely multiplied its ridiculous pretensions and generalized its vices.

Let us follow instead the example of America. There the men, at least, are self-made, are honored for it and, in fact, gain esteem only on that condition. Without patronage, without privilege, without hope of sinecures or inherited fortunes, they have learned to face the battles of life without fear. They honor work as we honor idleness. Even the richest young men are expected to find useful employment. They enter trade, industry or the law, not out of necessity nor because the work attracts them, but only because public opinion demands it. Every American loves to boast that he knows how to earn his own living and that of his wife and children.

You will insult him if you doubt it. From one day to the next he may be a lawyer or a carpenter, a journalist or a trader, a school teacher or a member of the Cabinet, a tailor's apprentice[10] or President of the United States. He never feels out of place and never complains of his situation. This is true democracy, for it makes free men and citizens; ours makes men who love equality only out of jealousy, people who are so weak and envious that they are afraid of liberty.

January 5, 1865

INTERESTING NEWS came from Savannah this morning. The government of the United States has gone back there as though returning home. Officials of the Post Office and Treasury have lost no time in resuming their duties. The Adams shipping company is back in the offices it occupied before the war and has registered $300,000 worth of merchandise in four days. The restoration of the old order seems so easy that one is tempted to believe the intervening years have left no trace. The residents accept the supremacy of the Union without hesitation. The fortunes of war, by causing them to fall into the hands of the enemy, have excused them from keeping up the hypocritical pretense of Confederate patriotism any longer. They are eager to recover their former trade, to care for their poor and to retain their municipal self-government. General Sherman has respected all their rights except that he has temporarily denied them freedom of the press. (Why has he done this? I have no idea—what harm could

---

[10] President Andrew Johnson was supposed to have begun life as a tailor's apprentice.

it do him?) He even offers, if they find his rule unbearable, to transport them to the enemy lines. A public meeting called by Mayor [Richard D.] Arnold, has unanimously affirmed the general wish to remain faithful [to the United States]. These resolutions, contrasting with the insane diatribes which the papers of the city were printing a few days earlier, show very clearly how much empty bravado and official bluster there is in the arrogant attitude of the Confederates.

"Whereas owing to the fortunes of war and the capitulation of the city, Savannah has again come under the authority of the United States, . . . we, the people of Savannah, in general assembly, do hereby resolve:

"That we accept our position and that, pursuant to the offer of the President of the United States, we desire to obtain peace by laying down our arms and submitting to the national government under the authority of the Constitution, leaving all other unsettled questions to the peaceful arbitration of the laws, to negotiation and to future elections. . . .

"That, furthermore, *we do not assume the posture of a conquered city asking mercy of her conqueror*, but claim all the immunities and privileges set forth in the proclamation and message of the President of the United States, and also in Acts of Congress relative to our present situation—and that, in return for a *strict observance of the laws of the United States*, we ask for ourselves and our property the protection afforded by those laws. . . .

"That we respectfully petition his Excellency the Governor to call *a convention of the people of Georgia* to decide whether this state wishes to continue the war *between the two sections of our country*.[11]

[11] Italics added by Duvergier de Hauranne.

Such are the people who are said to be ready to die rather than agree to a new union with the "Yankees." From the other side, the people of the North reach out a helping hand; they want the South to submit, but not to be humiliated. General Sherman is feeding the starving people of Savannah. The city government sent Colonel Allen to New York to buy food and clothing in exchange for rice, with payments guaranteed by the city of Savannah. But the New York Chamber of Commerce has declined to accept anything in return and has opened a public subscription. Boston is already organizing meetings to raise money. Everywhere people want to contribute to this fraternal charity. This magnanimity is at the same time a clever political move in that the conquered city, as it returns to life, will become a center of Unionist feeling. The old rivalry between Savannah and Charleston can also be exploited effectively.

When its port is re-opened and its trade expands, when agricultural produce from all parts of the South starts flowing into its markets, Savannah will congratulate itself on having changed masters and will take pleasure in observing the jealousy of its ruined rival. Georgia will follow the example of its chief commercial city, and Governor Brown will finally make up his mind to merit the accusations [of defeatism] that have been so freely made against him in Richmond.

He was recently attacked in the Rebel Congress for having exempted from military service 15,000 men who would now be very useful in Richmond. Brown haughtily replied that if he were to accept

any blame, it would be for having yielded too much
to the demands of military tyrants and for having
allowed the laws of his state to be trampled under
foot. If Georgia, instead of sending the last remaining contingents of her male population to defend
Virginia, had turned a deaf ear to the appeals of the
[Confederate] President, Sherman would not have
invaded the state, leaving it devastated and half-
conquered. It ill becomes the Richmond legislators
to make complaints against Georgia after having
stripped her of her last defenders and left her at the
enemy's mercy. She has sent fifty regiments to perish on distant fields of battle and these 15,000 men
she is accused of having withheld—and who at present make up her entire militia—consist entirely of
old men and young boys. The law requires military
service only by healthy men from sixteen to fifty
years of age. There remain barely 800 of military
age and those are priests, judges and state officials,
all indispensable to the government and legally exempt. Georgia will not agree to dismantle her government, draft her legislators and close her courts of
justice; she took up arms to maintain her freedom
and she will be quite capable of defending it.

These are the two factions that are quarreling
over the mutilated remains of the Rebel Confederacy. The strength of a powerful hand on the bridle
can force the country to go forward into one last
battle, prolonging a useless struggle at the cost of a
gigantic sacrifice. Virginia, in all likelihood, does
not have 600 white men who are not under arms,
but she can still send her blacks to be slaughtered.
The government pays for only a fifth of the value of

what it requisitions by force, but it can stop paying anything at all. The risky trade through the blockade has enriched some traders, so there is talk of confiscating their ships, of turning their business into a monopoly run by the government, which could then pocket the profits. Then, with the blacks seized and mustered into the army in spite of their masters, a blow could be struck against Maryland, Pennsylvania and perhaps Washington; but after that, if victory still proved elusive, they would have no choice but to surrender, to be killed or to die of hunger. This strategy is the one General Lee is expected to adopt; but some prefer to see him as the peace-maker sent by providence. It is known that "the Old Virginian" was drawn into the Rebellion only by his chivalrous feelings of loyalty [to his native Virginia] and by misguided patriotism. Will he now have the courage to admit that he is beaten? Whether he does or not, the collapse of the Rebel cause is near at hand. "Never," says [Edmund] Burke, "has a nation been obliterated,"[12] and the Southerners try to keep up their courage by invoking this saying. The question, however, is whether they have had enough time to found a nation. I am aware that today nations are in fashion and that this sonorous word is considered the answer to everything. Slavery is doubtless an abominable institution, but no matter—slavery is a national cause! It doesn't take much more than this to confuse the vast multitudes who feed their minds on words instead of ideas.

[12]The idea is developed more fully in Burke's *Speech on Conciliation.*

I am perfectly willing to admit that a nation should be inviolable when its roots are profoundly planted in history. But it needs at least some time to take shape; it can't be improvised in four years. Not without reason is it said that the nationhood of the United States is still in process of formation. Mr. Davis, who thinks he has made a nation, already feels the pieces coming apart in his hands. The process of "reconstruction" is far from being as difficult as had been thought. No doubt there are profound differences in interests and customs between the two sections; but there are fewer differences, all things considered, that between Gascons and Flemings, Alsatians and Bretons or between northern and southern Italians. Economic interests and social prejudices were what divided them; slavery, in a word, was the sole obstacle to Union. Once this obstacle is removed, the same interests that separated them will bring them together. Their antagonism should end with the institution that was its cause. For the American people, weary of provocation, war was the only possible course to take, the only one consistent with its dignity and the only one that gives it the right to call itself a nation. It would be interesting to know whether, even without the war, national unity would not have triumphed. The policy of the South's friends, who hypocritically urged acceptance of an accomplished fact, might very well have turned against them in the end. That is what Mr. [George H.] Pendleton foretold in his celebrated speech urging the assembly [the Federal Congress] to say a tender farewell to the Rebel states in the expectation that, like the

prodigal son, they would return to the fold again.[13]
His prophesy was truer than even he believed, because—though it is true that the rest of the United
States would soon have been absorbed by a Confederacy that was mistress of the West, of Maryland,
Washington and Kentucky, squeezing the remnant
of the Union between the Mississippi, the Great
Lakes and the Mason-Dixon line—a Confederacy
demarcated by the ocean, the Mississippi and the
uncertain line of the Potomac would soon have per-
ished. Given a lasting peace with the old ties re-es-
tablished, there would have been an inevitable
blending of a population drawn from the same ethnic stocks and their natural family relationships
would promptly have reasserted themselves.

Even the violence of this war has not dug an
abyss of national hatred between the two sides. On
the contrary, the thing that gave rise to hostility was
destroyed without generating among the Rebels—
whatever may be said to the contrary—the incalculable moral force that enables defeated nations to
rise again. Many secret Unionists are being uncovered for whom conquest is a deliverance from the
Rebels. How many prisoners have escaped from the
South thanks to the covert assistance of these unknown friends! General Sherman found a number
of Federal officers who were sheltered and hidden
by families in Savannah. A whole population of

[13] Pendleton was a leading "Peace Democrat" and Southern sympathizer. In 1864 he was the Democratic candidate
for Vice President on the ticket headed by General George
B. McClellan. His attitude toward secession was summed up
in his appeal to the North to "let our erring sisters go."

deserters and draft-evaders has taken refuge in the mountains of North Carolina. The fanatics will gain nothing by putting out childish fables to the effect that the Yankees are burning children and attacking women, that Sherman, like Pharaoh, gave an express order to cut the throats of all little boys. These ridiculous stories are not credible, and rebellion is extinguished wherever the victorious army shows itself.

Like all civil wars in which men have been motivated by passion rather than obedience, this war has been implacable and fierce. The proverbial violence of the American character is not enough to explain these excesses. We ourselves, less than a hundred years ago, experienced the criminal extremes to which civil and class conflicts could push a nation known for its humanity.[14] But massacres in the Vendée, mass drownings in Brittany, mass executions by cannon-fire and the guillotine have not prevented us from continuing to be a single people, even though we may have been temporarily alienated from one another by the convulsions of a great revolution. Except for a handful of émigrés who died in exile, France emerged from the Revolution to find itself once again a nation, as united as in the past. Civil wars may bathe a nation in blood and may even dismember it, but they never completely destroy it. Although more cruel [than other wars],

[14] The conflicts referred to are those that accompanied the French Revolution of 1789-1794. The Vendée and Brittany in western France were the scene of a bloody civil war; mass executions by cannon-fire took place in Lyon; the guillotine is associated with the Reign of Terror.

they are also more quickly forgotten. Hasn't English national unity survived centuries of civil war? Hasn't Italy, absent so long from the family of nations, miraculously recovered her identity and unity in our own day? I believe more than ever in the natural unity of the United States; I believe them to be geographically, morally and politically indivisible. Like the new territories, the Southern states will be repopulated after the war by people from all parts of the country; the free men of the North will bring their labor and capital to the land redeemed from slavery and the "eternal antipathy" of the two supposedly hostile sections will be dissipated along with the smoke of burning towns and cannon-fire.

The story is told of 300 [Union] soldiers entering Milledgeville who gathered at the State House to "reconstruct" the state of Georgia according to their own lights. They chose a legislature, a governor, a secretary of state and even members of Congress. Resolutions were voted; it was unanimously proclaimed that secession was "a damned piece of nonsense;" and then the assembly dispersed, having restored a state to the Union. The governor was from Ohio, the secretary of state from New Hampshire, one senator from Illinois, the other from New York; all the states were represented in the vest-pocket government. This masquerade prefigures the restoration that will follow the Union's victory.

9

Washington and Congress

Washington
January 11, 1865

YESTERDAY EVENING in New York, when I got to the Cortland Street ferry, I learned that the departure schedules had been changed and that I would have to wait for the midnight train. I spent the evening with friends and, at the appointed hour, set out for Fifth Avenue where I expected to board an omnibus. But there wasn't one to be seen, and I soon lost my way in the meandering streets in this very irregular part of the city. I decided to head toward West Street—which borders the West River [the Hudson]—where there is a line of horsecars that serves the whole waterfront. Little by little the darkness grew more complete, the street-lights were more widely spaced, houses gave way to tall warehouses in whose shadows one could imagine all sorts of dangers.

At last the sidewalk came to an end and there were no more people in the streets. I walked through muddy building-lots covered with the debris of structures in the process of being torn down; there were excavations and piles of lumber. Here and there a black shape prowled silently in the dark alley-ways; frequently there was a sinister-looking shack through the cracks of whose closed shutters filtered a few rays of fire-light and the sound of drunken voices. At length I reached the docks, where I found a long stretch of broken sidewalk shadowed by tall wooden fences. I passed street after street and pier after pier until I reached the meat market, where my path led into a labyrinth of raw flesh, winding between two deep, compact arrays of skinned carcasses. This midnight stroll through the almost-deserted slums of the city's West Side was certainly exciting—the scenes might have come from Victor Hugo or Dickens. The market was especially fascinating, its main gallery running like a tunnel between two walls of bloody meat in the murky half-light thrown by a few smoking lamps. I heard only the muffled footsteps of a solitary passerby. All this had a fantastic and horrible resemblance to the bone-filled den of Polyphemus the Cyclops.[1] But for a stranger with no guide, pressed for time and unable to retrace his steps, having only his umbrella for self-defense and—to cap the climax—carrying a sackful of gold coins on his person, this stroll was filled with a wholly different and no less intense kind of excitement, and I was extremely glad to observe from time to time on a street corner the tall silhouette, the huge hands gloved in buffalo-hide, the large black boots and the square-cut uniform of a policeman.

In great cities like Paris, London and New

---

[1] In Homer's *Odyssey*, Book IX, Ulysses and his sailors were captured by the one-eyed giant Polyphemus who shut them up in a vast cave and ate them a few at a time, flinging their bones into a corner. Ulysses succeeded in blinding the giant, after which he and his followers escaped by clinging to the bellies of Polyphemus's huge sheep as the latter were being turned out of the cavern to graze.

York new, hideous and terrifying aspects of reality are uncovered every day. Whenever we get beneath the shining mask of the city's public face we discover what is squirming about in the depths of the sewers. New York has its "Five Points" neighborhood, corresponding to our ancient Cité;[2] as in certain parts of London, no one ventures there except in the company of a policeman. Boston also has its quarter from Dante's Inferno at whose entrance a person may well say, "All hope abandon, ye who enter here," unless he is prepared to defend himself or is accompanied by his guardian angel in the shape of a police officer. You will find such conditions wherever commerce heaps up the riches of the world but also deposits its scum and dregs.

The courageous charity of the ladies of New York has not shrunk from entering these horrible precincts, and they have built a school here in the midst of a slimy, rotting slum with the aim of reclaiming the residents. The Five Points Institute[3] prospers as much as one could wish and it will not take many years to raise the intellectual and moral level of this population of drifters who have been driven here by debauchery and then instructed by poverty in all the vices known to man. Schooling—

[2] This term refers to the medieval center of Paris with its twisting, narrow streets and dense, mostly poor population; it includes the Ile de la Cité, together with small portions of the right and left banks that were also enclosed within the city walls at the time.

[3] The Five Points Institute, which combined education and moral uplift with social service, was founded with money furnished by a number of society women. It anticipated Jane Addams's work in Chicago.

or, as it is now more modish to say in figurative style, "enlightenment"—is without doubt the best means of making sure that the human spirit is healthy and fruitful.

There is a great deal of talk here about the imminent resignation of Mr. [William P.] Fessenden. It is said that he plans to resume his seat in the Senate on leaving the Treasury Department. The latter is a heavy and ungrateful burden which, like the rock of Sisyphus,[4] must ceaselessly be rolled uphill only to slide to the bottom again under the weight of a new loan. Who will now be courageous enough to venture out onto the fragile tight-rope from which so many political acrobats have fallen? I can think of only one man who seems ready to take the risk: it is Representative [Thaddeus] Stevens, at least if one can take any stock in his incredibly rash proposals. The defeat of his bill providing for the forced circulation of paper money at par inflicted a cruel blow to his self-esteem. Just the other day, and for no reason other than a wish to rake over old grievances, he reintroduced his bill regardless of the desire of the House and, in a lively, witty and arrogant speech, turned back on his opponents the accusations of ineptness and absurdity which they had been lavishing on him. He invoked historical precedents, including the example of England, to prove that his proposals were not unreasonable and that

[4] In Greek mythology Sisyphus, King of Corinth, showed contempt for Zeus and was condemned in the afterlife to roll a heavy stone up a hill through all eternity. The stone always rolled back down and had to be pushed up again the next day.

Engraving   From *Harper's History of the Great Rebellion*

Thaddeus Stevens

the temperature can be regulated by changing the scale on the thermometer. But it was rightly pointed out in reply that although in England in 1815 the forced circulation of the Bank of England's notes, in spite of the suspension of [gold] payments, had not brought on a catastrophe, this fact was due to special circumstances which England owed solely to her good luck. At the very moment the bill was passed, [the battle of] Waterloo was bringing the war to an end. If peace comes to the United States, Mr. Steven's bill will be neither necessary nor dangerous. England, moreover, had placed a limit on the printing of paper money. But to impose a fixed value on banknotes while reserving the right to print an indefinite quantity of them is like trying to fill a barrel that has no bottom.

Rest assured that Mr. Stevens will not be the next Secretary of the Treasury. The creditors of the United States can sleep in peace. He himself perhaps finds the independent and less responsible role of legislator preferable to the burden borne by a Cabinet member. It is a difficult position in any country, but in America it is crushing. A man can recover from the loss of a Cabinet post, as Mr. Chase has done, but his ship is becalmed for some time. The higher his position, the less a democracy is willing to pardon a man who has been unable to stay on top.

Most former Presidents have had to live out their lives in obscurity. Who recognizes today the names of Fillmore, Pierce or Buchanan? They are mentioned only as objects of ridicule. Today's forgotten man [General McClellan], lost in obscurity, is the

one who only yesterday was hailed as the victor of
Antietam. Democracy is a quicksand that swallows
up famous men who have been stranded on the
shore. I think of Victor Hugo's comment: "How
dreadful for a man to become nobody!"

While I'm on the subject of Congress let me tell
you where matters stand in the great debate about
slavery and the [proposed] new amendment to the
Constitution.[5] In the House the two-thirds majority
necessary for passage is still difficult to find. The
Senate, for its part, has just voted on the bill proposed by Senator [Henry] Wilson of Massachusetts
to emancipate wives and children of black soldiers,
so that the same question is now being considered
by both houses, though in different forms. In the
Senate the opponents of the measure number 10
against 27: an amendment by Senator [Garret] Davis
[of Kentucky] making the law non-retroactive obtained only seven votes. Senator [Reverdy] Johnson
of Maryland spoke against the bill with a very pronounced moderation which indicates how much
progress the abolitionist cause has made. The pro-
slavery party will fade away as slavery itself disappears. The change is so great that old-time Southern
Democrats, who were once so adamant, are now defending the cause of moderation and common sense
against the uncompromising extremism of the Radicals. While the latter, with Senator [Benjamin F.]

[5] The Thirteenth Amendment abolishing slavery had been
passed by the Senate, 38-6, on April 8, 1864, but defeated in
the House, 95-66, on June 15. It was later reconsidered and
passed by the House, 119-56, on January 31, 1865. Ratification was completed December 6, 1865.

Wade of Ohio at their head, go on nursing—even though they are victorious—all the animosities they formed when they were an oppressed minority and often place their grudges ahead of the public interest, the pro-slavery party, now humbled and meek because of its weakness, offers only feeble resistance to the inevitable. They are temporizing, hoping to delay rather than prevent abolition. I must say they are often more conspicuous than their opponents for prudence and calm rationality. "Better thirty years of war," cries Senator Wade, "than peace without absolute abolition!"

The Radicals remember that only a few years ago they felt the weight of public opprobrium and I can easily excuse them for taking revenge on those who heaped scorn upon them. But their vocabulary leads one to believe that the goal of their party—declared in their manifestoes and in the resolutions of the Baltimore convention [of 1864]—is not so much the preservation of the Union as it is Abolition. The Democrats have often attacked them on this score and the Republicans have always repudiated their attacks as slanderous. But let them take care. The tide is carrying them to power, public opinion is on their side and the very moderation of their opponents proves that their victory is uncontested. But if they don't show moderation themselves, public opinion could well shift in midstream and the Democrats could get the upper hand by coming forward with a compromise.

In the House the debate is even weightier. A number of Democrats, including Representative [George] Yeaman of Kentucky and Representative

[Moses F.] Odell of New York, think it is time to finish once and for all with the accursed question of slavery and sweep it ruthlessly out of the way. When Jefferson Davis himself abandons it and threatens to become the most radical abolitionist of all,[6] how can the Northern Democrats persist in defending this lost cause? Once this obstacle is done away with, the opposing forces will again be on an equal footing and that is probably not the least important reason for this unexpected change of alignment. If you're trying to win a race, you mustn't try to carry your dead horse on your own back; instead, you should abandon his useless carcass and, if you can, steal your rival's horse. Moreover, Abolition is a good cause in its own right, for slavery is, after all, a great injustice. The game is lost, so let's change the rules and try to recoup our fortunes!

Even those who are fighting the amendment don't attach much importance to their resistance and will easily resign themselves to its adoption. As Mr. [Daniel] Vorhees, the well-known Indiana Copperhead, roundly denounces the amendment as unconstitutional, he says it isn't needed because the slavery issue is dead. The real debate is taking place on the battlefields. If the South is defeated, slavery

[6] During the closing months of the Civil War the Richmond Congress discussed and finally rejected a proposal associated with spokesmen for Jefferson Davis for alleviating the South's increasingly desperate shortage of military manpower by offering emancipation to slaves who would volunteer to fight for the Confederacy. Duvergier de Hauranne refers several times to this proposal, which he interpreted as a *de facto* renunciation of slavery by the leading officials of the Confederate government.

will have been abolished in fact, whatever Congress decides; if the South wins, what will be the use of the amendment? Still, as a good Copperhead faithful to the Southern cause, even though his patriotic colleagues favor the law, he is against it, and for precisely that reason.

Willard's Hotel is the same as ever, the worst and most expensive hotel in the United States. It is profiting from the influx of transients by raising its prices higher than those of the Tremont Hotel in Boston or the Fifth Avenue Hotel in New York. The service is abominable; the meals are hasty and penny-pinching despite the elaborate menu; the portions are trimmed down by thrifty hands and it is all too evident that they serve left-overs from other people's plates. The clientele makes a better appearance than it did last summer: the mainstay of the hotel's trade consists of members of Congress, governors of states and general officers. Nevertheless, the noisy, ill-assorted crowd that throngs the corridors and parlors of the ground floor presents a rather dismal appearance and the place is like a hive always full of buzzing bees that perpetually come and go without ever alighting.

January 12, 1865

WASHINGTON has certainly changed with the season, though the outward aspects of the city have not altered very much. On the outskirts there are still vast, level spaces that have been turned into wastelands by military encampments; everything has been scraped clean to the ground; there remains not a tree, not a blade of grass, nothing but tents and

barracks. Inside the city are the same monotonous
stretches of mud and the same vain and pitiful attempts at grandeur; but instead of the death-like
sleep that paralyzed the city under the summer sun
I now find the most astonishingly intense activity.
What with the clatter of carriages, the screeching of
the horsecars on their iron rails and the hum of
conversation among the pedestrians who crowd the
sidewalks, one could imagine oneself in a populous
commercial city.

To be sure, this motion is only on the surface; the
crowding is only temporary; and if everything that
isn't a permanent part of the city were taken away,
scarcely anything but a desert would remain. Never
has the government employed so many people, never has its sovereign influence attracted so many interested persons. Furthermore, the war has added a
large number of troops to the population. If the
Federal government continues to expand and grow,
this capital city will grow along with it. If it falls
back into its earlier insignificance, the city will
wither away. For it is a cardboard city like Berlin,
which exists only because of the presence of the
government; its future is bound up with the unity of
America. The tighter the national bonds, the more
importance will be attached to the place where for a
century it has been traditional to join together all
the strands of politics and government.

One can, however, foresee the day when the expansion of the United States toward the west, and
the meeting of the two legions of civilization that
are advancing upon the Rocky Mountains from two
sides, will—in obedience to the laws of physical

equilibrium—displace this badly situated fulcrum of the American nation. St. Louis or some other city perhaps still unknown would become the capital and Washington would continue to be important only if the Republic were to split up. Such a division must inevitably occur, moreover, though not until some far-distant future time. The separation of North and South, which was represented as necessary, certainly has nothing natural about it. I see as inseparable the states of the South, those of the North as far as Maine and all the western states on this side of the Rocky Mountains. I mean that the valley of the Mississippi forms a single great geographic region of which the Atlantic states are merely the edge or border. Once slavery is dead, no antagonism of races, interests or institutions seems to me capable of compromising that unity.

It is not the same for the vast settlements on the other slope beyond the mountains. Soon these will be linked with this part of the continent by railroad; they already communicate with it by telegraph; but if I am not greatly mistaken, the dozen or so states being created there will one day form a separate federation. When the two growing communities meet at the crest of the Rockies, crushing between them the last scattered tribes of Indians, it will be the signal for a violent conflict over possession of the land, as happened earlier in Michigan and Kansas.[7]

---

[7] Duvergier de Hauranne may have been thinking of Nebraska (rather than Michigan) and Kansas, since he is presumably referring to violent clashes between opponents and defenders of slavery.

Settlers sent out from New England will be exchanging rifle fire with the pioneers coming from Oregon and California. As for the Mormons, that strange people, they are growing more numerous in an interior basin enclosed by mountains between the two slopes of the Rockies. Their rights are respected at present by the Federal government which admits their delegates to Congress, but they have no future other than extermination or conquest in the event the Union is completed and joined together; they will doubtless choose to join forces with the men of the West. . . . But you are probably laughing at my bold prophecies, so I'll pass on to the news of the day.

The chief and most astonishing news is that General Butler has been relieved of his command; this event has fallen like a thunderbolt from the mysterious cloud that conceals the government's august summit. Butler received orders to retire to Lowell, in his home state [Massachusetts], to turn over all the papers, documents and public funds in his possession to General [Edward O. C.] Ord, chosen by Grant to fulfill the duties of temporary commander of the Army of the James. It is predicted that within a week he will be imprisoned in Fort Warren. This sudden disgrace is the explosive result of patience long tried by his abuses of power, frauds and cruelties of all sorts. General Grant, who is all-powerful in all that relates to his army, had up to now lent Butler the protection of his own supreme authority. Since the not-very-glorious retreat of the expeditionary forces sent to take Wilmington (of which, it seems, Butler took command without orders to do

so) and the fiasco of Dutch Gap,[8] a huge, useless
canal he had built between two elbows of the James
River in the style of a Xerxes or a Marius,[9] Grant
seems to have withdrawn his protection and this is
the immediate result. I can't work up much pity for
him on account of his abrupt fall. Let it serve as a
lesson to all the ambitious and undisciplined soldiers who might be tempted to follow his example.
Let the New England abolitionists, who sing his
praises because he comes from their region, finally
turn their backs on this poor imitation of a hero! I
have heard his friends say in extenuation of his
greed, "It isn't for himself; it's for his brother. His
only failing is that he's too soft on his family." Truly a touching weakness!

His political career proves he is only an adventurer with no scruples and no principles. Formerly
an ardent Democrat, he became an enthusiastic abolitionist at the exact moment when he first felt the
wind blowing in a new direction. His brutality is

[8] General Butler conceived the idea of digging a short canal across a bend in the James River so that Federal gun-
boats could approach Richmond more closely; but when the
canal was finally washed clear of debris by floods the Federal
navy was unprepared and Confederate ironclads came downstream to launch a surprise attack. Butler was widely criticised for his grandiose plan, though it was probably a sound
idea in itself.

[9] Xerxes I, King of Persia, a great conqueror famous for his
feats of military engineering which included cutting a canal
through the isthmus of Athos and constructing a bridge of
boats across the Hellespont in order to invade Greece. Caius
Marius was a Roman general of plebeian origin who fought a
number of campaigns against the Senatorial oligarchy; his
wife, Julia, was the aunt of Julius Caesar.

General Benjamin F. Butler

equalled, I am told, only by his lack of delicacy. In New Orleans he wanted to crush the hostility of women whose brothers and sons were fighting in the Southern army. In their anger at being defeated, these ladies had showered their conquerors with something very different from garlands and bunches of flowers—so he threatened to send them to the prostitutes' prison, the local St.-Lazare,[10] and he actually carried out this threat. Many people thought it was the right thing to do. Again, just recently in Virginia, he expelled from Federally-held territory a woman, an old man and three children who, when ordered to take an oath of allegiance to the United States government, answered that they were willing to promise good behavior, but that the form of the oath itself was repugnant to their consciences inasmuch as their families were on the other side. He had them driven out with an ignominious and insulting letter in which he compared their scruples with those of Hindu women who have themselves burned on their husbands' funeral pyres. Another time he quoted Shakespeare in support of an act of cruelty he had ordered. But now he has been laid low, and what is the good of hitting a man when he's down? It might, indeed, do harm, for it would make him seem a victim, a false martyr; he might someday come to be—can you guess what?—President of the United States.

In the South the process of dissolution goes on. The quarrel between the [Richmond] government and the states grows more envenomed with each

[10] A Paris prison and house of correction, formerly a monastery, where prostitutes were detained.

passing day. It is a question of whether the militia will be taken away from the states and put under Lee's command, or whether (as the law now provides) the governor of each state will remain commander of his militia. The governor and legislature of Mississippi have categorically refused to send their militiamen to the Confederate President. The governor of Alabama declares that he intends to exempt from service clergymen, druggists, public officials and journalists. You already know what is happening in Georgia. Now South[11] Carolina and Governor [Zebulon B.] Vance are taking the same position. The legislature refuses to suspend *habeas corpus* and is debating the question: "Whether it be reasonable to secede [from the Confederacy]" while North Carolina, still abstaining from separate action, resolves "to initiate negotiations for an honorable peace," urging the President to take the first steps to this end. Meanwhile Richmond itself is full of turmoil and discord. The Rebel Congress is discussing, by implication, the great plan for a dictatorship about which I have written you. The main issue is whether General Lee will have sole power of appointing all the officers of the army or whether his choices will remain subject to ratification by the government and Congress. As you can see, dictatorship lies on one side and disunity on the other, and everywhere a spirit of resistance and liberty is combatting the despotism of Richmond. The rebellion will perish from the very same tensions that have threatened the American

[11] This is obviously a slip of the pen; North Carolina is meant.

nation with extinction. The guilty ones will be punished by the same impulses that prompted their original transgressions.

Much is said of the secret mission of Mr. [Francis P.] Blair [Sr.], a close friend of President Lincoln who, according to official sources, is traveling to Richmond to recover certain family papers that were carried off last summer when his country house was looted during the Confederate raid into Maryland. Everyone thinks this pretext [is a cover for] a peace mission. The government is strongly criticized by some members of the Republican party who, foreseeing the futility of such attempts, fear that the South will see them as a sign of weariness or weakness. They are strongly approved, though, by another party faction led by Horace Greeley, the editor of the [New York] *Tribune*. As for me, I hope for their complete success. I believe that by making these repeated overtures—even though they come to nothing—and by not being put off by the insulting replies of the Confederates, they [the Federal authorities] are simply doing their duty and are acting with the magnanimity that befits the stronger side at the same time that they are gaining supporters by it. Mr. Blair's mission has no official status because it has been disavowed. Anyone who makes allowance for the blind obstinacy of the Richmond government knows that this new peace meteor will fade away like the others.

The weather is sunny and mild, which reconciles me to the Washington climate. From my window, open to the east and high up on the sixth floor, I see on the horizon the majestic dome of the Capitol

raised on a natural pedestal that adds even more to
its grandeur. It is wrapped in mist like a distant
mountain. This morning it loomed up over the city
in superb isolation, washed by the purple-violet
color of dawn. I am going there in a little while to
hear a debate in the Senate about abrogating the
treaty of reciprocity with Canada and, in the House,
a debate on the [proposed thirteenth] amendment
to the Constitution.

January 13, 1865

MY VISIT to Congress was a waste of time. To begin
with, I couldn't hear the speakers clearly in the
public galleries and, in addition, Congress is not a
festival of eloquence every day in the week. It is
said that American oratory has degenerated and
that in the old days there were real virtuosi. The
most one can claim for it today is that speakers are
incredibly glib and long-winded. There are two
styles, one might even say two contrasting schools.
One, the Senatorial style, resembles a conversation
interrupted by courteous, muted disagreements.
Many seats are empty, the galleries are sparsely occupied and the presiding officer dozes in his chair.
Everything conduces to the calm and sober transaction of business. The House, in contrast, is a storm-
tossed sea; the floor is surrounded by huge galleries
full of spectators. The number of members is small
in comparison with the British House of Commons
or even with our own assemblies, but every one of
them makes enough noise for four.

The hum of conversation, the sound of footsteps,
the chattering of groups in corners, the incessant

clapping of hands to flag down the "waiters"—I hesitate to call them "ushers," for they have neither ceremonial chains nor rods of office—all these things contribute to the general atmosphere of indiscipline, insubordination and irreverence. Few speakers are accorded more than five minutes of attentive silence; the debates are carried on at one end of the room, while at the other end no one is any longer paying the slightest heed. It is therefore necessary to speak like Demosthenes[12] so as to be heard above the sound of the waves, to go right on speaking without giving any thought to ones audience and to shout loudly enough for the stenographers to hear. Hence the oratory of the House is full of long-winded bluster, accompanied by gesticulations—in fact, the very image of a public meeting.

In our country the orator seeks to guide his audience and his hearers, in turn, accept his control like a horse that may be docile or restless, that may even rear or buck, but feels the bridle at every moment and always knows what the rider is about. From this intimate relationship flow an infinite number of mutual concessions, delicate expressions and polite phrases which give our debates the interest and feeling of a stage performance.

In the United States Congress the audience is like a herd of runaway horses and the orator lashes out

[12]Demosthenes was the most famous orator of ancient Greece. It is said that he learned to correct a tendency to stammer by practicing his speeches with pebbles in his mouth while walking along the beach and in this way learned to make himself heard even above the sound of the breaking waves.

at them brutally to left and right, using all his strength to skin them alive in order to make them kick up their heels or settle down to a steady gallop. Signs of approval or disapproval are equally rare. A member speaks and then sits down again amidst the continual buzzing of the noisy and inattentive crowd. What sort of public speaking do you imagine one gets under such conditions? The speaker will bellow or else he will remain silent. The only way to put an end to this disorder would be to fire point-blank into the middle of the crowd. This whole scene would no doubt be instructive for timid, delicate souls who are afraid of fire and shrink from the aggression of the crowd—but Americans do not have this failing. I could wish for the sake of their oratory that their nerves were a little less battle-hardened.

In the Senate the emancipation of the wives and children of black soldiers was voted by a large majority. Afterwards, Mr. Sumner introduced his bill calling for denunciation of the commercial treaty with Canada as amended by the Committee on Foreign Relations. You will recall that some weeks ago the Senate, in a moment of anger, almost voted the immediate termination of the treaty. Today tempers have been cooled by the passage of time and by the satisfaction given by the Governor-General of Canada, so they hesitate to vote even for the peaceful and legal abrogation proposed by Mr. Sumner. Not only the form but the substance of the measure are under attack. It is being argued that it would hurt the United States more than its neighbors, that the bullet might ricochet and wound the marksman himself. To break the treaty now, after the injury has been repaired, would no longer be a matter of taking just reprisals; it would be acting like a bad neighbor and it would be pointless in the bargain since there is no longer anything to avenge; the United States would be acting foolishly because it would lose more than Canada.

Trade between the two countries has grown tenfold since the treaty was signed and the ratio of exports to imports is greatly to the advantage of the United States. Raising tariffs would mean losing this profit. The revenue the Treasury would receive from the export duties to be levied under the terms of the bill would therefore be gained only at the cost of great sacrifices. If several million dollars are needed, it would be much better to take them directly from the taxpayer's pocket, for tariffs are the most costly way to raise revenue. What remains is nothing but bitterness, an anger that people want to satisfy no matter what the price: this is a mean and despicable motive, as unworthy of a great nation as it is poor policy. Even though they are rightly jealous of their honor, Americans should never inflict a needless injury on their neighbors nor do them a deliberate injustice. Breaking the trade treaty could have been excused as a reprisal, almost an act of war, at the moment when Canada seemed to be provoking the United States. There is no such occasion for it today and it can only be seen as part of a spiteful policy that will bring little honor to this country.*

* The treaty's abrogation was voted a short time afterwards by a large majority in both Houses. Mr. Sumner and

In the House of Representatives slavery is still being discussed. The attempt to amend the bill seems to have failed, for it hasn't gained an inch of ground for several days despite the energetic efforts of its supporters. It is probable, from the turn the discussion seems to be taking, that the wrangling will be dragged out until everyone is tired of it, whereupon some sort of vote will send it to gather dust until the next session. Barely five votes are needed to obtain the necessary two-thirds, but they are becoming extremely difficult to win over and the advance is one step at a time.

Meanwhile, the fight between the two wings of the Democratic party is becoming more bitter. Some, like Yeaman, Odell and [Nathaniel B.] Smithers [of Delaware], accept abolition as an accomplished fact and the [constitutional] amendment as a necessity. Others, the perennial standard-bearers of the party like [Fernando] Wood, Voorhees

---

the authors of the bill saw in it only a financial expedient for increasing revenue. They disavowed any hostile motive or thought of annexation. In the spring of 1865 the Detroit International Convention, by expressing a wish to return to former trade relations, bore witness once again to the interests the two countries have in common. Everything leads to the belief that the present high tariffs will be maintained only to cover the financial needs that caused their adoption and that the United States does not want to use them as a weapon against the Canadian nation. Despite the threats of the Irish Fenians and their armed encampments south of the border, Canada can put its fears to rest. Its independence is not yet really endangered. This is more likely to happen when the United States decides to use its commercial power as a means of conquest and declares a complete blockade of its neighbor beyond the frontier of the Great Lakes.

and Pendleton, mostly backed by the rank-and-file, repudiate indignantly or with a half-smile of disheartened skepticism what they call a violation of the constitutional rights of the states.

I admit that I don't understand their reasoning because, since the Constitution itself provides for future changes, it can't be said that it is unconstitutional to amend it according to the rules it lays down. They may deplore the existence of the right of amendment because it threatens slavery and because they want to preserve forever the equivocal silence of the Constitution on the question and thus retain the pretext it offers for rebellion. But they can neither make this right disappear nor forbid its use by their opponents unless they abrogate it for themselves, following the legal forms, by a majority which they are unlikely to find. It is too easy at the moment to use the Constitution to defeat the national will and then repudiate the Constitution when it agrees with what the people want.

Some people point out that the South is not present to defend her own interests. She is not regarded as a party to the social contract and her fate is to be settled without giving her a voice in the decision. But if representatives of the South are not in Congress today to oppose the amendment, whose fault is that? Who drove them out? And then they trot out the great, eternally serviceable bromide—the excellence of slavery! Fernando Wood, in a speech that he ended as usual with his eyes raised to heaven in an unctuous prayer for peace, declared that slavery is a blessing for the black race, a gift of Providence so that they may be raised up from their primitive savagery and so that the Negro may attain his highest level of development under slavery. Some others are less shameless and stop short of singing a paean of praise to the institution. They are content to invoke for its protection the need to respect property rights. Still others claim to be very zealous to maintain national unity and denounce the amendment as tending to perpetuate secession. Several seem to oppose it only from habit and fidelity to old opinions. Some even plead conscientious scruples as an excuse for their opposition.

Fernando Wood has no such squeamish fears. He frankly admits he is a secessionist and denies that the Union can be saved by any means other than the reinstatement of slavery. His beloved institution, nevertheless, is collapsing everywhere, both in the North and in the South. A representative from Missouri, a former slave state and himself a slaveowner, recently spoke in favor of immediate total emancipation in bold language that reflects deep conviction. The next day it was learned that the extraordinary constituent assembly, or "constitutional convention," of Missouri had just summarily swept away the last remnants of servitude even before beginning work on the new constitution or naming committees to draft its detailed provisions. So the last-ditch defenders of slavery have little solid ground to stand on and if the South, or rather, the Richmond government, imposing its law on the Southern states, decides finally to go through with the plan of military emancipation it is considering, they will no longer have any pretext and all their weapons will have been struck from their hands.

They will have to choose between a total loss of influence and the new role that is being forced upon them by events.

The Republicans are not very much involved in this quarrel. They are letting their adversaries tear each other to pieces, secure in their confidence that they will emerge as the ultimate winners. In general, the opponents of the amendment sound a note of despondent fatalism or resort to their standard rhetoric of exasperated denunciation which uses insult in lieu of argument. They give the impression of merely going through the motions of debate like men who know their cause is hopeless. In contrast, the abolitionists, who are now to be found in all parties, speak with an accent of passionate sincerity. It is not the minority that now appears to be on the side of the angels; no one listens to its cries of rage or its complaints of oppression. The day after the vote you will see their indignation fade away as their ship veers around so as to sail before the wind. Nor is the abolitionist cause altogether free from petty foibles. For instance, the dispatch in the *Tribune* announcing the unanimous vote of the Missouri convention was couched in these terms: "At three o'clock this afternoon, Wednesday the 11th of January, in this year of grace 1865, every slave in Missouri immediately became unconditionally free by vote of the state convention. Amen!" Farther along an article ended with a verse from the Bible: "The Lord reigneth in heaven: let the earth rejoice!"[13]

[13]The reference is to the 96th Psalm, verses 10-11: ". . . the Lord reigneth: . . . Let the heavens rejoice, and let the earth be glad . . ."

No, the Lord doesn't yet reign in America and in spite of Abolition the millenium is still a dream of the distant future. And indeed these very measures of abolition, which are said to right the wrongs of slavery, have their darker side. What will become of the poor blacks who from one day to the next are being thrown out onto the street without a crust of bread? The army rolls, the nameless graves on every battlefield, the gallows erected by the Southern authorities to hang black prisoners, the forced-labor gangs organized [in Louisiana] by General Banks, the hospitals and the workhouses provide the answer. Abolition is no more a cure for the evils of slavery than amputation is a cure for a gangrenous leg. In whatever form it comes about, it is now virtually synonymous with the extermination of the black race. It is one of those heroic reforms that are just and necessary even though they cost the lives of innocent as well as guilty people. Doubtless it would have been much better if the South itself had understood its compelling necessity, for it is by means of slow education and gradual emancipation that the black people should have been assisted from slavery to freedom. But does that mean that under the color of humanitarianism slavery should now be perpetuated and injustice prolonged simply because there are dangers?

If emancipation does cost millions of human lives, then let the full and entire responsibility for the crime fall upon the blind originators and the stubborn defenders of slavery. But let them not presume, at the end of this unholy war, to speak in the name of humanity and philanthropy!

There are some new details on the cashiering of General Butler. The order to relieve him of his command was signed after a conference between Lieutenant-General Grant and Secretary of War Stanton. Butler, on taking leave of his army, issued an order-of-the-day in the style of Napoleon in which he boasted of having spared the lives of his soldiers. Then this great and noble citizen left for his place of exile.

The Radicals, as I expected, are trying to make him out to be the victim of political scheming and the unfortunate truth is that personal motives seem to have played a big part in General Grant's decision. It is said that he had begun to resent Butler's popularity.

A noted Radical, Butler was contrasted with Grant, who is a Democrat, and he was seriously spoken of as a possible Secretary of War in a future anti-Seward or anti-Stanton Cabinet.

That was a prospect calculated to be extremely displeasing both to the Lieutenant-General and to the present Secretary [Stanton], who joined forces, says the *Tribune*, to strike Butler down in good time and thus nip his schemes in the bud. But whatever the personal motives of General Butler's enemies may be, justice has nonetheless been done and the public is awaiting the piquant details.

January 14, 1865

I HAVE BEEN again to Congress, this time I was taken by Mr. Sumner onto the floor of the House of Representatives where Mr. [Thomas D.] Eliot of Massachusetts got me a seat near the Speaker's

dais. Mr. [Henry] Winter Davis, the chairman of the
Foreign Affairs Committee, lent me his seat while
Mr. [Thaddeus] Stevens was speaking. This detail
alone shows you how well I was treated.

The session was interesting and lively; speakers
for the most part were given a respectful hearing.
The first to speak was Mr. [James Sidney] Rollins of
Missouri, formerly a War Democrat and once the
owner of many slaves. He has the rough exterior
one expects of men from the [Middle] West, but
along with that there is a strain of candor and native
tact that raises him above the ordinary. A long-time
opponent of the abolitionist amendment, he rose
today to speak in favor of it. Though he personally
has been a heavy loser from the emancipation proclaimed by the convention in his own state, he
nonetheless defended and praised the decision. He
would have agreed, he said, to the preservation or
even the expansion of slavery if that would have
saved the Union. He agreed now to accept abolition
because it had become necessary to win the war and
restore the public peace. It was strange to hear this
slave-owner, impoverished only yesterday by the
new principles, defying the Democrats to find any
religious, moral or even economic or political argument to justify slavery. He then went on to make a
vehement plea for the general freeing of the slaves
without conditions or pecuniary compensation but
solely in the name of justice and the public welfare.

Why is it that Missouri, which was settled long
before its neighbor Illinois, has remained a poor
state, only half cultivated, while Illinois, after only
a few years, now has a population of two million? It

is because slavery prevailed in Missouri, discouraging commercial, industrial and even agricultural enterprise among its inhabitants; it is because slavery is a deadly germ, because it discourages European immigration and because free labor cannot exist alongside slave labor. Thank God, the irresistible tide of modern civilization is sweeping away the last remnants of this barbarous institution. Already Missouri is showing new signs of life and—by their own admission—the most recalcitrant states of the Rebel Confederacy will soon do the same. This natural and peaceful victory of liberty in the South is inevitable and the same result would have followed if the South had won its independence and had immured itself in its so-called nationhood. Why, then, do we see such futile resistance to the force of events? Maryland and Missouri have accepted the amendment in advance. The Kentucky legislature, in the same session that sent the Democrat James Guthrie to the Senate, has declared immediate emancipation to be in the interest of public order.

Some people speak of military oppression and of forcing opinions down people's throats in such cases. No, it was the free, authentic voice of the people that spoke in these elections; it was the popular will which, in the Missouri convention, decided by 60 votes against 4 to put an end to the moribund institution of slavery at a single stroke. As for the constitutional validity [of the amendment], no one can deny it except in bad faith. Certainly there are limits to the power of amendment which is being invoked, above all, the two-thirds majority required in Congress and ratification by three-fourths of the states. (But who dreams of violating these safe-guards?) Besides, the Preamble to the Constitution sets forth its own purposes and principles. It says the Constitution was instituted in order to secure to the American people the blessings of liberty, unity, justice and peace. Who would dare to assert today that slavery is just, that it is not a public enemy, a cause of war and, whatever its friends may say, an arrogant denial of human liberty?

The objection is made that the amendment is contrary to the spirit of the Constitution. Who is to say what that spirit is if not each individual's con-science? Furthermore, where did the authors of the Constitution proclaim that slavery is sacred? They tolerated it as an unavoidable evil which it would have been dangerous to try to remove, but they took care to enact a solemn prohibition against the extension of this criminal practice and to put an end to the slave trade until the time should be ripe for total emancipation, which alone is compatible with the principles of liberty and justice pro-claimed by the Declaration of Independence and the Preamble to the Constitution.

I have often told you that the Democratic party was at bottom the party of slavery and disunity. I did, of course, recognize that it embraces a large number of honest but deluded men, beginning with its leader [General McClellan]. I did not then see that it included such a large number of people who were already in sympathy with the abolitionist cause, who were deeply devoted to their country and who differed from the Republicans only over timing and procedure. I attached too little weight to the profound loyalty to the Union which, in spite of individual treacheries and the party's equivocal behavior, was still decisive for most Democrats. Respect for the Union and a will to maintain it are the great moving forces behind public opinion; their effect will be to make it unanimous when the time is ripe. What better example of patriotism could there be than the attitude of those who, putting aside the recriminations and rancor of the past, ask that their sacrifices be recognized only by pardon and forgetfulness on both sides. They have a right to claim their share of the credit for the revolution. Their efforts are helping to bring it about as much as—and perhaps even more than—those who, having always desired it, are now basking in the glow of its triumph.

As with us in 1789, it is the privileged class itself that is destroying the old regime. The most fanatical defenders of slavery come from states that abolished it long ago. America, after its military "1793," is now making great strides toward a peaceful "1789."[14] It is certainly better to win the rights of man by a civil war than to lose them as we did in bloody anarchy. The cannon is preferable to the guillotine; it does less to degrade the character of a nation. France emerged from the First Empire with a great hunger for liberty; she emerged from the period of the Convention [1792-1795] with a servile

[14] Two references to the French Revolution: great reforms were brought about with relatively little violence in 1789, while 1793 was the year of the civil war that crushed provincial resistance (particularly in the Vendée) to the Revolutionary program; 1793 also saw the beginning of the Terror.

and irresistible yearning for despotism. Among us, moreover, ideas ran ahead of events and exploded like a mine, leaving nothing but rubble. Here they have followed events and appear upon the scene just in time to cement the foundations of the new edifice. The future will eventually tell us which is the better way.

I will pass in silence over the speech made by a loud-mouthed representative who delivered himself of a string of anti-slavery platitudes. He seems to be one of those who don't believe they are speaking eloquently until they are blue in the face and have bloodshot eyes.

The final incident that day was a short speech by Mr. Stevens, famous as the author of the gold bill, who rose this time to reply to a personal allusion by Mr. [George H.] Pendleton. At his very first word I was able to recognize a born orator. Mr. Stevens is a strong, vigorous old man with deep-set eyes whose expressive, haughty face is heavily furrowed by wrinkles. A rather awkward wig, which lets fall some brown locks onto his bald forehead, does not—as one might suppose—give him the grotesque look of someone trying to look young. And when, as he recalled his past and his unvarying opinions, he spoke of his "enfeebled old age," his tremulous and plaintive voice justified this appeal for everyone's respect. His phrasing is well-rounded, ample, unforced and lively; his sentences are always sure of where they are going. Upright and calm while he speaks, sparing of gesture, the whole force of his eloquence is in his look and tone of voice.

He is one of the last of that elder generation of

orators that included Clay, Webster and Calhoun, whose proud, dignified manner so little resembles the shouting and arm-waving of today. Passionate as he is in getting his own way, rough and pitiless as he may be to his adversaries, Mr. Stevens was raised, like Mr. [John] Bright,[15] in the religion of "brotherly love." In fact, he resembles the Pennsylvania Quakers of former times who could be militant in political struggles but without putting aside their austere gravity or their tone of quasi-religious earnestness. An undefinable power seems to emanate from certain men and makes itself felt everywhere. The House of Representatives, which is usually so disorderly, lending only half an ear to partisan clamor, suddenly grows quiet when Mr. Stevens rises to speak, rendering an involuntary tribute to an eloquence and dignity whose secret it has lost.

One also hears a great deal about another orator of the old school, this one a younger man. He is Mr. [Henry] Winter Davis, the abolitionist, a charming man who gives an impression of modesty, candor and intelligence. His power, as so often happens, is revealed only on the speaker's platform. I have not actually heard him speak.

To sum up, the House of Representatives is not, as I may sometimes have led you to believe, made up entirely of opportunists and barroom politi-

[15] British Quaker and free-trade reformer who, with Richard Cobden, founded and led the Anti-Corn Law League in the years preceding the successful repeal of the Corn Laws in 1846; the League served as a model for many subsequent efforts to enact or repeal legislation by mobilizing public opinion.

cians. This type is undoubtedly more numerous than it should be, and for one Davis or one Stevens there are many like C. of Ohio or W. of Illinois. Ugly faces and home-made haircuts abound there, but when you are once accustomed to the typical American face and costume—a strange mixture of stiff formality and unbuttoned negligence—you realize that the greater part of the House is composed of "gentlemen."

Here and there, among the white-haired elders, your eye will be caught by the rough, undistinguished features of a young politician from the [Middle] West, a farmer or wagon-driver pushed into politics by a newly-rich father. Dressed like an apprentice in his Sunday best, he has long hair and his manner is a blend of boldness and awkwardness; he awakens in me a vague memory. I have heard this young gentleman in St. Louis, shouting at the top of his falsetto voice the most insignificant and least eloquent of speeches at a meeting to which he was introduced as "the Honorable Mr. Blank, Representative from Kansas." Here, as in England, there is a distinct class of politicians, and these precocious darlings of democracy, who come to the halls of Congress still wearing a schoolboy's impertinent, vacant expression on their faces, remind me of some of the junior members of the House of Commons who haven't a single hair on their chins and attend the evening sessions only to display their polished boots and white ties. Democracy also has its spoiled children whose fortunes have been made a ridiculously long time before they have done anything to earn them.

10

The Men in Power

[Washington]
January 15, 1865

I HAVE just visited the warehouses and administrative headquarters of the [United States] Sanitary Commission, that marvelous organization founded and carried on by private initiative which performs three-fourths of a task the government should do but doesn't. It is run by a regular hierarchy directed by a central committee with complete authority. It is organized into departments, armies and services, just like the Federal [War] Department. It employs a legion of doctors, nurses, administrators and inspectors, most of them volunteers devoting themselves without pay to these onerous duties, rewarded only by the austere pleasure of doing good works and rendering a necessary service to their country.

I have seen the chart representing this ingenious and complicated organization, which was created entirely by the private initiative in which the Americans have a right to take pride. All the branches are interconnected and all the powers are balanced with the nicely adjusted, rational consistency of a constitution drawn up by the Abbé Siéyès.[1]

[1] Emmanuel-Joseph Siéyès (1748-1836), author of the famous pamphlet, "What Is the Third Estate?" which exerted much influence on the early phase of the French Revolution.

The director of the Eastern Department, which embraces three armies, is a young man from Boston[2] whose fortune runs into the millions. He has interrupted a brilliant university career to devote two years of his life to this difficult and unpublicized work. "The Commission," he once told me, "has assumed the obligation of caring for the soldiers and providing for all their needs. It goes out and gathers them up as they lie bleeding on the battlefield or prostrate with fever in a swamp and cares for them in its hospitals, looks after them when they travel or when they are convalescing in a "Soldier's Home" where they can always get room and board. It helps them with the often complex formalities the government insists on for obtaining a furlough, establishing the right to a pension or claiming back pay. It even defends them against the suspicion of having deserted—and because of the great disorder of the military bureaucracy discharged soldiers are often harassed on this pretext."

Thanks to this independent organization, founded no one knows quite how and supported by voluntary contributions, the American soldier does not realize that his government is poorly organized and

---

Later he drafted or else had a hand in drafting a number of important constitutional texts, including *The Declaration of the Rights of Man and of the Citizen* and the French Constitution of the Year VIII (1800) under which Napoleon ruled as First Consul.

[2] Efforts to arrive at positive identification of this young man have not been successful. Duvergier de Hauranne may have spoken with an official less important than he indicates, but misunderstood the actual position occupied by his informant.

inept. At the same time, the books of the Commission furnish exact and detailed statistics on all those matters of which the government is ignorant. Each soldier is listed in a triple register, and the Commission is often able to find soldiers mislaid by the army's clerical staff after all trace of them seemed to have been lost.

I have learned from their summary tables a curious fact that is worth reporting: three-fourths of the army's losses were not sustained on the battlefield, but resulted from illness. In summer and in winter the death rate is frightful—so horrible that in McClellan's army just during the month of July, 1862, 262 men out of every thousand died, that is, more than one in four on the rolls. Still this American war, murderous as it is, cannot come close to matching, even in its worst moments, the losses of the Crimean War;[3] there, during the winter spent besieging Sebastopol, some regiments reported that more than 1,100 men out of 2,000 died in the month of January alone. I've just managed to learn this fact here in America.

The Sanitary Commission has records of a million soldiers who have passed through its hospitals in the last three years. It has given them medicine,

[3] The Crimean War (1854-1856), in which British and French armies invaded the Crimean peninsula and laid siege to the Russian fortress of Sebastopol, was notable for the scandalous insufficiency of the services of supply, particularly hospitals and medical facilities. It was the well-publicized sufferings of the sick and wounded that prompted Florence Nightingale to organize the first modern military nursing service. Her example was followed in America during the Civil War by women like Clara Barton and Dorothea Dix.

food, clothing and shoes. In the city of Washington alone, the expenses of the Soldier's Home, where discharged or furloughed soldiers stay during the long time it takes to get their papers in order, amount to $12,000 a week. What is even more astonishing than these large donations is the order, the dependability and the perfect discipline of this improvised administration. Most astonishing of all is the dedication of those who are giving several years of their lives to this great work of patriotism and charity. This achievement teaches us to admire America and the philanthropists of the Old World would do well to take some lessons from it.

I have visited Mr. [William H.] Seward several more times in his little house on Lafayette Square a few steps away from the White House and the Department of State, a modest dwelling for such an important person. I have found him sometimes alone, sometimes with his family, occasionally surrounded by people seeking favors. You should hear him in the evening when, wearied by the cares of the day, he stretches out in his armchair, crossing his legs and swinging one foot from the ankle as he tells in his guttural, muffled voice about various incidents in his political life. His mobile features are often enlivened by a smile. Though he gives the impression of never caring what he says, he always takes care to remain within the bounds of propriety and politeness. He speaks of his opponents in a friendly way, without rancor, with a pleasing mixture of diplomatic subtlety and sincere good nature. Furthermore, his view of things is just and clear; he sees beyond the events of the day, beyond partisan beliefs and emotions. Above all, he has the rare good taste not to make a great parade of his own opinions. This is apparently the reason he is unjustly considered to be a skeptic and a hypocrite. What people mistake for indifference is really only a mixture of moderation, impartiality and good will. Believe me, he is not the tiger with velvet claws, the practicing Machiavellian that he is represented to be. He has neither that much strength nor that much ferocity, and his misdeeds are probably limited to the incidental killing of a few mice that have slyly taken refuge under the presidential chair.

January 16, 1865

THE BUTLER REPORT has just been published. Mr. Seward, observing official discretion, seems not to know the reasons for his disgrace and speaks as if it were due entirely to the displeasure of General Grant at Butler's failure to take Wilmington. "I blame nobody," he said with his customary adroitness. "It may very well be that General Butler, although a tried and true patriot, is no better a soldier than I myself would have been, if I had taken a fancy like so many others to put on a general's uniform four years ago." It seems clear to me that behind this excuse there is to be found some dirty linen that no one wants washed in public. Butler's report, considering only the facts he alleges—facts that are confirmed by other generals, vindicates him completely. General Grant has nonetheless repeated to General [E. O. C.] Ord, Butler's successor, the order to take Wilmington. A new secret expedition, about which the newspapers were urged to say nothing for fear of alerting the enemy, has gone to bombard Fort Fisher or to take it by assault. Grant is a stubborn man who always seems at first to be dashing himself to pieces against an impregnable position, but in the end he batters his way through the wall.

Admiral Farragut claims that one of two things will happen. The Rebels may be taken by surprise and defeated before their reinforcements can come up. Or, if the fall of Wilmington is not achieved at one stroke, it can be taken only by long and bloody fighting. Everything leads one to think that the enemy is now on guard and that much blood will be shed. So far there is no news, although word is expected from hour to hour at the War Department.

I have renewed acquaintance here with Admiral Farragut, inasmuch as he has been staying at this hotel for several days. I have had little trouble getting on friendly terms with this excellent and cordial man, and I want to sketch him for you. His face is so frank, so open, so perfectly sympathetic, that you know at a glance what manner of man you have to deal with. He is a real sailor down to his fingertips, upright and good-natured, heroic without being conscious of it and likable without thinking about it, just because of the simple goodness of his unspoiled nature. A cabin boy at eight years of age, he has made his way for himself and is now reaping his reward for a life of hardship. Fearless and simple, he speaks about the remarkable exploits of his career without vanity or ostentation, taking a purely professional point of view and seeing in them only practical examples and lessons. He is so accustomed to being brave that he doesn't even think of putting himself in a good light; it evidently seems to him that anyone in his place would have done the same. Listening to him, one can imagine that fear would be impossible in his presence. I realize that in time his stories of maneuvering, of being under fire, his judgments on naval engagements about which I know nothing, would be as tiring as trying to follow a foreign language; but there is no need to be an expert to see his calm, quick intelligence shining out from under the unadorned simplicity of his conversation.

Admiral Farragut was born in Tennessee. He is one of the heroic defenders the Union has recruited from among those hard-working people of the South who have left their families and homes and sacrificed everything to follow the Union flag. To him, at least, the country has not been ungrateful: to honor him the obsolete rank of Vice Admiral has been reinstated. Just recently the leading citizens of New York contributed to a $50,000 fund that was presented to him as a token of their admiration and gratitude. In France such a gift would be seen as alms. Here it is accepted as the payment of a reward by a grateful nation and as a mark of honor. What difference is there, after all, between this gift to an individual and our accepted custom of begging for a pension or a state grant? Which is less demeaning? Every country has its customs; in the old days no one was ashamed to be the king's valet or to live off his bounty. In America the people reign; therefore one courts the favor of the people and accepts their largesse.

One hears about refugees from the South. The wife of [the Confederate] Senator [Henry Stuart] Foote of Tennessee,[4] is being held as a prisoner of war here at Willard's Hotel. Mr. and Mrs. Foote tried to escape from the South, but a Confederate patrol recaptured them just as they were crossing the lines. After being involved in a skirmish, Mrs. Foote fell into the hands of Federal troops along with the enemy's supplies. The unlucky Mr. Foote is at present in a Richmond prison. Mr. Seward, who was for a long time one of his adversaries in the United States Senate, has personally installed Mrs. Foote in this hotel and is paying her expenses for the time being. Everyone is kind to her and tries to cheer her up. If Mr. Foote succeeds in escaping from the South, he will probably be tried for the sake of form and then pardoned by the President.

The Richmond newspapers are indignant at the proposals of Mr. Blair, at least the ones he is supposed to be bringing from the North, for according to the latest reports he has not yet appeared in Richmond. The newspapers consider it an outrage for the North to suggest that the South should return to the Union. All well and good! But then they will have no right to complain when the troops of the North rule over their land as conquerors.

The number of people like the Footes increases every day. Patriots who have had to be put into prison to assure their good and loyal services are not much help in an extremity such as this. It is said that local elections now taking place in various parts of Georgia are giving results that are more

[4]On Senator Foote, see above, pp. 173-4.

than pleasing to the Unionists. Yet I have the impression that Savannah is more humiliated and cowed than genuinely acquiescent. Besides the toadies, the place-seekers and the speculators there are many proud people who do not wish to bow in submission. Nor will Citizen Sherman, Plenipotentiary of the Republic,[5] make them bow in the French fashion under the blade of the guillotine. Those who hate the "Yankees" have been able to slip behind the Rebel lines. The children of Savannah are allowed to sing verses that insult Lincoln. By remaining in the city the inhabitants have nonetheless submitted to the Union and, in their own way, betrayed the Confederate government.

Flags on all public buildings are lowered today in mourning for the death of Mr. [Edward] Everett. He became ill on leaving a meeting where he had spoken [to raise money] for the poor of Savannah. He died an orator, like a soldier under arms; his last words were an appeal to patriotism, concord and charity. He was a noble spirit and a good man. He fully deserved the honors rendered by the President to his memory.

January 17, 1865

FORT FISHER has fallen after a seven-hour battle that was stubbornly fought and murderous. Cannons were fired here to announce both the expedition

[5]Duvergier de Hauranne uses the term, *commissaire de la République*, which is an allusion to the all-powerful delegates sent into the provinces during the French Revolution and again after the Liberation in 1944-1945 to punish treason and reassert the authority of the central government.

and its success. There was, however, nothing unusual to be seen in the streets or in the hotel lobby—no excited talk, no posters—only the newsboy selling a special edition of the morning paper and shouting the news at the top of his lungs. Americans have become so accustomed to the war that victories and defeats no longer stir their emotions. With their imperturbable, almost arrogant confidence, they would watch without being alarmed while their own walls were levelled by artillery fire; on the other hand, they greet the most welcome news without giving much sign of joy like people who are used to hearing nothing else.

There is a man in the hotel whose ears must be burning at the news of this victory—General Butler. The Senate voted the other day for an inquiry into the first Wilmington expedition, and Butler appeared before the Committee on the Conduct of the War[6] this very morning. He was just demonstrating from a mass of documents that the fortress was impregnable when a War Department clerk came running in with the dispatch which was read to the accompaniment of loud cheers. Staggered by this

[6] This committee, consisting of three senators and four representatives, was established in December, 1861, to report on the Ball's Bluff disaster in which a force under Colonel E. D. Baker was seemingly sacrificed needlessly. The committee's proceedings were frequently high-handed and partisan, notably in the case of General Charles P. Stone who was unjustly removed from command and imprisoned without charges for 189 days. But the Radicals dominating the committee may have achieved some of their purpose, which was to winnow out incompetent, sluggish or disloyal officers.

crushing argument, Butler kept up his bold front and, without being disconcerted, cried out in a loud voice, "Praise be to God! May I always be wrong in the same way!"[7] His defense has become difficult now that events themselves have resolved the issue. He continues, however, to keep up a good countenance, and even takes the offensive in the battle against his enemies.

Among the "boarders" or permanent guests at the hotel there is a certain Mrs. X., whose son is in the army; since the war began, she has formed the habit of spending the winter in Washington. Restless and fond of intrigue, she is up to her ears in politics. This same officious spirit has moved her to take over the hotel parlor in the evening to hold her little assemblies; she introduces to one another the guests whom chance has thrown together here and usurps the role of mistress of this public house. She spends her time writing letters left and right—to cabinet officers, to generals, to the President; letters recommending, advising or accusing somebody or other. This busybody sometimes makes a lucky guess, and among her many accusations it happens

[7] The Committee on the Conduct of the War, after hearing testimony from General Grant, Admiral Porter and General Weitzel as well as that of Butler and others principally concerned, reached a unanimous conclusion that ". . . the determination of General Butler not to assault the fort seems to have been fully justified by all the facts and circumstances then known or afterwards ascertained." (*Autobiography and Personal Reminiscences of Major General Benj. F. Butler*, Boston, 1892, p. 821). Butler claimed that his removal from command was due partly to a cabal against him by West Point officers and partly to the hostility of Admiral Porter and Secretary of the Navy Welles.

that some of her shots have hit the mark.[8] She is friendly with a certain Protestant chaplain who was accused by General Butler of deserting his post and overstaying by two months a brief leave that had been granted him. The chaplain, for his part, complains bitterly that the general shut him up for several days without food in a powder magazine under enemy fire merely for having delayed his return by less than two days owing to the death of an uncle.[9] On hearing this, Mrs. X. wrote immediately to General Grant to demand that Butler be punished. Though this drop of water could have had little influence on the already overflowing cup of Butler's troubles, his dismissal—coming by pure accident at that very moment—has been hailed by this vain and fatuous person as the grand outcome of her puny efforts. As for Butler, he was happy enough to disguise the real or supposed reasons for his disgrace by putting the blame on Mrs. X. and her pitiable

[8] The French expression, "la mouche du coche," here translated "busybody," refers to the fly in La Fontaine's *Fables* (Livre VII, Fable VIII) who felt sure it was only his buzzing around the driver and horses that made the coach go uphill.

[9] This was a certain Chaplain Hudson of the First New York Volunteer Engineers who, according to Butler's account, had been sent in late May, 1864, by General Quincy Adams Gillmore to superintend the printing of a book by the latter about the siege of Charleston; though ordered to return to duty July 25, the chaplain did not do so until September 20, having published some letters in the New York *Evening Post*, highly critical of Butler, at the behest of Gillmore. Butler denied that Hudson was maltreated in any way during the time he was under close arrest for having overstayed his leave. (B. F. Butler, *Autobiography*, pp. 833-6)

protégé. Yesterday, therefore, while Mrs. X. was carrying out her self-appointed duties as mistress of ceremonies in the hotel parlor, Butler came strolling through the crowd and took care to say in a very loud voice when he was passing quite close to her, "So, I am relieved of my command on the charge of a runaway parson!"

The remark was heard and noted, and there followed a most curious and comic scene. Butler, who has a rough tongue and boasts of being a lawyer, was the winner; thus he has taken his revenge for Wilmington on Mrs. X.

In general, I should say, the people here at the hotel are on his side. A delegation of pro-Union men from Kentucky has come to tell him they hope the President will appoint him military governor of their state. He himself is so good-natured, so straightforward, so approachable that I don't doubt he is adding a large number of personal friends to the ranks of his political sympathizers. I was much amused by the spectacle he put on this evening in the lobby with his square-cut, sturdy figure, his frock-coat buttoned in military style, his flamboyant cap tilted to the back of his head, his heavy, fighter's mustache and the perpetual smile on his thick, ironical lips. He shook hands vigorously and tossed out friendly remarks while a crowd of curious people gathered in a circle around him. There is a certain studied roughness in his manner, a certain disdainful expression in his sardonic, slightly sinister glance, and his whole personality is a blend of vulgarity and pride, boorishness and elegance, so that he has the air of a shrewd, popular adventurer, an actor playing the part of a soldier, a political mountebank who is also an enterprising buccaneer, as arrogant in spirit as he is supple in character, as bold in public life as he is cautious on the battle-field. Taking all his qualities together, there is much about this man that both attracts and repels, as though he were in fact the "Beast Butler" who is referred to with horror by those he has governed— as though he were about to pull out of his pocket a hairy paw armed with sharp claws. Looking at him, you tell yourself that he would be a dangerous man if he had as much courage and moral force as he has vanity and effrontery.

January 18, 1865

I SAW General Butler again at Mr. Seward's reception in a numerous company of diplomats who were obviously not overjoyed at his presence. He seemed to me entirely different from the man I had just seen holding forth at the hotel, applauded and almost acclaimed by the crowd. He seemed less proud and less at his ease on this small stage than he had been in the midst of the popular tumult. On the contrary, he cut a rather poor figure as he moved awkwardly from one group to another, maintaining an embarrassed silence like a country bumpkin in a great city where he feels out of his natural element. He seemed uncomfortable in his splendid dress uniform; with his sword hanging down, his golden spurs and his pistol holster strapped to his side, the impression he gave was about as martial as a country lawyer in national guard uniform.

Diplomatic society is, to be truthful, a world of

gloves and white ties; it is disdainful, superstitious even, when it comes to matters of etiquette. They are less likely than any other group to make allowances for adventurers and demogogues. However well accustomed they are to dealing with the democratic element, professional diplomats always retain an invincible dislike for everything and everyone connected with democracy. I have met very few of them on this side of the Atlantic who have much confidence in the future of American liberty—or indeed, of liberty in general. They are used to thinking of foreign affairs as the only things that make much fundamental difference to a nation, and they view themselves as the agents of an executive power to which alone they have to account. In addition, they have an instinctive preference for secret diplomacy, the element in which they feel most at home. To their way of thinking, government is a matter to be worked out—quietly and without useless bickering—among the members of a small inner circle of polite, well-bred gentlemen presided over by an all-powerful minister. Diplomacy is not easy in a democratic government where it is continuously at the mercy of public opinion, obliged to give an account of its doings, to caress the majority, to flatter it with fine words, to follow its impulses just far enough to moderate its acts and to be always on hand to remove the monkey-wrenches thrown into the works by elected assemblies. A wise minister, caught as Mr. Seward is between the hammer and the anvil, has a difficult and self-sacrificing role to play. It is not astonishing that diplomats do not understand very well the greater good that flows from these small nuisances. To each his trade: the chimney-sweep knows nothing but the price of soot, the mason that of plaster, and the price of bread is the political thermometer of our peasants. It is human nature to see no farther than the end of ones nose. People are puppets hung by threads; they imagine that by virtue of their own independent thoughts they are able to walk freely upon the stage of the world, when in reality all their opinions depend on the hand that supports them and makes them dance.

January 19, 1865

I LEAD A NOISY, hectic life. Continually running up and down six flights of stairs, tramping back and forth through the hundred-yard-long corridor that leads to my hideaway, the frightful hubbub that fills this great building, all this keeps ones nerves in a perpetual state of agitation and discomfort. Finally—and worst of all—the indescribable uproar of the dining-room intensifies ones irritation to such a degree that he too falls into the convulsive rhythm that has gripped everyone around him and leaves the table still half-starved, with an aching head and a cramp in his muscles, having succeeded only in snatching a few half-chewed mouthfuls. Everything here makes me think, by contrast, of the delights of "home," of its intimate, tranquil atmosphere which calms and refreshes the weary spirit. I marvel at the Americans who can live like this for months at a time without losing their sanity, without longing for the family hearth. The pigeon-coop is often deserted for long periods of time while the birds are out competing for their livelihood amidst shouts and tumult, with flocks of crows and vultures ready to swoop down on anything that ventures into the open. I have made the acquaintance here of several people from New York and Boston who have quiet, comfortable homes waiting for them, but stay on at Willard's Hotel to enjoy this witches' sabbath. There are some who regularly spend half the year in Washington and do not even dream of seeking a little peace in a quieter "boarding-house." This whirlpool lures them and sucks them in.

One of Washington's attractions is that during the winter political activity brings together a great number of people who all the rest of the year are scattered to the four corners of the country. This motley, ill-assorted throng takes on the appearance of a mob, much like the one I saw earlier at Saratoga Springs. Here, however, there is more chance of meeting notable people and I am constantly hearing some famous name that catches my attention. Naturally, I do not gain much from a hasty glance at those whose images follow one another across the screen of this magic-lantern show, but it amuses the mind to see new faces and to label those faces with names that are already familiar. Last night, for example, I saw Senators Sprague, Trumbull and Sherman, General Burnside, General Banks, Judge Holt of Kentucky and many others. I also saw a striking portrait of General Sherman, whose high, square forehead, firm mouth and muscular face full of proud and rather ruthless energy makes a remarkable contrast with the crafty smile and false candor of Butler.

At last I have seen and been able to form an

opinion—not merely of Boston or of New York high society, nor of any other limited group—but of American society in general, whose still confused elements form what may be called the political élite of the country. A time must surely come when Washington society will predominate over that of all the other great cities of the Union as, in England, London society has eclipsed that of the provincial towns. I won't even make a comparison with Paris, the universal city that contains twenty diverse kinds of polite society and absorbs into itself the life of the whole nation. Unlike France, America will never have a true capital, a sort of sovereign queen imposing down to the smallest detail the rule of her whims on the inert body she drags behind her. It is more appropriate to compare London with the future capital of the United States because in London there is only one society, gathered together for just one purpose—politics. Apart from this select circle, London is really nothing but a particularly large provincial city, a gigantic Manchester piled on top of a colossal Liverpool.

If the social gatherings of Washington are to be compared with anything, it would be what the English call "routs." They display the same monotony, the same mania for cramming crowds of people into houses that are too small, inasmuch as they serve only as temporary quarters for the season. Washington has everything except London's irreproachable elegance and phlegmatic stiffness. In England inherited social position, the continuity of political alignments and the centuries-old institution of an aristocratic ruling class combine to give cohesion and unity to the temporary gathering that is called London Society. In America, on the contrary, even allowing for the passage of several hundred years and even supposing that by that time customs and manners will have become uniform, I cannot imagine anything but a nomadic high society, full of shocking contrasts, with great diversity of dress and behavior, the faithful image of the democratic society in whose womb it was formed. The political milieu will always be a grab-bag of people from all classes and backgrounds, united today only to be dispersed tomorrow, too fluid for habits to be fixed or for traditions to be passed on. It will always be a patchwork affair, its members drawn from the four corners of the nation by the accidents of popular election.

There will never be any possibility of identifying any common trait or of finding any principle of unity unless it may be that of a country inn where all sorts of men rub elbows together, some with muddy boots and dusty traveling clothes, others dressed in the height of fashion, the latter as serious and reserved as they would be in a cabinet officer's reception room, the others as careless and slipshod in dress and manner as people who come down to breakfast in the hotel dining room wearing a bathrobe and carpet slippers. And I do not even mention all those pretentious and vulgar persons whose attempts at elegance misfire, who lay claim to good taste without being able to recognize it, like actors who try to convey the atmosphere of high society on a stage-set made for a play about bohemians. Seen through the eyes of a European, Washington society in general—no matter how distinguished a few individuals may be—can only be regarded as a clumsy, jostling masquerade, a gallery of eccentrics who put themselves on display like freaks in a circus side-show.

I am superstitious about clothes. I admit it without a blush because, all things considered, dress is part of manners and Mr. [Ralph Waldo] Emerson is right in saying that one must have uncommon natural superiority to be able to neglect it. I therefore think that its rules should be strictly observed, and that no one except truly outstanding people can disregard them without penalty. A person with perfect manners can even wear a peasant's jacket and make it seem in good taste, but I shudder when I see some common lout wearing splendid, highly polished boots, a pair of loosely-cut, colored trousers and a light overcoat shaped like a sack and made from a horse blanket. I grate my teeth when I see women from the West wearing dresses of the gaudiest, most screaming colors they can find, in skirts that don't quite hide the muddy hems of petticoats they dragged in the streets that morning, and also when I see their square-cut, plunging necklines, their bodices clumsily padded with cotton, their high-necked, sleeveless blouses with ruffles over their shoulders and bare arms, their "waterfalls" or cascades of false curls, topped with a basketful of poppies or peonies. I wince at these dandies with vests buttoned up to their chins, wearing blue or brown ties and gloves of every color in the rainbow.

Bewildered by this chaos of colors and forms, I long for the anonymous uniform of European fash-

ion. At the same time I wish that Americans of all
sorts could acquire a little more polish over their
rough exteriors. I can hear you exclaiming that I've
turned into a haberdasher or a wig-maker, and reminding me that I should not judge people by what
they wear. I freely admit that the crudeness of
American fashions is not a condemnation of democracy; but it is still true that these petty details give
one some insight into the intimate nature and spirit
of a society. The [New York] *Herald* mentioned
yesterday, in an article on Mr. Everett, that his artistic sense, his taste for the beautiful, was evident
even in his clothing. I have never seen him dressed
otherwise than very simply in the European style,
like you or me. If fastidious people naturally imitate us in these little ways, doesn't that show that
these are signs of intellectual superiority and a
keener, more reliable esthetic sense? I maintain that
there isn't a street-urchin in Paris who doesn't show
himself to be a better judge of art than nine out of
ten Americans, however admirable—and even envi-
able—they are in their own way.

There are, moreover, two distinct types among
the residents of Washington: the Easterners who are
much like us Europeans—the most distinguished
among them unconsciously copy British ways—and
the Westerners who, almost to a man, are six-foot
giants, coarse-featured, robust in build, and have
mops of hair as thick as horses' manes. The latter
are more countrified and their manners are less polished, but they have in their favor an originality and
a certain aura of sheer power that I find admirable.
The specimens one encounters at the homes of Mr.

Chase and Mr. Sherman are, of course, selected with care. I have not seen there the flattened skull and carnivore's snout of Mr. W. nor the gold-buttoned blue suit of the future Senator Y.

On the contrary, almost all these vigorous Westerners have something very attractive and likable about them. You musn't expect them to exhibit refinement of language nor politeness carried to the point of foolish exaggeration; but for frankness, openness and good fellowship mixed with shrewdness they have no equals. I am not talking about Mr. Chase, who is not so much typical of the West as he is of New England, where he was born. As an excellent example of the Westerner at his best I propose a certain Mr. [James M.] Ashley, of Ohio, one of the most influential members of the House, a tireless foe of slavery, a man of generous, jovial aspect who cuts a lively, even a heroic figure; he is cordial, obliging, informal without being rude, courtly in his relations with women, and pleasing in his speech. He also shows more genuine zest for living than any man I've ever met. Powerful, elemental natures such as his continually fill me with amazement and make me feel like the small, stunted fruit of a kitchen-garden civilization. When I stand near the entrance to the Senate at the end of a session and watch all these lusty, raw-boned fellows come striding out, I feel the same twinge of awe as if a troop of Horse Guards were parading in front of me. The trouble is that many of these giants are unlike Mirabeau except in appearance, and there is often more real intellectual power in the sharp, lively features of a Guizot or in the plump, dimpled

hand of a Thiers than in these great, imposing as-
semblages of flesh and bone.[10]

I haven't as yet really seen President Lincoln
because so far I have only caught a glimpse of a
long-legged giant who was leaving the White House
lobby wrapped up to his nose in an enormous scarf.
It is the fashion for European visitors to go to ogle the
President as they would go to stare at a strange animal, and to make endless disparaging comments
at his expense. I know of an English journalist
who asked for the honor of being presented to
him and then, the very next day, wrote an insulting,
comic account of his interview with "Abe" Lincoln,
as he called him.

As for myself, I have been inside the White
House several times and I have seen nothing so far
that might justify such raucous mirth. If only the
slanderers would content themselves with epigrams
in execrable taste! Or if they would attack only the
President's public acts, decently stopping at the
threshold of his private life! No such thing—even
the President's family is not spared. People insinuate
that Mrs. Lincoln makes a financial profit from all
her little perquisites, that she sells flowers from the
presidential greenhouse, that she makes the government pay for the most modest dinners she gives
from time to time, that she has retained the habits

[10] Henri Gabriel Riqueti, comte de Mirabeau, was a leader
of the French Revolution between 1789 and 1791; he was
tall and stout and spoke in a powerful voice. François Guizot
and Adolphe Thiers were the two most prominent statesmen
of the July Monarchy under King Louis-Philippe (reigned
1830-1848); Prosper Duvergier de Hauranne, our author's
father, also served as a cabinet minister during this period.

of an economical housewife who haggles over a cabbage to save a penny. At the same time, it is said that she doesn't pay her bills promptly enough. The newspapers print the tradesmen's letters and her replies. They have gone to the length of charging that Mrs. McClellan bought a shawl with money entrusted to her by a charitable organization for helping wounded soldiers.

Yet in spite of all the thievery they are accused of, these American leaders are not very rich. Mr. Lincoln has refused to have his meager salary of $25,000 paid in gold, as provided by law, rather than in paper money. I asked his eldest son [Robert Todd Lincoln] if he didn't plan to make a trip to Europe soon. "I am waiting," he said, "for the end of the war. At the present price of gold, the journey would cost too much." What modesty in his answers, and what noble austerity! I know that in Roman times, the dictator Cincinnatus plowed his own field and dined on onions with black bread, but that sort of self-abnegation is not in fashion nowadays, and I know of no other country where the Chief of State is too poor to afford a trip abroad for his son.

Nevertheless, the tenants of the White House are reproached for living in tawdry splendor and for making a display typical of the newly-rich. People speak especially of Mrs. Lincoln's extravagant taste in dresses. I have read the ridiculous descriptions she allows to be published by fawning journals that probably think they have found the key to her favor. "The President wore a simple black suit with white gloves; Mrs. Lincoln wore a delightful gown of white silk, a charming coiffure with ribbons of gold and a 'lovely' pearl necklace."

Let them talk, and come with me to one of Mrs. Lincoln's receptions. You arrive on foot, you enter the huge, bare vestibule of the White House. There are no honor guards with golden breastplates, no swarms of glittering lackeys, not even a sentry at the door. A lone servant in a black coat asks for your card and opens the drawing-room door for you. It is a simple, plain room, hung with red damask. The mistress of the house rises and comes forward; her welcome is so open and friendly that you think she is going to offer you her hand like an old acquaintance. The heavy stiffness of your formal bow recalls her to the cold conventions of official etiquette. This former country-woman looks no worse in her velvet gown than any other aging lady who is a little bit plump and middle-class. Her manner is dignified, kindly, reserved and almost shy; I must admit that her conversation is not phenomenally brilliant, and it seems that she feels an easily understandable diffidence when speaking with strangers from Europe, thought by her to be very severe judges—especially after all the indecent mockery that has been showered upon her. The joke is on those who scoff at her, for there is nothing to laugh at in this respectable household, and I have a poor opinion of those who jeer at this modest simplicity as though the Lincolns were crude backwoodsmen.*

* I hope I may be forgiven for my indiscretion in reporting these intimate details. I didn't want to change my original impressions for fear that people might accuse me of painting a portrait of the residents of the White House that would be

As for the President himself, I still suspend judgment. But how can I believe in the reputation for incompetence that is imputed to him in Europe? This man who has raised himself by his own unaided efforts from a "log cabin" deep in the Indiana woods to the presidency of the United States cannot possibly be a run-of-the-mill person. He needed a great deal more than just intelligence—a gift less rare than we commonly realize—which counts for nothing without character. He also needed that moral force, those virtues of perseverance and resolution which are, indeed, the American virtues *par excellence*. There is in his life-history a great lesson for refined souls like ourselves, mandarins of the mind, who consider intelligence to be the monopoly of the learned, a delicate flower that opens only when given infinite care in the artificial atmosphere of a closed hot-house: it proves that in American democracy great minds are ripened naturally by the sunshine of liberty.

Six months of primary instruction in a poor country school—that is all the education ever given this man who was one day to stand on an equal footing with the crowned heads of the world. He has been successively a farm worker, a rail-splitter, a day laborer living by the strength of his arm, then a carpenter, a Mississippi boatman, a miller, a soldier

either too imaginative or too conventional. The familiarity and outspokenness of this account show the profound sincerity of my respect better than a more elaborate portrait could. Furthermore, the name of Abraham Lincoln no longer needs to be defended against ridicule. Envious and impotent sneers cannot leave a mark upon that brow, now crowned by a martyr's aureole.

and a store clerk. At last he was elected to the Illinois legislature by the town of New Salem where he had won the esteem and affection of everyone. His mind, developed by solitary study and by the practical education that "self-government" gives to all citizens, had acquired the strong temper, the simple, straightforward nobility and the piquant originality that from the first made him stand out from the common crowd of political orators. It was there that he studied law and became an attorney. He soon became indispensable to the success of the Whig party in Illinois.

As early as the year 1837 he presented to the state legislature a petition against slavery. Later [1846], he was sent to Congress. He became an influential member of the convention of 1848,[11] then a candidate for the United States Senate and the formidable opponent of the famous orator [Stephen A.] Douglas in an election campaign that was talked about all over America. The two candidates traveled together from city to city, competing with their eloquence on the same platforms before crowds of assembled citizens. Finally he was elected President of the United States.

His talents as an orator and statesman have gone on growing with his success. One day, speaking[12] of

[11] This is undoubtedly a slip of the pen or a typographical error, and the author meant to write "1858" because in that year Lincoln was nominated to run for the U.S. Senate by the Illinois Republican convention meeting in Springfield. His Democratic opponent was Stephen A. Douglas.

[12] In an address to an Indiana regiment delivered March 17, 1865 (Abraham Lincoln, *Speeches and Letters*, Everyman's Library ed., London, 1907, pp. 225-6)

slavery, he said with the grave, penetrating irony that is one of his best-known traits:

" . . . I may incidentally remark, that having in my life heard many arguments—or strings of words meant to pass for arguments,—intended to show that the Negro ought to be a slave,—if he shall now really fight to keep himself a slave, it will be a far better argument why he should remain a slave than I have ever before heard. He, perhaps, ought to be a slave if he desires it ardently enough to fight for it. Or, if one out of four will, for his own freedom, fight to keep the other three in slavery, he ought to be a slave for his selfish meanness. I have always thought that all men should be free; but if any should be slaves, it should be first those who desire it for themselves, and secondly those who desire it for others. Whenever I hear anyone arguing for slavery, I feel a strong impulse to see it tried on him personally."

I do not believe that modern eloquence has ever produced anything more noble than the address he delivered over the graves of the soldiers who died at Gettysburg. He attained the sublime simplicity, the inspired detachment, of antique patriotism, but one feels at the same time the emotion of a human being and a Christian face to face with the horrors of civil war.[13] I have been told that this "illiterate buffoon" or, as the New York *Herald* scornfully calls him, "our very classical President"—knows by heart all of Shakespeare and I also hear that when he goes to hear it performed, no one is more quick to notice omissions from the original text or to catch mistakes by the actors. I begin to believe that his only fault

[13] Here the author inserts a French translation of the Gettysburg Address, which is so familiar that it has not seemed necessary to include it.

was to have been a lumberjack, a rail-splitter, and a man of all work. For my part, I only honor him the more for it.

January 20, 1865

AT LAST I have met the President. I was presented to him in his office by Mr. Sumner at the hour when, like St. Louis under his oak tree, he receives petitions from his people.[14] For a foreigner the White House possesses a certain prestige; and besides, I have been taught discretion by our customs to the point where I wouldn't dare go past its threshold without a guide or without a special invitation from the great personage who lives there. Yet its doors stand open to every American: like a church, it is everybody's house. At all hours of the day, you will find curious or idle people milling about in the great reception room where the President holds his popular audiences. It is said that some visitors—country bumpkins, no doubt—cut pieces from the silk curtains to take home as souvenirs of their pilgrimage. You may think that a policeman or at least a guard has been posted. Not at all! There is only a notice asking visitors to respect the furnishings, which belong to the government.

We went up a flight of stairs, we opened a door, and suddenly we were in the majestic presence of

[14] King Louis IX (Saint Louis) of France, according to tradition, frequently sat under a great oak tree in the forest of Vincennes, then a few miles east of Paris, to receive petitions and complaints from even the humblest of his subjects and to render judgment on the spot in the interests of justice or for the relief of the oppressed.

the President. At the far end of the room, his back to the window behind a huge desk piled so high with papers that it seemed to enclose him like the walls of a confessional, "Father Abraham" was seated on a low chair and writing on his knees with his long legs bent double. In front of him stood a woman who had come to ask a favor; dressed in her best attire and standing respectfully before him, she leaned forward and whispered into his ear something that he proceeded to write down on his pad. Mingling pertness with humility, she favored him with her sweetest smiles and most penetrating glances; but the President, a grave and somewhat hurried judge, urged her to come to the point, questioned her briefly and rather brusquely, diligently scribbling at his notes all the while, his attitude clearly indicating by his manner that she was wasting his time and that he was neither stupid nor easygoing enough to be taken in by her wiles.

Five or six other people, soldiers and lower-class women, were silently awaiting their turn, sitting in a row along the wall. The lady in velvet was soon sent away, and the President rose to receive us; it was then that his great height was revealed. I looked up and saw a bony face, framed by a shock of carelessly combed hair, a flat nose and a wide mouth with tightly closed lips. His face was angular and furrowed by deep wrinkles. His eyes were strangely penetrating and held a sardonic expression; he seemed sad and preoccupied, bent under the burden of his immense task. His posture was awkward and like nothing I've ever seen before—partly rigid and partly loose-jointed; he doesn't seem to know how to carry his great height. We all opened our mouths after the customary handshake, I to pay him a compliment, Mr. Sumner to explain who I was, and he himself to respond to my remark and to pretend that he already knew my name. His voice is far from musical; his language is not flowery; he speaks more or less like an ordinary person from the [Middle] West and slang comes easily to his tongue.

Beyond this, he is simple, serious and full of good sense. He made some comments on Mr. Everett and on the unrealistic hopes the Democratic party entertained four years ago that it could impose its policies on the victorious Republicans. These remarks may have been lacking in sparkle, but the thought behind them was subtle and witty. There was not a single burst of clownish laughter, not a single remark in doubtful taste, not one of the "jokes" for which he is famous. We shook hands again and left him to his chores. I took away from this ten-minute interview an impression of a man who is doubtless not very brilliant, not very polished, but worthy, honest, capable, and hard-working. I think the Europeans who have spoken and written about him have been predisposed to consider it amusing to exaggerate his odd ways—either that or else they went to the White House expecting to see some splendid, decorative figure, wearing a white tie and behaving in a manner both courteous and condescending like some sort of republican monarch. What a stupid and egregious error to expect that Abraham Lincoln, the former Mississippi boatman, could have the manners of a king or a prince!

In order to judge people rightly it is first of all necessary to understand the realities of life and remember that in a democracy nobody has any use for the pomp and circumstance of high society. If a nation is so sensitive to superficial forms that it needs the trappings of a monarchy—the guards, chamberlains and an inaccessible sovereign loaded with gold and embroidery—then it may as well keep the name of royalty along with its substance. In a republic people are more practical and down to earth. The President is chosen to perform his political functions, not to dance royal quadrilles nor to gallop up and down in a plumed hat at military reviews. It is not necessary that he be a man of letters or a scholar; he need not have written philosophical treatises, nor published a ten-volume set of collected works. He doesn't even have to be what Americans call "a fine gentleman." Uncalloused, perfumed hands are useless in the rough game of American politics. Provided he does his job well and honestly, no one troubles to ask whether he writes in a "classical" style or whether he is dressed in the height of fashion. Despotism holds up little idols for the crowd's adoration; but republics fill positions of general esteem and power with carpenters like Abraham Lincoln.

There is a great deal of talk about the investigation demanded by Senator [Lazarus W.] Powell of Kentucky into the conduct of General [Eleazer A.] Paine. Mr. [Henry] Wilson and some others support this high-handed patriot out of party loyalties, while Senator Powell attacks him in language that is incredibly violent and crude. When Mr. [John]

Engraving

The Old Brick Capitol Building, Washington, D. C.
Used as a Prison during the Civil War

Courtesy of the New York Public Library

Conness of California referred to him in uncomplimentary terms, he replied with a furious outpouring of personal insults. In France such an exchange could only have resulted in an exchange of slaps [and a duel], but the composure of Americans is as great as their intemperance and I would not be astonished, even after this brawl, to see the two opponents shake hands.

In the House an inquiry already launched against General Paine and Representative [Lucian] Anderson of Kentucky, both accused of corruption and abuse of power, has awakened public attention to the many injustices the military authorities feel they can commit in the name of the President since the suspension of *habeas corpus.** Mr. [John] Ganson, a New York Democrat, touched off the scandal. The abuses are so flagrant, the arbitrary arrests are so often followed by indeterminate detention, and the number of victims imprisoned in Fort Lafayette or the old Capitol building is said to be so shocking, that the whole Republican party—except for an obstinate group of five men inspired by the pitiless Thaddeus Stevens—has joined in a campaign to put

* The suspension of the writ of *habeas corpus*, permitted by the United States Constitution " . . . when in Cases of Rebellion or Invasion the public safety may require it" [Art. I, Sec. 9, Par. 2], was proclaimed by President Lincoln on September 15, 1863; it was revoked by President Johnson at the end of November of last year [1865] for the whole territory of the Union except the District of Columbia, Virginia, South Carolina, North Carolina, Kentucky, Tennessee, Georgia, Florida, Alabama, Mississippi, Louisiana, Texas, Arkansas and the territories that took part in the rebellion where law and order have not yet been fully restored.

things to rights. Mr. [Henry] Winter Davis of Maryland, and Mr. [Henry L.] Dawes, a representative from Massachusetts have denounced the stubborn old Pennsylvania mule's motion to table the matter as an intolerable denial of justice.

It will be interesting to watch the reactions of the American people as the secrets of the prisons are brought to light and they learn, thanks to Congress, that under a façade of liberty they have gradually handed over to bureaucrats, to junior officers and to armed men acting with scarcely any judicial oversight, the right to imprison citizens who may be innocent or guilty, but who have not been given a proper trial. It is said that these arrests took place in such a hit-or-miss fashion that it is often difficult to find the persons originally responsible for the injustice. So they are going to clean the skeletons from the government's closets because the elected representatives of the American people have no fear of the truth. They do not believe that they can remedy an abuse by closing their ears to the voices of those who reveal it to them, like ostriches who believe they become invisible when they bury their heads in the sand.

11

Prison Camps of the South

Washington, D.C.
January 21, 1865

THIS MORNING there was a reception, or official receiving line, at the White House. There was no need to have a formal invitation nor to be wearing a frock coat in order to be admitted. It was not even necessary to take off ones wet overcoat, dripping with icy rain. Any respectable person—that is, anyone of halfway decent appearance—was allowed in on his looks. I don't even know whether the servants on duty in the vestibule would have had the authority to refuse admittance on the ground of muddy boots or disreputable clothes to any patriotic citizen eager to meet his President.

The visitors filed in one by one. Standing near the door, dressed in a tight-fitting frock-coat and towering over two aides in military uniform, was the President and Commander-in-Chief of all the armed forces of the United States of America, tirelessly shaking hands with everyone who came along, his arm moving stiffly up and down in a rhythm as regular as clockwork. Farther along and a little to his rear, Mrs. Lincoln, flanked by two solemn individuals dressed in black, dutifully greeted the visitors as the line moved past. All the while the noise of a military band assailed our ears with loud drum-rolls and clashing of cymbals.

This affair, please note, was only an ordinary reception, hardly more than an informal get-together, such as takes place every month. For the President's "Grand Levees" everyone in town tries to elbow his way into the entrance hall and the railroads bring in crowds of out-of-town visitors. The enthusiasm is so great that after a few hours, when the diplomatic corps in its embroidered uniforms, the members of Congress and their wives and all the other important men and their elaborately gowned ladies have passed through the receiving line, the great double doors are thrown open. Mrs. Lincoln retires, the other fine ladies take to their heels and the unlucky chief magistrate of the nation is left alone to be assaulted by the mob. Fortunately for him, he has been a farmer and a lumberjack and has long ago been forced to develop powerful hands that can take this terrible punishment.*

* Last November a committee of important New Yorkers invited General Grant to an immense reception to introduce the people of New York to him. I have taken the following account from the New York *Times*—it will give you an idea of democratic politics and its festive occasions:

General Grant stood facing a basketful of flowers, with the members of the committee buzzing about him like bees around a piece of sugar. To his right stood Mrs. Grant and some other ladies. . . . In front of him was the crowd, shouting, shoving, gasping for breath, staggering with fatigue, groaning, overcome by heat and lack of air. People were pushed and tugged, jostled and butted by the hapless members of the committee as they emerged from the throng. As each couple approached, a little man asked their name. He scarcely ever heard it right and announced to the General all sorts of bizarre names as amusing to the people being presented as they were unintelligible to the General. Every man and woman was absolutely determined to shake his hand,

I have several new figures to add to my portrait gallery. One is a Mr. ***, especially interesting as a representative of that class of wealthy plantation owners whom they call "Virginia gentlemen." He is half farmer, half lawyer, a perfect specimen of the rural gentry, shrewd and keenly aware of his own interests, more an intriguing politician than an influential statesman. Another new acquaintance is a cashiered military man, General [Ambrose E.] Burnside. You may recall that two years ago (late in 1862) during that frightful slaughter where generals and their armies melted away like snow, Burnside had a brief hour of glory when he was momentarily singled out from among the unlucky leaders who kept replacing one another without a let-up in command of the Army of the Potomac. After the blood-bath of Antietam, McClellan—who with great difficulty had just driven ["Stonewall"] Jackson and Lee

---

with the result that before the ceremony was over his hand was swollen and distorted. Pious and obsequious people said little prayers for him as they passed; others found it a good occasion to make little speeches. "I am very happy to meet you, General. May God bless and keep you!" "General, this is my eldest son, William Mason. Willie, tell General Grant the little prayer you say for him each night." (Willie is about to oblige, but the committee member is dragging him away.) "I knew you were going to win, General." "May I kiss you, General?" The General excuses himself. "Don't you remember me, General? Last year at West Point?" "A lot of people here, General! It's only right, General; it's no more than what you deserve!" "Hello, old comrade! Let's trade a few yarns about Chattanooga!" "I had a brother in the 29th—did you know him?" These remarks and many others were made to the General, who solemnly and patiently let everyone "pump his hand up and down," helpless to resist the onslaught of his well-wishers.

out of Maryland—was too lethargic to follow up his victory. Burnside assumed command and crossed the Rappahannock, but then dashed his army to bits at Fredericksburg where Jackson and [General James] Longstreet had taken up strong defensive positions. In his retirement he retains—along with the last rays of his former glory—the only fame that can't be denied him: that of being one of the handsomest men in America. He really is a fine figure of a man—fleshy without being fat, dapper although thick-necked, broad-shouldered and full-cheeked; he has warm, melting black eyes. He is very carefully, even impeccably turned out and looks very much like a resplendent colonel of the English Horse Guards. His manners are refined and graceful—indeed, almost effeminate. At dinner where I met him he had a finicky way of handling his knife and spoon which shows off his plump hands. He is not the usual type of democratic general. He would show to better advantage, it seems to me, on the parade ground or in the finicky protocol of peacetime maneuvers than in the rough-and-ready close combat of American warfare.

I could also describe to you the bristling mustache, the self-satisfied expression, the peremptory and overbearing manner of General [Nathaniel P.] Banks, a former lawyer and the former Speaker of the House of Representatives, who has recently turned warrior. But I should like first to tell you about Congress and an extraordinary debate that gives an excellent insight into the American character—its ruthless brutality as well as its imperturbable generosity.

You are doubtless aware of the systematic cruelty the Rebels have shown to Federal prisoners-of-war. The latter have literally been spared nothing, for their lot has included starvation, nakedness, exposure to cold and the severity of the other elements, mistreatment of all sorts, execution by a firing-squad on the slightest pretext and moral degradation even worse than physical suffering. They have been forced to wallow like pigs, without clothing or shelter, in stinking ditches into which they had been driven by rifle-fire like a herd of animals. I believe that no modern nation has ever displayed such barbaric behavior. These atrocities have created in the North a very natural reaction of hatred and desire for vengeance. Last year the authorities began to reduce rations to Rebel prisoners, refuse them blankets or to furnish these only in exchange for cotton delivered by the Confederate government and, in general, to institute harsher and more oppressive disciplinary rules and to choose victims for those human sacrifices called "reprisals."[1]

---

[1] In this paragraph and in much of this chapter Duvergier de Hauranne here presents a distinctly Northern view of the prisoner-of-war problem and of Southern prison camps in particular. In fact, conditions were very nearly as bad as he describes, but grave abuses existed in Northern camps such as Elmira, New York, and Camp Douglas in Chicago, as well as at Libby Prison, Belle Isle and Andersonville. The statistics are unsatisfactory, but they show that the mortality rate was a little over 12 percent in Northern prisons and 15.5 percent for Southern camps. Disease, caused by the lack of sanitation, and exposure seem to have been the main causes of death in all Civil War prison camps. See William B. Hesseltine, *Civil War Prisons* (Columbus: Ohio State University Press, 1930) p. 256.

Today the Senate is preparing to adopt measures specifying the kinds of retaliatory suffering to be inflicted upon these hostages who must suffer for the crimes of others. Senator [Henry Smith] Lane of Indiana has presented a petition from the citizens of Fort Wayne asking that Rebel prisoners be guarded exclusively by Union soldiers formerly interned in Southern camps so that the Rebels may receive similar treatment.

"Some people fear," he said, "that reprisals will make the war even bloodier. I don't give a damn how much blood is spilled! I'd like to make every river run red with the blood of traitors!"

Mr. [Benjamin F.] Wade [of Ohio] then expressed regret for the sympathy shown by the people of the North toward the population of Rebel Savannah. The President has seen fit to stretch out his hand to protect a fugitive Rebel, Mr. Foote[2]—threatening the Confederate government with reprisals if a hair of his head is harmed. "As for me," said Mr. Wade, "I wouldn't hit a dog in reprisal if he was caught biting a traitor!"

Finally, in spite of all the humanitarian opposition of Mr. Sumner, the Committee on the Conduct of the War has recommended that the measures be adopted, and has urged the President to exact an eye for an eye and a tooth for a tooth from the Rebels. I am not surprised at an exasperation that is so well justified. Nevertheless, there is something terrifying in this wholesale cruelty which Americans are taking too much for granted. They are less intemperate in their deeds than in their words, and

[2]See above, pp. 173-4 and 328.

their motives are even less extreme than their actions. The day after adopting these implacable resolutions, they will shake hands [with the enemy] like
courteous duellists or even embrace one another
like old friends who have been reconciled. In the
Army of the James soldiers from the two camps
meet peaceably between the lines, talk with one
another, trade supplies and play cards. Francis P.
Blair—the elder Blair—of "Lincolndom" (as the
Rebel papers call the Union) was seen the other day
on the streets of Richmond where he was recognized and greeted with joy by many old friends,
though for the local newspapers he has become a
sworn enemy whom they insult in print every
morning. Certainly it is a fine thing not to hold
grudges; but I believe that toleration, when carried
to such extremes, is a little too much like indifference or insensitivity.

Another important vote in Congress, though disguised under the innocuous cloak of a simple
amendment to the budget, is one that makes the
Republic of Mexico the only government [of that
country] recognized by the United States, thus denying to the [French-supported] Empire even the
partial satisfaction of an implied American neutrality between the two belligerents. This measure was
introduced without fanfare and was offered as an
innocent change in wording. The item covering the
expenses of the American legation in Mexico came
up quietly in its turn along with several similar
items for Senate approval. The original text read
"legation in Mexico." A senator rose and asked
that the "Republic of Mexico" be substituted

for "Mexican government," and this was accepted without debate, without incident, by a unanimous, tacit agreement that provides a significant clue to public opinion. This resolution, the newspapers are saying, is the Emperor Maximilian's death warrant and "seals the doom of the so-called empire of Mexico"; it will put an end to all intervention by European monarchial powers on this republican continent.

Already popular writers are advising Jefferson Davis to earn a pardon for his crimes by going to Mexico to fight in defense of democracy's threatened principles. These half-serious proposals will be translated into a mandate of the people the moment conditions become favorable. A policy of invasion and annexation is not an exclusive privilege of despotic governments. Republics can even boast of having over monarchies the advantage that, because the majority of the people is sovereign, it is in fact responsible to no one and is free to break faith without compunctions since its plighted word binds too many consciences to have effective power over any single one. In absolute monarchies there is always a dissident minority that will accuse the ruler of bad faith; but in a democracy right and wrong are just a matter of majority votes and it can be truly said that in that case the very idea of what is just flows from the general consent of the citizenry.

Therefore I will concede, if you like, that certain European states have reason to watch with a suspicious eye this vigorous reëstablishment of the American nation at the very moment when it threatens to become warlike and imperialistic. Unhappily the only constant motive for the behavior of nations is self-interest and will remain so until that distant day when all mankind comes to form one vast federation on the model of the United States. Until then, and as long as the world continues to muddle along from one civil war or international conflict to another, each one will simply be playing its assigned part if it casts jealous eyes on its neighbors—the Europeans will be mistrustful of American power, while the Americans will annex neighboring territories in the name of liberty and will drive Europe back to the Old World in order to remain in full possession of the New. I save all my anger for those who hide their hostile designs behind a mask of neutrality and hypocritical good will, only to stab in the back an enemy they dare not attack face to face.

January 22, 1865

MR. SUMNER has made an eloquent speech opposing reprisals. He stands firm with generosity and moderation and rejects vengeance in the name of strict justice. He says that the commission of one crime does not excuse a second one and that the reply to the enemy can only be one that is consistent with the principles of humanity and Christian charity. Congress only half agrees and I begin to think that, if I were an American, I should agree with them. I've just read the report of the detailed inquiry made at the expense of the Sanitary Commission on the actual condition of the [Federal] prisoners. This is not some collection of vague charges; it is an array of authenticated facts attested to under oath by a thousand eye-witnesses. The men who gathered them are doctors, judges, members of the clergy— persons of known veracity and integrity. The witnesses' depositions have been carefully compared and checked with each other. These are merely facts, but what a shocking light they shed on the rebellion and its defenders! You shall judge for yourself from the following details.

When the Rebels capture a prisoner, they begin by taking his money, his coat, his blanket and all his most necessary clothing. He is left nearly naked, or else they give him in exchange some filthy rags. He is then taken to a prison. In Libby Prison in Richmond[3] there are four thousand men. These "Yankee dogs" are lucky to be there because they are mercifully provided with shelter. One of them, Joseph Grider, reports that he was one of 214 men held in a single room, the windows of which were without glass, where they were so crowded they could scarcely move and were compelled to jump up and down at night in order to keep from freezing. During all of last winter, twelve hundred officers of all ranks lived shut up in low, damp rooms, each man having a space of about ten by two feet in which to move about.

They had to keep away from the windows because, if anyone carelessly chanced to get near them and showed so much as a head or an arm, sentries

[3] Libby Prison, used mainly for Union officers, was brought to Chicago in the 1880's and reassembled stone for stone. Its walls were subsequently incorporated into the Coliseum and it became what it now is, a museum of Civil War memorabilia.

Engraving, after a Photograph

From *Harper's History of the Great Rebellion*

Libby Prison, Richmond, Virginia

stationed outside would fire on them without pity, waiting for the opportunity with rifles at the ready, eyes glued to the sights, like hunters lying in wait for game. For the Rebel soldiers it became an amusing sport that they relished greatly. They would challenge one another as at a pigeon-shoot, each one laying a bet that he would bag a Yankee while on duty, and the winners gained great fame for their marksmanship. Not a day passed without someone being wounded or killed. Sometimes, carried away by enthusiasm for the game, the guards would leave their posts at the foot of the wall in order to find a better vantage-point from which to aim more accurately. When a complaint was made to Major [Thomas P.] Turner, the commandant of the prison, he made this charming reply: "Our boys have to keep in practice." Dick Turner, his underling and apt apprentice, added with a string of oaths, "You damned Yankees get better treatment than you deserve!"

But all that was only a minor annoyance. The prisoners hardly noticed it, for they were starving to death. In the officers' cells at Libby Prison the daily ration was a piece of corn bread the size of a man's fist, full of straw and worms, weighing about half a pound, and two ounces of beef. The bread was so hard they called it "Ironclad" (like the armored cruisers) and they could eat it only by scraping off a few crumbs at a time. In the beginning, as provided by the exchange-of-prisoners agreement signed by both armies, they sometimes received clothing, food or tobacco which they chewed to kill the pangs of hunger. These supplies were sent to them from the

North by their wives and mothers or by the Sanitary Commission, that marvelous institution that carefully watches over them all like one big family.

Suddenly, in January, 1864, the distribution of parcels was stopped and the guards seized the provisions. One day a certain Lieutenant McGinnis recognized a piece of his own clothing being worn by a prison employee. By then the hunger was frightful. The high-ranking officers who had been allowed to keep their blankets offered to sell them to the guards for a handful of rice; the latter simply snatched them and had a good laugh at their own cleverness. The prisoners were reduced to hunting for bones they could gnaw.* Once, by lifting a beam that ran under the floor, they got into a cellar where there was a great quantity of provisions—flour, turnips and potatoes. They had a great feast, but were caught. As punishment they were thrown

---

* All these details were vouched for to me personally by a French soldier serving in the Union army who was captured in January, 1865, at the very moment I was writing the above lines. By a miracle he was able to escape. "When I was taken," he told me, "the Confederates took everything I had on me, leaving me just enough to cover my nakedness. I was put into a low-ceilinged, crowded, stinking room where the floor was covered with mud and offal. I'll never forget the sight that first met my eyes—pale ghosts, all skin and bones, half naked, unshaven, with sunken eyes, squatting or sprawling in the muck. Several of them were snarling at one another like dogs over old bones they were trying to gnaw. They were no longer human beings. The daily ration consisted of a small portion of rice broth, mostly water, two mouthfuls of mouldy corn bread hard as a rock and a piece of meat no bigger than my thumb. I was there only two weeks. I'm sure that if it had been a month, I'd have died of hunger."

into cells at the river level, so crowded they all had to remain standing up. As men died, their corpses were thrown into a cellar open to animals running loose in the streets so that pigs, dogs and rats came to feed on them.

Finally, the supreme touch of horror, we are assured that explosives had been placed beneath the prison. At any rate, the guards made no secret of their intention to "blow it all to Hell" with its inmates inside if Richmond should be taken. When General [Judson] Kilpatrick made his daring raid into Virginia, Major Turner told his captives that "if Kilpatrick comes to free you, it won't do you any good because I'll blast you to pieces first." These, it seems, are the atrocities being committed just a few steps from President Davis's official residence, practically under the eyes of General Lee!

In the prison for ordinary soldiers at Belle Isle [Virginia] it is even worse. Belle Isle is a sandy, low-lying island without vegetation in the James River, not far from Richmond. Earthen walls have been built there surrounding a small camp covering two to three acres into which ten or twelve thousand men are crowded. Each one has a space about three by eight feet to move around in, hardly enough room to make a grave. Here the wretched men don't even have a roof over their heads, neither wooden huts nor lean-tos made of branches. They have been given nothing but a few old pieces of torn, worn-out, rotten canvas which have wound up in the hands of the strongest or luckiest. In that part of the country, covered by some of the finest forests in the world, there is apparently not one scrap of wood that can be given them to keep off the sun and rain. Most of the prisoners must go bare-headed, with no protection against either the scorching summer sun or the icy winds of winter, with no coats, no shoes, no blankets, dressed only in disintegrating rags that scarcely suffice to cover their loins.

Picture to yourself the horrors of such a life in this cruel season on that bare island exposed to frost and snow; imagine the gray water of the river that carries corpses and blocks of ice as it swirls along, with two inches of ice forming on the water barrels every night, with the north wind blowing at gale force, and these miserable wretches blue with cold, shivering and huddling together in the ditches to keep the spark of life glowing faintly in their bodies and lying down at night in close rows "like pigs in winter." Every morning there are stiff, frozen bodies that will never rise again at the ends of the rows! Some dig pits in the sand, while others run in place throughout the night to keep from freezing. How horrible!

And this is still only a part of their sufferings, for they are also dying of hunger. Their rations are a grisly joke: twelve ounces of under-cooked corn bread full of sand, straw and mould, sometimes a kind of sour-tasting soup containing spiders and caterpillars and, more rarely, a little spoiled meat, hardly a mouthful. As one of them said on his death-bed, "There is no name for our sufferings." One Hiram Neal reports: "I woke up one night and realized I was chewing on my sleeve." Sometimes they had the good fortune to pick up morsels of stale bread their guards threw to them. A dog that had wandered into the camp was torn apart and devoured in an instant. The cold, the starvation and the vermin cause all sorts of dreadful diseases: fever, dysentery, scurvy and tuberculosis make gaps each day in their ranks and these are soon filled by newcomers. The only hospital in the prison was a tent with a bare earthen floor where the invalids lay on straw with logs for pillows. "If you saw a dying horse," said one of these unfortunates to the commissioners conducting the investigation, "wouldn't you put a little straw under his head? Would you allow him, in his death-throes, to beat his head against a block of wood?"

Sometimes, when prisons like Libby, Belle Isle and Danville were too full, some of their inmates were loaded along with their blood and filth into cattle cars and sent by railroad to Andersonville in Georgia, notorious for the glorious exploits of General [John H.] Winder and of Captain [Henry] Wirz.[4] It covers a large parallelogram of swampy land, some twenty-five acres in extent, through which runs a small stream that half covers the area. For upwards of a year, 28,000, 30,000 and finally close to 35,000 men had to crouch in this quagmire under the muzzles of five batteries of cannon loaded with canister shot. There was no shelter of any kind, few prisoners had any clothes and many were completely naked; they were given eight ounces of

---

[4] Winder died before the end of the war; Wirz was brought to trial before a court-martial of Northern officers who did not accept his defense that he acted under orders from Winder and did his best to mitigate their harshness; he was executed by hanging.

the usual mouldy bread, two ounces of spoiled pork, sometimes a little rice. Having no way to cook anything, they often bolted their food raw.

The water of the brook was contaminated, and the swamp soon became an open sewer. Yet this was their only drinking water, and they died by thousands. Every day more than a hundred corpses were collected. Since those sent out to bury them were allowed to bring back a little wood, the cadavers were fought over as beasts fight over their prey. If anyone took a step over the boundary line, even though he was only leaning over to pick a blade of grass or gather a piece of dead wood, he was instantly shot dead. Men overcome with despair were seen to cross the line deliberately so the guards would shoot them. Others fell into insensibility or imbecility. I would never finish if I tried to tell you all the hideous and horrifying details. On top of everything else, the torturers are often infamous bandits who strip their victims' bodies and hold them for ransom. And these are the humane ways of the "knight-errants" of slavery!

You have been told that the North itself was to blame for the sufferings of its soldier-prisoners, that by refusing for such a long time to exchange prisoners they were deliberately abandoning them to the tortures of the Southern prison camps. But recall to mind the conditions under which the exchanges were broken off, the insulting and provocative arrogance of the South in refusing to treat the officers and men of black regiments as prisoners-of-war. In their view, the black soldiers in the armies of the United States were merely fugitive slaves and they

claimed the right either to shoot them for disobedi-
ence or to use them or sell them as slaves. As for the
officers, they were considered to be criminals and
were handed over to the state authorities to be shot
or hung. Could the North put up with that? Wasn't
it the Federal government's duty to protest by every
means against a treacherous enemy who treated the
soldiers and citizens of the United States as criminals or slaves? Who would claim that President
Lincoln could have acted otherwise without forfeit-
ing his dignity and the nation's honor?

The South then falls back on a plea of poverty,
claiming that its own troops are no better fed than
the prisoners. But is that any excuse for so many
needless atrocities, committed wantonly out of a
mad desire for revenge or for the pleasure of inflicting pain? We have heard altogether too much talk
about this "fratricidal" war and about the abominable deeds on both sides. But you should save your
indignation for the ferocity of the South. I concede
that one could point to atrocities committed by the
North in reprisal, to revolting and deplorable acts
that also deserve the name of murder and torture. It
is true that in Missouri ten men were recently shot
to death for crimes of which they were innocent,
crimes for which a so-called court of justice decreed
that they were to pay the price. It is true that in this
guerrilla warfare, where the fighters are more like
wild beasts than men, the combatants on both sides
have given free rein to their most savage impulses. It
is likewise true that Congress has come close to voting systematic measures of retaliation; but these
harsh acts would be no more than a delayed and

reluctant response to long and intolerable provocations. At the very beginning of the war the cruelty practiced by the South did nothing to diminish the feelings of brotherly humanity which the men of the North felt for the wounded or captive enemy. On the battlefield of Gettysburg fallen soldiers of both armies were gathered up without discrimination and cared for together. Hospitals for war prisoners were set up with the same charity, in the same numbers and with the same concern as for patriot-soldiers. Near Baltimore there still exists a hospital for prisoners where the pro-Confederate ladies of the city make visits of mercy. Even in the camps, where it became necessary to place them under the guard of armed regiments, they had houses, beds, books, games, schools, food in every way comparable to that of the [Union] army. Even today, what is being done in retaliation for the atrocities committed by the enemy? What is the policy of the [Federal] government, which is accused of starving its prisoners? Congress orders it to give them everything they really need and to deny them only what is superfluous. Apparently nobody claims they are being treated with excessive tenderness.

In the South half the prisoners die within a year. Those who survive reap no benefit, for the most part, except a more protracted period in which to wait for death. In the North, in the large prisons at Fort Delaware, Johnson's Island and Point Lookout, the Rebels seem able to regain their strength for future campaigns. Yesterday, right here in Washington, I went to have a look at Lincoln Hospital, a huge and admirably run establishment

where friends and foes are mingled in the same
wards and receive equally good care. It is in the
field when prisoners are exchanged between the
two armies that the contrast is so striking between
the healthy, well nourished men, newly clothed at
the expense of the United States, and the walking
cadavers, some crawling on their knees, eaten up by
vermin, covered with sores, their feet frozen, their
hands benumbed, blind, deaf, mute or reduced to
idiocy and all showing the effects of starvation, who
are returning from the prisons of the South. You
should read the report made by the commissioners
on their recent visit to the Annapolis hospital! "No
words," they said, "can give the frightful, hideous
spectacle of these human skeletons, with their skin
stretched tight over their skulls, with every rib
showing, with no flesh on their bones, who manage
somehow to move and turn themselves over feebly
like living creatures. . . . " I have in front of me as I
write some photographs of these walking ghosts.

Have I told you how, if some of these wretches
tried to cling to life by betraying their flag and enlisting in the Rebel army so as to get something to
eat, their jailers scornfully referred to them as "gal-
vanized [resurrected] Yankees?" The Rebel government, which claims lack of resources as an excuse
for barbarities worthy of Tamerlane or Soulouque,[5]

[5] Faustin Soulouque (1782-1867) was a Haitian black who
was proclaimed Emperor in 1849 as Faustin I; he was noted
for his wanton cruelty. Tamerlane (c.1336-1404) was a
Mongol conqueror, also celebrated for extreme cruelty; after
taking certain cities, he slaughtered thousands of the defenders (perhaps 80,000 at Delhi) and built pyramids of
their skulls.

on the other hand, treats [Federal] deserters very
well, pays them a bounty, gives them free passage to
Europe or Canada or wherever they want to go.

Now consider the reprisals discussed by Congress, the pressing need for them, the opposition
that has been raised against them—unyielding opposition by Mr. Sumner and some others with less
bold but nevertheless real opposition by tougher-
minded colleagues. Note the limitation put upon
Mr. Lane's proposal by these words which remove
virtually all its sting: "Provided that they are in
conformity with the customs of war among civilized
peoples." Recall that *carte blanche* as to the means
to be adopted was given to this good-hearted President, whose humane principles are well known to
you. Doesn't all this add up to a *threat* to take reprisals rather than actual retaliation? Don't forget, either, that there are a hundred thousand families
who have had a father, a brother or a son killed an
inch at a time or maimed for life far away from the
field of battle by an enemy who has neither honor
nor pity. And if, once the war is over, those who are
chiefly to blame for these crimes escape their well-
deserved punishment, then you may wonder at the
clemency of the American people.

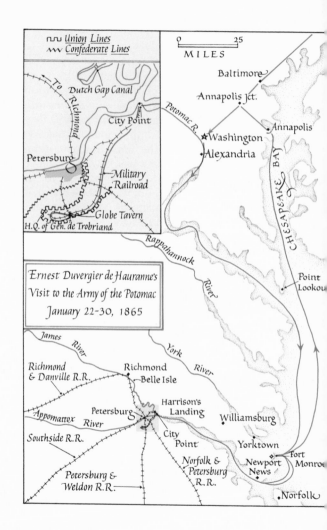

Union Lines
Confederate Lines

0   25
MILES

Baltimore

Annapolis Jct.

Annapolis

Potomac R.

★Washington
Alexandria

CHESAPEAKE BAY

To Richmond

Dutch Gap Canal

City Point

Petersburg

Military
Railroad

Globe Tavern

H.Q. of Gen. de Trobriand

Rappahannock

River

Point
Lookout

Ernest Duvergier de Hauranne's
Visit to the Army of the Potomac
January 22-30, 1865

James

River

York

River

Richmond

Richmond
& Danville R.R.

Belle Isle

Harrison's
Landing

Williamsburg

Appomattox

Petersburg

River

City
Point

Yorktown

Southside R.R.

Newport
News

Fort
Monroe

Norfolk &
Petersburg
R.R.

Petersburg &
Weldon R.R.

Norfolk

12

With the Army of the Potomac

FOR THREE DAYS I have been with the Army of the Potomac. The day before my departure from New York, General de Trobriand[1] who, despite his long residence in America, has lost none of his French manners or attitudes, came to spend ten days' leave with his family. He invited me to visit him at his headquarters on the extreme left wing of General Grant's forces. I knew the two armies were in winter quarters and that except for daily shelling near Dutch Gap, on the far right of the Army of the James (from which [General Benjamin F.] Butler was just removed), there was a tacit agreement not to waste ammunition before the great battles begin. The only enemy to be found at that time in the camp of General Grant was the clear, cold weather, which kept the soldiers shivering in their tents and stiffened my fingers inside my fur-lined gloves. For

---

[1] Brigadier-General Régis de Trobriand was a naturalized American whose French forbears boasted of strong military traditions. Coming to the United States in 1850, he had made a successful career in journalism as theatrical and society editor of the *Courrier des Etats-Unis*, a French-language newspaper in New York. At the outbreak of the Civil War he obtained an army commission with the help of influential New York friends and rose through his own exceptional ability to command a brigade in the Army of the Potomac during the last year of the war.

some months now, the most peace-loving people have come here, even women, and it took a special order from the commanding general to keep the officers from setting up housekeeping with their families. I gratefully accepted the kind offer of hospitality, and last Sunday, supplied with a pass in the handwriting of President Lincoln, I left with the general on the steamboat for City Point.

The trip was long and monotonous. Instead of the twenty-four hours usually needed for the voyage, it took us at least forty. The Potomac was partly blocked by ice through which we had to make a path with our thrashing paddle wheels and the fog which settled down in the evening obliged us to spend the night at anchor near the mouth of the river. Along those low, flat shores indented by deep inlets where the waves break on long, sandy beaches, the tide flows gently up the length of the estuaries and is neither violent nor rapid enough to break and scatter the ice. In winter, boats must break their way through a solid crust of ice that surrounds them and sometimes grips them as in a vice.

The previous day the weather had been the worst of the year, a kind of bad weather that is typical of the American climate and is totally unlike anything experienced under our European skies. The wind was icy and there fell in gusts something which was not rain, nor hail, nor melting snow, nor fine, light sleet, but bits of solid ice which covered the ground with a slippery sand that soon formed a thick crust. Nothing more miserable can be imagined than the Siberian aspect this coating gave to objects and men. One could imagine that they were clothed in snowy rags, stained remnants of a curtain of hoar-frost reduced to tatters by rain and sun. Horses' manes were encrusted with ice which formed an armor on their backs and icicles on their tails. Trees were completely covered with a coating of ice like flies enclosed in amber or fruits preserved in syrup. If there had been a ray of sunshine, it would have caused a diamond to sparkle at the end of each twig, making the countryside glitter like a box of jewels, but the sky was gray and leaden. The banks of the Potomac, which I saw last year resplendent with foliage, were instead a dull, dirty white. Its waters, which I saw one evening at sunset reflecting all the many colors of a painter's palette, now lay yellow and muddy under a pale crust. The ice broke and cracked under our weight, the pieces floating in our wake, but we moved forward only at a snail's pace. We went past the old commercial port of Alexandria, standing like a sentinel on the Virginia bank; it was retaken from the Rebels at the beginning of the war. We passed Mount Vernon, once the home and now the tomb of the father of the American Republic. Then there was only darkness, lack of motion, silence, impatience and boredom.

The only passengers were officers, soldiers and army employees. I saw the young, beardless face of a veteran, still of school age, almost a child, who had already taken part in six campaigns. I saw the strong, square-cut figure of a gray-bearded Indiana farmer, who enlisted as a soldier at the age of fifty and has won a colonel's epaulettes at sword-point. There was also a Canadian adventurer full of jokes and a German artillery-man, slow-moving and

phlegmatic, awkward and remote behind his large
blonde moustache, his long saber hanging down to
his heels. Then there was a whole crowd of hangers-
on in odds and ends of uniforms and a number of
suppliers and merchants in city clothes.

As happens everywhere, I was observed with curiosity, the object of much speculation; soon I was
assailed with questions. "Who is that general? From
which corps, which division, which brigade? Are
you his aide-de-camp or a member of his staff? How
did you come to be so friendly with him?" I briefly
satisfied their curiosity with all the dignity lent to
me by my traveling companion's rank. While our
companions gathered around the stove beneath one
of the two lamps, thriftily turned low by the captain, the general and I enjoyed a meandering conversation which in a few hours made us firm friends,
although we had been strangers the day before.

This well-educated soldier and man of the world
is a very attractive person. He has not been false to
the tradition of his military ancestors, but in addition he combines the sensitivity of an artist with the
fearlessness of his new profession. When an old soldier tells about his campaigns, it is clear that long
years of experience have made him insensitive to
the awe-inspiring horrors of his occupation. He inspires in us more astonishment than sympathy, and
we come close to being repelled by such inhuman
courage. Grapeshot is his element; to his hardened
senses, death and mutilation are just a game. He
speaks of the dead, of the wounded, of carnage, as
an executioner can talk about torture or a sur-
geon about operations. He describes a mine that

Engraving by A. H. Ritchie   Courtesy of Albert Krebs, Paris

General P. Régis de Trobriand

explodes, blowing up hundreds of men in a blast, a
sinking ship riddled with cannon-balls, an assault
column decimated by artillery-fire, mowed down
by canister-shot, the bloody breeches made in this
human mass, which in order to get out of danger
can only rush forward, furious and out of breath,
over the bodies of the dead and wounded. He tells
of a battle lasting two days and two nights in which
friends and enemies hunt and kill each other in the
darkness, of a regiment that goes into battle 600
strong and returns with only 50 men. All these details in the mouth of an old soldier seem only a
cold, dry statement of fact. But when a man is new
to this trade of war, he experiences poignant emotions that color his words. His descriptions are ani-
mated and vivid at the same time that they are horrifying. After witnessing the heroic effects of the
will-power that holds them under control, it is good
to see the expression of natural human emotions.

The next day we awoke on the Potomac River.
We raised anchor, reached Point Lookout, a sandy
promontory on Chesapeake Bay at the end of the
Maryland peninsula, where 10,000 Rebel prisoners
are imprisoned, then rounded the cape and went on
to Fortress Monroe[2] on our right. The dark, flat
coast of Virginia showed up as a line on the horizon. We met occasional gun-boats on patrol and

[2]South of the entrance to Chesapeake Bay, Fortress Monroe—or as it is now invariably called, Fort Monroe—was usually referred to by the former name during the Civil War, a
usage followed by Generals U. S. Grant and B. F. Butler as
well as Duvergier de Hauranne. The present-day usage will
be substituted in the ensuing pages.

flotillas of supply barges, like floating islands, set in motion by a small steamship in their center. The coastline fell away, the sea became heavier and we rounded Point Comfort. We sailed past the mouth of the York River, made famous by the siege of Yorktown, and we entered the calm waters of the harbor at Fort Monroe, whose banks were visible at night because of the lights burning everywhere. After another night's rest, we left at daybreak.

We were then on the James River; on the left was Norfolk, a small piece of eastern Virginia that has been brought under the authority of the Federal government once again. Behind Norfolk lies an immense area of swampy forest known by the mournful name of Dismal Swamp, a place of terror in which many a lost traveler has sunk without a trace; this is the setting in which the poet Longfellow has his old fugitive slave seek safety amid the underbrush and poisonous snakes of the swamp.[3] To our right lies the peninsula made famous by McClellan's bloody campaign, scene of the first costly lesson learned by the inexperienced army of America. The river itself is as wide as a bay, yellow and rough, dotted with floating chunks of ice. Farther along it becomes narrower, and one can take in at a glance the harmonious tableau framed by its banks. There are immense forests of pine, cliffs of brittle rocks with piles of debris at their base, leafless oaks with sturdy branches mingling with the sombre tufts of the pines, gray lines of tall, symmetrical

[3] The allusion is to Longfellow's poem *The Fugitive Slave* in which the runaway slave takes refuge from the bloodhounds pursuing him in the depths of the Dismal Swamp.

trees with their branches spread out like fans, without a single yellow or brown leaf to festoon the bare grayness of trunks and branches, and everywhere a thick mantle of green undergrowth spread over the hills. That scene, revealed to us by the cold light of the winter sun, was hard to reconcile in my mind with the splendor of the summer season in this region of lush natural fertility. The river meandered through the valley; on its banks one could see that land had once been cultivated, but today it is lying fallow and exposed to winter floods. On the shore, and even extending out into the river, rose strange trees whose massive, knotted trunks, rising above pyramids of roots, look out across the waters that wash over or cover their bizarre pedestals. These misshapen giants of the valley might have been supports of some huge breakwaters uprooted by the river. In summer when covered with leaves their dense green crowns must form an archipelago of grace and freshness against the watery background.

A few white houses line the banks on our left, and traces of deserted plantations are seen everywhere; but on the right even huts are rare, and one can see the tangled, impenetrable forest where McClellan's army had to cut its way with axes, dragging cannons and wagons over the fallen trunks of great trees. Here the ruined settlers, reduced to demi-savagery, still harass the few outposts stationed here and there along the shore with ambushes and guerrilla warfare.

At Harrison's Landing, we saw a jetty made of pilings, a fort, a village of tents and cabins, still guarded by a Federal regiment, and a huge swath of grey earth laid bare in the forest by cannon-fire for colonists still to come. It was here that the whole [of McClellan's] army came, worn out by its victories, in that heroic though disastrous retreat which you doubtless remember. Here, within reach of the sea, it reformed itself regiment by regiment and brigade by brigade, waiting month after month for the start of a new campaign that never was fought. The very name of Harrison's Landing recalls to the few survivors of that epic struggle the suffering, anxiety, humiliation, anger and the black and deadly boredom suffered during a long period of idleness while the army's indecisive leaders kept the impatient and disheartened troops in suspense.

The peninsula is full of memories of those already legendary times. People, things and ideas—all have changed almost beyond recognition in three years. The war has swept away more than one generation of soldiers. More than one army has melted away in a single campaign like snow on a warm, sunny day. The survivors of an entire army corps, men who have not finished their three years of service, are no longer numerous enough to fill even one regiment, and the few scarred veterans who survive in the ranks of the new recruits—like people who lived during our Revolution or under the Ancien Régime—are objects of astonishment and respect; they stand out like the remaining isolated columns of a ruined temple which serve to hold up a wall in which some modern builder has incorporated them. Some who were children at the outbreak of war are still nearly beardless, but can say that they have lived a whole century and that death has cut down around them more heads than if their own were white and bowed with years.

Finally we came to City Point, an improvised city, General Grant's great arsenal, the capital of the province consisting of the combined armies of the James and Potomac. For about an hour we had heard in the northwest a series of muffled explosions, sometimes slow-paced, sometimes hurried. It was a cannonade, a very ordinary kind of noise in these parts, but more violent at this moment and more persistent than is customary during these idle days of winter. People hardly bothered to wonder what it meant; the merchant fleet remained at anchor in the estuary; the steamers of all sorts and sizes continued to send out waves as their paths crossed. The docks were littered with bales and boxes; a busy swarm of white and black workers in blue uniforms rushed to and fro and, behind the wooden warehouses bordering the pilings of the jetties, a large locomotive with a clanging bell chugged along, pushing a long train of heavy freight cars. It was running on the Army of the Potomac's own railroad, 19 miles long, which was hastily built in five days by the Corps of Engineers.

This is the way war is waged today. It has little in common with the older warfare of fortresses, of distant expeditions, of tedious sieges and battles in the open countryside, of campaigns decided by the capture of some isolated stronghold or by a strategic victory on some glorious battlefield. We are no longer living in the age of Gustavus Adolphus[4] or

[4] King Gustavus Adolphus of Sweden was one of the greatest commanders of the Thirty Years War (1618-1648).

even Napoleon. The armies themselves form the strongholds which must be taken, and wherever they are stationed the whole region is transformed into a citadel. They do not move freely from one day to the next with their arms and baggage, supplies and munitions, tents and trenching shovels, all carried on the soldiers' backs as Caesar's legions did. The new armies need wagons, long trains of wagons, each drawn by a team of six mules, and temporary railroads. They need whole fleets to keep them supplied, and for this they need seaports. For shelter they need whole cities which rise like magic out of the wilderness. One can play the role of Hannibal or Alexander only in a defenseless country where one's halfhearted opponent is a man like Governor [Joseph E.] Brown in a Georgia as rich in food supplies as it is poor in manpower. Woe to General Sherman if he had found General Lee's army facing him or if he had found it necessary to survive without railroads in a Virginia ravaged and laid waste by war! Impatient people ask why the Army of the Potomac has not yet captured Petersburg when the Army of the West has been able to occupy Georgia. Let them come here before passing judgment and then they will realize how much blood has been paid for every inch of ground won from the narrow and strongly defended circle in which the rebellion is now concentrated.

City Point is located on a small promontory that rises above the confluence of the James and Appomattox Rivers. It is the Balaklava[5] of the American

[5]Balaklava was the principal supply port for the British army operating in the Crimea, 1854-1856.

army and the center of the combined operations
against Richmond and Petersburg. It is here that
Grant, the supreme commander of all the armies,
has established his headquarters. Farther along, on
the James River, first Butler and then his successor,
[General E. O. C.] Ord, occupied the area between
that river and its tributary, the Appomattox; this
river runs in front of the enemy lines up to the
point where the Rebel front crosses it to defend the
southern outskirts of Petersburg. Towards the
southeast [General George G.] Meade commands
the Army of the Potomac which is stretched out in a
semi-circle around that city with its right flank resting on the Appomattox and its left fortified behind
a small stream, Hatcher's Run. [General Philip H.]
Sheridan in the Shenandoah Valley northwest of
Richmond is, as you know, under the command of
General Grant, who went to Washington last week
to coordinate plans with him. Even Sherman himself has only limited discretion in carrying out the
plans made by this "Grand Constable"[6] of the Federal armies.

In recent weeks General Grant has been trying to
extend his left wing, hoping to surround[7] Johnston
and Lee. It is in this area that Richmond has its last
remaining line of communication with the rest of
the South, the railroad to Danville, which the Fed-

[6] The title given under the old French monarchy to the
royal official having nominal command of the armies as well
as general responsibility for military affairs.

[7] Grant's object was to force Lee to extend his lines,
threaten him with encirclement and then prevent him from
joining forces with Johnston in southern Virginia or North
Carolina. This strategy was successful in all respects.

eral troops are approaching step by step. It is now the only artery feeding the Rebel government. It possessed two last year, including the Weldon railroad, twice destroyed, and only six weeks ago torn up by General de Trobriand himself for a distance of thirty miles. The Danville line is now threatened by his outposts and doubtless he will soon attempt to cut it completely. Once this last thread is broken, the Confederate capital will die of starvation, while each part of the fragmented South will be left to shift for itself.

The Federal forces have just captured Fort Fisher, the key to Wilmington, the last commercial port held by the Confederates. The only harbor now open to them is the dangerous and distant port of Galveston, in Texas. Each new movement of the Federal armies is like the stroke of an axe which cuts off another portion of their strength. They claim that these mutilated segments will come to life again like the pieces of a snake, but attempts to regain their unity are in vain and their strength is being used up in agonized convulsions. When once the head is crushed at Richmond, the blind and exhausted body will thenceforward be an easy prey for the conqueror.

But I have wandered far from City Point. The village itself is not very remarkable, being made up of a few recently-built warehouses, some old wooden houses where the generals live, a few canteens under canvas where by strict order neither wine nor brandy is sold, but where we lunched on oyster stew. Beyond, as far as you can see, there are rows of huts, covered for the most part with canvas or branches, interspersed among groves of trees and fortifications. This encampment extends all the way to the other flank of the army, twenty-five or thirty miles from here. I was shown General Grant's headquarters, a small group of rustic cottages in a grove of pine trees. I have not seen the great man himself. My companion visited him and planned to introduce me to General Meade, who would have sent me on, by ricochet, to General Grant, but we learned that Meade has left suddenly for Philadelphia where his son is ill. I regret not having seen these two interesting personages. I had already been obliged to decline an invitation to dine with the President at the White House. You have to expect that some opportunities will slip through your fingers in times as exciting as these.

The military railroad of the Army of the Potomac extends over a distance of twenty miles from City Point to Patrick Station, crossing a plateau across which flow several small streams in their gently sloping valleys. The roadbed is rough and erratic with many rises and dips and it crosses the valleys on crude trestles rather than solid fill. Still, everything runs without difficulty and the only accident has been the explosion of a locomotive which killed five or six men, a mere bagatelle in a war that is devouring lives by the thousands.

We clambered into a freight car for lack of anything better and there we bounced along, sometimes seated on our baggage, sometimes on our feet with our backs braced against the side of the car in order to absorb the engine's wild and unpredictable jerks. Soldiers, officers, generals and civilians were

Photograph, 1865

Wharves and Railroad Terminal at City Point, Virginia

all huddled together in democratic fashion, shivering in the wintry north wind that blew in upon us through the wide-open doors. Some were chewing tobacco and spitting, bombarding us with their liquid projectiles at the fast tempo of one or two shots per minute. Others, including myself, were smoking large cigars in order to keep warm. The soldiers who were clinging to the roof stamped their feet with desperate energy. From time to time there was a sudden lurch and we were thrown forward by an irresistible force, falling over each other in a heap, or else we all lost our balance at the same time and, in our efforts to regain it, found ourselves sitting on the floor before we knew it. Meanwhile, the general and I continued our conversation about the lower realms of philosophy and literature and were descending in a leisurely way from the heights of esthetics to the charming valleys of modern art, when a poor devil of a Negro, having fallen asleep in a squatting position, relaxed his knee-joints and came rolling in between us. Thus rudely awakened, he showed us his large white teeth in one of those broad grins that are so expressive in a black face.

I then began to look about and to consider the strange, monotonous aspect of this broad, treeless plateau, covered just a few months ago by age-old forests. I found it so arid, so trampled, so violated that it seemed to have been slowly devastated over a long succession of centuries. Here and there we came across sparse groves of tall pines, but even these survivors seem to have been affected by the destruction. Huge fallen trunks lie at their feet, chopped down by repeated strokes of the axe. Long

Engraving

*Train about to Cross a Bridge on the U. S. Military Railroad
near Petersburg, Virginia*

From *Harper's History of the Great Rebellion*

mule teams were dragging away their mutilated sections. In one place we saw wagons stuck in mudholes; elsewhere carts bounced painfully over the scraped roots that protruded from the gray, sterile earth. In still another place we saw a small fort complete with ditches, log walls and yellow sand, the outer ramparts protected by *chevaux-de-frise* [rows of pointed stakes driven into logs from four sides] with a tattered flag flying from atop a pole. Everywhere we saw endless rows of huts. They were made of wood and branches with roofs made of canvas and with clay chimneys surmounted by pierced barrels so that only thin streamers of smoke could escape. Every so often there were headquarters surrounded by a fence, and scattered throughout the area was a swarm of men in blue uniforms armed with shovels, spades, axes or guns. This is what a camp of one hundred thousand men is like.

No poor village, no forgotten hamlet, no crumbling peasant's hut offers so dismal a sight as this immense city of mud spread out over the countryside with low, sprawling, mud-plastered burrows like those of a mole, these being frequently half-drowned in a swamp through which the miserable inhabitants plod their way. One always thinks of an army camp as a picturesque and romantic place with rows of white tents, sparkling banners, stacked rifles, convivial groups around the campfire and a fresh, unspoiled wilderness all around. But we see here what war is really like; here the horrors of the battlefield are augmented by misery, ugliness and boredom. "A bivouac," the general said to me, "is gay and picturesque in summer, when you make camp in a new place, pitching your tents on fresh grass or in the shade of a pine forest." But war makes a desert out of a once beautiful and fertile region in a few weeks. It wears out men and materials in a few hours and nations in a few years. I can understand that one might get used to—and even enjoy—the hurricane of battle, but the worst hardship is to have to live afterwards amidst the debris.

We finally neared our destination. Not far away we could see a white house inside the enemy lines. I saw the Confederates' huts, their tents and their earthworks on the other side of the valley. I could see two distant church spires in Petersburg. How many times last year did we hear foolishly premature rumors of the capture of Petersburg! Then it was being attacked from the north; now they are attempting to envelop it from the south so as to sweep the Rebels back toward Richmond. I saw the "Boynton [Boydton] Plank Road," one of the few lines of communication dating back to before the war and the scene since then of so many battles. I saw the railroad leading to Petersburg, the tracks torn up since last summer. On the horizon to my right a conical silhouette loomed up against the sky; this is the observatory built by General Butler opposite his canal at Dutch Gap. Then we crossed the Weldon Railroad, destroyed in December. On the left lay the dark line of the Virginia forests.

It was even more interesting to see flesh-and-blood Rebels. I got a quick look at them as they were running up and down the roadway to keep from freezing while waiting to be taken off to a camp. Are they prisoners? No—they are deserters

who presumably slipped through the lines last
night despite the danger of being shot by both sides.
An empty stomach gives a man courage, and it is
better to run the risk of the bayonet or the gallows
than to freeze or starve to death in the terrible cold
of these winter nights. Now they are content because they are certain at least to eat their fill. However, these fellows are not leaving empty-handed.
See—each one has a blanket draped over his shoulders in place of an overcoat to cover his rags. Where
did they get these articles of luxury? Apparently
the quartermaster has just furnished them at the expense of the Federal authorities since it is known
that the Confederate government gives its defenders
only one blanket for four men. They drank Yankee
coffee this morning and found it better than the
slop made of boiled rye substituted for it by the
ingenious penny-pinching of their rulers. These
poor creatures have their trousers worn out at the
knees, their jackets worn out at the elbows, the
whole outfit without shape or color other than a
muddy yellow. Is that really their uniform? It seems
more like a street-sweeper's tatters. It is the color of
"butternut," which they use because other dyes are
unavailable and it has now become a nickname.
They are still called "graybacks," from the name of
their money[8] and the fact is that they have the dog-

[8]The term "grayback" referred not to the Confederate
money but to the color of the uniform, which was gray as
long as dyestuffs to make gray cloth were available; then
makeshift dyes were used and the most common color was
"butternut" brown. The Confederate currency was predominantly blue.

eared look, the undescribable filth of an old bank-note. Several are mere children, while others are bent and gray. Their long hair, their moronic expressions and their heavy, awkward demeanor make a striking contrast with the smart, martial appearance of their guards. Yet these are the "chivalrous warriors of the South;" the others are only idle Yankees, nothing but mercenaries. Among these "citizen-soldiers" there are few, I am told, who know how to read, so great is the ignorance and inertia of the lower classes in the happy land of slavery. This is the second cornerstone on which Southern aristocracy rests. The poor farmers in Georgia or Carolina are mere tools, almost beasts of burden like the Negroes, who are made to vote like automata and are herded off to the slaughter. To nerve them up to this they are told a thousand stupid lies which they believe implicitly. They are convinced that the Yankees intend to reduce them to slavery, that the black man will soon be exploiting the white man as his property, that the Yankees massacre all new-born infants and that they rape women only to kill them afterwards. Such is the credulity of the Southern "poor white," another sort of slave who will be emancipated and educated by this revolution. These pitiable creatures owe their low state of civilization to the social conditions that spawn slavery and the fine results are no doubt greatly admired by Southern sympathisers.

At last we have arrived. An ambulance drawn by two strong horses, shaggy as bears, jerked us through mud holes and over a corduroy road to the headquarters of the First Brigade, Third Division,

Second Corps of the Army of the Potomac, an exceptionally large brigade and one whose general speaks of it with pride because it can put about 3,000 men into the line of battle. Other brigades, allowing for illness, absence and deaths, can hardly muster 1,500 to 1,600 men. This is true of any army seen close-up, especially those which, like the American army, do not have our useful institution of a replacement battalion [which can be drawn upon] to fill up empty places in the various regiments. An army is a gulf into which men are thrown by the thousands to return only by the hundreds, if indeed they return at all.

The First Brigade is encamped outside the fortified lines of the Army of the Potomac, on recently occupied terrain that is a little less desolate than the neighborhood of City Point. The ground here is firm and dry, which makes the camp healthier and more comfortable. Even the stumps of the great pines that were felled have not yet lost their bark or their pitch, and the grass and undergrowth are still growing roundabout. The headquarters are surrounded by a fence of interwoven green boughs cut from the pines. Over the arched entrance decorated with garlands the general's initials appear in green letters. Inside, along the edges of a small parade ground, are the cabins of the staff officers with the canvas of their tents attached to pointed posts and stretched over the roofs. Another screen of branches with two gates built into it shields the private quarters of the general.

These consist of a corridor or rather an unroofed wooden runway connecting two cabins that have been made as attractive as possible by the rough but ingenious hands of amateur builders. The interior of the little house is hung with oat sacks that have been cut open and nailed to the walls. A sort of flooring has been pieced together out of boards salvaged from empty crates and carefully arranged to cover the well-leveled ground. A bright, crackling fire giving off a piny odor was burning on the hearth, which is made of moulded clay and has two green beams for its chimney throat, and a real chimney with planed pine lumber for the facing and mantelpiece. The door is made of four or five crosspieces covered by stretched canvas; the latch is a thin, flexible piece of lath. The roof is an awning of canvas nailed to the frame of the cabin. This is the sitting-room, furnished with a plain pine table, three folding chairs and a row of hooks to serve as a closet. The bedroom, which opens off the back of the sitting-room, is simply a tent with a small cast-iron stove that is lighted on below-freezing nights. The bed, a foot and a half wide, is made entirely of straps and blankets.

What I've just described is a palace for a soldier. The other cabin, similar to the first, but without chairs, with only a slat bed mounted on four rickety legs, is reserved for guests and "distinguished foreigners." Each of these little cottages has its screen of greenery and its own outhouse whose ingenious and simple construction combines comfort with economy. Farther along is the officers' mess, less solidly built, always full of acrid fumes on account of a smoking chimney; its roof was made from a discarded tent through which the sky is visible. I spent most of my time there, hunched over a bed of oak-wood coals that did little to keep off the penetrating chill, roasting one side without warming the other. We tried in vain to warm ourselves by drinking boiled coffee, whiskey and "bitters," meanwhile breathing the country air and working up the appetite of an ogre without leaving the fireside. In back, at a respectful distance from the little enclosed area, is a roughly-built stable made like the "corrals" of the Argentine plains: it consists of a narrow enclosure fenced in by tall posts driven into the ground and is surmounted by a rustic roof made of pine boughs whose needles are still green.

A bed of wooden boards covered with five blankets under such a roof is not very warm on nights when a glass of water turns to solid ice and even the ink freezes in its bottle inside my portable writing-desk. My first night in camp was therefore rather unpleasant. It is said that cold makes you dull, but I found that on the contrary it woke me up. Furthermore, all the unaccustomed noises of an army, the drums answering each other, the fifes and bass drums parading through the whole camp playing strange music, the trumpets sounding assembly calls and alarms from time to time, the echoing hooves of horses galloping over the frozen ground, the clacking of scabbards and sabers, the loud footsteps of patrols and sentries, the sound of conversation and laughter, the officers' commands, the rowdy noise made by a passing battalion, but especially the crescendo of bugles and drums, beating out in unison a sort of warrior's march while distant cannon added their solemn, rolling tones in a voice like thunder—

all this put me on the alert for some order from our commanders summoning us unexpectedly to action.

I got up and opened the door. The night was beautiful, starry and clear, but there was no sign of approaching dawn. This could not be the ordinary camp reveille. The cold sent me back to my blankets, but the uproar did not let up. The cannon spoke more and more loudly; the salvoes followed each other at a faster tempo and without let-up. What was happening? Was I going to witness a battle? I tried, during intervals in the cannonade, to see if I could identify the sound of imaginary rifle-fire in the distant drum-beat. Unable to tell what was happening, I finally fell asleep. When I opened my eyes again, it was almost dawn. Everything was quiet and serene; no one was yet moving about in the neighboring tents. Had I dreamed it all?

Later I was told that there had in fact been "heavy firing" during the night near Dutch Gap, no doubt set off by a salvo fired by Rebel cannoneers at the Federal batteries. High water has finally cleared from the canal the debris that had originally encumbered it following the great underground blast, with the result that Butler's huge excavation now offers not only a clear line of fire to the Confederate artillery, but also a direct and poorly defended passage through our lines.[9] For two days we have been waiting for the newspapers to learn the details of the business, but no papers or letters have arrived. Tonight the cannon fire has started again, but I won't be able to tell you the reason until I get back to Washington.

[9] See Chapter 9, footnote 8, p. 298.

You would expect the army to be the best place in the world to keep track of the events of a war. Nowhere, in fact, can news be more up-to-date or more complete than at the headquarters of the commanding general at City Point. But as for the corps commanders and lesser officers, they are only machines that control other machines. They perhaps may be allowed a certain discretion in the execution of general orders given them, but they know only their own assigned task and do not even know the nature of the larger operation in which they are taking part. As for the great maneuvers that had impressed me so much, I learned that during the night 300 men of the brigade had received an order to man the advance posts. That was what had troubled my untrained ear and disturbed my sleep as though I had been a raw recruit.

We mounted horses after lunch to visit various nearby headquarters. First we saw Major-General [Gershom] Mott, commander of our division, a tall handsome man with beautiful manners, a gentle face expressive of good will and the appearance of a true gentleman. He is said to be immensely rich and his sacrifice is a remarkable example of patriotism on the part of a fifty-year-old man for whom life has always been very easy. He began four years ago as the colonel of a regiment he had raised himself and his general's epaulettes, won at sword's point, are only a feeble repayment for all he gave up. Our second visit was to General [A. A.] Humphreys, commanding the Second Corps. He is a West Pointer and so has had a thorough military education, but he is as unmilitary in appearance as possible, with myopic eyes, glasses, head held forward and wearing an incomplete uniform along with knitted gloves and a round cap. For the rest, he is likable and knowledgeable; his manners have a slight European flavor and he has a very agreeable conversational style. This man, who seems so gentle with his half-smile and his courteous poise, is one of the toughest fighters in the army. Under fire, during a charge, under a hail of bullets and cannon-balls, he maintains the same pleasant calm, smoking cigarettes and adjusting his glasses on his nose with the serenity of a man meditating at his own fireside.

His headquarters, no less than his person, merit a brief description. These reflect the fastidious good taste of the commander. In the middle of an empty plain stands a clump of tall pines surrounded by a fence made of branches. Inside the enclosure a double row of neat cabins is built around a rather French-looking formal garden, in which sprigs of holly and pine branches stuck in the ground take the place of flowers and grass. The spaces between the beds are covered with white sand. At the far end the general's tent, protected by a double partition that provides a kind of vestibule, has red wallpaper and is luxuriously furnished with chairs woven of rushes; it also has a handsome brick fireplace. The interior of this retreat could hardly be more pleasant when the sun shines on the tent which serves as a roof. Large trees, three times as high as our stunted French pines, sighed in the wind as they waved their feathery branches against the bright blue winter sky. It was a green oasis in the midst of this man-made Sahara, for the contrast was pleasing and restful to weary eyes. I can't think of any planting of hornbeam trees, any beautiful park or majestic meadow shaded by oak trees, any public gardens at the Tuileries, Windsor or Versailles, that have given me as much pleasure as General Humphreys's little enclosure.

From there we went to the front lines. Across from us, a few hundred yards away, were the enemy's trenches. In between were the pickets of the two armies. We crossed the levelled ground, plowed and harrowed by exchanges of artillery fire and bristling with *abatis* [felled trees] and *chevaux-de-frise* [structures of pointed stakes]. A path running along the far side indicated the army's outer edge, the space within which it is permitted to move freely, but beyond which it is forbidden, under pain of being shot, to go without an officer's order. Every twenty yards or so there are breastworks about half as tall as a man, made of tree trunks, branches and earth. These protect the small, scattered detachments from enemy fire. The men take shelter behind them, lying flat on the ground, and exchange shots with the enemy. About thirty yards in front of each of these little redoubts is posted a sentry who is relieved in turn by his four or five comrades. Anyone who ventures onto this forbidden ground is considered a deserter.

At the moment, the pickets are peacefully seated around their campfire. Some of them, rolled up in their blankets, are warming themselves in the sun. This sentry duty is long and monotonous, lasting twenty-four hours at a stretch, and it becomes cruel during the cold night. Brown dots a little farther

Photograph

From *Harper's History of the Great Rebellion*

Chevaux-de-frise, Part of Fortifications
near Petersburg, Virginia

away are Rebel sentries. While the Yankees keep the terrain in front of them cleared, the Rebels prefer to remain in the cover of the forest hidden among the undergrowth and brush. There is a point where the two lines pass through woods and there, in spite of its being strictly forbidden, soldiers from the two armies have often been seen fraternizing— talking, trading, exchanging Federal coffee for Rebel tobacco, or even playing cards after eating a meal together. There exists between the two sides a tacit understanding not to fire without giving warning to the enemy. "Hey! Yankees, get into your pits! We are ordered to begin to fire."[10]

Then the sentries fall back; they crouch in their "rifle-pits"; one or two shots are fired into the air as a salute; then the bloody work commences. Each man is ready, lying in ambush, his gun to his cheek, his eye alert, his hand ready, and from then on anything that is visible, whether an arm, a leg or a head, is shot at without pity. Two minutes ago, these men were amicably talking together. Now they are killing each other like wild animals with ferocious delight. What is it that makes them enemies? Neither hate nor anger, not even a deep resentment, but simply their orders and the indifference of a soldier for the lives of others as well as for his own. They kill because it is their job, with no more passion than a hunter shooting a hare or a marksman aiming at a target.

The war presents other contrasts that are sadly comic. There is a house off to our left, situated between the two lines, spacious, even luxurious for

[10] These words are given in English in the original text.

this wild section of Virginia. An old man lived there and he preferred to remain there under fire rather than abandon his home; the soldiers feed him like a beggar. When we were passing a redoubt after having forded a stream, breaking the ice under the hooves of our horses, we saw two strange, bent figures, apparently planting wheat or colza by hand. They were scratching the sandy soil with little sticks and seemed to be either burying or digging up something we were unable to see. They might have been a couple of lunatics determined to sow imaginary crops in what had been their field. They were the owners of the estate, perhaps rich in former times, who had no other resource than to gather up spent bullets so as to sell them by weight for lead. These two lonely old people lead a poor and unhappy existence on the blood-stained confines of the two armies, harvesting deadly bullets in the very place where last year, perhaps, they had planted corn or sweet potatoes.

The next day, booted and spurred, I galloped to review the Second Division with the general's staff. It is always splendid to see the long, symmetrical formations in front of which the glittering troop of mounted general officers and aides-de-camp goes trotting past. When at last our turn came, we took our appointed places in a compact body with the generals at the front and the troops marched past us. The flags were riddled with holes made by shell fragments, torn to shapeless rags, the poles sometimes almost bare, with hardly a threadbare scrap still floating. Old soldiers will tell you this is often a deceptive sign, because it takes only a few months of campaigning to wear even the newest flag to shreds and tatters.

What is more blood-chilling is the fact that the regiments themselves are no less used up than their banners. Filled with new recruits, having at the most one man in two a veteran, several regiments have fallen below the size of a company. I saw some that didn't have as many as fifty men. They were commanded by a captain, a major, or even by a second lieutenant if he was the only officer to survive the previous campaign. After certain battles, some regiments were commanded only by a sergeant. In our armies the ranks of a decimated regiment would be filled in a week. Here their numbers are allowed to dwindle until they get around to consolidate several units; that is, until a number of depleted regiments are gathered together to form a new one. This is the natural consequence of the volunteer system that prevailed at the beginning of the war, traces of which still remain in the stubborn individuality of the old corps. There may be a company of some regiment that is made up of all the survivors of some brigade or division; and even in the membership of squads you can still find the traces of the original regiments and battalions.

But let us return to the review. General Humphreys noticed me and called me to his side while the regiments passed before us, each ragged flag dipping before the general who each time removed his cap in respect. The uniforms were faded and discolored from age; the men, of unequal and ill-matched stature, were for the most part hardened veterans marching in good order, keeping step smartly with a martial air. Some laggards in the last rows—new recruits, I suppose—moved awkwardly as though stiffened by the cold. The marching forest of blue uniforms and bayonets slowly dispersed and spread out across the field to the sound of military music.

We then stopped at the headquarters of Brigadier-General X., acting commander of the division.[11] We crowded into his tent and the drinks began to flow—whiskey, grog, cocktails, "milk punch," mint julep, egg-nog and other tasty products of American ingenuity. Everyone there was a general or a colonel commanding a brigade except for myself and another civilian. You should know that in America the civilian is not regarded with the same disdain as in French military circles. All American officers remember having been civilians themselves—merchants, lawyers, engineers or clergymen—and, though they wear uniforms, they still have the mild, well-behaved ways that went with their former professions. I watched them attentively and, in spite of the effects of strong liquor, which they were drinking in liberal quantities, in spite of the freedom of a gathering where there were no constraints, not one (except our host) forgot for a single instant the language and manners of a gentleman. The latter, a small, thin, ordinary-looking man who has lost a hand, apparently fearless, but foul-mouthed, became over-excited and began to tell us all about his regiment's exploits. He talked so much we couldn't get a word in edgewise, which

[11] This was Brigadier General Thomas A. Smyth, commanding in the absence of Major General John Gibbon, who was on leave.

was rather tiresome. But Mott, Humphreys, Madill and a certain General Smith,[12] one of the handsomest, most heroic figures of the army, behaved better than many of their compatriots do in a drawing-room. It almost seemed as if the uniform, the military life, habits of obedience and command had made them more reserved and dignified. God knows that boors are found everywhere, and there are as many among us as in America. But to judge by the ones I've met here, the general officers of the American army are certainly not inferior to those of any other army.

The visit ended with a little comic scene which General X. performed for us when somewhat in his cups. "Gentlemen," he said, "We are fighting for the emancipation of the blacks. I am going to show you what we've accomplished so far." At this the door opened and a small Negro boy about thirteen years old entered the tent. This unfortunate lad's story is rather interesting and reveals his character. One day, General X., during a tour of the lines, was approached by a child who gave him a smart military salute and cried out: "I've flanked them, General, I've flanked them!"

It seems he was a deserter from the enemy lines who had escaped unaided from his master and come all by himself to seek his fortune in the land of liberty. They made him a servant and an officer took him to Washington.

[12]General Henry J. Madill and General W. F. ("Baldy") Smith; the latter was an officer in whom General Grant placed much reliance; he is not to be confused with General Thomas A. Smyth referred to by the author as "General X."

"What a marvelous city!" he said on his return. "What a marvelous city, where a white man will polish my shoes for ten cents!"

But he had only exchanged one form of servitude for another, and that was not what this little African Gavroche[13] had been led to hope for by the vague hearsay that had reached the astonished, anxious ears of the slaves. He had been turned into an amusement, a toy, a sort of trained dog. There he was among us, somewhat apprehensive in spite of his brave exterior, forcing himself to smile and cavort. He was made to sing and imitate the cries of animals. His master, the general, had a whip brought in and cracked it to make him dance faster. Suddenly the child stopped, overcome with pain; his eyes filled and large tears rolled down his cheeks. The lash had touched him; it had only grazed him; but it was the touch of a whip, the symbol of slavery and humiliation. Some of the spectators expressed sympathy in low voices, but didn't dare to speak out in his defense. The others burst out laughing. He slowly got the better of his distress, dried his tears and began to dance to the accompaniment of a banjo that was brought in.

The banjo is an instrument of African origin, and its sound is as unusual as its shape. It is a four-stringed guitar with a small drum for a sounding-box. When the plucked strings resonate with this parchment-covered box, the sound is primitive and harsh, recalling both the guitar and the drum.

[13]Gavroche, a character in Victor Hugo's *Les Misérables,* was a street urchin of Paris who hid a heart of gold under a mocking exterior.

The tune being played was simple, even childish, consisting of a phrase of two measures repeated over and over, and yet this is enough to cause this naturally musical race to be overcome by a sort of voluptuous ecstasy.

The door was opened, a black face peeped in and, encouraged by a burst of laughter, its owner came confidently into the tent. A soldier began plucking the banjo. A Negro playing the castanets let himself be carried away by the flow of music. Eyes closed, head thrown back, body undulating, he clacked out a light, rapid, varied, insidious rhythm with agile and languishing movements the equal of which will never be found in any Spanish gypsy or ballet dancer. I can't quite explain why, but there was something intoxicating and strangely harmonious in the rhythms created by those bits of wood. The dancer's arms, in constant undulating movement like that of a garden snake, had a morbid, sensual grace that neither the Taglioni nor a Petipa[14] can ever teach.

Watching this black figure and its ever-changing shapes made me think of Indian dancing girls or Oriental *almahs*[15]—but even more it suggested the

---

[14]Celebrated artists of the ballet stage who had long, triumphant engagements with the Paris Opéra and made tours of the leading European capitals. Marius Petipa was a noted French dancer and choreographer.

[15]Young women trained as public entertainers; their specialties are singing and dancing. Although the author uses the term Oriental, the cultural area referred to is the Muslim civilization of the Near East, Middle East and North Africa. The *"bayadères"* of India were also famed as singers and dancers at entertainments.

African sun, the warm, moist land of his fathers and a whole tribe of uninhibited black people moving in a frenzied dance to the sound of primitive music. We had fallen completely under his musical spell, for this poor abused creature had his share of inspiration and genius.

Moment by moment the emotional pitch rose higher; the enthusiasm became more irresistible; the roll of the castanets grew louder and more insistent, more brilliant and fantastic. The musician's head drooped as in a swoon, his legs began to jerk in a shiver of pleasure. At last he could keep still no longer and began to dance with the lively imps who had rushed in from all directions at the sound of the music. Encouraged and excited by our laughter, they went on dancing until they were exhausted. Then the poor devils were sent on their way, and the drinking began again in earnest.

When I went out to mount my horse, although I was otherwise "rational," the ground moved under my feet, which weighed a hundred tons, and my numb fingers obstinately refused in the darkness of night to disentangle the bridle straps from the reins. Thanks to the marvelous sure-footedness of these army horses, I managed to get home without difficulty. Once there, I gravely tried to puzzle out by fire-light the letters of a newspaper that were dancing a sarabande in spite of my efforts to read calmly.

Three long days have passed without my feeling any inclination to write. The reason is that in a military encampment nothing is more unnatural than to do any serious thinking. The fresh air, so sharp and overpowering in this cold season, the log fire which I kept going while I crouched shivering beside it, the continual playing of fifes and drums in the background, the sleepless nights spent curled into a ball underneath a heap of blankets, my hours of wakefulness marked by drums, bugles and the noisy marching of squads moving up to the outposts, even the slow, measured step of the sentry on duty at the entrance to headquarters, even the wind striking the canvas roof and singing in the tall pines—all these physical and moral influences disposed me to inaction, silence, torpor and boredom. I am not surprised that soldiers like to go into battle. Any kind of action is pleasant to them after the monotonous routine of winter quarters. You have no news, no ideas, no books—not even the desire to read; whiskey, tobacco, long drowsy mornings and long evenings in your tent; an occasional review or parade; and then, week after week, you spend two hours on picket duty with a blanket draped around your shoulders and a carbine in your hand, watching the Rebels a hundred paces away. There is nothing in all that—even if you throw in the prospect of glory and the chance to get your head blown off—to inflame the imagination of a man accustomed to the comforts of civilian life. I have known a major-general to cry out against his idleness and boredom, beg for newspapers and books, and finally, in order to kill time, fling himself on his horse to make purposeless visits to neighboring headquarters. Only my host has lost nothing of the animation and brilliance of his charming character. He has been able, even in this glacial air, to keep alive the spark of intelligence and good humor.

January 28, 1865

I HAVE just gone out with the general to review the ambulances and supply wagons of this division. Usually the great weakness of improvised armies lies in these logistical departments. The Americans learned this at the beginning of the war when they sent their half-trained batallions forward into an area that was hostile or without supplies. They have profited from the lessons of experience, and I don't believe there is an army in the world whose services of supply are better managed. The enormous parade-ground, the long black lines of caissons and wagons three rows deep, the good order and perfect condition of the hundreds of six-mule teams, the animals' manes cut short and their black drivers sitting firmly astride their mounts, holding the reins in their hands—all this gave me the impression of a discipline and organization far superior to what Europeans imagine when they hear the term "volunteer army."

The most complete order reigns today in the mass that was formerly so chaotic. Americans, perhaps more than any other people in the world, have a genius for organization and discipline. What we do after long training, they do by an instantaneous and intelligent agreement of everyone's will and they improvise in a few weeks what it has taken us centuries to create. The so-called "volunteer" army now has all the earmarks of a *regular* army. In reality, it is a volunteer force only in name, for it was raised by presidential decree with the attraction of enlistment bonuses and under the threat of conscription. It is composed, to tell the truth, solely of mercenaries and conscripts. Its officers hold their ranks as long as the war lasts alongside those of the regular army. The only observable difference is in the manner of recruitment and the length of service. The volunteer army is recruited by the individual states and then mustered into service by the Federal government. Its officers are appointed by the governors. Enlistments last only one, two or three years at most; this temporary, volunteer army will be disbanded as soon as possible after peace is proclaimed and its officers and soldiers will hasten to resume their places in civilian life.

In contrast, the permanent army, which is in fact the only United States army, is recruited directly by the Federal government and its members will retain for life their right to their rank and pay. Hence there are many strange contrasts and duplications of status. Since not all the officers holding rank in the regular army are on active service, some of them have accepted commissions in the volunteer army, so that a captain of the regular army may be a general of volunteers; or a captain of volunteers may have the rank of colonel in the regular army. All this is provisional anyway, and at the end of the war there will probably be a radical change in the military system of the United States.

It is doubtful that, when the Union is faced with a conquered and discontented South, it can send all the volunteers home or reduce the regular army to 10,000 regular troops. I have heard that at least 100,000 to 150,000 men will be kept under arms and that these will be permanently enrolled. At the same time it will be necessary to decide on a new legal basis for recruitment because a permanent organization cannot be established without rules. The stop-gap system of enlistment bonuses and hired substitutes cannot be used indefinitely. In a country like America, where everyone easily finds employment, bounties—even very high ones—will not fill the ranks of a peacetime army of 100,000. Will it be necessary to resort to periodic discretionary draft calls, which single men out by chance and never produce what is wanted?

Assuming the hiring of substitutes [by the well-to-do] could fill the army's ranks, would the authorities keep those odious practices of impressment and constraint which are doubtless excusable in times of urgent necessity, but in the long run dishonor the government of the United States? Should press-gangs prowl continually in seaports, waylaying foreign sailors, taking them to saloons or brothels, slipping into their drinks a drug which renders them helpless in five minutes? Should herds of cannon fodder be lured from Ireland, Germany and Canada, thus repeating with whites the traffic from which the blacks have been rescued?

I know several states—Massachusetts is the chief among them—that would not have any scruples against such a commerce. Off the coast of New England there is a small island where men recruited in Europe as workers are held and threatened until they give in and consent to become soldiers. But such an infamous scheme could not become the official post-war system. Nor, after the war, could one swindle soldiers out of half their bonus on the pretext of paying it at the end of their service, a debt

often left unpaid because of the death of the cred-
itor. Nor could recruiting agents, once the attention
of the country and Congress was drawn to the situation, pocket the hundred-dollar bonus allowed
them for each man who enlists, throwing back onto
the government the responsibility for their entrap-
ments and lies. The day of justice must come after
peace is declared, for any responsible government
that encourages these shameful practices would deserve ostracism from civilization and humanity. If,
as is reported, the army is to be maintained at more
than 100,000 men, Congress will have to vote a just,
orderly recruitment law, for no trace of inequity
can be allowed to remain in this terrible and inevitable levy of blood.*

The mercenary [substitute] system does not produce a reliable army. It mobilizes temporarily for
monetary gain a small number of individuals who
later disappear in the hope of collecting a new bonus. No mercenary army can exist for three years
without being constantly renewed. It is hardly organized before it begins to fall apart. Nothing but the
firing-squad—tough discipline and high risks for
deserters—can keep it in order and then only for a
few months. The Rebels fire their cannon every
night to prevent the desertion of their soldiers. In

* Reductions in the size of the army have been greater and
easier than the Americans dared to hope. Today [1866] the
volunteer army has diminished by 800,000 men and President Johnson wants the military forces of the United States
reduced in the near future to 50,000 men while leaving open
the possibility of increasing them on short notice to 82,600.
This reduction will take place when Federal forces in the
Southern states are replaced by local militia.

fact, however, desertion causes as many gaps in the ranks of the Federal army as it does among the Rebels. From the month of May, 1863, to the month of September, 1864, there were as many as 60,000 deserters. There is a type of adventurer whose game is to enlist and re-enlist many times, each time placing the bounty money in a safe place, until the day he is caught and executed. Some scoundrels are known to have stolen no less than seventeen bounties. Not a week passes in the army without the execution of several of these "bounty-jumpers," as they are called, but it is rare to find the man's real identity under the thick layers of false names he has adopted. They wander through the army from regiment to regiment.

If soldiers have simply deserted, they are shot as deserters; if they have gone over to the enemy, they are hung as traitors. The Richmond government has done all it could to encourage their defection. It offers good meals, comfortable lodging and free passage on a "blockade-runner" to return to their own country. Most of these hirelings are Irish, Canadian or German. The very fact of their existence, irrespective of their origins, remains the strongest condemnation of a system which attempts to fill the army with foreign mercenaries instead of with a patriotic body of citizen-soldiers.

As a matter of fact, however, these expedients have not helped very much. The American army remains basically American. Except for the 100,000 Negro soldiers, who cannot be called foreigners and who, more than anyone else, are fighting for their own cause, those under arms are all citizens of the

United States. Some Northern states have tried to fill their quotas with fugitive slaves; but they have not been able, in spite of their best efforts, to enroll more than about 2,000 during the past year, and the average price of each black soldier obtained in this way is about $3,500. The Army of the James has, along with its ten black regiments, some foreign or international regiments. There are some Indians in the contingents from the Western states and even some Chinese in the New York and California units, but the great strength of the American army is in the rugged batallions from the [Middle] West, which are made up of healthy farmers' sons already hardened by the rigors of a harsh, laborious life. The Union's strength comes also from the idealistic youth of the Eastern states who, in a unanimous outburst of patriotism, have abandoned their counters, factories, school benches, lawyers' offices, even their pulpits,—all the hopes and promise of their lives—to go and die an obscure death on some distant battlefield. In a single year 400 young men, students from the university in Cambridge [Harvard], many of them sons of the country's leading families, have enlisted in the army as ordinary soldiers. Teachers, an influential and enlightened group, have furnished perhaps as many as 100,000 men to the Federal army. Conscription has not dampened this patriotic enthusiasm. On the contrary, it has aroused the citizens' altruism and given a new impetus to the prodigious voluntary subscriptions contributed in every city, in every parish, at every new appeal made by the President, to recruit men or to hire substitutes for men chosen by lot. It is calculated that, of the nearly three million soldiers raised during the war,* only 35,000 were furnished by conscription.

This immense effort by a free nation is perhaps due to the character of a dynamic, fearless and determined people. Substitute for the Americans, the Chinese, the Mexicans or the Russians, and unless an absolute authority imposed discipline by physical force, they would soon be tired of so many sacrifices and setbacks. It is necessary, in the main, to give credit to the virtues of liberty itself. Do you think the American people would have given this great example to the world if they had been deprived of initiative and spirit by the existence of a centralized bureaucracy and a large standing army? Once more democracy has proved its strength, already made manifest during our Revolution [of 1789] when our people were able to stand firm against all Europe, sending to our frontiers fourteen armies of conscripts who were the equals of any veterans. Unhappily, in the aftermath of this triumph, we fell exhausted into the grip of absolutism. The wisdom, perseverance and virtue of democracy

---

* The authentic, official statistics of the War Department give a total of 2,759,049 men called to the colors by the President between April 15, 1861, and April 4, 1865. Of these only 2,656,553 men have actually served in the army or navy. The first period of enlistment was for only three months; this was successively extended to six and nine months, then to a year, two years and three years. This last term was the one that proved to be permanent. The figures I have cited do not include the militia mobilized in the summer of 1863 which served for only a few weeks; its strength amounted to more than 120,000 men.

remained to be demonstrated; and the present experience of the United States does this service by
remaining faithful, even after four years of internal
warfare, to its traditions of liberty. That is what
they will prove to the world after the war when, as
is hoped, the army of one million men will vanish,
returning to civilian life and laying down their arms
as willingly as they took them up on the day of
their country's danger.*

* The forces of the United States Army were estimated on
May 1, 1865, at 1,000,516 men. On March 1 the figure was
965,591 men of whom 602,599 were fit for battle. The rest
were scattered in garrisons, hospitals and Southern prisons,
or were home on leave. The total number of men listed on
the army and navy rolls during the last sixteen months of the
war was 675,452. Losses in the North, both wounded and
dead, have amounted to more than a million. At least
326,000 of these were deaths. On last November 15, only
seven months after the peace, the volunteer army was already reduced by 800,000 men. This large number of soldiers was discharged in only a few months, almost without
disorder and, except in the Southern states, when its protection of the newly-freed blacks was necessary, all trace of
military authority has already disappeared. The veterans
who wish to remain in uniform now serve in the regular
army. The others, by far the greater number, preferred to
return to their homes. Mr. Stanton, the Secretary of War, at
first wanted to keep under arms, at least until Congress was
in session, the "Veteran Reserve Corps," composed of veterans who re-enlisted during the war after the expiration of
their first term of service. However, he realized it would be
difficult to keep them, and that it would be better to release
them as quickly as possible. An English traveler, Sir Morton
Peto, who visited the United States at the end of last year,
reports that he saw in Chicago a print-shop run by a former
secretary of the London Embassy. The owner escorted him
through the different departments and showed him the
workers on the job. "They are all former soldiers," he said;

Aboard the steamer *Webster*
on the James River
January 29, 1865

I HAVE HAD ENOUGH of military life. Nothing unusual has happened in the last two days. Horseback
rides, visits, some lectures on strategy of which I
understood very little, long reveries in front of the
general's hearth listening to the mournful sound of
the tall pines moaning in the north wind—such is
the daily program. In the evening our only entertainment has been to play cards or checkers on a
rickety table in the smoky dining room, or else we
solemnly smoked our pipes between glasses of
brandy. Unconsciously the mind goes to sleep and
even the body grows numb. Sometimes I left the
general's tent to talk with the young men on the
staff. They were eager to please, mild-mannered
and serious; a number of them come from good families and upper-class backgrounds. I had no fault to
find with them—only with the inevitable dullness of
the season. I encouraged them to tell me all about
the campaigns they had taken part in.

One of them was wounded last year and taken
prisoner. He was sent to Libby prison, so weak he
couldn't stand up. He lost a great deal of blood but
he told me, "I was determined not to die." By good
luck, he belonged to an order of Free Masons which

"That one was a major, this one a captain, the one over there
a lieutenant and this fellow here was an infantryman. They
left their jobs here three years ago, making me promise to
rehire any of them who might return from the war. They
were discharged a few days ago and there they are back at
work as though they had never left the shop."

has many lodges in the Southern states. He gave the secret sign calling for help, and one of his guards, a Confederate officer, responded. He took care of him, fed him and nursed him back to health.

Another young officer, brave but a little naïve, said without pretentiousness: "I love to take part in great battles!" They are indeed thrilling occasions! During the murderous campaign that took Grant from the Potomac to the James, there was fighting nearly every day. Thirty thousand men met their death in the forests of the "Wilderness." For five days soldiers killed each other day and night, often without seeing the enemy in the impenetrable thickets, advancing hardly at all. At night, the exhausted survivors lay down to sleep next to the bodies of the dead. At Chancellorsville the battlefield was set afire and the dead and wounded were burned together in the tall grass. The Americans, who do everything on a large scale and boast of it, can well say that this is a war of giants.

This is the school in which their generals have learned their trade. You may like to make fun of the hand-to-mouth military education of American officers. I can assure you that the time has passed when journalists, lawyers or clergymen who had perhaps never held a rifle or a sword can suddenly become colonels or captains; ready-made generals no longer fall from the sky. The West Pointers, graduates of the military academy, who are, so to speak, the aristocrats of the army, at first enjoyed humiliating the other officers, but they are certainly forced to accept them today as their equals. Four years of tough, practical experience have made them better officers than many of our garrison veterans who have reached the rank of general without ever having been under fire. After all, did our great captains of the Republic and the Empire attend any other school than that of experience? These young men, many in their early twenties, have been in the army for four years. One has been wounded five times in one year. Another enlisted as an ordinary soldier. Only one was a lieutenant at the outset. The list of their dead comrades is longer by far than that of the living. They wage war neither for pleasure nor out of ambition nor to win advancement, medals or pensions. They dream of their families, their studies, their suspended careers, and they look forward impatiently to the day when they will be mustered out. One of them told me that his fiancée was waiting for him at home and that he hoped to marry her one day if God spared his life. War is not a career for them; it is a stern duty to which they are sacrificing the best part of their youth. Compare these patriot-soldiers to some of our sword-wearers, the handsome, idle sons of good families, who take up the trade of arms for the pleasure of wearing a uniform or an officer's epaulettes, and you will understand the distance that separates a military nation from a nation of citizens.

Now let us visit the tent of an ordinary soldier. It is smaller and lower than that of an officer. Four men sleep together on a sort of low table and share all their blankets. During this cold winter weather, they huddle together over their fires. Furthermore, the regulations forbid them to wander about and discipline is at present very strict in the American army. The habit of obedience and unified command have been adopted along with a single uniform. Still, the "Yankees" do not have the awkward correctness and mechanical stiffness of British troops, an army of automata as admirable under fire as on parade. No soldiers, not even those in our army, have more initiative or ingenuity. Give the American an axe, some nails and a plane; he will make you tables, chairs, any kind of furniture—all designed in his own imagination. Give him some clay and a few strips of wood—he will make fireproof chimneys. He is a blacksmith, mechanic, gunsmith, saddler, tailor or civil engineer as the occasion demands. He reads, he spends the winter days writing long letters to his family. He even carries his writing paper to the outposts and reports on the battle between rifle shots. He is the most civilized and knowledgeable soldier in the world.

However, the order of ranks is as well observed as in the Russian or the Austrian army, where absolute docility prevails. Officers who let themselves be treated too democratically by their men are cited as bad examples.

As for the physical aspects of life, the food is abundant and healthy. The soldiers eat three meals a day. Rations are generous, especially in fresh meat, vegetables and coffee, which is the drink that replaces strong liquor here. Brandy, wine, beer and all other alcoholic beverages are strictly forbidden. In this connection, it is said that the general-in-chief himself sets an example of the sobriety he has ordained by allowing nothing but pure water to be drunk at his table. Sometimes the commissary dis-

tributes an extraordinary ration of whiskey to the
men, but only on days when they are on the march
or engaged in battle. The presence of women is not
tolerated, and the general has said that other officers
could invite their wives on the day when Mrs. Grant
comes to visit him. If it happens that soldiers molest
the Virginia farm women by exercising their rights
as conquerors too vigorously, they are hung without
mercy as an example to others, it is said, and also to
give the lie to Rebel slander. Several colonels forbid
cardplaying in their regiments and want to make a
monk of the soldier and a monastery out of an army
camp. Such strictness is excessive and results from a
puerile display of authority. The wiser officers manage without this kind of tyranny and don't try to
snuff out good humor, that great morale-builder.

Yesterday there was a rumor that General Lee
had just been invested by the Rebels with powers
equal to those of General Grant, which in the desperate situation prevailing in Virginia would be
equivalent to dictatorship and absolute authority.
Johnston is said to have taken over command of the
army defending Richmond and President Davis
may well be reduced, if Lee so decides, to a very
small role. Those who know the characters of those
two men think, however, that the dictatorship of
Lee would be only another name for the omnipo-
tence of Davis. This is what I was told the other day
at the headquarters of General M. between drinks
and cigars by a certain Mr. C., who was formerly an
intimate friend of the "Arch-Rebel," for whom he
has kept a great deal of sympathy and a certain
amount of admiration. He is certainly a proud and

highly gifted person, this son of an unscrupulous horse-trader, this "Yankee" who became a son of the South, this successful offspring of democracy adopted by the aristocrats of slavery as their leader, this ambitious and obstinate man who, after four years of needless and criminal war, when everything is weakening and falling apart, continues to carry on his own shoulders the weight of universal ruin without being crushed by the terrible weight of his dreadful responsibility.

Mr. C. tells me Davis is a "noble fellow," even in his crimes. As good, simple and gentle in private as he is violent and intractable in his public life, he has the violent passions, the autocratic will, and the irresistible power over others that belong only to superior men. He is certainly not, like his colleague, Vice President Stephens, a man to follow a criminal example without daring to take the initiative himself, a man who does not deserve the honor of a spectacular punishment. No one thinks of striking at someone who is so subservient. Davis is the sort of man whose very haughtiness arouses a desire for vengeance. The more desperate his cause becomes, the more he infuriates his opponents as though he took pleasure in braving their anger and blinding their sense of justice.

He may be a criminal, but he is not despicable, and the tragic grandeur of his character is very different from the weak, timorous decency of General Lee. The latter was for the Union, yet he served the Rebels; he desired peace, yet he waged war. Full power lies within his grasp; yet rather than seize it, he prefers to obey a despotic government that is leading his country to disaster. An unselfish man of integrity, he is always misled by his generous feelings—and these are totally unsuitable for the role of savior he is being asked to play and only make him the pliant instrument of a stronger will.

Rumors of peace continue to circulate. There are reports of a second trip to Richmond by Mr. Blair; hence it is not true that his unofficial overtures were contemptuously rejected. He is a Virginian by birth and was formerly a close friend of Davis; he will be better able than anyone else, it is said, to have some influence on that stubborn, proud spirit. Isn't it in fact a sign of the times and a good omen to see even the army hoping for peace with all its heart? One last campaign is expected, one or two great battles with heavy casualties, but no one doubts that this year will see an end to this great war, or that the Federal troops will, in the end, pitch their tents beside the Capitol in Richmond.

No more for the present. It has been an hour since we cast off [from City Point]. The boat creaks, the deck bobs up and down, the crowd mills around me. I get a little amusement from a Negro who is singing and playing the banjo. The afternoon is almost over and it will soon be night. We have passed Fort Monroe and are heading not for Washington, since the ice in the Potomac bars our way, but for Annapolis, the only open port along Maryland.

Washington

January 31, 1865

I HAVE YET TO TELL you about my return from the army. The day before yesterday at daybreak I boarded the officers' railroad car with a group of exuberant aides-de-camp on leave, heading back the way I had come. Here is the cut along which they have built a wall of sand to protect the railroad from the artillery fire—usually ineffectual—which the enemy directs at passing trains.

At City Point in the barracks of the "Provost Marshal" everyone eagerly crowds together in front of the window where passes were being handed out and then at the bottom of the hill around the steamboat ticket-window. It took two hours of marking time in the freezing air to obtain the necessary papers.

One of General de Trobriand's aides-de-camp introduced me to another general who was returning to Washington. All the other officers of our brigade who were present—about eight or ten in number—joined us and, to the astonishment of the onlookers, we transformed ourselves into his staff. During the whole trip General Madill kept us under his protection and, with the greatest kindness, shared with us the prerogatives of his rank. It was thanks to him that I found a berth on the steamer, a seat on the train and shelter from the cold when we had a long wait at Annapolis Junction during my journey back to Washington.

We spent the night at Fort Monroe, not a very picturesque or attractive spot. The thick walls of the fort stretched along the flat shore and warships rocked slowly on the waves. Everything was gray, black or yellowish, seeming pale and gloomy in the cold. It was amusing to see how my companions, who had not left the army for perhaps as long as two years, espied with delight a figure wearing a woman's dress on the shore and how they studied it covetously like some rare, marvelous object. Afterwards these fine young fellows crammed themselves like sardines into the general's cabin, squatting down to play cards on the floor.

The next morning was cold and bright as we entered the harbor at Annapolis. The site is gracious and charming: there is a small city surrounded by trees; it doesn't make a big impression when seen from the water, but it looks cheerful, almost rural, even in this icy winter weather. You will recall that this is the capital of Maryland and one of the oldest cities in America. It is the home of several colleges, including the United States Naval Academy; it has a great many splendid memories, for it was here at Annapolis that Washington resigned his command after the War of Independence. The port is open the year round and is located on a nearly landlocked bay sheltered by the Delaware peninsula; it is protected by curving promontories and is one of the best along the coast. Annapolis would be a rival of Baltimore except for the sleepy inertia into which it has sunk by reason of the institution of slavery and long-established habits of idleness. Steamboats that have been diverted here by the icy weather lend animation to the scene and jostle one another alongside docks that are too small to accommodate all of them at once.

The city itself, once we had disembarked, was like a village. Some of the old paved streets remind me of the stagnation and boredom of our provincial cities where grass grows under one's feet between the cobblestones. One can see that there is, as in our country towns, a small bourgeois aristocracy living on its income and dragging out its sterile existence between the café and the club. These are perhaps over-hasty conclusions I have drawn after a few minutes' observation and conversation during the course of a luncheon. But I send you my impressions, such as they are, without considering whether it is my state of mind that has made me see things in this light or whether it is the reality itself that has caused these ideas to take shape in my mind.

At the railroad station we found a crowd of soldiers on leave besieging the tiny, pocket-sized waiting-room, fighting for places on the few crowded trains. Whenever a car appears, it is instantly filled to overflowing. The station employees, who are not at all used to this confusion, don't know what to do. There are some unfortunate soldiers who have already spent five days of their fortnight's leave attempting to get the free transportation they have a right to. The plight of these poor fellows is heartbreaking: they don't have a penny in their pockets because they won't receive their pay until they get to Washington; they are wasting their time in a vain effort to obtain what is due them and nobody wants to give them.

Here one sees the worst flaw in the American military establishment: in matters of pay, railroad tickets and travel papers everything is uncertain and lacking in system. The rights of the government and the obligations of the railway companies are not yet clearly fixed. Instead of reaching their destination under the care and protection of the government, soldiers (including the wounded) are left entirely to their own devices and must shift for themselves. How many times have I seen them in crowded waiting rooms, where hardly a place can be found to sit down, or standing patiently for long hours in rain or snow, or jostled by uncaring crowds, painfully making their way to a railroad car into which they hope to hoist themselves with their feeble hands—how many times have I seen soldiers who were ill, wounded, legless, on crutches, with expressions of suffering on their pale faces, but with not a word or even a murmur of complaint against the negligence of their government which discharges them in this condition from its hospitals! Just now these poor fellows don't know where to turn or whom to ask for help. For lack of anyone else, they appeal to the general who can do nothing for them. This example of *laissez-faire* makes me regret our fussy, omnipotent civil service, but the Americans don't feel its lack.

After long delays, helpless impatience and interminable discussions, we were finally able to leave, packed without room to breathe into a "car" where our fellow-officers resumed their noisy card-game. Soon bottles of whiskey were produced from various pockets and passed around, making the circuit time after time and receiving a cordial greeting from everyone in turn—such are the simple pleasures and diversions of soldiers!

We arrived at Annapolis Junction, a lonely place where one has to change to the train for Washington. Here we endured three hours of waiting, frozen by an icy north wind. We found the two inns, the only buildings, closed by order of the Secretary of

War—this is obligatory while troops are here in transit. We pounded in vain at the closed doors and shuttered windows. Finally Captain H., half by diplomacy and half by threats, managed to have one of them opened for the general and his "staff," and about thirty of us rushed inside. Women and wounded men were admitted to one room, and the rest of us, with our whiskey and cigars, took possession of a large damp room from which all the chairs had been removed. First we went through the customary forms of etiquette—introductions accompanied by hand-shaking, American style, followed by a toast to everyone's health. All these gentlemen were forthright, hearty good fellows.

Four of us were in civilian dress, including myself and a certain General [James W.] Singleton, a "Peace Democrat" from Illinois, who is a member of the unofficial mission led by Mr. Blair that left Richmond the day before yesterday. He is a real Westerner, with a long mane of reddish hair, an unkempt beard, a large otter-skin cap and the general awkwardness of a workman on holiday. There was also a huge Yankee with a goatee that curled forward from his chin, a small round head on an elephantine body and a tiny, almost invisible hat stuck over one ear. This delightful personage threshed his arms and legs about and made grimaces with his wide-open, toothless mouth; his small eyes were full of tears on account of the whiskey with which he had filled himself. The fourth was a "gentleman" of ludicrously solemn gravity, putting on a show of lordly manners as a joke and uttering pompous foolishness in a thick, slurred voice. His

eyes were glassy and unfocussed but shone with the
secret joy a drunkard can never completely hide.
Little Lieutenant W., assigned by General Ord as
escort to Singleton and some ladies he was bringing
back from Richmond, introduced me to these two
men, who were chaplains in his army corps. The
solemn one, with many handshakes and portentous
greetings, said to me, "So you're from Paris? I was
there for a long time, engaged in a great work."

"What great work was that?"

"The Christian society!" was the answer.

"Well," said I to the little lieutenant, "your men
of the cloth seem in very good humor. That one is
especially jovial."

"Oh," he answered, "he's tight, that's all."[16]

This will show you how some chaplains of the
American army behave, and the strange thing is that
no one seems surprised. It is taken for granted that
men of God also have their little human weaknesses
like the chaplain whom General T. kicked out of
his brigade for offenses that in Europe would draw a
life sentence at hard labor. The Americans, though
the most religious people in the world, do not prostrate themselves before a preacher. They pay his
salary, give him a comfortable lodging, and require
him to write sermons, but ask nothing beyond that.
He is considered hardly more than an orator for
hire, for Sunday edification, and his talent rather
than his morals determines his worth. Military
camps, moreover, are a poor school for manners.

In Annapolis I had already observed young Lieutenant W., whose beardless, almost feminine, face,

[16] This phrase is in English in the original text.

mild expression and slender, youthful figure made
such a startling contrast with the heavy, begrimed
appearance of most soldiers on campaign. I couldn't
help taking an interest in this frail, still-boyish
youngster who had been thrown into the brutish
environment in which I saw him. When I learned
that he was the son of a Cabinet member, the scion
of one of the best families in the country, I was no
longer astonished that he carried himself with such
distinction and grace that all the inevitable crudeness of military life could not efface them. I felt
extreme distaste to see him cram a big piece bitten
from a plug of tobacco into his delicate, beardless
mouth, spitting a jet of yellowish saliva with all the
aplomb of an old sea dog, and to hear his childish
lips spouting the stream of foul language that is the
usual speech of soldiers.

This greenhorn, however, is more of a man than
many a bewhiskered ninny fresh out of seminary or
college. Though barely twenty years old, he has
sailed around the world on a ship of the American
navy, in which he enlisted as cabin-boy when he
was fourteen. When war broke out, he transferred
to the army and is already a veteran. I regarded him
with sympathy and almost with pity, thinking it
a shame that such a handsome sapling should be
cut down.

I met him again that evening when we went together to visit Mrs. Blair. In her company all his
soldier's manners—pipe, tobacco plug, brandy, profanity and military swagger—disappeared. He appeared to be merely a soft-spoken, smiling young
man, a schoolboy on vacation, almost as modest,

inoffensive and shy as a young girl. The next day, however, he had to resume his saber, his uniform, his hob-nailed boots and the rough, chancy life of his cruel trade.

He led me into the adjoining room to present me to the fugitive ladies from Richmond. Although they seemed little disposed to carry on a normal conversation, I did draw from them a few interesting details about life in the Rebel capital. The way they pretended to take patriotic offense at the very suggestion that Richmond might be suffering misery and mourning, their enthusiastic accounts of its parties and entertainments, were in themselves amusing traits of character. Even while proudly waving the Rebel banner in their talk, they have lowered it in reality by coming to take refuge with the enemy and their prudent flight spoke all too eloquently about the solidity of the house whose splendors they were praising to the skies. To hear them tell it, life in Richmond is as calm, as comfortable as in New York; staples are even cheaper there; and only toilet articles are worth their weight in gold. Aside from that, they claim that the capital of Virginia has never been so gay or so full of luxuries. Carriages, horses, concerts, balls, even the theater—nothing is lacking to the general picture of prosperity.

"But when you hear the cannon," I started to say.

"Cannon! Why, we hear it sometimes when the air is very clear; but Richmond is a long way from the war!"

In this way do societies accustom themselves to a precarious and storm-tossed existence and believe themselves safe when enemy armies are but fifteen miles away, as oblivious of danger as a sailor in a fragile boat or a tight-rope walker on a cable stretched over Niagara Falls.

But let's take a look at the crowd that has leaked in, one person at a time, until the whole house is full. You can't imagine a sadder collection of faces. Here, stretched out on a bench, is a man suffering from dysentery and more dead than alive. His eyes, however, still move, even though he can no longer turn his head; soon he stumbles out between his two guides, no longer having strength enough to support himself on their shoulders with his arms. There are also amputees, jostled by the crowd without regard for the pain this gives to their still-tender stumps. They have not yet learned to use their crutches and move hesitantly, with little short steps, but even so, they don't want anyone to help them.

Outside a crowd of about five or six hundred people patiently waits in the cold and snow. Some of the officers are collecting money for the sick and the needy. In the other room the voices have all fallen silent. The men of our brigade, one after the other, have stretched out on the floor all along the walls and, aided by the whiskey, are sleeping the deep, easy sleep of a soldier, a sleep that is disturbed by neither bugle nor drum. Some are dreaming with their eyes open and a pipe or cigar between their teeth. Some others have formed a circle in the middle of the room and, crouching near the stove, go on contentedly playing cards. At the back of the room Singleton and the general, my protector, are seated on the only two chairs; they engage intermittently in desultory conversation.

Speaking about Richmond, Singleton gives some details on life in the Confederate capital. He reports that nowhere are prices of foodstuffs lower in terms of gold. The relative cheapness I have noticed in the United States is a result of the monetary crisis caused by [the depreciation of] paper money; this effect is even greater in the Confederacy. On the other hand, clothing, cloth, manufactured goods in general and all foreign imports are expensive. High and low prices both have the same cause—a surplus of unneeded raw materials—and are, as in the [northern] United States, a sign of the same difficulty or, one could say, of the same distress. While cotton, turpentine and tobacco pile up on the plantations or in warehouses, and farmers, unable to realize their usual profits, sow mostly corn, potatoes and wheat, manufactured products from Europe pile up on the British island of Nassau for want of vessels to take them to the Confederate States.

Meanwhile one gold dollar is worth between forty and sixty paper dollars, and Confederate "graybacks" are worth at most three cents on the dollar, the average rate being only two cents. General Singleton drew from his pocket the bill for a dinner he had eaten three days before at Spottswood House, the most elegant hotel in Richmond. The dinner itself cost eighty dollars for each person, that is, $320 for four, plus wine, liqueurs, coffee and Havana cigars, making a total of over $800. On the other hand, he brought back a huge cube of chewing tobacco, weighing a quintal [225 pounds] and hard as wood, from which the knives of General Ord's officers have already carved out a number of pieces.

This tobacco of prime quality and exquisite aroma was purchased for twenty-five cents in United States currency. Thanks to this great discrepancy in prices, huge fortunes are being made by speculators and traders in Richmond, Wilmington and Charleston, and no doubt also in Liverpool and New York.

The "steamers" made in England to run the blockade cost less than half the profit they make from one successful trip. The value of cotton varies so much between the Charleston market and Nassau that it is like the difference in value between British gold and Confederate paper money. Just suppose the operation succeeds in both directions and the boat, having disposed of its cargo of cotton, tobacco and resinous products to British buyers, carries back to Wilmington a load of arms, lead, steel, shoes, sheeting, cloth and the hundred thousand trifles the Richmond ladies have not yet learned to do without. The rarity of such arrivals makes the lucky ship-owner the master of the market and however extravagant a price he demands for his goods, he is certain to find buyers. His fortune is thus made at one stroke. Even if he is satisfied with only the export profit, and brings back to Richmond the amount the English paid him in gold sovereigns, he still finds himself much richer than he was in Nassau, thanks to the exchange value of gold.

Gold is the only stable foundation of business in the Confederacy as in the United States, with the difference that legal tender here has real value based on a serious hope of redemption [in gold], while Confederate notes have no other value than the commodities they will buy at a given moment and, beyond that, their usefulness as a medium of exchange. Only in America do you find people willing to accept paper money with no present value whatever and no possible value in the future. The Americans have become so accustomed to this fictitious money that they willingly accept it, planning to pass it on as soon as possible without looking further ahead than the immediate use they intend to make of it. When they accept Confederate paper money, they see in it not a twentieth, a fortieth, a hundredth or any other fraction of a dollar in gold, but simply the lawful means of payment in their markets. It matters little whether gold is selling at 65 or 30 to one; these variations indicate neither catastrophes nor the resurrection of Rebel finances but simply the ups and downs of day-to-day speculation and the temporary abundance or rarity of the precious metals. Beyond a certain point there is no longer any possible connection or proportion between credit and hard money. The Confederate money passed that point long ago and is maintained in the face of twenty-fold bankruptcy only by legal compulsion and the isolation caused by the war.

So it is that skillful and daring speculators fish in troubled waters and traffic shamefully in public misery. If they are afraid of seizure at the hands of Federal cruisers which always threaten their ships, they can find insurance companies in Nassau or in England to share the risks and the profits with them. Nevertheless, as the blockade grows tighter and the principal Confederate ports are occupied by the enemy, this trade becomes more difficult and dangerous. The capture of Fort Fisher, which closed

Wilmington to the "blockade-runners," struck an irreparable blow. On Nassau there are huge shiploads of goods for the Confederate States, but now that there are no means of getting them, these goods must be sent to the New York market.

Mr. Singleton said the closing of Wilmington was an insignificant loss, amply compensated for by the unexpected revival of activity in Charleston in spite of shelling and Federal cruisers, but I mistrust the too-rosy judgments of this "Peace Democrat" who is almost an accomplice of the Rebels, and his comments are even less impartial than his judgments. Singleton, like all those who want peace at any price, is trying to make people think the war will never end, that the resources of the Confederacy are still unimpaired. One might as well listen to an emissary of Jefferson Davis as take Singleton's word on the size and strength of his Southern friends' forces. In reality, his trip and his semi-official mission as negotiator—or rather as a scout for peace, sent to reconnoiter the enemy's terrain—show how much the Union cause has gained in the last year; as well as how close the patriotic hopes of the Republican administration and those of the most intransigent Democrats have come to coinciding. But that old devil, human nature itself, has not changed enough so that he [Singleton] is beyond suspicion of bias. I believe, though, that he is sincere when he states that the South still has enough strength to fight one last dreadful campaign and that the Richmond government has in its warehouses 1,070,000 bales of cotton, a huge quantity of tobacco and enough corn to feed its armies.

The fertility of the soil is so great in most of the Southern states that many crops will grow there almost without cultivation. They will never lack for "Indian corn," sweet potatoes and rye unless the land is left to lie fallow. A few thousand slaves and a few hundred thousand pigs, which take care of themselves, can come close to feeding the Southern population, including the fighting forces, but it is not enough to have corn bread to put in people's mouths and satisfy a soldier's hunger more or less. A civilized people has many other, no less insistent needs which go unsatisfied because of the blockade. No matter how good the crops may be, if there are no highways or railroads to distribute them, nor hands to harvest them, nor markets in which to sell them, misery and hunger will eventually subdue the most stubborn resistance and dampen the most heroic resolution.

I didn't want to quiz Mr. Singleton on the prospects for peace. Furthermore, it didn't take long to see that he and Mr. Blair considered the subject a state secret. Last night, when visiting Mrs. Blair, I hazarded a timid avowal of modest curiosity. She immediately answered, without my having directly evoked the response, that she herself knew nothing and that her father-in-law had said nothing about it. In spite of the insults in the Richmond papers and the wounding taunts of the newspaper that publishes the President's own opinions; in spite of the disdainful announcement that Francis P. Blair of "Lincolndom" had come to spy on them in their own capital, his old friend Davis had welcomed him with open arms on his first visit, had spoken with him cordially and had invited him to tea with his family. Mr. Blair, after conferring with President Lincoln, has just left for City Point, but I have heard nothing about the negotiations which he claims to have undertaken on his own responsibility and in his own name.

There are rumors that matters are really much further advanced, that this week General Grant has received peace overtures which he has sent on to President Lincoln, since he did not want to reply himself. The Lieutenant General is said merely to have told the envoys from the South that he had no authority to negotiate, or even to conclude an armistice unless the President empowered him to do so. This victorious soldier, the stern chief of an army of 100,000 men, the supreme commander of all the military forces of the United States, does not believe he can take on any civil authority or usurp any powers illegally, although a popular vote would doubtless grant them to him. The absolute master of the army, where even the President's wishes take second place, he feels obliged to obey the sovereign majesty of his country's laws. In this proud, noble modesty, General Grant's magnanimous character and his complete and disinterested patriotism certainly count for a great deal. Perhaps other popular generals would not be so reserved nor so honest,*

* General Sherman, for example, cannot be accused of Caesarean ambitions; yet after the capture of Richmond and Lee's surrender he took it upon himself to grant General Johnston, whose army was at his mercy, a kind of general political amnesty which was, to say the least, premature. It was an act which his government was obliged to disavow in dramatic fashion.

but the influence of republican institutions and customs must also be given their share of the credit. America is perhaps the only country in the world where one can see this admirable but rare spectacle of a military power yielding voluntarily to civil authority, plotting none of those disastrous usurpations which, in France, are crowning achievements bought by great men at the expense of the morale and liberty of the people.

The fact is that Americans do not have a taste for obedience or military domination. Although patriotic sentiment has made it possible to call millions of men to arms and to create ten armies, one after the other, over the past four years, it doesn't follow that the civil war has given birth to a military or "Praetorian"[17] spirit which flourishes by preference in countries where under the veil of a false democracy a type of degenerate aristocratic sentiment continues to reign. I am thinking of a society that is apparently democratic but where, by a strange anomaly, flamboyant and unproductive idleness is still the object of public admiration, where blind resentment and ridiculous class prejudice have survived egalitarian leveling and where common, everyday honesty is valued less than a superficial and frivolous affectation of honor. Such a society is fated to fall prey to military domination, to charlatans

[17] Refers to the Praetorian Guard of ancient Rome. As the Empire declined, these troops, which formed the garrison of Rome and the Emperor's bodyguard, frequently rebelled and replaced one ruler with another who promised them greater benefits. Their indiscipline and propensity for meddling in politics have often been included among the reasons for the fall of Rome.

and to the intrigues of underlings, to despotism and individual caprice, until the day comes when it will blush at its vices. What is the original of this portrait? God forbid that it should be our own country! It is certainly not the portrait of the American people. No other country practices in a more complete and natural way the principles of modern equality.

It could be said that there is only one class in America—the working, trading and industrial class which includes everybody. Men so unmetaphysical by nature and by habit, interested only in the useful or practical aspects of things, do not waste their time in a vain display of punctilio. An American officer beaten by the enemy will not try to cover up his defeat with vainglorious boasting like a Chinese mandarin or a Mexican hidalgo and no one will consider his artless admission of defeat a proof of cynicism or cowardice. Is there any other country in the world where one finds more scorn for those habits of aristocratic and wasteful idleness in which we Frenchmen still take pride?

For all these reasons, the military spirit will never enter into their customs. For Americans war is not an occasion to display their brilliant abilities nor a chance to be applauded on a vast stage nor an art like that of the musician or the ship-builder. It is a necessity which they endure courageously and will be able to bring to a successful conclusion.

Pay no attention to the false prophets who predict for America a military dictatorship that will soon give way to a monarchy. That is only a dream of reactionary supporters of slavery or the bitter mockery of a few ambitious men whose hopes have been disappointed. The American army could not become either a durable political force or the instrument of a long-lasting dictatorship. The independence of some and the patriotism of others would never permit it. If a victorious general tried to turn his arms against the liberty of his country, his troops would refuse to follow him or would themselves take charge of his punishment. If after the war some ex-soldiers become bandits instead of returning to civilian life, the firing-squad and the gallows, which the Americans know how to use as well as anyone, will quickly take care of the problem. The permanent army, which will certainly be enlarged, will never be strong enough to be dangerous. In addition, even if a Caesar (and American democracy doesn't produce such men) did seize power in Washington to the sound of military drums, the Republic's foundations would not be shaken. In order to change a democratic nation into a monarchy or even a dictatorship, it would be necessary for a long, slow revolution to have concentrated all power in one place. It it not surprising that the Roman republic fell, when only two forces, the citizens of the capital and the army, controlled everything. Any general popular with the Roman people was master of the empire. If we in France fall so easily from one hand into another, it is because we have one national political center, and whoever controls it has the power to dictate our laws. America is right not to envy us our centralization, believing as she does that the maintenance of the federal form of her institutions is as necessary to preserve her liberty as national unity itself.

13

A Southern City

Baltimore
January 31, 1865

I'VE just arrived here from Washington. Following my usual custom on coming to a new city, I
have been strolling at random through the streets of
Baltimore to get a general idea of its principal features. I wound up my voyage of discovery by climbing the monument to Washington which stands on
top of the highest of the hills on which the city is
built in the fashionable neighborhood of Mount
Vernon Square and Charles Street. Situated at the
center of a park in the form of a Greek cross and
facing south, it is a massive block of masonry surmounted by a tall, plain column topped by a colossal statue of Washington. The base has a variety of
inscriptions referring to the great man himself and
to the state of Maryland which has dedicated this
monument to him. The custodian lighted a lantern
and in the semi-darkness like a miner I ascended
the narrow spiral staircase that leads to the top of
the column.

From such a height the nearby houses seemed to
flatten out, almost to disappear, and pedestrians
looked like black dots. It was truly a bird's-eye
view, and a higher one than the sparrows have.
Poised on the overhanging capital of the column,
with empty space under my feet, I couldn't help

being gripped by the fear that a gust of wind might blow down this tall, slender shaft which seems so precariously balanced. But the view was delightful. The red houses of the city extended into the distance to the south; they seem to be built on the steps of a great amphitheater all along the range of low hills that borders the Chesapeake. Here and there the line of hills is broken by steep valleys down the sides of which the houses and streets seem to be tumbling. A hundred church-towers, steeples, belfries and turrets, their size enlarged by the evening mist, thrust their gray or brown needles upward against an undulating background.

To my left lay the harbor with its forest of bristling masts and the white expanse of the bay closed in by distant promontories. Straight ahead of me was the Patapsco River where thin black lines [of barges] were moving, unrolling behind them slender ribbons of smoke. On my right were hills and fields covered with snow and with black silhouettes along the edges, but keeping, even on this cold evening, an air of grace and gaiety. This is half of the panorama of Baltimore. To the north the houses were less numerous, and one could see where streets ended or else continued as long, straight lines through suburbs yet to be finished. A small stream meandered through the bottom of a curving valley. Factories, smoking chimneys and the long brick-colored roofs of warehouses and workshops bore witness to an industry that was once thriving but is now stifled by the competition of the enterprising Yankees who are held in such contempt in Baltimore, perhaps because they are such rivals.

Various confused sounds floated up to me from the city. I could make out the metallic clatter and the high-pitched bells of the locomotives I saw down in the valley like fat, shiny insects banded with iron. It is oddly agreeable to look down on the microscopic stirrings of this busy anthill with its two hundred thousand inhabitants.

But let us now descend from our aerial perch and take a walk through the city. First you go through the aristocratic quarter with its handsome English-style residences, its small parks and its streets laid out uniformly on the standard American plan in which lots measure 25 by 100 feet. A great silence reigns here as though the world were plunged in a deep sleep. Well-dressed women are sitting at their ground-floor windows, watching through the pane the few people who pass by in the street. The latter are all fashionably clothed and behave politely; many are in mourning, and all seem to be suffering from idleness and boredom. The Civil War has sadly diminished the gay social life of Baltimore. It is divided into two hostile factions, its mood is gloomy and irritable, it has been decimated by many painful losses and it is embittered by political discords that have torn families apart. Finally conquered and dominated by the Unionists, Baltimore has all the attitudes we tend to associate with a dethroned aristocracy, maintaining a proud reserve while awaiting a revenge that will never come. The upper town, in short, is like a tomb. One by one, solitary strollers leave their houses to take the air. On Charles Street I met the same people two or three times as they walked back and forth in an absent-minded way. Americans don't go in much for strolling idly about, so this indicates a social milieu quite different from that of the busy North. Baltimore is essentially a Southern city with all the inertia and lazy somnolence of the South. This is intensified nowadays by private and public mourning and by the stubborn pride, not unmixed with fear, that always haunts the losing side during a revolution when they won't admit their cause is lost. This slave-holding aristocracy formerly lived only for amusement and pleasure, and now public calamities, instead of arousing its energies, have only condemned it to impotence and paralysis.

As I went down into the lower part of the town there were more people on the streets and everything was livelier. Here Charles Street is bordered by shops and soon it is given over entirely to commerce. At last I came to Baltimore's "Broadway," a wide street full of heavy traffic that reminds one of other large Eastern cities. This is the realm of the foreigner and the immigrant, of the Yankee who, undismayed by the hostility of his snobbish, idle brethren of the Southern states, has come here as though to a conquered country to take charge of the commerce they can't be bothered to look after. They treat him more or less the way feudal society treated the Jews and Lombards or the way our nobles treated lawyers.[1] But of what importance are

[1] Duvergier de Hauranne is speaking here of the French nobility before the Revolution of 1789. He no doubt exaggerates their antipathy for the middle classes, especially for those who had attained high office or great wealth. Nor were the nobles as completely averse to money-making as his

the archaic pretentions of an impotent caste? The
Jews and Lombards, with their gold, couldn't be
prevented from dominating the world, nor the merchants of Venice and Holland from dictating laws
to the rest of Europe. And as for the lawyers and
attorneys whom the Old Regime held in such contempt, they have nevertheless become the ruling
class, the only class governments have to reckon
with, while those who obstinately held aloof have
become as powerless as they are useless; they are
like people who have left their country by choice,
or who have become voluntary exiles in the midst
of their fellow citizens, excluded from all participation in economic life or even the political and cultural affairs of the nation. So it is that the Yankees,
after completing the military conquest of the South,
will go on to make peaceful conquests there. This is
inevitable, foreseeable, and the people of the South,
by seeking to forestall these [conquests] by war,
have only made it certain that they will be more
rapid and far-reaching. There's no use talking about
tyranny and spoliation: it is the force of circumstances, the justice of history, that has ordained this
outcome. Idle, unproductive classes must not expect that their power will last forever; the privileges
of this world will always go to those who are able to
take them, to the only ones who deserve them. It is
always the busiest and most forceful who win out.

Except for this commercial street the lower part
of Baltimore is ugly and dirty like the New York

comments suggest. His interpretation, however, was the one
most widely current in his time and was one shared by the
Southern "aristocracy."

waterfront. Narrow, muddy little alleys thread their way at irregular intervals through the huge blocks that lie between the main thoroughfares. Even the latter are laid out in a twisting, whimsical pattern. This is the part of the city where sailors, Negroes, "castaways" and, in general, the entire impoverished class of the city lives. On impulse I turn to the right and Liberty Street takes me straight back to my hotel.

Tomorrow I will give you a brief description of Baltimore high society seen from within. I want to show you the city of brick and plaster before introducing you to its moral side. But we will not leave the physical Baltimore until I have taken you on another tour of exploration out beyond the main streets into the remote southern parts of the city.

These are noisy, crowded and muddy; much more than the rest of the city, they are like our European seaports. Ships are tied up alongside wharves in basins that have been dug by manual labor as at Le Havre or Marseille. There is some indefinable southern quality here that makes me think especially of the latter. There is a large black population that is always imaginative even in its ugliness and here it lends a picturesque appearance even to the dirt. A little farther on there is a district with broad streets and wretched, low houses that are occupied by the poorer people and by immigrants. The German language is the one most frequently heard. The dullness of this neighborhood sends me hurrying back toward the upper city.

In the domestic architecture of Baltimore there is only one unusual and characteristic feature: the houses are often decorated from top to bottom with wide wrought-iron verandas, with open-work columns, entablatures and cast-iron tracery, often making a balcony that goes all around the house on every floor. The façade of the Hotel Barnum is made in this way, as are those of a number of other buildings with pretentions to elegance. I am told that this style of ornamentation is also very common in Charleston, Savannah and Augusta as well as in other Southern cities, particularly in upper-class neighborhoods. And the cities themselves take on some of the gaiety of the open fields thanks to the fact that homes are surrounded by gardens in which the fence railings are overgrown with climbing flowers and vines.

February 1, 1865

THERE IS GREAT and glorious news! Yesterday evening at the very hour when I was strolling through the streets of Baltimore, the constitutional amendment abolishing slavery[2] was triumphantly voted by Congress amid the excited shouts of joy of a huge crowd. This wholly peaceful victory is worth more than the capture of Savannah or even the taking of Richmond. The victories of the Federal armies merely reduce the physical power of the rebellion, but the amendment to the Constitution destroys its reason for being and makes another rebellion forever impossible. As Mr. Sumner has said, the rebellion is, after all, nothing but slavery in arms, and the Union will never be entirely secure until the

[2] The Thirteenth Amendment (see Chapter 9, p. 291, footnote 5.

day slavery is totally eradicated. The country's salvation is bound up with this measure, at once radical and prudent, by which Congress today sets an example; the news is being acclaimed everywhere from one end of America to the other.

But in order for the amendment to become the law of the land it will still have to be ratified by three-fourths of the state legislatures. This is only a question of time, and the definitive adoption of the amendment is as certain as the victory of the Northern states. For the past five years the tide of events and opinions has been flowing constantly in this direction. Once scoffed at as a handful of troublemakers, the abolitionists gained their first foothold in the Senate; now they have swept into the House of Representatives, rallied the Republicans to their banner and converted two-thirds of Congress to their views. Little by little they have been raised up by the flood tide of public opinion with the result that they have now become the majority in the country and can steer the ship of state in the direction they choose. Even the Democrats are beginning to follow their leadership. If in the future a new conservative party should arise to inherit the name "Democrat," it will be no more than a bastard child of the one whose collapse and dissolution we are witnessing today. Such a regenerated Democratic party could perhaps someday raise the liberal banner against a Radicalism grown too demanding and too friendly to centralization, but it can never do this until it has rejected slavery once and for all, accepted sincerely the victories of abolitionism and solemnly recognized the national government's

right to maintain territorial unity by answering insurrection with war.*

Besides, the constitutional amendment is only
the first step along the road of egalitarian progress
and national assimilation down which the forces of
history are sweeping all America. The Radicals who
wrote it have designedly included an elastic clause
that will permit them in the future to broaden its
scope and facilitate its enforcement. According to
the first paragraph, "[Section 1.] Neither slavery nor
involuntary servitude, except as a punishment for
crime whereof the party shall have been duly convicted, shall exist within the United States, or any
place subject to their jurisdiction." And the second
paragraph goes on: "[Section 2.] Congress shall have
power to enforce this article by appropriate legislation." This opens the door wide to the reforms desired by the Radicals.

* It is now well known that several months ago the legislatures of South Carolina, North Carolina and Georgia voted
to give legal force to the constitutional amendment, thus
completing the number of twenty-seven states required for
ratification; thus slavery, already abolished in fact in the majority of the Southern states, has now ceased to have legal
existence there. Strange to relate, the ratification of the
amendment met with greater resistance in some of the
Northern states and in certain "border states" where, moreover, the Unionist cause had numerous supporters, than in
the Southern states, humbled by their defeat and in a hurry
to fulfill the conditions placed by President Johnson upon
the withdrawal of their provisional governors. The states of
New Jersey, Delaware and even Kentucky (which nevertheless had come close to abolishing slavery by state law the
previous year, so far as the state itself was concerned, in
order to put an end to the anarchy of a half-emancipation
that was as unsatisfactory to white proprietors as to black

In fact, in order to emancipate the black race it is not enough to rebuild the constitutional façade and change, as it were, the costume of slavery. Even if the day comes when the Southern states, conquered and pacified, give their assent to the great reform, it will still be necessary to sweep away a great mass of legislation that had its origin in slavery and was meant to perpetuate it. What meaning would the word "liberty" have if all these specific laws were to be maintained and even reinforced, making emancipation merely a new form of servitude? What is the good of proclaiming slavery's abolition if the blacks are still to be excluded from civil and political life, systematically kept out of the schools, banished workers) have held out to the bitter end in refusing to adopt it. But from this time forward the abolition of slavery is an accomplished fact. The old political parties have reorganized and adopted new "platforms." It only remains to be seen whether success will go to the Democrats, who are for readmission pure and simple and without conditions of Southern members of Congress and the abandonment of the freed blacks to the tender mercies of their former masters; or to the Radicals, who wish to obtain for the blacks complete equality, of which the suffrage is the symbol, treating the Southern states meanwhile as "territories" and as a conquered country, even to the point of paying off the debt contracted during the war [by the Union] out of the proceeds of a general confiscation of all property belonging to rebels; or, finally, to the moderate Republicans who, with President Johnson as their leader, are content to obtain from the South the indispensable guarantees that the liberty of the blacks will be respected, while leaving it to future developments to settle peacefully those issues which it would be dangerous to resolve by violence. It is no longer possible to return to the past, and whether the moderates or the Radicals are the ones whose position prevails this year, every day will see a new step forward in the direction of equality.

from the law courts, hunted down like wild animals on the pretext that they are beggars or vagabonds, prevented by force from leaving the plantations and bound to their former toil (though bearing the name of free workers) and forced to work for tiny wages fixed by their old masters—whipped, mal-treated and exposed without any defense to all the whims of the whites?

It is absolutely necessary that those former slaves be protected against the violence of the dispos-sessed master who will have become their enemy, and this is exactly what Congress intends to do if the Southern states do not decide of their own free will to safeguard the liberty of the freed slaves with solid guarantees. The second part of the constitu-tional amendment gives [Congress] the necessary power and even helps the Radicals by providing them with a good excuse for extending the right to vote to blacks if they can demonstrate that it is in-dispensable to give them political power in order to make them truly free men.*

Perhaps, indeed, there will be no other alterna-tive. In the Southern states there is a whole system of political and social institutions, a whole network of habits and traditional behavior that must be de-stroyed before anyone can boast that the blacks have really been freed. Law and conscience have

* This is very well understood in the Southern states and it is for this reason that a number of them have voluntarily abolished slavery by state law without yet, however, taking the formal decision to ratify the constitutional amendment. Some of them, among others the state of Mississippi, have even ratified the first article of the amendment although they have rejected the second.

been molded by slavery, it is deeply rooted in private life and it serves as the foundation for all social distinctions. A comparison of the North with the South is one of the best methods of demonstrating the incalculable influence, the overriding importance, of social realities compared with the interplay of political institutions. Here are two countries living under democratic and republican institutions that are very nearly identical; they are inhabited by people of the same ethnic stocks and often of the same families. The principles of democracy are as fully accepted in the South as in the North; [white] people have the same liberties; the laws are inspired by the same spirit; the forms of government are the same—and yet there are such profound differences between the two peoples that an American can tell at a glance whether he is in a slave state or a free state. As early as thirty years ago Tocqueville was aware of this difference when, on a boat on the Ohio River, he heard from one shore the noise of cities, the hum of industry and human activity, and on the opposite shore saw nothing but solitude, savagery and death.

It is slavery that condemns the South to this fatal stagnation. If the South's wealth up to now has been entirely agricultural, that is because nothing but agriculture can flourish under the system of slave labor. Only two sources of value are known: the land and the human livestock that cultivates it. And even the land, since it is not the object of competition by free labor, has no other value than that of the slaves put to work upon it. Hence the only true wealth in the Southern states is the slave himself; he is the only instrument of labor and the only productive agent. The most opulent planters of the South frequently have no capital and are obliged to borrow from Northern financiers and wholesale merchants against the profits of future crops. The latter can lend only on burdensome terms, for all trade is difficult in isolated regions where there are no good means of communication, where the only way to market may be a small river that isn't even navigable every year. As a result, the land is often mortgaged and its produce sold far in advance. Those great landed fortunes which appear to be so solid are nearly all built on shaky foundations, ready to collapse like houses of cards. This becomes evident at the owner's death when creditors slap liens on all the family's possessions and proceed to sell off chattels, animals and human beings to a horde of eager speculators who come running to be in at the death like a pack of wolves. Such catastrophes are not infrequent in the great plantation families of the South, and it is on such occasions that one may see in all its horror the true character of the holy, patriarchal institution of slavery.

Even when the slave lives at his master's side on the plantation where he was born, his condition is certainly nothing to be envied; it is comparable to that of a beast of burden or that of a man condemned to the galleys for life. He is told to go here or there, herded about in a gang and made to work by being flogged with a whip; he is forced to beget children at his master's orders, he is denied all religious, intellectual or moral education, and, as you know, there are very strict laws in the South that even make it a crime to teach a Negro to read. If, as a last resort, he should try to escape, he is hunted down with rifle fire, with fierce dogs trained especially to follow his trail; he may be beaten or even killed without any legal formalities. This patriarchal justice is the only one in effect and the only kind possible in a region where, to be sure, the letter of the law pretends to defend the life of the black man against the homicidal whim of the white man, but where the oppressed have no right to lodge a complaint or to appeal to the protection of the laws.* In short, the slave is excluded from the human family; he is entirely dependent on his master's harsh or gentle disposition; sometimes he may be lucky enough to enjoy the modest happiness of the well-fed ox that can repair the day's fatigue by chewing its cud as it lies on a pile of straw; he may even aspire to the happy lot of a favorite dog or docile horse that is petted by its master. All those who have lived in the Southern states say that the planter's slaves are members of his family in more than one sense. Sometimes for the sake of pleasure, sometimes through calculation and greed, he works hard, they say, to enlarge these families so that the product may be sold at a later time. Some of these great aristocratic proprietors are real human stud animals who make a profit even on their pleasures;

* It is well known that the old laws of the Southern states denied to colored people the right to appear or to testify in court against a white man. Even the new legislatures that have repealed this odious exception have not yet authorized the presence of blacks in the courtroom except in cases where the interests of a black person are involved.

the majority maintain in their homes, alongside their legal families, one or two more or less secret families from which they choose their personal servants. I have been told of more than one "gentleman" of noble race who has as his "body servant" (a kind of *valet de chambre* or attendant who never leaves his master's presence) a brother or a son who is still his slave. After a number of generations this race of hereditary servants has become almost white. Then, if the head of the family is a generous man, he has them educated, gives them their freedom and sends them to live in Europe so they may escape discrimination on account of their birth and color. But not all masters assume such an obligation, and more than once it has been known to happen that at the father's death young men brought up to think of themselves as masters wake up to find themselves the slaves of a greedy or jealous heir; young women who have grown up amidst all the luxury of modern life may fall into the clutches of a resentful mother-in-law who, to get revenge, has them sold to city debauchees whether young or old.

What the slave dreads most is being sold to a far-away owner, for then all his memories, all his affections and family ties, are broken forever; husbands are separated from wives; little children are torn from their mothers' arms. A slave who is forced in this way to knock about the world without ever taking root anywhere soon loses all faith, all conscience, and feels a disinclination to form any durable relationships. Moreover, his master is no less demoralized than he is: the great Jefferson, harassed by his creditors, was obliged to rent out his slaves and sold his own children. I know of a rich planter who confessed, naïvely and without embarrassment, that he had done the same. "I had so many, you see! How could I keep them all?" To find morals like this you would have to go to China or Turkey! And even the Chinese, who have been accused of drowning their children, or the Turks who abandon them or send them out to beg their livelihood, haven't yet hit upon the horrifying idea of selling them for hard cash. The apologists for slavery think they can shrug all this off by saying that such atrocities are, after all, not very common. It's comforting to know that human nature, however perverted it may be by laws and customs, doesn't allow such things to happen every day! But the fact remains that they are part and parcel of the morality of slavery and are unavoidable under an institution that will allow parenthood to be turned into a commodity to be infamously bought and sold.

It is above all when the law lays a cold hand on private fortunes that one must bow down in admiration of the partriarchal system! The law knows nothing of hidden love affairs, of secret bonds of affection; it spells out with all its pitiless rigor the logic of the institution. [To understand slavery] you must attend the public auctions where men, women, children and old people, including both the inarticulate black giant who knows nothing but how to swing an axe and the lovely, white-skinned girl brought up under her father's eyes, all of whom are exhibited on the infamous block for the inspection of connoisseurs along with horses and household furnishings! Then you'd see how all the most predatory types gather around: first and foremost, the slave-dealer, always armed with a huge whip, two loaded pistols and a cutlass—a jolly individual full of effrontery who shouts jokes and blasphemies at the top of his lungs. He pinches the merchandise, he glowers, he drives down the price. This old woman he will send off to the cotton field, this tall, husky fellow to the rice paddies, this other one to the killing toil of the swamps and this last one, a lad of fifteen, he will send to the great central market in New Orleans where he expects to get $3,000 for him. In a little while, when he has rounded up all his victims, you will see him ride away, whip in hand, driving before him his gang of prisoners who walk dejectedly chained together in groups of four toward the unknown place of their unending exile.

Yes, this is the reality of slavery, which has been portrayed as the nursery of all chivalrous feelings and of all manly virtues! The "Southern aristocracy," as it calls itself, has two faithful agents: the slave-driver and the slave-dealer. It has an affection for both these estimable personages; it invites them to its table; and they are proud of having their assigned place in the hierarchy. They are right, for this whole aristocracy has no other basis than slavery, and they are its indispensable servitors. Every man's power and influence, like his wealth, is determined by the number of slaves he owns. As for the poor whites and ne'er-do-wells, they feel that they have an ineffaceable title of nobility in the color of their skins. No one insists so vehemently on the distinction between himself and a black or yellow person as these "poor whites," even though their physical degeneracy and loose morals make them far more brutish than the slaves they reject with such lordly contempt. Their racial vanity is incredible—worse, even, than that of the great planters—and with them, even more than with the Yankees, all women are "ladies" and all males are "gentlemen." Living in wretched hovels, dressed in filthy rags, sleeping like pigs on the bare ground, living like wolves by hunting and thievery or by begging scraps from their rich neighbors, they are still aristocrats because they enjoy the noble prerogatives of idleness and ignorance. Owning scarcely anything in the whole world but their knives and rifles, they live with their arms folded on their breasts in arrogant indolence and sincerely believe themselves far superior to the vile Yankee.

The great planters, whose influence rests on their support, carefully maintain them in this state of abject savagery. Though they too are victims of the slave system and of a social structure that condemns them to poverty and idleness, they take more pride in it than anyone else and have shown themselves to be its most fanatical defenders. At the outset of the war they were made to believe that the Yankees would not dare to fight and that the Southerners would have only to show themselves to be victorious. They were told, and they believed unquestioningly, that President Lincoln was part Negro, as were all his abolitionist friends. In most of their lonely hamlets there are neither schools nor churches within a radius of thirty or forty miles. The Yankee adventurers who teach them to sing psalms or mumble the alphabet are all spineless hirelings of the aristocracy and preach or teach whatever it commands. Ignorance and mental torpor and a fierce pride in their own poverty and servility—all these are fruits of slavery and help to perpetuate it. How much progress and how much liberty are possible under a system that makes labor despicable because synonymous with servitude?

It is said nevertheless that in appearance the manners and customs of the South are the most democratic and egalitarian in the world. The half-savage peasant who comes to beg at the rich man's door speaks to the planter with the pride of a brother and an equal. He does not put aside his dignity as a member of the sovereign people. Families of this class often come together at "camp meetings" to sing hymns or to "barbecues" to listen to "stump speeches"; on these occasions they get drunk, they fight, they strut about and empty their purses in a day. When elections take place the whole citizenry turns out armed to the teeth, and the parties wage a sort of civil war on one another around the polling-place. One might think they were moved by a fierce spirit of personal independence, but these orgies have no real significance and in the end everyone takes orders from the aristocracy. The planters feel unbounded contempt for the common people they make use of even while allowing them to retain the illusion of an empty sovereignty. They also keep at their beck and call all the middle-class small property-owners who reside in the country towns and are too poor to live on their incomes but too lazy to make them bigger, who live in idleness by owning a few slaves whom they rent out to the great landed proprietors on whose alms and gratuities they eke out an existence. This indolent but turbulent class dominates all the Southern cities, where it constitutes the most oppressive kind of oligarchy. It enforces orthodox opinions, persecutes Unionists, drives out the opponents of slavery, suppresses, burns or confiscates newspapers and books that come from the North and exercises an unbearable tyranny in the service of slavery.

Such are the influences that must fall to the ground along with slavery. On the other side of the account, there is a new class in the Southern states that has been silently growing these past twenty years: this is the class of poor whites who have gained wealth and independence through their labor and have come to be property-owners in their own right, cultivating the soil with their own hands. For long years they have been enemies of the secessionist aristocracy and followed it only with the greatest reluctance into the present rebellion. It is with this class, as with the working farmers of the North, that the future of American liberty rests, together with the safety of the Federal union. Hard-working, independent, asking only to be educated, augmented continually by recruits from the Northern states, it is the proud destiny of this class to build the new South on the ruins of slavery.

February 2, 1865

IF EVER I have been sorry to leave a city, it was this evening when I said farewell to the people who have shown me such splendid hospitality here in Baltimore. I have especially grateful feelings toward

Messrs. Eaton and Morris,[3] two of the most respected gentlemen of the place, both pre-eminent in ability and highly cultivated as well. They are both Unionists, though in different degrees and with very different effects on their standing in this society.

Mr. Eaton is a Republican, candid and definite in his opinions, without ifs or buts and adopts a firm, just—though moderate—view of the necessities and duties of the present. He was a supporter of Mr. Lincoln in the recent electoral campaign; he takes satisfaction in the total abolition of slavery; and, even while according him involuntary respect, the secessionist faction has put him on their bad books as a tool of the Yankees.

Mr. Morris is less decided and less firm in his policy. He is a former slaveowner, a Democrat who supported McClellan, the son-in-law of the secessionist Senator Reverdy Johnson and a brother-in-law of the Radical Congressman [Henry] Winter Davis, but he is also subject to a conflict of loyalties on account of his other Southern friends and relatives. He is a man who expresses regret more frequently than condemnation, and it was only with a heavy heart that he accepted the necessity of war, emancipation and the subjugation of the South. What he believes in most strongly is the Union— the integrity of the American nation and its restoration at any cost, but he also has many sympathetic sighs and much tender concern for the chivalrous

[3] Probably John T. Morris, businessman and president of the Board of Commissioners of Public Schools. Mr. Eaton was probably George Nathaniel Eaton, a merchant and civic leader.

aristocrats of the South. In coöperation with declared secessionists he supported the candidacy of McClellan, but he did this in the hope and belief that his favorite would govern with greater firmness as well as more leniency, that he would do a better job both of making war and of concluding peace. As a result he has a foot in both parties: first, in the Republican party, which he only half opposes and in which he counts his best friends, and then among the Rebels, with whom he has long-standing family and social ties as well as a temporary political alliance dating from the last elections. But in spite of all this the Unionists of the city count him as one of their own, for here the issue is not posed—as in the North—as a choice between two political parties, each of which proposes or pretends to propose the same objective to be attained by different means; rather, it is posed here as an opposition between patriots and the declared enemies of American nationhood who do not even take the trouble to disguise their treason. Among the people, that is, among the laboring and merchant classes, there is Unionist sentiment that weighs decisively in the electoral scales; but the rich and fashionable classes have taken as their password—in a sense, as a test of social acceptability—a blind and implacable hatred for the Republicans and an unflagging readiness to conspire against the government of their country.

Yesterday Mr. Eaton invited me to dinner at his beautiful house on Mount Vernon Square. He keeps a bachelor's establishment and is well-known for his hospitality to newcomers. We were six at table. There was Mr. Eaton's brother, a man of great can-

dor and cordiality who has his feet firmly on the
ground. Right at the outset he told me that he
agrees as completely with me on French politics as I
do with him on American affairs. There was also a
Mr. Kennedy,[4] the Everett or Motley[5] of Baltimore, a
politician who has become a man of letters in retirement. I had the misfortune to be unaware of his
great reputation. He is a former Secretary of the
Navy and was an influential member of Congress, a
participant in all the great events of the previous
generation and a man who remembers Calhoun,
Webster and Jackson. He is also the author of a
series of novels which Americans rank among the
best examples of their literature. He is getting on in
years and his health is none too good, though you
would not know it from his exterior, which is still
robust; he wears a white beard, has courtly manners
and an open, intelligent, kindly face. I have seldom
met anyone I've liked more at first sight.

He regaled us with anecdotes that were vivid and
original, both about President Jackson, that strange
backwoodsman who has assumed a large place in
history because of the events of his administration,

[4] John Pendleton Kennedy (1795-1870), in addition to
writing three novels of plantation life in Virginia, books that
were highly regarded and widely read in his own day (the
best being *Horse-Shoe Robinson*, published in 1835), was
Secretary of the Navy in the administration of Millard P.
Fillmore. A prominent Whig, he was a member of Congress
(1838-44). He was a friend of Edgar Allan Poe.

[5] Edward Everett (1794-1865) and John Lothrop Motley
(1814-1877) were leading literary lights of the period, the
former as a famous orator and the latter as author of *The
Rise of the Dutch Republic* (3 vols., 1856).

and about the actually barbarous customs of "Southern chivalry." We heard, for example, of the Kentucky "free fight," a sport that consists of a brawl in which two good friends attempt to kill each other, while drunk, in a locked, dark room. He told us also about public duels in which the two principals agree to meet at an inn and there, before a crowd gathered as if for a spectacle, let fly at one another with pistols and knives until one of them is left for good on the undertaker's slab. These half-civilized folk seem superbly indifferent to human life and hold murder in great respect; they think it a duty to spill blood to show one's manhood.

He told of a thousand more traits of that anarchic and violent region and illustrated them with a compelling verve that gave me an understanding of the bloodthirsty brutality of the Texas and Missouri [guerrilla] bands. Such are the ferocious ways that give rise to the humane institution of slavery! These are the men who herd Federal prisoners together in open sewers, without shelter, clothing, fire or bread, leaving them there to rot like a pack of pariah dogs, hardly even allowing them to bury their dead and whiling the time away in the barbarous sport of taking pot-shots at the Yankees. These are the men who, in the West, have shot down whole villages just for the fun of it, carrying off scalps as trophies and leaving nothing but mutilated corpses in the burning houses. They are the same ones who, in Kentucky and Tennessee and all the border states, have strung up patriots in order to terrorize the Unionist party and who, even now, murder even without pleading retaliation as a pretext all the former

[Union] soldiers who fall into their hands. Finally, it is this same spirit that drives on the leaders of the Rebel government when they encourage and even order atrocities, and then have the effrontery to complain when the government of the United States, in a timid effort at reprisal, deprives Southern prisoners of sugar and coffee or refuses to issue them blankets unless the Confederacy sends money to pay for them!

The table conversation, which at first ran along in a series of whimsical digressions, at last settled down to the great—indeed, the unique—subject that monopolizes everyone's thoughts here: the basic and always controversial question of whether the Rebels were right in claiming a right of secession. There again, Mr. Kennedy's voice compelled our attention. His lucid, eloquent, passionate words brought life and warmth into the narrow and subtle scholasticism of constitutional law. I shall not weary you with his conclusions, which are identical with my own, but in all the discussions of this hackneyed question that I have heard, no one has ever made the truth of the matter more clear, more luminous or more convincing. Mr. Morris, whose assent was given only with great reluctance, objected to the vivacity of Mr. Kennedy's language and told me as we were leaving: "Although, as you can see, he is a stormy petrel, he is the most generous and well-intentioned man alive. He doesn't harbor the shadow of a personal resentment against those guilty people he was denouncing and holding up to public opprobrium." Mr. Eaton, too, when speaking to me of his friend's poor health and the fears it had more than once given rise to, paid tribute to his magnanimity, which is rare among men who are so full of passionate conviction. "Every time a Rebel needs a protector," he told me, "whether because he is threatened with imprisonment or because his property is endangered or because he wants a favor from the government he is conspiring against, he always turns to Mr. Kennedy, who will then move heaven and earth to be of assistance to him."

In the evening Mr. Morris took me to a ball attended by the flower of secessionist society. Since the coming of the war life has changed greatly, and private receptions have grown more and more infrequent; but once or twice a week people still come together in a large ballroom where there is a chance to get some relief from the prevailing gloom. On these occasions, I was told, the company may be rather mixed, and in fact not all those present had the fine manners, the Parisian dress or the impeccable command of French possessed by my companion. Still, I was impressed by the good manners as well as the educational attainments of the women present. As for the men—brothers, fathers and sons—the majority are at Richmond or on the high seas in some pirate vessel flying the Confederate ensign. In any event, I can't speak as an expert on a group of people in whose company I have spent only two hours, ten minutes of which, at most, was with the same person.

Today from morning to night I have not been out of Mr. Eaton's sight. He has put himself at my disposal with a courtesy and kindness that are quite rare even in this hospitable land of America. I won't

tell you about his books, his art objects, his draw-
ings, his many memories of the long trips he has
taken. It is the man himself I want to make you
acquainted with, for he is a remarkable specimen of
that enlightened class of American travelers and
cosmopolites who are the real high nobility of this
mercantile society. Possessing a comfortable fortune, he retired from business at the age of thirty
and became a globe-trotter. I can't think of a single
country in the world that he hasn't seen nor a great
city of Europe where he hasn't made a long stay. He
is independent of all political parties and is free of
any personal ambition, seeking to exert his influence only for the benefit of the national cause; he
devotes most of his time these days to running the
Peabody Institute, a private foundation for the encouragement of literature that will one day take on
the dimensions of a great university. You may well
imagine that such a man cannot entertain any of the
anti-European prejudices that often render the
company of his fellow-countrymen so unpleasant.
As a person he has little in common with the New
York gold merchants or with the "cock-fighters"
and "Negro-whippers" of the South.[6] Though he is
inclined to deplore the Yankee character as too
pragmatic and grasping, he condemns even more
sharply the frivolity and contemptuous nullity of
planters who have the pride of aristocrats without
having their culture or dignity. I think I've explained to you that in the current American revolution the great landed proprietors of Maryland have
played an anti-patriotic role similar to that of our

[6] These expressions are in English in the original text.

noble *émigrés*[7] and that their stubbornness has been punished by a similar ostracism from public affairs. Even though they still have social gatherings to dance and show off their ladies' toilettes, they have systematically withdrawn from all useful or benevolent enterprises. This rule of abstention—stupid, obstinate and carried to the point of inertia—has become for them a point of honor. Many of them don't even want to take part in elections; they are too proud to mix with the vile multitude that has taken power away from them. They are afraid that if they played any role in public affairs, even that of a legal opposition, they would be acknowledging their citizenship and hence the shameful supremacy of the Yankees. If they were members of some charitable association, they now withdraw their advice and financial support; if they are officers of a bank, they make it a matter of pride to work against their Republican colleagues; although there are ten secessionists on a board of twenty-seven trustees of the Peabody Institute, these are ten inanimate bodies who, by their absence, protest—but against what? They don't even know themselves. They try to create an empty space around their enemies without suspecting that the desert is really around themselves and that their spitefulness only harms their own interests. Well, they're welcome to play dead and doze off into a feigned lethargy; their opponents are only too happy to march over their supine

[7] Another reference to the French Revolution of 1789 in which many nobles emigrated to take up arms against the Republic or to engage in other forms of counter-Revolutionary activity.

bodies and to add a fresh shovelful of dirt to their graves every day. When they tire of this ungrateful role they will want to get up and live again, but will find that they have been buried once and for all.

I'm sure you haven't forgotten that Maryland came very close to being a Rebel state. The Confederates claim that they still haven't given up hope of reclaiming it. The famous Mason-Dixon line, which is the northern frontier of slavery, took in the state of Maryland. To keep it in the Union it was necessary for Butler, secure in the inexperience of an amateur soldier, to charge with his regiment into the midst of this hostile population: when he marched through the streets of Baltimore his troops were fired on from the windows.[8] It was necessary also for General McClellan (and Maryland has not forgotten this) to seize the Rebel legislature by the throat and put it under lock and key[9] to prevent it

[8] Troops of the 6th Massachusetts militia regiment, commanded by Butler and ordered to the defense of Washington, were fired on in Baltimore while changing trains in the late evening of April 19, 1861. Butler was not present, the detachment being led by Colonel Edward F. Jones; 6 men were killed and 30 wounded. On May 14, 1861, Butler occupied Baltimore in a surprise move by night without orders, without informing his superior, General Winfield Scott, and without firing a shot. Duvergier de Hauranne seems to confuse the two incidents.

[9] On September 12, 1861, the Federal government ordered the arrest of allegedly disloyal members of the Maryland legislature, scheduled to convene in Frederick September 17. McClellan carried out numerous arrests from the 12th to the 17th, strongly discouraging the secessionists. The author exaggerates both the threat to the Unionist cause and the extent of McClellan's counter-measures.

from following the contagious example of [Southern] ordinances of secession.

These revolutionary proceedings have left deep resentments. There is in Maryland a whole class who regard themselves as conquered people. Left to themselves, they would not be content, like certain Democrats, to let the Confederacy "depart in peace," but would actively embrace the Rebel cause and would add one more great heap of debris to its ruins. Four years ago these people were in the majority, but events since then have put things in a new light and, as always, the influence of the majority in the nation has helped to enlarge the local minority on which the Union depends in this state. I doubt that at the present time, despite all their clamor against the tyranny of the Union, there are any secessionists in Baltimore who sincerely wish to be transported to Richmond. They express a lot of good wishes for the [Southern] cause, but they limit themselves to good wishes, along with a few random acts of treason that have no effect but to prolong the agony without making it any less desperate. For as much longer as the war lasts, Maryland will remain in a state of half-suppressed civil agitation kept under control only by force.

Mr. Eaton would be the first to concede that without the presence of military power there would have been fighting in the streets during the elections; he even doubts that the vote was perfectly honest and does not dare affirm that Lincoln would have carried the state without the soldiers' vote and the presence of the army. As for the new constitution, which abolishes slavery in the state, there is no

question in his mind that it would have been rejected had it not been for the pressure and the tireless
efforts of the Federal troops.

So great is the power of a *fait accompli* that the
abolitionist majority, formerly counted in hundreds
of votes, would today amount to several thousand.
Resentment is no less great on that account among
those who have lost their property as a result, but
they failed to understand the necessity for this in
good time. Today the Unionist cause and the abolitionist cause are tending to coalesce, and the time
for equivocation by the parties is past: one must
either put the Union above slavery and reëstablish a
following in the Rebel states by advocating [volun-
tary] emancipation, or else declare against national
unity and embrace the South as ones country. It is
the latter choice that has been made by Baltimore
high society, with all the implacable fury that goes
with lost causes. The women are the most rabid and
the most fearless. They defy General [Lew] Wallace, the military governor of Maryland, with a
heroism worthy of a better cause.

I have been asking myself all along how it comes
about that the women of the South are so passion-
ately dedicated to a domestic institution that turns
the family into a you-know-what and, under the
wife's very eyes, fills the house with a swarm of ille-
gitimate little creatures whose parentage is perfectly
well known to them. No doubt they read the Bible
and find it quite natural that Hagar should share the
patriarch with Sarah, assuming, of course, that Ish-
mael is later sold or turned out of doors like a dog.
A Baltimore lady, the grave and respectable mother

of a family, the wife of a New England Yankee, told me one day in a joking manner, though at bottom very seriously, that she never would have married him if she had foreseen this civil war and had known in advance what detestable opinions her husband held.

"But how, then, does it happen," I asked, "that you women like slave owners so much and that you are so fanatical for the cause of slavery? Don't you know better than anyone else what little domestic difficulties it gives rise to?"

"Oh!" she replied with a laugh, "it isn't always the best men that we love the best."

The fact is that one is not a gentleman in the eyes of these ladies unless one is a buyer and seller of human beings.

"Whom have you seen in Washington?" a Rebel lady asked me the other day. This lady is descended on both her father's and her mother's side from two of the leading families of the slaveholding aristocracy and is immoderately proud of her pedigree, though she is now the wife of an ordinary commission-merchant.

"I have seen Mr. Chase (a cry of surprise), Mr. Sherman[10] (a cry of disgust)—'Sherman! Sherman! Why do you associate with people like that?'

"I beg your pardon, but Mr. Sherman seemed to me a respectable man and very well mannered." More expressions of contempt.

"But just because a man is a Republican, is he no longer a gentleman?"

[10] Salmon P. Chase and Senator John Sherman, a Republican from Ohio, a moderate leaning toward the Radicals.

"Goodness gracious yes! It almost comes to that."

Doesn't that sound like some Ultra-royalist under the Restoration?[11] Such scornful attitudes come naturally to those who have come down in life, to people who feel diminished and have no consolation left except to be meanly contemptuous of everything and everyone. This same lady, when I rang the doorbell of the house in which we had this memorable conversation, made a wry face when she heard I was there "because she had heard it said that I was a Unionist."

So it seems that here in Baltimore the very word "Union" is outlawed and the name of "Unionist" is a shameful one. "Be very careful," said another lady who is equally pro-Rebel at heart, but whose secessionism is more tolerant for the very good reason that her whole family is in the Federal administration, navy or army or is in government service in the North. "Be very careful about admitting that you are a Unionist in Baltimore—people won't like it. I am sorry for you that you came here with that reputation: it will close all doors to you."

It must be said that a few of these heroic ladies have been handled a bit roughly by General Wallace. The one I have been telling you about was summoned before him one day and, upon being asked the question, "Madam, are you a Unionist?" boldly replied: "No, I am not."

"Your family," he went on, "is under suspicion;

[11] The Restoration of the Bourbon monarchy in the person of Louis XVIII after the fall of Napoleon in 1815. Ultra-royalists (who were "more royalist than the king") controlled the assemblies and the ministry.

you have relatives in the South." "Well, I won't disown them."

"We have an eye on you. Be careful how you behave."

The courtesy of a Yankee officer is not always exquisitely refined, even in dealing with women, especially when it is overlaid with patriotic gruffness. I don't pretend to find excuses for General Wallace. But it must be admitted that these ladies have shown themselves so far superior to the weaknesses of their sex that they have earned the right to be accorded all the honors due to masculinity. They are not satisfied merely to collect money, sell subscriptions and make charitable gifts to help Rebel prisoners, whereas the soldiers of the Union don't get a dollar of their money and their opposition brought about the failure of the "Sanitary Fair"[12] in Baltimore.

It is their right to behave this way and nobody challenges it. But what is worse is that the majority of overt acts of treason are committed by women. How can you account for the fact that up to now not a single military plan has been kept secret for more than a week? Whose ear is it that listens for the South in those secret councils of war where no one is present except a few military leaders, the Secretary of War and the President? Who is the

[12] This was part of the fund-raising efforts of the U.S. Sanitary Commission. In his first volume Duvergier de Hauranne gave an enthusiastic description of a highly successful "Sanitary Fair" held in Philadelphia in June, 1864. (*A Frenchman in Lincoln's America*, Vol. I, pp. 43-46.) Similar fairs were held in the other large cities of the North.

subtle and elusive spy that slips invisibly into their midst? It is a woman, often a Rebel, who once more plucks Eve's apple and gets men to eat it in order to wheedle their secrets from them. There is hardly a family in Baltimore that does not have a relative or an intimate friend working for the Confederacy. You overhear scraps of conversation: "My brother, who is in the Southern army," "My brother, who is in the navy—the *Southern* navy, of course." This is the kind of chatter you hear from the young misses I danced with yesterday evening. They are taught to venerate slavery as they are taught to love God, and to hate the Union as they are taught to flee the devil. What other government would not lose patience after all these poisoned pin-pricks and send, now and then, a few of these rabid lambs to employ their patriotic fervor on a wider stage?

Even the oath of allegiance, that oppressive, revolutionary measure, is excusable, given this incessant small-scale civil war and these daily acts of treason. Do you remember what was done by our National Convention[13] when confronted with an enemy that was much weaker and much less guilty? Suspect persons were sent to the scaffold; long lists of proscribed individuals were sent to the guillotine; in a word, the most civilized nation in the world acted with the harshest brutality toward victims begging

[13] During the French Revolution the National Convention (1792-1795), dominated after mid-1793 by the radical Jacobins, governed France through the Committee of Public Safety led by Maximilien Robespierre. This was a period of severe economic crisis, invasion and civil war; suspected traitors and enemies of the Revolution were ruthlessly dealt with.

for mercy. Think about all this, and you will have a greater respect for the ill-mannered Yankee who doesn't make a fetish of politeness but is capable of such moderation in inflicting well-justified punishment and unobtrusively shows so much humanity in his dealings with the vanquished.

Finally, I want to tell you about the great news of the day—peace, or at least negotiations looking toward peace—Mr. Stephens's mission (for he has been sent by President Davis as an ambassador to President Lincoln), Mr. Seward's departure to go and meet him at Fort Monroe and finally the departure by special train of the President himself, the eagerness of the two governments to exchange visits and the question that is to be decided: Will they exchange a kiss of peace? But with all my gossiping I have lost track of the time. So I shall take leave of Baltimore and of Mr. Eaton, who has already accepted me among the number of his close friends and said to me "God bless you!" as he hastily shook my hand in farewell. I must run to catch the train for Philadelphia.

14

Philadelphia

Philadelphia
February 3, 1865

I MUST be allowed to vent my spleen one more time on the railroads of America. Last night I arrived here from Baltimore; never had a passenger coach seemed more asphyxiating, more nauseating. Picture a cargo of peasants and soldiers crammed into a third-class carriage and raised to a white heat by a cast-iron stove. Every sort of miasma, beginning with the fumes of whiskey and going on to include the stench of tobacco and the exhalations of human grease, were blended together in an atmosphere of carbon dioxide that pressed down on ones lungs and eyes like a crushing weight. If you are not provided with a magical talisman in the form of a petticoat at your side so as to gain admission to the "ladies' car," you have no choice but to go into this cavern and squeeze yourself into a seat beside a drunken soldier or a farmer reeking with manure, for it is freezing outside and it wouldn't take more than an hour on the platform to turn you into a block of ice.

But where to find a seat? Here is half a seat vacant beside a big fat fellow sprawled at full length on a bench where he is pretending to be asleep so people will leave him alone. Give him a shake, make him reluctantly yield you a tiny space, and

don't by any means allow yourself to be put off by
the filth he spreads around him, for he will scrape
his heavy boots back and forth along your legs,
pound you into your corner like the iron under a
trip-hammer and from time to time will give you a
savage jab in the chest with his elbow. Soldiers on
leave, who for three days have been amply compen-
sating themselves for the disciplined sobriety of the
army, curse, shout, exchange fisticuffs and slap you
on the back, fraternally offering you a kiss from the
divine bottle. Some are very amusing in their state
of intoxication, heaping insults upon themselves,
spouting grandiloquent political or military orations, taking anyone who comes along for an old
friend and confiding in him, letting themselves be
led along like children by everyone who takes a
fancy to listen to their talk, reminding one, by their
communicative ardor, of Rousseau's praise for the
good fellowship and openness of drunkards.[1] I finally got off and appeared at four o'clock in the morning more dead than alive in the great marble lobby
of the Continental Hotel.

February 6, 1865

I'M STILL HERE in Philadelphia, detained by the gracious and hospitable cordiality I have found here.
Besides, it would be making a useless stop on the
journey from Baltimore to New York if I were to
leave Philadelphia without seeing its schools, its

[1] Jean-Jacques Rousseau wrote in his *Nouvelle Héloise* in a
passage describing the merriment of the grape harvest at
Clarens in Switzerland that drunkenness dissolves constraint
and makes people affable.

churches, its prisons or any of the other public buildings that house its cultural institutions. So I have given in to the friendly urgings of my new friends, Mr. Field[2] and Mr. [James Henry] Haseltine. When I accepted their obliging offer to be of service, the least I could do was to put myself entirely in their hands. First, Mr. Field took me for a walk from one side of the city to the other. It is remarkable that in America the things they show first to visitors are not the churches, the great mansions or the palaces dedicated to luxury, but buildings of public utility, which are, in truth, the only works of art that are known here, or at least they are the only ones that express the industrial genius of the country. Therefore Mr. Field took me first to see the drinking-water reservoirs of Philadelphia. These are built beside the Schuylkill in a place called Fairmount at the top of a little hill to which the water is raised by enormous pumps connected to huge wheels that are turned by the river's current. The site is lovely and cheerful, and the Philadelphians love to come here to skate in winter or to enjoy in summer the cool shade of the arbors that have been planted round about. The Schuylkill, impounded here behind a dam over which it flows in a cascade, runs down clear and copious from a pretty little valley full of tall trees, gardens and summer-houses.

Then Mr. R. takes charge of me. He is a young man of twenty-six, studious, somewhat solemn, well

[2] Perhaps this was J. H. Haseltine's younger brother, Charles Field Haseltine. No Philadelphian prominent in 1865 had Field as a family name.

educated and the owner of a substantial fortune. For the last year he has worked as a volunteer at the hard and ungrateful task of recruiting soldiers for the city. For two years he served in the army as a staff officer, and he told me that he had never learned so much as when he was in the army and had to spend his hours of idleness crouched in his tent reading the books his family sent him every week, now scattered along the roadsides of Virginia.

First we visited the law courts. There I saw an elderly attorney with all the mannerisms of a country man—my guide told me he was one of the leading lights of the Philadelphia bar. On learning that I was a foreigner and that I had just come from the Army of the Potomac, he said to me with the inimitable naïveté of American national pride: "What an army we have! You have nothing to compare with it; it has no equal in the whole world. Isn't it true, Sir," he went on emphatically, "Isn't it true that we are a great nation?"

My reply must have struck him as rather cool, for nothing is better calculated to dampen my enthusiasm than this kind of naïve fishing for praise. Yet how can one be annoyed with so sincere and ingenuous an admiration of oneself. In every country patriotism is next-of-kin to chauvinism.

I shall only mention in passing the Franklin Library, whose director, according to the rule laid down by the statutes, is a descendant of its illustrious founder. There, however, I saw a map and a bird's-eye-view of Philadelphia as it was in the time of William Penn, with its widely spaced houses with pointed gables and a few small ships moored along the river bank. From there we went on to Girard College a huge structure of marble with a Doric façade. This is a home for orphan children founded by Etienne Girard,[3] a wealthy Frenchman whose name has remained famous throughout America as would be the case in our country for some financier worth several hundred millions. It is interesting that the founder, an eighteenth-century freethinker, put into his will a provision that expressly forbids ministers of any organized religion to enter the school. But don't conclude from this that the three hundred poor youngsters who are being raised in this palace with all the luxury that wealth affords are absolutely deprived of religious education. Every Sunday the director gives them a lecture on morals and natural religion in which he comments on the Gospels and the Old Testament. They sing hymns and recite psalms just as in a Protestant temple. At the time of my visit to the chapel the congregation was just on the point of assembling to attend a commemorative service for one of the young men belonging to the school. This pure Deism is in reality very close to Christian beliefs.

The reason is that it is very difficult to build up any following in the United States for the French

[3]Stephen Girard (1750-1831) was a native of Bordeaux. Coming to New York in 1774, he moved to Philadelphia in 1776 and accumulated a sizable fortune as a merchant and shipowner. He was a shareholder in the Bank of the United States and set up his own bank when its charter was not renewed. He left several million dollars to found a nonsectarian home, secondary school and junior college for orphan boys. Girard College opened in 1848; it combines academic and vocational teaching.

style of free-thought with its philosophical scorn for religion, which it treats as a pure illusion. On the other hand, the abstract lay religion they practice here, despite the wishes of the founder, in the temple he built to atheism has nothing in it that clashes with the American idea of religion and nothing unacceptable to the liberal instincts of its most fervent sectarians. The average American is equally opposed to the great zeal of intolerant sects and to the philosophic rebellion that flourishes only in countries where some religion is forced upon people. He considers that faith proceeds from the individual conscience and, because he sees the source of religion in the testimony of each person's conscience, he leaves religion alone even while he respects it. There are plenty of sects in Philadelphia: Quakers, Wesleyans, Swedenborgians, Congregationalists, Anabaptists and a large number of others bearing more or less barbarous names, not to mention the Catholic church and the four or five great Protestant denominations. I have already explained to you how this extreme dispersion leads to the lowering of doctrinal barriers and how a broad, philosophical type of Christianity emerges from the infinite diversity of religious organizations in the United States. I have told you about the churches where, as at Girard College, they do not hold themselves bound by the formulae of any particular sect but simply come together to pray and to read the Bible aloud. This is the only form of official worship that is permitted in public establishments. When congregations multiply to the point where one may say that every pastor is the father of his own church, preoccupations with orthodoxy become blurred and Christianity falls into the public domain. This is the logical outcome and the most purified form of positive religion; it is the ultimate result of the great Protestant revolution that has been able to attain its full development only in America thanks to its unrestricted religious freedom. If the American feels a repugnance for anyone who says he has no religious beliefs, this is merely the hostility for the wrecker and the arsonist felt by the man who has made his bed and wants to lie comfortably in it. But as long as you are some kind of Christian, people will pay little attention to the denomination in which you were born and people will gladly unite with you in common prayer like property-owners, who build their houses on plans different from those of their neighbors, but are still unanimous in wishing to preserve and defend their possessions against all marauders.

Nor did I see anything remarkable at the famous cellular penitentiary of Cherry Hill,[4] a model for many of those in the Old World and the object of obligatory pilgrimages by all foreign visitors. It is a kind of Mazas[5] with the outer walls of a fortress,

[4]This prison was almost an obligatory stop on the itineraries of European visitors to the United States at this period because it represented an advanced principle of penology, the idea that each prisoner should have the privacy of an individual cell instead of being herded together with a large number of other criminals as in traditional prisons.

[5]Built in Paris in 1845-50 on the Boulevard Mazas (now Boulevard Diderot), near the Gare de Lyon, this prison was another early example of the cellular design. It was demolished in 1898.

narrow cells, exercise spaces twelve feet in length and long, vaulted galleries in the form of a cross. Let us pause only at the house of correction, or "reform school," for young children. We were taken into a courtyard where about twenty small black children were glistening with sweat as they played in the sun. Upon a sign from the teacher their noisy game instantly comes to an end; with one last frolic and one last funny face, they line up in marching order to return to work: they are making umbrella handles. Later they leave the shop to attend school, which takes up at least half their time. The teacher told us that he finds them just as intelligent as white children, but less attentive and less persevering.

Then we crossed over into the wing reserved for whites—for here they do not yet, as in Massachusetts, think of mingling the two races. I walk along panelled corridors where the floor is covered with woolen carpets, into fine dormitories, spacious and well heated; on each side there is a row of pretty little cubicles with beds and white curtains. The parlor also is a handsome room decorated with etchings and engravings. The children I met there were clean and well-dressed—more so than is generally the case in our boarding-schools. However, these are only unruly children, youngsters who have repeatedly been in difficulties with the law, or else they are abandoned children whom the city is charitably maintaining and educating. Like the young blacks, they are required to work with their hands so that they may learn a trade. I went into several of their workshops: in one place they make children's shoes, or else big, hob-nailed boots for the army or the Sanitary Commission; elsewhere they make boxes of chemical matches or brushes of heather,[6] and all with incredible speed and dexterity. They are set to work, insofar as possible, on articles of small value in which private business has little interest; thus they can be of use to the consumer without hurting the working man by their competition. Moreover, the establishment is forbidden by law to make any profit.

On my way back I go through vast, monotonous neighborhoods made up of little two-storey brick houses that look exactly identical, with their front steps of stone and their red façades. I am told that the artisans and lower middle classes of the city live here. These very up-to-date residences show what the power of association can do. A number of working men join together and pool their resources to buy a piece of land, mortgaging it to make up the purchase price; then, in the slack season, they assess themselves to buy materials and after that, each in his turn, they get their houses built, the masons raise the walls, the carpenters put in the beams, the plumbers make the roofs and rain-spouts. It is a communal industry working for profit, for the association sells the houses its members don't need. The others are divided among the members according to the plan drawn up in advance. At last, when everything is finished, the association dissolves itself and everyone takes possession of his own property. As you can see, it is a practical sort of association rather than a permanent, theoretically designed

[6]The French term is *chiendent*, which is a type of Scotch grass sometimes called "twitch." It is similar to heather.

organization run by philanthropic economists who like to promote the people's welfare by handing out ready-cooked morsels and subjecting their clients to regulations they happen to fancy. To anyone familiar with the industrial and agricultural development of America—the shortage of labor, the high rate of wages—it must seem unlikely that any considerable number of families will be driven by need to commit themselves to that sort of workhouse. The "alms-house" is open to invalids; children are placed in schools; and the able-bodied have no need to seek the charity nor to undergo the tutelage of anyone. Here they do not have much use for administrative reports, detailed inquiries nor learned theories. That sort of thing is all very well for us Frenchmen who love statistics and paper work, spillers of ink and wasters of valuable time, who prefer ideas to realities and are then astonished at the practical impotence that keeps us paralyzed. We are as formalistic as the Chinese who spend an hour in preliminary ceremonies before they finally sit down at the table. The Americans come to the point more quickly; they go directly to work hewing something out of a rough block without losing time drawing up symmetrical but unnecessary plans. They begin with the foundations, that is, with an actual investment of money. They will never be tempted to enlist a fine-sounding but hollow science in the service of an empty treasury.

I wound up my day in a natural history museum founded by public subscription. There Mr. H. exerted all his efforts to get me to admire, despite my ignorance, the most beautiful collection of birds in the whole world. After that he insisted that I go to inspect, from cellar to garret, the splendid new building of the Union League Club, a society of fifteen hundred members and a political association that rendered great services to President Lincoln in the recent elections.

Tomorrow I will tell you about the schools.

February 7, 1865

MR. FIELD introduced me yesterday to his friend, Mr. [Edward] Shippen, one of the most influential members [actually president, 1864-69] of the Board of Controllers elected by the people and, as in Boston, charged with running the city's schools. Mr. Shippen, who belongs to one of Philadelphia's oldest families, did not decline to woo popular favor so as to win the right to serve his fellow citizens. He told me himself that the system of direct popular election—which anywhere except in America would be regarded as madness—results here in the best and wisest choices possible. In this country, where social hatreds do not render the rich and enlightened classes suspect to the mass of the voters, the people are very well aware that for them the crucial thing is public education, the true method of increasing ones influence and dignity, and they elect to it the most capable men they can find without regard for personalities or opinions.

The first school district of Pennsylvania, comprising the city of Philadelphia, is divided into twenty-five sections, each of which elects one delegate to the general assembly. The Board of Controllers, chosen by this mode of election, names a set of officers which includes a president, a secretary, an assistant secretary and a "messenger," and these form, as it were, the government of this little republic. In addition, there are ten committees, each executing some special task, of which the president of the Board is always an *ex-officio* member; these committees share with him the work of administration. Nevertheless, there is still a board of twelve members elected by the people in each of the twenty-five sections; these local assemblies are, so to speak, the state legislatures of the public educational system, deliberating under the control and guidance of the central council. This body assigns them their functions, defines their powers, audits their expenditures, exercises over them a right of inspection and tutelage and even absolutely reserves to itself the final decision in all matters of general policy. But it cannot authorize any expenditure except on the proposal and with the consent of the individual section boards, except in the running of the High School, over which it has exclusive authority, or in the spending of special funds voted for purposes other than the regular services. As you can see, it is a parliamentary government on federal lines, built on the model of the United States government.

This whole republican government resembles very strongly the one in Boston which I have already described. The course of study is pretty much the same, and the schools are also divided into several levels to which pupils gain access only in order of merit and after taking a series of examinations. But to the three levels familiar to us—primary school, grammar school and high school—the city of

Philadelphia adds a "secondary" school, which serves as a useful transitional stage between the humble beginnings of the primary school and the already-rigorous studies of the grammar school. Moreover, the best students can make their way through several of these levels in a few months' time. In Philadelphia there are two high schools, 58 grammar schools, 70 secondary schools and 177 primary schools, as well as 59 unclassified schools, making a grand total of 366 schools attended by 72,000 pupils and taught by 1,239 schoolmasters and schoolmistresses. As in Boston, the teachers of the male sex are extremely rare and occupy only the highest ranks. The personnel of each school consists of a "principal," who is frequently a woman, and of several assistant teachers, or adjunct mistresses, according to the number of pupils and the needs of the establishment. The starting salary for the lowest-ranking teacher in the primary school is $300 [a year], or about 1,500 francs in our money. It is $320 in the secondary school and $310 in the grammar school; in the latter, a "first assistant" earns as much as $450. The primary school principals receive $400; those in the secondary schools get $450 and those in the grammar school $750. In the boys' grammar schools the principal is always a man and is paid $1,500. As for high school teachers in the boys' division and those in the High and Normal School for Girls, their salaries are much higher: the lowest is $1,200 for male teachers and $600 for women; the principals receive as much as $1,800 to $2,500. As a general rule, the lowest salary for a male teacher is likely to amount to at least $400.

In the primary and secondary schools boys and girls are together or separated according to their numbers, the rooms available and the convenience of the teachers. They are always separated in the high schools and in the grammar schools. Here and there, moreover, one finds an unclassified school where young men and women are admitted to pursue special courses of study without having to go through the normal routine of examinations and promotions. In the lower grades pupils are promoted by the teachers themselves, but when it comes to the transition from grammar school to higher education there is a committee of the Board of Controllers that administers the examinations. Besides, girls are not admitted until they are fourteen years old, and boys must be thirteen. Not until the age of seventeen may those who have chosen a teaching career present themselves before another committee of the Board, the Committee on Qualifications of Teachers, whose special task it is to pass judgment on the candidates. The diplomas it delivers are first, second or third class, according to the individual's merit, and these give access to the various ranks in the different levels of the system. One only attains the rank of principal after twenty-one years in the secondary school and twenty years in the primary school.

Finally, one must have a year's service in an inferior rank in order to obtain the second-class diploma and two years for the first-class one. You can see how much wholesome competition is stimulated by this system of ingenious regulations, awakening it in the pupil from the very beginning and sustaining it for the teacher until the end of his career: throughout the system one finds examinations and competitions at every level.

The physical organization of the schools is no less admirable than their intellectual discipline. Of the $737,000—a little more than ten dollars per pupil—which the city spends annually for public education, it allows about $226,000 for the upkeep of its offices and school buildings. With Mr. Field and Mr. Shippen I have visited some of these schools, and I shall always remember them with affection and pleasure. Once you have seen these splendid edifices you can never forget their spacious and tastefully decorated rooms, the troops of quiet, attentive, clean and well-dressed children—whom one could compare to their advantage with those of our provincial middle-class families although they come from the poorest homes in the city—the teachers, so simple in their manners and modest in their behavior, though proud of the fruits of their labors, many of whom come from the same social origins as their pupils. I saw a frail young woman of seventeen dictating to big boys of fourteen the lessons that prepare them for the composition part of the competition that will decide which ones can go on to high school. What a healthy moral atmosphere one breathes here! Everywhere the attitudes are studious and sober and one feels that there is a serious will to rise by ones merits.

Last week, indeed, was devoted to the semester examinations, a long and grueling competition in which less than a quarter of the aspirants are admitted to the normal school where teachers are trained.

A hundred girls came before us to sing patriotic hymns, each taking a turn as accompanist at the piano. Just at that moment the contestants came running into the hall bringing the results of the examinations. The school we were in had been outstanding among all those in the city, for it had carried off all the highest scores. The young girls came in one after the other, all out of breath from running so hard in the snow, and threw themselves into the arms of the head-mistress who hugged them as though they were her own children. Mr. S., the inspector-general, played a very paternal part in the celebration: they all remained respectfully standing in his presence, but no one seemed to be surprised or frightened to see him there. Among the students there were pale, drawn faces, though radiant with great happiness, that testified to the labor these triumphs had cost. "The girl with the highest grade," the head-mistress told us, "has been spending half the night with her books for the past two months." But then there was a disappointment following on this scene of joy: the inspector told the girls that now they had been admitted to the normal school they could no longer come back here to attend the grammar school since they didn't belong to it any more. The head-mistress interceded and obtained the concession that at least the doors of her school would remain open to them, and the young people lowered their eyes in sadness.

How little all this resembles our schools, where children are continually being threatened with the rod or the switch, where the rasping voice of an angry master is always echoing unless it is drowned out by the tumult of heedless scholars! I insist once again that free peoples are formed by free public schools—or, if they do not form them, at least they are the measure and symbol of their freedom.

Never has this truth been brought home to me in such a self-evident manner. There are some people afflicted with either a natural or an acquired pessimism who consequently see all progress as a snare, all science as a delusion; they love to poke fun at this universal remedy. They believe we should stingily measure out knowledge to people and reduce everyone's portion to the bare minimum he must have. A working man, they say, has no need to know all a rich man knows; a farmhand doesn't need much science to spread his manure. Give them a smattering of reading and arithmetic and just enough writing to sign their names—this will amply suffice for all their needs. More education than this would be dangerous—dangerous indeed (and why not say so?) for those who would like to chain the common man to his humble occupation, dangerous to the handful of people who would like, in the name of the rights of the newly-rich, to forbid him to raise himself beyond the narrow sphere they have marked out for him, and dangerous, finally, because it would let him escape from the bondage of his class and from the leading-strings of a paternalistic society, bonds that could no longer be justified by conservatives on the plea of protecting him from his own weaknesses!

Shall we never learn in France what democracy means? We have introduced to the world a form of government that was hitherto unknown, one that

America itself has never heard of—unlimited universal [manhood] suffrage, the right of every human being, acquired at birth, to exercise through his vote a share (often imaginary) in the government of his country. We have treated as completely theoretical a question that everyone else treats as a matter of experience, utility and social progress. We have preferred barren abstractions to the reality of liberty, the only thing that can make it fruitful. We ask of universal suffrage that it provide us with constitutions and even with crowned heads—but we are still debating whether or not we should teach all French citizens to read!

February 8, 1865

I HAVE just come back from a ball and in an hour I am to leave for New York. Yesterday evening, as I was on my way to a dinner to which Mr. Field had invited me at his house, I firmly decided to leave that very night. But a heavy snowstorm has blanketed the entire region, and the flakes were falling so thickly that I was afraid I might be snowed in along the route. My hosts thereupon enlarged upon the charms of a sojourn of two or three days shut up in a passenger coach trapped in the snow in company with a whole trainload of famished, frozen travelers like myself.

In short, instead of leaving for the railroad station, I allowed myself to be taken to the ball. There I was introduced by a lady who greatly annoyed me by her obstinacy in calling me "Count;" but I finally gave in and answered to the title when I saw that people were bent on applying it to me. You must realize that in American polite society a Frenchman with good manners cannot escape being at least a count or a marquis, for it can only be his modesty or his respect for American democratic manners that makes him descend momentarily to the level of ordinary mortals. Just as ordinary folk always call me "Captain" when they want to be polite, so the matrons and debutantes call me "Count"—for it is inconceivable that so distinguished a gentleman should be nothing more than just Pete or Johnny. I have gotten used to these involuntary usurpations and I now put up with them with an imperturbable gravity, without even frowning.

Well, then, here I am at the ball, tricked out with a title, introduced right and left, the darling of the young ladies—and all this without any calculation of self-interest on their part, for no other reason than their desire to be kind to a passing stranger who won't be with them tomorrow. This earnest good will, this solicitous hospitality, deserves in return some effort on my part to be courteous. Besides, I greatly enjoyed myself in this very amiable, almost European gathering. The ladies spoke elegant, correct French and seemed proud of their ability to do so to the satisfaction of such a good and appreciative judge. Their conversation was perhaps not very knowledgeable, but this is typical of all small-talk, and at least they were able to talk about some serious things, so I could not bring myself to regret the hours of sleep I was losing. Two or three times I made an attempt to escape only to be brought back by force. To make a long story short, I didn't leave the party until three o'clock in the morning, carrying away with me highly favorable impressions of this city's polite society, which is perhaps more provincial and less in fashion than that of New York, but is more serious and essentially more discriminating.

Meanwhile the snow had melted. All that remained in the streets was a pasty porridge like a melting "*granite*,"[7] and on the paving stones of the sidewalks, wherever a lot of water had accumulated, there were arabesque patterns of wet ice, the most slippery and dangerous footing a person can walk on. I had come there in a carriage in company with several ladies, and I had no idea where I was. I asked someone how to get to Chestnut Street and he pointed vaguely in the general direction. So I began to walk, now splashing with my dancing shoes in puddles of slush, now sliding—despite infinite precautions—on paving stones encrusted with melting ice. Even in the daytime, the streets of Philadelphia all look alike and you have to have a practiced eye to tell one from another. At night it is a vast labyrinth. I soon lost my way, and for a long time I walked on tiptoe, making superhuman efforts to keep my balance. There were no gaslights burning, no signs at the street-corners. Here and there shone a pale lantern in the midst of a dark wilderness, and none of my ill-tempered shouts were successful in calling forth a single policeman from the silent depths. The Philadelphia city government, which does so much for public instruction, does precious little to maintain the streets or to police them. It

[7] A kind of hard-frozen ice cream flavored with chocolate or fruit syrup.

allows holes to form between the broken paving stones which become muddy man-traps after dark; it allows water and snow to accumulate in this great city without providing sewers or any other way for it to run off, without natural slopes, without any method of clearing it away except for the limited absorptive power of the earth and the evaporative power of the winter sun's feeble rays.

At that very moment the red glow of an immense conflagration began to light up the horizon and half the sky; then the slow, mournful sound of the alarm bells came floating from afar over the great sleeping city. From time to time one could hear strident shouting or the footsteps of hurrying squads of firemen clattering over the pavement to the fireworks display. It was a storage depot for petroleum, and it burned completely to the ground in less than an hour; but then the flaming oil spilled out into the streets and flooded an entire neighborhood with a rapidly spreading sea of fire.

In the end a nocturnal passerby showed me the way to go and I finally got back to my hotel soaked and frozen after many a fall and many a false step, with my dress suit bedraggled and my shoes in ribbons. Now I must dash off to the railroad station and tonight I shall be in New York.

February 12, 1865

FOR the past three days I haven't touched either a pen or a book. New York is an immense gulf that swallows up all ones time. Yet events are now pressing hard upon one another and tension is building up. There is anxiety over whether there is to be peace or war; there are contradictory rumors about negotiations being opened, being broken off, about Davis's unexpected somersaults, about one or more great battles that are said to be imminent. Finally, there seems to be evidence that a dénouement is approaching, that the demonic fury of the Confederate government may, out of necessity, be abating somewhat. All this is like a tragi-comedy being played out before my eyes, and it grows more absorbing with every day that goes by. Inasmuch as the mysterious bomb finally went off today and the two presidents' reports to their peoples have just laid bare for us the secret history [of their negotiations], I can now tell you about these matters as I see them, as public opinion has judged them—and, finally, as the outcome has revealed them to our disappointed hopes.

During my stay with the army there was talk of nothing but Mr. Blair's mission. Everybody thought that it augured, if not immediate peace, at least a great step toward an amicable agreement and the restoration of the Union. As for me, I had scarcely any hopes of this kind, for in the Richmond newspapers I had read so much invective against anyone who would not make the full independence of the Confederate states the condition *sine qua non* of any peace settlement that I was forced to assume that the Rebel government, which dictates the opinions of the Virginia press, was not at all disposed to sacrifice itself to the public good. Furthermore, Horace Greeley was mixed up in the business, and however much respect I have for his tireless and persevering efforts to awaken in the Confederates a spirit of peace and submission, the Niagara negotiations are still too recent to allow me to have very much confidence in the fuzzy diplomacy of that noble and dedicated—but utopian and fantastic—personage.[8] What I found it easier to imagine, and what my reason was able to accept, was that Blair's mission or any similar gesture would strengthen in the South the steadily growing peace party whose growing restiveness has been threatening to overthrow Mr. Davis. Alexander Stephens, the reluctant Vice President of the self-styled republic, might seize this occasion to place himself at the head of the party converted [to peace], thus confronting the obstinate dictator with an internal opposition that would soon completely paralyze the wounded and moribund body of the rebellion. But I counted without the weakness of the one and the domineering energy of the other. What ought to have been President Davis's downfall has become for that extraordinary man an occasion to retrieve all his former ascendancy over the faint-hearted ones and to drive before him the flock of rabid sheep he has bitten.

Mr. Blair returned, then he went back [to Richmond], then he returned again, and already no one seems to be paying any further attention to the business. Only New York, like all great financial centers whose instability is disturbed by the slightest

[8] Held at Niagara Falls, Ontario, these negotiations took place in the early summer of 1864 between emissaries of the Confederacy and Horace Greeley, the editor of the New York *Tribune*, acting unofficially for President Lincoln. The outcome was insignificant except for Greeley's embarrassment. Details are given in Volume I of this work, pp. 124, 164-7.

shock, still hesitates between hope and fear and, while wishing for peace, already begins to hope that it won't come too soon. The newspapers, on the alert for every rumor that might serve to fill their columns, produced as if by machine twenty contradictory reports and conjectures for the benefit of an unbelieving and indifferent public. Some, pooh-poohing the current rumors, amused themselves by pretending that it was all just part of some financial maneuver and even denied that Blair had gone at all. Then, all of a sudden, a dispatch arrived from Fort Monroe stating that Vice President Stephens, Judge [J. A.] Campbell and Senator [R. M. T.] Hunter had crossed through the Federal lines and were seeking permission to go on to Washington as bearers of [Rebel] peace proposals. Mr. Seward went to meet them, empowered to negotiate for the President. The report even goes so far as to spell out the conditions he is taking with him: he demands in the first place that the Rebels lay down their arms, that they submit themselves to the laws of the United States as these have been modified by the revolutionary crisis; in compensation he offers an indemnity for the emancipated slaves and the assumption of the Confederate debt by the government of the United States.

These concessions are exorbitant, but it is explained that the indemnity would be minimal because it would be figured on the basis of the present market value of the slaves and these are nowadays a form of property that is more burdensome than profitable. It is also said that the United States government would never bind itself to fulfill all the wild promises that the [Richmond] government, in its desperation, has made. But they will assume the principal of the debt and this all by itself would be an immense boon, giving real value and a certainty of repayment to capital sums that were borrowed at extravagantly usurious rates of interest and have been considered worthless for a long time. As for the ten percent interest promised by the Confederate government, it would be reduced to three percent in Federal money, and this would still be worth twenty times the current rate of return. Thus the United States would purchase the Rebels' submission—or rather, having disarmed them and reduced them to helplessness, would welcome them back into the Union with a magnificent gift that would help them repair the destruction which their own folly has drawn upon them! This is the intolerable yoke they have wanted to impose on the Rebels, this is the insult, the indignity they have been trying to inflict upon them! It almost amounted to paying all their war costs for them, punishing their criminal obstinacy by admitting them, like prodigal children, to an even greater share of the public revenue [than before the war].*

---

*These details have since been confirmed by the account Vice President Stephens himself has given of the Hampton Roads conferences. It appears that President Lincoln offered him an indemnity of $100,000,000 for the abolition of slavery and promised that the South would have six years to carry it through. Mr. Stephens, who would have liked to accept these proposals, was obliged to reject them on Mr. Davis's orders. As for the Rebel debt, the Confederates no longer have the right to complain of being forced into repudiation, for they made it certain the day they rejected the

Nevertheless, the Richmond newspapers, taking their marching orders from a single source, put on an elaborate pretence of disdain and skepticism. The *Sentinel*, usually the mouthpiece of President Davis, referred to Stephens and to the others as "the self-styled commissioners of the Confederate government." "We shall never," they said, "make peace on any terms except independence, and any other proposal from the enemy will be taken as an insult. Our government has neither the intention nor indeed the right to treat with the Yankees. The unofficial mission of the Vice President will serve only to show that peace is impossible and that war to the last ditch is the only policy that can save us." These rantings, seasoned with a few chivalrous insults in the style of the Rebel aristocrats, appear in the official paper of Jefferson Davis at the very hour when his emissaries are carrying words of peace and hints of surrender to the Federal capital. What, then, could his policy be aiming at? What hidden design was wrapped up in this double language, and which half of it consisted of lies?

We told ourselves that there had always been two parties contending with one another in Richmond, among the people, in the army, in the legislative chambers and even within the executive branch:

---

too-generous offer of President Lincoln. Besides, they have never had any illusions about the probable outcome of their financial expedients. The speech Mr. Stephens gave some time ago before the Georgia legislature, exhorting it to assume its part of the Confederate loans, proves quite conclusively that when the Rebel states sold their bonds they knew very well that these would be worthless if the war turned against them.

one favoring surrender pure and simple and a humble return to the Union—this party included the enlightened and far-seeing people who realized that the stretched cord couldn't bear the weight of the war much longer—and the other, that of the "fire-eaters," consisting of an ignorant mass guided by ambitious and fanatical leaders, men who had deliberately blinded themselves in their efforts to prevent the crowd from seeing the truth. Between these extreme factions floated the undecided multitude of those who desired peace without daring to make it, who made war without really wanting to do so, that soft and docile multitude of which Vice President Stephens, an intelligent man without character or willpower, was at the same time the leader and the typical example.

These reluctant Rebels have passively obeyed those who have governed them for the past four years, and from obeying they have formed the habit of showing a sort of devotion to the cause they are defending. One remembers Alexander Stephens's eloquent speech against secession in the Georgia convention [of 1861], as well as the uncharacteristic violence with which he then branded as ambitious criminals those whose humble satellite he has been ever since. Today, when his original opposition to secession has been justified by the disasters that have overtaken the Rebel Confederacy—now that the day of his vindication has come—Mr. Stephens and all the weaklings who followed his example still don't dare to raise their heads or to repudiate a loyalty that was never sincere. Instead of revealing to the people what they foresee and what they understand—the inevitable catastrophe that is drawing near—instead of repudiating insane delusions of [Southern] independence, they still do not dare speak of peace unless they immediately add that visionary word which keeps alive so many fatal illusions. They know that peace cannot be had without surrender, without returning to the old national unity, without abolishing the last traces of slavery—without forgetting the word "Confederacy." They know that the war can lead only to extermination and that no other course remains to the survivors of this mortal combat but to throw themselves, in an act of repentance, upon the generosity of the United States. Otherwise they must make a futile display of false heroism and let themselves be swallowed up in a theatrical and criminal shipwreck. They know all this, but they still don't dare say it, and they go on giving credence to the vain hope of a peace settlement on equal terms; even their timid opposition serves the purposes of the opponent whom they are trying to overthrow. But no matter: the number of these shamefaced partisans of peace has grown so much since the recent defeats, and they have set up such a clamor in the [Confederate] Congress and press that the government must be afraid they are about to come out into the open. Davis, despite his dictatorial powers and the dependable support of General Lee, begins to totter on his presidential chair which he is accused of wishing to transform into a throne. The Stephens-Campbell mission, whether or not sincere, was obviously calculated to rally the malcontents around him and consolidate his grip on power.

But at this point people began to wonder again. Was this nothing but a ruse of war, a feint, as the Richmond papers said, and should one take literally the article in the *Sentinel* which, so as to camouflage the truth more completely, may have adopted the clever tactic of shouting the whole thing from the rooftops? Had Davis not perhaps intended to catch the "peacemakers" in their own net by momentarily adopting their policy, counting on reducing them to silence later on by revealing to them how impossible of fulfillment their hopes were? When the Confederate commissioners crossed the battle lines, both armies acclaimed them with enthusiasm, joining in a cheer for peace the voices hitherto accustomed only to provocative taunts and shouts of war. But there is no warrant for believing that the Rebel army, though it cheers the prospect of peace, has any thought of applauding the idea of surrender. The ignorant class in the South has been assured so many times that it is invincible, that its resources will never be exhausted and that the Confederate nation will never be subjugated by the Yankee conqueror, that they have finally come to believe in its permanence and to have faith that peace will assure to them that independence which now has no meaning but which they consider precious as people always cling to worthless trinkets for which they have fought.

Davis himself, even before he had lost all hope and all his energy, could not from one day to the next confess his defeat to his people. The popular current, if suddenly blocked, would have turned against him with all the furor of unexpected reactions, and peace commissioners could only have gone to meet the enemy over the dead body of the detested criminal who instigated the rebellion, for abrupt changes of policy bring about the ruin of the very ones who advocate them and the disillusioned populace sees in the former servants of its mad folly the leaders who were first responsible for leading it astray and causing its destruction. This is a harsh but rigorous kind of justice from which Davis can't escape unless he is able to conjure the demon by delay, by indirection and by lies prudently calculated to wean his people away from their fanatical errors to a more calm and rational view of reality.

But the fact remains that the first conference took place. It is reported that Stephens spoke nothing but conciliatory words throughout the talks and that he took leave of the officers assigned to escort him back saying that he "hoped to meet them again under happier circumstances," and that he even said "We are one and the same people." Anxiety grew when it was learned that President Lincoln, acting on a message from his Secretary of State, had suddenly left for Fort Monroe. Was peace, then, so near? The hardiest skeptics half believed it, and surprise was expressed that on the strength of this great piece of news the price of gold did not fall by fifty percent.

To tell the truth, gold was well advised to wait and see. The *Herald* and the *Express*, the quibblers and the hysterics of the press, were right in throwing onto the universal optimism the cold water of their mocking incredulity. The next day, negotiations were broken off. Lincoln and Seward returned to Washington, saying flatly that peace was not yet possible. Stephens and Hunter are now behind their own lines and, according to the well-worn cliché so much employed by the reporters, "Grant, Thomas and Sherman are now once again the real peace commissioners and the real peace negotiators." What had gone wrong? There was no lack of rumors, but, until we read the message which the President is preparing to send to Congress, we are obliged to be content with the bare facts and the imaginative speculation that fills the newspapers. The first details have come from Richmond. Scarcely had the commissioners reappeared in the city than all the newspapers in a solid phalanx opened up with all their biggest guns in a barrage that had clearly been planned in advance. I can't begin to describe to you that delirium of calculated indignation, that flood of invective and insults, that they began to spew out like cannon loaded to the muzzle which the gunner sets off at the first signal. One might have thought that at the last moment the North had suddenly unveiled claims so unexpected, so despicably exorbitant, that the ambassadors had reeled back in horror. Lincoln, the Yankee tyrant, had set an abominable pit-trap for them. He had refused to recognize the independence of the Southern states, he had required of the Rebels an immediate and unconditional resumption of obedience to the laws of the United States, carrying his insolence even to the point of promising them, should they surrender, the merciful treatment that is owed to an erring brother.

What! Mercy from a vile Yankee? The Yankees

dare to call themselves brothers of the chivalrous Southern nation? It was obvious that this ambush was designed in order to afford to the "ignoble Lincoln" and the "bloodthirsty Seward" an occasion to give a slap in the face to the noble citizens and the sublime people of the Confederate States: the outrage must be washed out with blood and avenged by the total extermination of all the armies that have dared to violate the sacred soil of the rebellious Confederacy.

But fury and insults do not excuse people from thinking clearly. The day before, these same newspapers, this same Davis who tells them what to think, had been speaking scornfully of those so-called negotiations that would serve only to reveal the enemy's incorrigible arrogance and the need to press on ruthlessly with the war. Today they are vociferous in their claims that the enemy has deceived them, that Lincoln, in order to induce their emissaries to cross over into his territory, let them believe he was going to submit humbly to their conditions for peace. If it is true that anyone tried to deceive them, they certainly did not fall into any snares, and this pretence of innocence is unbecoming to them after the haughty condescension of their previous boasting. Besides, it would be real cause for astonishment if, having fought them for four years through all the ups and downs of fortune, the North would now decide to admit defeat at the very moment when it holds the wolf by its ears and is getting ready to wring its neck. But it's a waste of time to demonstrate their madness and convict them of bad faith.

President Lincoln's report to Congress has finally been made public along with a letter written by Mr. Seward to Mr. [Charles Francis] Adams, Minister of the United States at the Court of St. James, and the world can judge to what lengths this Tiberius and this Sejanus[9] have carried their tyrannical fury. The Rebel plenipotentiaries and the President of the United States met at Hampton Roads on the James River on board the steamboat that had brought them there. Their discussions were cordial, frank and amicable; they drank champagne together, and when they parted, Seward was so shameless as to say, American-style, to his old friend Hunter, who was grasping his hands, "God bless you, Hunter!" "It would have been better," screams the Richmond *Dispatch*, "to have damned Seward to hell instead of blessing him!"

Mr. Stephens had opened the conference by expressing his sincere wish that peace might be concluded. But he still clung to a great illusion, for he imagined that the government of the United States might temporarily recognize the legitimate existence of the Rebel government, grant its members an amnesty, withdraw its armies, give back to it the territory that it still claims and then wait patiently, on the strength of a mere verbal promise, until people and circumstances should be ripe for the proposed reconstitution of the Union. Meanwhile, the

[9] Tiberius was the second Roman Emperor (reigned A.D. 14-37); since the hostile account of his reign given by the historian Tacitus he has often been portrayed as moody, suspicious, cruel and tyrannical. Seianus (or Sejanus) was his chief minister.

Confederacy would conclude an alliance with the United States to enforce the Monroe Doctrine in the Western hemisphere, that is, to free Mexico from French military occupation and perhaps even to take Canada from the British. President Lincoln said in his message that the Confederate commissioners did not positively reject the Union, but asked only for more time in which to resolve the differences [between the two sections]. Mr. Seward also said in so many words that Mr. Stephens proposed as a compromise the conclusion of a political alliance and the taking of common action against those powers that are violating the Monroe Doctrine. In this way, war against the European powers would have been used as a diversion to give the hatreds aroused by the Civil War time to fade away and disappear.

All this shows how much *bona fide* good will the chivalrous Confederates have for their good friends across the Atlantic—timid friends, to be sure, but friends who deserve a better reward for their secret hopes and half-complicity than this sweeping enmity that Richmond, even more than Washington, seems to have proclaimed against them. There is no longer any thought of flattering them in order to get their help, still less of rushing to their aid so as to get their protection. President Davis has decided that he has nothing to gain by crawling before Europe, so we now behold the real feelings that were hidden behind the curtain of official flattery which fooled us so long.

As for the United States, who for the present haven't the faintest desire to make war against the

European powers, the bargain the South is offering
them is as unprofitable as it is morally unacceptable
and incompatible with their dignity. In the purely
hypothetical event of a foreign war, the help of the
South's decimated population and its splendid financial resources would be precious indeed! And
then, is it not strange, after four years of bloody
struggle to maintain the Union, to offer as the prize
of victory nothing but a vague promise of alliance
while asking the North to give up the principle and
even the national name for which it has fought? It is
not for the vanquished to lay down the law to their
masters, and as for President Davis's letter to Mr.
Blair announcing that he was ready to make peace
"between the two nations," President Lincoln had
replied in the same indirect style that his intention
was to bring back peace to "the people of our common country," and it was abundantly clear that he
would hold to his word. The Confederate commissioners therefore knew, or ought to have known,
what proposals were going to be made to them, and
if there were arrogance or insults, they were rather
on the side of the conquered who want to dictate
conditions of peace to the victors who are offering it
to them.

They are saying also that Mr. Stephens tried to
find another escape hatch no less impracticable and
no less ridiculous than the first. He let it be understood that the Confederate States would return to
the Union at a time and under circumstances of
their own choosing if the government of the United
States would first recognize their absolute individual sovereignty and their inalienable right to secede.

This would amount to saying, "You will get us to admit you are right on condition that you admit you are wrong." To concede the absolute sovereignty of the states would not only be an act unworthy of a nation that has affirmed its sovereignty in a hundred battles; it would also be the most imprudent and fatal concession that could be made. That clause, though it may seem purely theoretical at first glance, would before much time had passed resurrect the whole noxious and superseded quarrel over "nullification" and the right of states to secede; it would have meant a revolution in the constitutional law of the United States and rendered the national government impotent in the face of the whims of some new rebellion.

These so-called compromises are nothing but ingenious attempts to disarm the government of the Union and to wring from it a *mea culpa* [admission of guilt] which they would not have failed to take advantage of later on. I doubt that in the entire Rebel government there is a single man so demented as to imagine that such terms could possibly be acceptable or that one could offer them with a straight face to a President who has just been re-elected because he promised that he would make the authority of the Federal government prevail throughout the nation. To these ridiculous proposals President Lincoln replied—as he ought to have replied—with an irrevocable *non possumus* [We cannot do it], and no one can honestly be surprised that he made this reply.

But on the other hand he did make all the concessions permitted by national honor and the mandate he has been given by the people, requiring only that the laws of the United States reign supreme in the so-called Confederate states, that the Confederate government be dissolved—but not those of the states—that the army lay down its arms, that the [Thirteenth] constitutional amendment be adopted as the foundation of public law, abolishing slavery in the Rebel states, with this event to occur on the day when, in accord with the Constitution, which must be the supreme law of the land, three-fourths of the states shall have ratified it. He went on to promise that in the practical enforcement of the laws, and especially in the application of the decree of confiscation which still hangs over the Rebels' heads, he would exercise all the mercy compatible with his duty and would commute any penalties that were too harsh, providing only that his right to impose them be acknowledged. It is even said that he gave his word that he would do all in his power to help the South to rise again from its ruins. But all this was not enough for the envoys of the South. Since their government is determined upon usurpation and war, let the guilt of future bloodshed fall upon them!

These are the facts as they emerge from the brief report made by President Lincoln and from the recriminations of the Rebels themselves. It is from the Richmond newspapers that I have taken the details that testify most eloquently to their intractable stubbornness. The accounts they have printed of the Hampton Roads meeting are the most telling indictment that could be brought against them and the clearest justification of the man whom they call "the tyrant Lincoln." The most criminal excesses are in their own eyes the noblest deeds of patriotic heroism one could imagine. Virginia's governor, William Smith, better known by his nickname "Extra-Billy,"[10] has called together all the citizens of Richmond in an immense public meeting "to make a fitting reply to the outrage the President of the United States has offered them"—meaning the people of the South—by not being more humble in his supplications to them to be content with independence and give up their determination to conquer the Northern states. General Lee and all the officers of his staff were present in full-dress uniform, and 10,000 people voted by acclamation that they rejected "this gross insult with the indignation it deserves" along with the conditions President Lincoln has laid down for peace between the two peoples. Jefferson Davis spoke. "Everything," he said, "must be sacrificed on the altar of our country. We will prove to Lincoln once and for all that we are the stronger side. He will see that Sherman has led his last army into Georgia. Before summer is over, it will be the enemy who will be begging us for conferences at which we will dictate our laws to him." Messrs. [Judah P.] Benjamin, Hunter, [Williamson S.] Oldham and a number of others took the floor, and the newspapers opened fire with all their batteries. The *Sentinel*, in a crazy, eloquent piece from the pen of Jefferson Davis himself, appealed to memories of Roman history and offered as

[10]The origin of this nickname is uncertain. It probably had to do with Governor Smith's proposing a number of "extra bills" as addenda to his program.

an example to the Rebels the heroic Romans defeated in the battle of Cannae.[11] "All cowards," cried the *Examiner*, "should be strung up on the nearest streetlamp." "They cannot," cried the *Enquirer*, "rob us of the right to fill a glorious tomb." Then followed a parody of indignation: "Are we rebels? Are we traitors?"

President Davis's aim in playing out this comedy around the theme of peace discussions can be seen underneath his bold and well-turned impudence: he wanted to stop the mouths of those who want peace so as to set public opinion afire once again. For the moment he has succeeded. Stephens, now resigned to continuing the war, has set out to revolutionize Georgia, acting as the docile servant of a policy he detests. Lee flourishes his sword. The people of Richmond are again as full of fanaticism as during the first days of the war. Unfortunately these great theatrical triumphs are by now only too well understood: the phrase for it is "to fire the Southern heart," and every one of those splendid conflagrations has left behind cinders and ruins. At this very moment, when Jefferson Davis is screaming his war cry in Richmond and hearing it repeated by ten thousand voices, Sherman is cutting at Branchville the railroad from Augusta to Charleston and the left wing of the Army of the Potomac is making in the vicinity of Petersburg one of those

[11] At the battle of Cannae (216 B.C.) the entire Roman army was encircled and annihilated by the Carthaginian general Hannibal. Though seemingly crushed and without an army, the Romans continued to resist and eventually emerged victorious.

modest movements which, if repeated a few times, will interrupt Lee's communications [with the rest of the Confederacy]. All the while they are getting ready to take draconian measures against deserters and draft-dodgers, the latter are nonetheless in full occupation of the North Carolina mountains from whence they stretch out a hand to the enemy. Finally, at the very hour when negotiations were officially broken off in Virginia, the legislature of North Carolina has peacefully chosen five negotiators from its own membership and has invited the other [Southern] states to follow its example. Even in Richmond, only two days after the President's fire-eating mass meeting, the Congress, which had taken part with great pomp and ceremony, unanimously voted down the proposal to arm the blacks. Negotiations conducted by Davis have failed, but they will succeed elsewhere and in the hands of others. Even those who are swearing that they will resist to their last breath will be the first to make their own peace with the enemy when the day comes to honor their reckless pledges.

15

After the War

W HEN I left the United States in the month of February, 1865, the war was approaching its end. Sherman's victorious campaign in Georgia had revealed the exhaustion of the Southern states and the hopeless fragility of Confederate patriotism. In vain did [Jefferson] Davis seek by means of theatrical diversions to prolong resistance, so costly to the South and so useless except to salvage his pride. Ten days after the breakdown of the Hampton Roads negotiations[1] Charleston, the heart of the rebellion, the city where the first spark of this great conflagration was struck, surrendered to Federal troops. The Union's flag already floating over Wilmington and Savannah, was now planted amid the smoking ruins of the Rebel citadel, its defenders having been sorely tried by six months of bombardment and starvation. Sherman marched north, clearing the coasts and threatening Virginia.

[1] The Hampton Roads peace discussions were held February 3, 1865, aboard the *River Queen*. President Lincoln and Secretary of State Seward spoke for the Union, while the Confederacy was represented by Vice President Stephens, former Supreme Court Justice John A. Campbell and R. M. T. Hunter of Virginia. The Federal demand was for unconditional restoration of the Union before discussing other questions, while the Confederates demanded terms for peace between two independent nations. The conference therefore ended without result.

Only two Rebel armies still remained in the field, that of [General Joseph E.] Johnston and that of Lee; these were perhaps strong enough to put up successful resistance if they joined forces, but too weak to hold out separately against enemy attack. Lee, who had long since given up all hope of winning the war, understood that his only salvation lay in linking up with Johnston by withdrawing [from Richmond] in the direction of Danville. But at this moment Grant struck the final blow. Massing the largest part of his forces on his left wing, he joined up with Sheridan's right, cutting off Lee's retreat. At the same time he made a thrust into Richmond through the lightly-held Confederate lines. Lee began a headlong retreat, abandoning the capital city almost without a fight. But when he saw that he was completely surrounded, he presented himself in person to General Grant whom he asked for terms of surrender; these were magnanimous.[2] What followed is well known—the flight of President Davis, his efforts to reassemble his cabinet at Augusta, Georgia, his hope of escaping with his government to the west of the Mississippi so as to reorganize the resistance there. Equally well known is General Sherman's overstepping of his authority in making an armistice with Johnston and the disavowal of his negotiations by the President. Finally, there came the surrender of Johnston's army on the same terms as Lee's. President Lincoln hastened to Richmond

[2]The Confederate troops were required merely to lay down their arms; officers were allowed to keep their side-arms and every man claiming ownership of a horse or mule was allowed to take it home with him.

at the first news of victory, but it was not to proclaim confiscations nor sentences of outlawry or
death. On the contrary, he came with his hands full
of pardons and writs of amnesty. It was even said
that he intended to offer a general pardon to all
who had fought for the Rebel cause. But before he
could do so he fell victim to the cruelest and most
cowardly assassination that the annals of history
thus far record.[3]

The whole world knows the details of this tragic
event. On the evening of the fourteenth of April the
President planned to go to Ford's Theater in company with General Grant and a party of Cabinet
members. For the first time in four years his mind
was at ease and his spirit was buoyant. He was tast-
ing at last the reward for his long exertions and
inner travail. The bloodshed of civil war, which had
weighed so heavily at all times on his charitable
heart, was at an end. He was now free to devote
himself to works of peace and preservation, conse-
crating his second presidency to healing the wounds
of the first. But he was not to know this satisfaction—yet one more victim must be claimed by the
fanaticism of slavery's defenders; the fates had decreed that there must be yet one more martyr to the
cause of liberty and patriotism.

Kept at home by urgent business, the Lieutenant-
General [Grant] and the Cabinet members were unable to accompany the President to Ford's Theater.

[3] President Lincoln was shot on Friday evening, April 14,
1865, by the actor John Wilkes Booth while attending a
light comedy, *Our American Cousin*, at Ford's Theater in
Washington. He died at 7:22 a.m. the following morning.

Only Mr. Lincoln considered that—even though he was overwhelmed with work—he could not beg off from his engagement because it had been announced that he would be present and he did not wish to disappoint the public. In truth, there were indeed those who were awaiting him, and all preparations had been made for the bloody scene in which he was to be the leading actor. Conspirators mingling with the crowd were watching the corridors and the approaches to the theater. At ten o'clock a man waving a revolver leaped into his box, shattered his skull with a pistol bullet fired at point-blank range and then, jumping onto the stage with a long saber in his hand, cried out with theatrical emotion: *Sic semper tyrannis!* [4] A moment later he had disappeared behind the scenery and in less than a minute, even before the crowd could recover from its astonishment and fright, there came from the street outside the hoofbeats of a horse galloping away at top speed. Meanwhile President Lincoln was taken to a house across the street where he died without regaining consciousness. His friends and the members of his Cabinet ran weeping to his death-bed and spent the night silently awaiting the end. The following morning his mutilated corpse was borne in sorrow to the White House.

And that was only part of the grisly work done

[4] These details are essentially correct, except that the weapon was a one-shot derringer—Wilkes had a second one in reserve which he later dropped while escaping across the stage—and he flourished a knife rather than "a long saber." He broke one leg in jumping from the presidential box, apparently because one of his spurs became entangled in the bunting draped over the front.

Photograph made in April, 1865   Courtesy of The Library of Congress

The President's Box, Ford's Theater,
Washington, D. C.

on that night of horrors. Just as President Lincoln was being struck down from behind by a cowardly assassin as he sat between his wife and his son, a second murderer, more daring and cold-blooded, forced his way into the home of Secretary Seward, who was lying ill in his bed.[5] Running up the stairs, stabbing the servant who tried to bar his path, he struck down the Secretary's son who had come running to his father's aid, and plunged his knife again and again into the face and throat of the old man who lay there defenseless, leaving him motionless and unconscious in a pool of blood. It appears, moreover, that these liberators of the nation had not planned to end their exploits so quickly. Their aim was to kill, all at once, the President, the Vice President and the members of the Cabinet, thus annihilating the whole administration at one stroke. Such was the reply of the expiring rebellion to the merciful and magnanimous intentions of the Federal government; it was like the revenge of a dying warrior who raises himself at his last gasp to strike a final blow at the generous victor who is leaning down to bandage his wounds.

Throughout the United States the public mourning was prodigious. At first, when the dreadful news spread from one city to another, people everywhere refused to believe it; but then, when the truth had become all too certain, there was such an explosion

[5] Seward's assailant was a burly accomplice of Booth named Lewis Payne (or Paine). The plot aimed at wiping out the whole Lincoln administration, including Vice President Johnson. Secretary Seward later recovered from his multiple stab wounds and resumed his duties.

of sorrow and anger as the world has never seen at the death of the greatest monarchs on earth. For an entire week New York and all the other large cities were draped in black, no business was transacted and the whole population put on black clothes. Woe to those who then indulged themselves in the malicious and stupid pleasure of affronting the general sorrow! In New York it was only with great difficulty that the police were able to rescue from the furor of an aroused crowd a rash secessionist who, upon hearing the news, had dared to say that the deed was well done. In Poughkeepsie the people nearly hanged an old woman who had screamed at the top of her voice that she was glad someone had finally "sent that wretch to Hell." Elsewhere there were violent incidents. And in many places furious crowds surrounded the homes of known secessionists whom they had reason to suspect of rejoicing. All party leaders forgot their quarrels long enough to unite their voices in one demand for vengeance. People spoke freely of spreading fire and execution to all the Rebel states, of raising to the memory of the martyred President a splendid funeral-pyre bearing the corpses of all the Rebel leaders. Had the assassins not been armed by the South? Nor was this the first of its many crimes, so its conquered chieftains scarcely had a right to dismiss this terrible accusation as an infamous slander and one undeserving of belief.* The banditry and pillaging

* Here is a strange advertisement that was published a few months earlier in an Alabama newspaper, the Selma *Dispatch;* I think it throws a great deal of light on the true feelings of the South: "*A million dollars to have peace by the*

along the border, the wholesale cruelty in the
Southern prison camps, the incendiary plots set on
foot the previous year by the Confederate government—all these seemed to have a striking family
resemblance to this act of blind and despicable revenge. At the very least it was natural that the South
should have been made to bear the guilt for a crime
committed in its name by a man known to have
maintained secret relations with the Rebels for four
years, serving them as spy and messenger, continually traveling from one of the two capitals to the
other and even planning with the leaders of the
Richmond government that strange plot to seize
President Lincoln which was abandoned at the last
minute in favor of assassination.[6] It is said that General Lee, on hearing the fatal news, shut himself up
in his house in Richmond and refused to talk with

---

first of March. If the citizens of the Southern Confederacy
will pay me, in specie and good securities, the sum of one
million dollars, I will see to it that the lives of Abr. Lincoln,
of W. H. Seward and of Andrew Johnson are taken before
the first of March of next year. This will bring us peace and
will show the world that tyrants cannot survive in a free
country. If this aim is not achieved, nothing will be demanded except the $50,000 advance which we consider necessary
to reach and kill the three culprits. I myself will contribute
$1,000 to this patriotic enterprise. All those wishing to sub-
scribe may address their contributions to Box X, General
Delivery, Cahaba, Alabama." The notice was dated December 1, 1864.

[6] This plan, which was apparently discussed with leaders
of the Confederacy though without their having given it any
tangible support, involved kidnapping the President as he
traveled, virtually unguarded, between the White House
and the Soldiers' Home, where he and his family sometimes
spent the night during the hottest summer weather.

even his closest friends; General [Richard] Ewell
wept like a child. The reason was that the crime of
April 14 could harm no one more than the people
of the South, and they now understood that they
had no reason to expect mercy from the conqueror.

Finally, the death of Mr. Lincoln called to the
presidency an honest and capable man, one worthy
on more than one score to play the great part entrusted to him. But he had always been famous,
both in the United States Senate and in the difficult
and dangerous post of Military Governor of a "border state," for the violence—even the brutality—of
his words and deeds. One of the "new men" of democracy, originating among that half-civilized population of "poor whites" whom a social system
founded on slavery has up to the present kept in a
state of ignorance and savagery, a furious enemy of
the slave-owning aristocracy whose interests and
prejudices he had once espoused, a rabble-rouser
rather than a cabinet statesman, Mr. [Andrew E.]
Johnson seemed fit to be a President to lead a civil
war rather than a man to pacify the country afterward by skillfully renewing contact with the traditions and memories of the former national union.
Although he had earlier been a Democrat and a
vehement defender of "states' rights," he had had
the reputation since the outbreak of war of being an
ardent abolitionist, a Radical of the most decided
stamp, and it was with the aim of conciliating its
own extremists that the Republican Convention in
Baltimore placed his name on the "ticket" along
with that of Lincoln. Therefore one might have
feared that he would let himself be carried away by

Engraving   From *Harper's History of the Great Rebellion*

President Andrew Johnson

his anger and by the general exasperation of public opinion, acting with pointless severity or engaging in unjust reprisals that might perhaps have the disastrous effect of compromising in advance the success of the great work of pacification that was about to begin.

As for Mr. Johnson, he seemed to take pleasure in giving grounds for these fears. In a speech replying to an Illinois delegation he said: "The American people must be taught, if they do not know it already, that treason is a crime—the greatest of crimes—and that the government will not always show patience towards its enemies, for it has power not only to protect but also to punish." On another occasion, replying to visitors from Pennsylvania, he seemed to be ready to cut off the heads of the leaders and instigators of the rebellion as a sacrifice to popular wrath: "To the ignorant crowd, to those who have been deceived or forced to take up arms—in a word, to the great mass of the people who have been misled, I will offer only clemency, reconciliation and restoration of the former government. But to the deceivers themselves, to the deliberate, influential traitors who threatened the nation's very existence, I shall say, 'May you bear the full measure of punishment for your crime.' "* At the same time he

* I think I should also cite several other passages from this address, remarkable as it is from more than one point of view, allowing us full insight into the intimate thoughts of President Johnson and showing from what a political rather than moral point of view this former slaveowner converted to abolition had arrived at the hatred for slavery he has demonstrated during the war: "I can say only one thing—my past life should give an indication of what my future conduct will

ordered the arrest of the principal Rebel leaders and he accused them publicly, with a somewhat rash vehemence, of having secretly had a hand in the assassination of April 14. Finally, he offered a reward for their capture and exchanged with them a correspondence carried on in the newspapers that was full of insulting language hardly befitting his rank. But in his proclamation of amnesty, especially, he gave the most revealing evidence of his penchant for egalitarian democracy and also of the long-standing resentment of a common man who has risen above his origins.

President Lincoln had offered during the war an amnesty proclamation granting full and unconditional pardon to all Rebels who would again accept the authority of the United States and take an oath of allegiance and fidelity. An offer as generous as this could be made in the middle of the war at a

---

be. . . . I know how easy it is to cry 'demagogue!' . . . If it is demagoguery to please the people, if it is demagoguery to contribute to their well-being and advancement—then, yes, I am a demagogue. . . . *A great monopoly existed, that of slavery, upon which rested an aristocracy. It is the duty of free men to tear down these monopolies . . . That is why I have always fought against aristocracy, against aristocracy in all its forms.* But there is a kind of aristocracy that has always won, and will always win, my approval and respect: the aristocracy of talent and virtue, the aristocracy of merit and public esteem, the aristocracy of labor that rests on honest industry—that aristocracy will always have my respect." [This citation, like the others from President Johnson's speeches and writings, was re-translated into English from the author's French version; the texts may therefore be found to vary slightly from the English original. Limitations of space make it impossible to give both texts for comparison.]

time when it could still seem to be a measure of pacification as well as a means of weakening the Rebels by bringing back to the fold some of the sheep that had gone astray. But President Lincoln's offer of amnesty naturally became inapplicable when the war ended, for it had only been extended as a means of securing a voluntary return to the Union, and it would have been too generous to obstinate Rebels who had resisted until the last minute; they had no claim to take advantage, after their defeat, of a pardon they had done nothing to deserve. Hence the new President had unimpaired power to pardon or to punish, and he was completely free to withhold the benefit of his amnesty from whatever category or from whatever individual he was pleased to except. Still, there can be no denying that the criterion on which he based the giving of pardons was bad and dangerous.

The whole world knows the terms of this amnesty. The President was not content merely to refuse its benefits to various classes of citizens who had been compromised by taking part in the civil or military service of the rebellion, depending on their rank, their importance and the more or less active role they might have played in the Confederate government's affairs. But, making wealth itself a crime, he excluded everybody worth more than $100,000, as if treason were merely a minor offense for poor people, for all who possess less than $100,000, but became an unforgivable crime for all those who had attained the fatal sum in excess of which a man somehow turns into a public enemy. It was all very well for Mr. Johnson to explain to a deputation from South Carolina, come to plead with him to rescind his invidious exception, that the great land-owners of the South were the true instigators of the Civil War and that it was perfectly proper to with-hold from them the forgiveness extended to the common people—this arbitrary distinction, which flies in the face of all reason and justice, obviously betrays a wish to despoil and level the upper ranks of society, a vague propensity for social revolution that Mr. Johnson himself scarcely tries to hide. How many times had he not declared that the unequal distribution of land ownership, was far more than slavery, the real cause of secession of the Southern states, and that the Union would never be firmly reëstablished until the day when all large property-holdings should be broken up and given to working men and small farmers!

The $100,000 exception, which left the lands of the rich planters subject to the laws of confiscation voted by Congress, could only be in his mind a memory or an effort to put into practice the equaliz-ing laws he had long admired. He made no bones about telling the delegates from South Carolina, displaying that harsh energy that no one but the Americans so well know how to use, a style that renders the mutual relations of citizens and officials so easy and clear: "Well, what are you complaining about? If you want to get around the $100,000 ex-ception, all you have to do is give away the balance of your fortune. I'll tell you quite frankly, gentle-men, that I think there would be no harm done if, instead of extending the amnesty to people like you, you were mercilessly taxed to the point where you would be forced under it. When I was military governor of Tennessee I used that system of taxation more than once, and never once that I know of did it fail to produce good results." At this point his strong language exceeded all permissible limits and, if one may say that President Lincoln could not have shown greater eloquence or manly resolution, at least one may be permitted to believe that he would have spoken with more moderation, propriety and dignity.

In a word, even the President's personal reputation left much to be desired. He was known to be a sincere and upright man; but the strange spectacle he had made in Congress on the fourth of April[7] had not been forgotten; nor, indeed, had the public meetings and the insulting speeches provoked by this scandalous incident, nor the advice—almost the imperious orders—he received to withdraw from an office which he had dishonored. It is true that these matters paled into insignificance compared with the terrible national misfortune that had called him to the Presidency, and that no American desirous of maintaining the national honor would now have taken it into his head to reawaken the ridicule with

[7] Presumably the author means March 4, Inauguration Day. When Johnson took the oath succeeding Hannibal Hamlin of Maine as Vice President, he had taken too much whiskey as medicine (as most historians now agree) and made a rambling, incoherent address that shocked many. It made an incongruous prelude to Lincoln's Second Inaugural Address ("With malice toward none; with charity for all; with firmness in the right as God gives us to see the right, let us strive on to finish the work we are in; to bind up the nation's wounds . . . ").

which that sad spectacle had covered a President of
the United States. Besides, people were well aware
that one example doesn't establish a rule and that
the Vice President, who was ill and exhausted by
the long trip he had just made, had done nothing
worse than to imbibe somewhat too freely of a cordial too strong for his weakened state of health. Did
not his difficulties on that occasion even go to prove
conclusively that he was a man of sober habits?

This is what his personal friends have been saying in extenuation of his conduct, and the arguments are echoed by all good citizens who would
like to give him support; but the Democrats and
secessionists never leave off insulting him and
throwing the incident of April [March] 4 in his face.
This freshly remembered incident, which made a
more painful and less easily effaced impression in
Europe than in the United States, taken together
with more distant though still fairly recent recollec-
tions of his administration in Tennessee, the too-
forceful roughness of his language and, finally, the
demagogic provisions of his amnesty proclamation
which he himself insisted upon emphasizing without any sort of apology—all this was enough to
cause concern among well-wishers of the American
Union and to make them fearful that the great example of forbearance and patriotism set by the late
President Lincoln might very well be lost on the
stubborn and belligerent man who has had to step
into his shoes.

It was in these terms that the world took note of
the policies of the man who was about to assume
the delicate task of directing the reconstruction of

the Southern states. We shall see how circumstances and needs, his experience and perhaps also his own sense of his heavy responsibilities before his contemporaries and in the eyes of history have changed this indomitable spirit to the point where he has become the idol of the conservative Democrats and the oftentimes blind opponent of the most necessary reforms being pressed by the Radicals—how, in a word, the raging demagogue, the former tailor's apprentice from Tennessee, has taken his place from the start of his term of office among the greatest and most capable Presidents the United States has ever had.

Not everything was settled on the day the Federal flag was raised once again over the capitol building in Richmond. A great many difficult problems remained unsolved. The nation had to go forward resolutely to complete the revolution begun by the Civil War; it had to enforce the abolition of slavery in the Southern states. It was needful not only to impose obedience on the conquered inhabitants but also to raise them up again after having subjugated them, to bring them back into the bosom of the Union, rebuild the devastated countryside and enlist the people's sincere acceptance of the great reform about to be inaugurated. They must be made to feel the firm hand of a determined government that would not, however, be a threat to their liberties. Armed repression must give way to politics and although its achievements would be less sensational, perhaps less glorious, than those of war, its tasks would be all the more difficult and dangerous to carry out.

There were two policies to choose from in dealing with the Rebel states. They might be considered a conquered territory and be told that when they left the Union they gave up all their rights under the Federal Constitution, that they had ceased to be sovereign states. In that case they must be treated as a conquered foreign people; their state and local governments must be destroyed or allowed to collapse and then reorganized as territories subject to the direct authority of Congress. Then some day, when the memory of the Civil War had been completely erased, they would be readmitted to the Union. This procedure, the Radicals argued, would be merely the literal application of the United States Constitution, the sole method of ensuring proper respect for national authority. It would be the only way to restore the former Union on a solid foundation, having levelled the ground beforehand by stamping out all tendencies to rebellion arising from slavery and the Civil War.

It would be a good thing for the Southern states to be subjected for a time to the rigors of military rule and arbitrary power, or at least for them to be kept for a number of years under the guardianship of Congress, that is to say, under the domination of the North. Their delegates might come, like those from the territories, and present their grievances or defend their interests; but they would have only a consultative voice in Congress and would have no share in the government. Great care must be taken not to give back to the South the preponderant influence it had exercised for so long. The rebellion is not yet dead, the Radical orators declared; it has only been knocked down and it may get back on its feet if we are not vigilant. Never has the Union been in such danger as in this moment of victory when peace seems to prevail, but when the future depends entirely on the decisions the people and the government now adopt. If the party of slavery and secession is once allowed to reorganize, if the Southerners renew their alliance with the Northern Democrats, it will be all up with national greatness and liberty. The same arrogant claims and the same quarrels will reappear as in the past and slavery, though abolished on paper, will be preserved in substance; all this will some day or other lead to another civil war which will encompass the total destruction of America.

The other policy corresponded to quite a different set of assumptions. It took as its major premise that the ordinances of secession voted by the Rebel states were null and void, that the Constitution of the United States had never ceased to be the fundamental law in the Southern states and that they had never had the legal power to leave the Union. Now, with the war at an end, they remain in possession of all their rights and privileges, retaining their former place in the structure they were unable to pull down. If the members of Congress from the South had temporarily abandoned their seats, they had nonetheless never ceased to have a right to them, and in their absence the two Houses had been just as legitimately empowered to pass laws as though they had still been taking part in the votes. The Confederate government had never had any legal existence; what went by that name was merely a cabal of rebels and usurpers. Therefore it was only necessary to annul all the measures taken during the war under the alleged authority of the so-called Confederate government: to repudiate the debt of the Confederacy and the debts contracted during the war by the state and local governments of the South,* to replace all the elected members of state governments chosen since the beginning of the war and, finally, to accept once and for all the abolition of slavery and the laws enacted by Congress and the President of the United States. Whereupon, the Southern states would recover all their constitutional prerogatives and their local liberties; they would elect governors and members of their legislatures, send Senators and Representatives to Congress. Participation in the national life had simply been suspended within their borders during the rebellion, but it was impossible that it should be destroyed— to treat them as territories, as a conquered region, would amount to a recognition of the possibility of destroying the Constitution.

This abstract theory, as one may well believe, was not constructed for the pure pleasure of system-building. Like the opposing one, it appealed to arguments of manifest practical utility as well as to party passions. The Democrats, who had been taught by events to change their tune, sought to drape themselves in the austere garments of pro-Unionist principle so as to be able to offer the states of the South one last plank on which to clamber to

---

*Naturally it could not be allowable for the *loyal* citizen of the Rebel states to be taxed to maintain the credit of the rebellion.

safety. The most reasonable spokesmen of the South were overjoyed to seize upon this occasion in order, in the first place, to recover at home the independence of their separate governments and perhaps to regain in the long run the influence they had formerly had on national affairs. In addition, a large number of moderate Republicans, desirous above all of bringing about reconciliation and forgetfulness of civil strife, believed that a policy of exclusions, of systematic harshness, would accomplish nothing and would merely keep wounds open indefinitely. It would be impossible to bring about durable reforms in the Southern states except with the consent and coöperation of the local population. The way to pacify the South and get it to accept the rule of the Union as a good thing was not to govern it by force nor to keep it in subjection as though to a foreign conqueror.

And besides, it was asked, even if a hundred thousand troops were kept there in occupation for ten years, would it really be possible to secure compliance with the will of Congress on the part of a sparse population scattered over an immense area, considering that there would be a universal conspiracy to violate or nullify those laws? In any event, even to attempt this would require a huge standing army, always on a war footing, and this would entail greater rather than less governmental expenditure. By taking over the government of the Rebel states, the North would simultaneously have to assume the heavy burden of providing for all their needs. It would be vain to expect agriculture and industry to regain their prosperity under the sway of a military regime sullenly accepted by people who would only obey when forced to do so. Hence the North would have to feed the South all the while it sought to keep it docile; it would have to go on indefinitely handing out charity, providing food to millions of famished persons—and this would be even more ruinous to the Federal government than the upkeep of its huge army during the war itself.

Would it be prudent to embark on this perilous venture and thus involve the national honor in its outcome? As for the renewal of the old alliance between the South and the Democrats, so perilous to the Radicals whose plans it could bring to grief, it would be the surest way to erase the memories of war between North and South by teaching the two former adversaries to remember that they are brothers living under the same roof. No one could hope to settle all the issues between the two sides in a single day. North and South must continue for a long time to be jealous rivals. But a resumption of the old legal forms of struggle within a new constitutional framework giving the last word to the Northern states would be far better than the indefinite persistence of the passions and resentments aroused by the Civil War.

President Johnson had to choose between these two policies, and in the United States hardly anyone doubted that he would declare himself with his customary violence in favor of the Radical solution. The Democrats, moreover, outdid themselves in their efforts to antagonize him. Following the execution of the assassins of President Lincoln, they actually went so far as to threaten him with "impeachment"* for what they call the "murder" of Mrs. [Mary E.] Surratt. After the arrest of Jefferson Davis there was a public meeting addressed by friends of the Rebel President; on that occasion several Democratic speakers openly declared that the Confederacy's defeat wasn't final, that the spirit that had brought it into being was still alive and that, with the help of its Northern friends, it might still triumph in a new form. They added that the execution of Mrs. Surratt had excited the whole world's indignation, that the government would never dare bring Jefferson Davis to trial and that "anyone who identified the Southern cause with treason could only be a madman or an imbecile."†

These insulting words were not calculated to soften the heart of President Johnson or to encourage him to make calm judgments. Nevertheless his policies tended more and more in the direction of extreme indulgence [toward the South], and many began to think that he was going too far. Even while publishing his drastic amnesty proclamation, even

---

* "Impeachment" is a sort of political trial which high officials of the government may be compelled by Congress to undergo. The House of Representatives draws up the indictment and the Senate tries the case. If found guilty, the defendant is deprived of his office and is incapacitated from holding any other position of trust under the authority of the United States.

† At this time the President daily received petitions couched in terms like these: "Mr. President and Dear Sir: We respectfully ask you to have President Davis hung because he deserves to be hung. If you don't hang him, there are plenty of people in Kansas who will do the job for you. Let us know your intentions, if you please. Very respectfully yours, A large number of citizens."

while obstinately refusing to modify it, he was displaying toward individuals a mildness at least equal to the violence of his language. Every pardon solicited by a former Rebel, however great his property holdings and however notorious a part he had taken in the secessionist cause, was promptly granted. When the [prosecuting] attorney of the Federal District Court in Norfolk, Virginia, brought an indictment against fifty-seven Rebels, including General Lee and all the military and civilian leaders of the Confederacy, the President exhibited the courage to issue summary orders quashing the proceedings in spite of the unyielding demand of Judge [John C.] Underwood—and, indeed, of the letter of the law— that justice take its course. It was almost as though he had only made so many blustering threats in order to be in a better position to keep the vanquished in check and confer more value, in their eyes, on the pardons they were able to obtain thanks to his unexpected clemency.

The truth is that public opinion had mellowed almost as much as the President himself. The leaders of the abolitionist party, Gerrit Smith, Horace Greeley, [Henry] Ward Beecher and even Wendell Phillips—all except the pitiless Thaddeus Stevens— preached clemency to the American people, and with all the more authority in that no one had ever seen them, like some of the Copperheads, trying belatedly to make up, by their bloody and indecent fury, for their long complicity with the enemies of the state. The *Tribune*, Mr. Greeley's newspaper, said in connection with the trial of Davis and the other political prisoners held at Fort Monroe that only two death sentences for complicity in the rebellion should be carried out—one against slavery and the other against "states' rights."

Mr. Johnson then began to be even more merciful. His own policies began to take shape with a clarity that alarmed the abolitionists and even made conservatives open their eyes wide in astonishment. Beginning at the end of June, 1865, he gave his most encouraging smiles to Southerners who came to seek his intervention in behalf of their local liberties. The first delegation from South Carolina, the state most guilty of inciting and then prolonging the rebellion, received the most favorable reply. The President told the delegates that he was an even stronger supporter of "states' rights" than they were; he urged them to make up their minds once and for all that slavery was dead, that there could no longer be the slightest question of reviving it; but with this proviso he promised to lend them his fullest coöperation in the work of restoration that was about to begin. "I say 'restoration,'" he added, "and not 'reconstruction,' because one can only reconstruct something that has been destroyed, and the Union has never ceased to exist." At the same time he appointed provisional governors in every state of the South, authorizing them only to fill the interregnum between the collapse of the Rebel governments and the reconstitution of governments recognized by the Federal authorities.

Except in Virginia, where a "loyal" government had already been reëstablished in several conquered districts and cities and needed only to be moved from Alexandria to Richmond, and except for the still-divided "border states," where governments approved by the Union therefore needed only to take the place of the Rebel authorities, all these temporary holders of such dangerous power were chosen from the ranks of former Rebels, even from the members of the Confederate Congress itself. In North Carolina there was Mr. [William W.] Holden, in South Carolina Mr. [Benjamin F.] Perry, in Mississippi Mr. [William L.] Sharkey, in Alabama Mr. [Lewis E.] Parsons, in Georgia Mr. [Herschel V.] Johnson, in Florida Mr. [William] Marvin and in Texas Mr. [Andrew J.] Hamilton.

Mr. Perry, in a speech delivered just a short time before taking office, declared that no one could feel more profoundly than he did the humiliation of entering into a new union with the "Yankees," but that—the God of battles having decided against the South's independence—the wisest course of action would be to resign oneself to the inevitable and coöperate with the Federal government in making good the war's destruction. No greater devotion than this to the Union by Southerners was asked by President Johnson; he required them only to understand that there could be no return to the past and that the future depended on their good behavior.

His plan, moreover, was a simple one. He would everywhere appoint provisional governors who would look after the most urgent business, hold elections in each Rebel state to a "constitutional convention," giving a vote to every citizen entitled to vote under the state's pre-war constitution provided he could give evidence of his loyalty. (This last clause was more or less illusory, but it was just as well to honor the principle.) The convention would revise the state constitution, repeal the ordinance of secession and resume normal relations between the state and the Federal government; this extraordinary assembly would go out of existence once it had finished its task. The provisional governor would then see to the election of a bi-cameral legislature by the people of the state, cause these bodies to repudiate the Confederate debt, ratify the [Thirteenth] Amendment abolishing slavery and adopt effective measures for protecting the freedmen. The provisional governor would then step aside, leaving the state to elect a governor of its own choice; he would end his tenure of office when he conducted the new Senators and Representatives into the two houses of Congress.

In brief summary, such was the simple and well-conceived method proposed by the President, doubtless the best and the most liberal that could be imagined for reorganizing the political life of the South. Mr. Johnson thus unexpectedly became the declared protector of the Southern states. As soon as his defection had become clear, the Radicals opened fire on him with all their batteries. Confident of their strength on account of their majorities in the two houses of Congress, they threatened in their turn to have him impeached in the House and removed from office by the Senate. They believed they had been betrayed and delivered into the enemy's hands by this new Buchanan,[8] by this renegade

[8] Many ardent Unionists believed that President James Buchanan had followed deliberately pro-Southern policies in the months before the outbreak of the Civil War,

from the cause of slavery who was now committing a second apostasy. Everywhere they set up a great cry of alarm, rushing from city to city and from meeting to meeting shouting that all was lost and that nothing short of the most heroic efforts could save the country from sliding into the abyss. According to them the policies of President Johnson amounted to an admission that the Rebel cause had been right from the beginning, raising it up from its defeat to make it more powerful and threatening than ever. If nothing was done to stop him, he would certainly go to the length of installing the Confederate leaders in their old seats of power in Washington, reviving the slain hydra of Democratic majorities. "We have no choice now," cried Wendell Phillips with his customary vehemence, "There can no longer be any parties save the two—the sycophants of Davis and the friends of the Union. Whoever wants reconstruction, the 'restoration' of the Southern states, can only be one of Davis's sycophants!" These monstrous exaggerations could only hurt the Radicals by offending the people's good sense. And while the orators were hurling their impotent thunderbolts at President Johnson, the majority of the Republicans remained faithful to him and followed him with confidence in the new path he had chosen.

But the terrors of the Radical party were not alto-

---

strengthening the future Confederacy by the transfer of arms and munitions and in other ways. These reproaches were unjust; Buchanan's great aim was conciliation and he went very far in that direction, but his loyalty to the Union should not be questioned.

gether imaginary. It was speaking sincerely when it accused President Johnson of making the Rebels a gift of victory and of sacrificing the national honor to the convenience of the moment. If this party was wrong in wishing to subordinate all the interests of the country to the immediate introduction of equality between the two races, one cannot find fault with its clearsighted perseverance in attacking slavery as the most dangerous enemy of the Union.

There are few persons in Europe who fully understand the nature of the American Civil War or the true importance of the obstinate and complicated question of slavery. Some wish to see in this complex struggle nothing but an idealistic crusade on behalf of moral principles and ideas, and they portray the men of the North as so many kindly, disinterested missionaries for the cause of humanitarianism. Others, flying in the face of common sense and irrefutable facts, claim that slavery was not really an issue in the war, that the Southerners are the blacks' best friends and the abolitionists their would-be exterminators. This is so revoltingly false that one can hardly believe in the good faith of those who argue it. Is it not all too well known that the founding fathers of the American Union themselves foresaw even then the dangers of an institution which they attempted to circumscribe without daring to end it? Is it not also notorious that toward the end of his life the great Washington read and reread repeatedly, with an assiduity that points to his extreme concern, a treatise on the social and moral effects of slavery?

For sixty years this fatal issue was the only cloud

that darkened the future of the Republic, and how
many times did it not come within a hair's breadth
of exploding before the date marked down by the
fates! As early as the year 1825 the Georgia House
of Representatives threatened the Northern states
with secession if they persisted in advocating the
abolition of slavery.* Later, when the evil had become many times greater, when the few thousand
slaves whose future had begun to trouble the patriotic conscience of the noble Washington had grown
in numbers to become a population of five million
souls, what signified those quarrels that arose between North and South? What signified the controversy over the rights of the states, the dispute over
fugitive slaves, the issue of [slavery in] the territories
and even the question of the tariff in which some
people have seen the sole cause of the war—what
did all these disputes signify if not slavery, always
slavery, the fatal source of discord between the two
societies which it kept separated by reason of their

*I think it desirable to cite a few passages from these
strange resolutions for the instruction of those who think
that slavery was not the real cause of the Civil War and that
the Southern states were not the aggressors: "The moment is
approaching when the States of the South must confederate
and say with one voice to the Union: 'We do not intend any
longer to submit our acquired rights to the insinuations of
perfidious and evil men in the halls of Congress, nor to put
our constitutional rights at the mercy of the labored and
obscure interpretation of self-seeking men occupying the judicial bench. . . . What Athens, Sparta and Rome were, we
wish to be: they had slaves; we have slaves. . . . Wherefore let
it be resolved . . . that having exhausted argument we will
have recourse to arms and that in support of this resolution
we pledge our lives, our fortunes and our sacred honor.' "

customs as well as their material interests? There had always been between them a commercial rivalry so intimately bound up with the issue of slavery that it finally became insuperable. The tariff dispute was doubtless just as important and had just as large a part as slavery in bringing on the Civil War for the very good reason that the two issues were intertwined.

For was it not slavery that caused industry to stagnate in the Southern states and made them dependent on European manufactured goods? Was it not free labor that made the Northern states an industrial region as well as a rich agricultural country and made it necessary for them to support their industries by means of protective tariffs that guaranteed them a monopoly of the markets of the South? Finally, was it not slavery that impoverished the South by turning away from it that fertilizing flood of immigration from Europe while the system of free labor was attracting to the North the surplus population of all the nations on earth? The alleged oppression of the South by the North was nothing more nor less than the natural consequence of slavery attempting to exist alongside free labor—in these two phrases lies the whole secret of the Civil War's origin.

Having said this, one must admit that often the black man's advocates and defenders don't really care very much, when all is said and done, what becomes of him. Except for a few intellectuals, to whose democratic consciences the whole idea of slavery is repugnant, the noisiest abolitionists do not, if the truth were known, feel much offended by slavery. When the Northerner gets hot under the collar at the single word "slavery," you may be sure he is thinking less about the moral wrong done to the blacks who are degraded by it than he is about the supremacy of the society he belongs to over the one of which slavery is the cornerstone. Nowhere is color prejudice more deeply rooted than in the regions permeated by abolitionist ideas. People there have discovered that the Negro is a human being, that he has as good a right as anyone to liberty and the protection of the laws, but the Christian brotherhood of the average American philanthropist doesn't go much beyond that.

While I was in Boston, the polite society of the town was deeply scandalised by an improbable story purporting to describe a dinner at the home of a mulatto merchant of the city at which it was said that Senator Sumner, Professor Longfellow and a number of other Boston celebrities were present, not to mention several Europeans emancipated from their prejudices, people known to be very set in their ways whose eccentricity came as a surprise to no one. The good Yankees were unable to entertain without embarrassment the notion that such honorable and respectable gentlemen, their fellow-citizens, could be so forgetful of social proprieties as to sit down at table and eat the bread of a colored man. I am told by an eyewitness that the following day Mr. Sumner was accosted in the street by an unknown "gentleman" who, with a distracted expression on his face, begged him to answer just one question: "Is it really true, Sir, that you dined yesterday at the home of Mr. S., the mulatto? Is it possible that someone may have misinformed me?" By this you can take the measure of the kind of social equality prevailing in the very citadel of the Negrophiles and in a state where black citizens are in full enjoyment of all their political rights. Accordingly, it was with profound admiration that I saw one day in a Washington horsecar an old gentleman with a white beard get up and offer his seat to a black woman. There was heroism in this silent, one-man protest against a prejudice whose authority he was the only person brave enough to challenge.

I don't believe that at the beginning of the war public opinion was as yet ripe for the great reform which events have precipitated. Had it not been for the blindness and ferocity of the Southern states, it is probable that emancipation would have been put off even longer than it was. To convince oneself of this, one has only to recall the words of President Lincoln on the subject of slavery: "If I could save the Union without freeing a single slave, I would do it." Recall, too, his reply to a delegation of black people: "We are of different races; it is better that we live separately." Yet the same man, driven by the war to take extreme measures, decreed the emancipation of all slaves belonging to Rebels and gave naturalization papers to the blacks[9] by letting them enroll in the armies of the Union.

[9] Black troops were enlisted in the Union forces in New Orleans by General Benjamin F. Butler as early as August 22, 1862, and the 1st S. C. Volunteer Infantry (of African descent) was organized in November, 1862. President Lincoln did not request the enlistment of black troops until July 21, 1863, and did not give orders to this effect until October 3.

The North has only struck down slavery in order to save the Union and, by way of compensation, it has allowed itself the pleasure of slandering to its heart's content the poor blacks whose unenthusiastic benefactor it has become. It may be truly said that the American people are abolitionists in spite of themselves. They will be glad enough to let the new freedmen get along as best they can with their former masters, even if in the end their glorious freedom turns out to look a little like their former servitude.

In the United States I have heard the saying on everyone's lips that God made America for the white man and not for blacks, which comes down to saying that the white man ought to look out for himself before bothering about his inferior brother. Therefore the Radicals play a useful role in stimulating the flagging energies of their countrymen and in reminding the American people of the debt of honor the government has accepted in their name.

It is most certainly something to have abolished slavery in principle and to have declared that involuntary servitude may no longer exist in the United States. But of what use would it be to have erased the word, "slavery," if the thing itself is to be retained? The Americans must understand this: by striking a death-blow at the slave system, they have set foot upon a path of gradual emancipation that can only end in full equality of the two races. By freeing the blacks, they assume a moral obligation to respect and fully safeguard the freedom they have conferred on them. Are the poor blacks to be released from bondage only to be handed over, tied hand and foot, to their former masters? The white people of the South have a very simple means of reasserting their former domination over the freedmen—all they need to do is make them a class apart, deprived of all political and judicial rights, restricted in the exercise of their civil rights, a class of pariahs or helots subject to special laws which they have no part in making. Under those conditions the planters of the South will have lost nothing and will have nothing to fear; they will scarcely be aware of the transition from slavery to a kind of innocuous, Platonic liberty that will be enough to comply with the law.

The Radicals want to ward off this danger by giving the freedmen the vote immediately. They think the best way to safeguard their liberty is to give them a share of political power so as to provide them with the means of defending themselves. They are certainly right if one judges in terms of abstract justice and the philosophy of republican institutions—but look at how many obstacles and disadvantages there are! Whether their policy can be enforced at all is very doubtful, and its immediate application is impossible. Perhaps it might have been just barely possible, by rallying all the forces of opinion that lean toward the Republicans to get Congress to adopt a constitutional amendment giving the suffrage to blacks and even to extort the necessary number of ratifications from the states. But how could such an unwillingly accepted law be enforced in practice or receive the sanction of public opinion? Rights that exist only on paper mean nothing unless they are backed up by force or toler-

ated by custom. Would the North itself set an example to the recalcitrant Southerners? Would its
people be willing to accept what they are talking of
imposing upon the Southern states? The conspicuous failure of Connecticut to allow black voting for
its constitutional convention raises serious questions about their zeal.

There are, of course, a few states where color is
not always an obstacle to the enjoyment of political
rights. Thus, in the state of New York Negroes may
vote in all elections if they have an [annual] income
of $250 or more; in Massachusetts the electoral law
does not draw any distinction between the two
races. There, however, it is notorious that blacks
hardly ever vote because they dare not challenge
local prejudice. How much more absolute and immovable would that prejudice be in the South
where there is still such strong antagonism between
the freed slave and the dispossessed master! Such
rights would be meaningless unless the new citizens
were to go about exercising them with arms in
hand. Or perhaps, indeed, one might see blacks
herded to the polls by their former masters in order
to vote for their own worst enemies. But apart from
voluntary abstention and sheeplike obedience there
seems to be no alternative to naked force and social
war between the races.

President Johnson was therefore right not to
yield to the impatience of the Radicals. It was both
more prudent and more convenient to leave the
states, as he said, to decide the question themselves
and beyond that to let the passage of time do its
work. But even so, he was wrong to think he had no

obligation to protect the freedmen from violent attacks that grew bolder and more outrageous day by day. But the President, who in this respect faithfully reflected the popular mind, seemed to harbor some sort of ill humor or childish resentment against the poor blacks. Apparently the blacks were making the accomplishment of his political designs more difficult and he would have been glad to get rid of them by shipping them off to some far-away country. He listened eagerly to all the most fantastic plans for founding a Negro state or for black emigration *en masse* to the West or to South America that were spun out of cobwebs by disenchanted philanthropists. He could hardly be induced to pay attention to pleas that he do something to protect the blacks and in the space of a few months he withdrew his troops from the Southern states, turned over all police duties to the local militia and abandoned the freedmen to the tender mercies of their former masters.

The fruits of this policy were exactly those one might have anticipated. The Southerners had always had contempt for the blacks; now this was reinforced by the hatred people feel for a dreaded enemy. As long as he was a slave, the black had been able to live on good terms with the white, for he was treated with the tolerance one shows for an unthinking animal, for a horse or ox whose rivalry one does not fear; but once he was a free man, the black became for the whites an enemy whom they persecuted with bitter ferocity. There is no mistreatment so extreme that they do not think it right to inflict it on him in revenge for his having been liberated. His slightest faults are punished as though they were crimes. If any serious misdeed is committed by a member of the black race, the whites retaliate against his brothers in an indiscriminate massacre of the innocent together with the guilty. In Tennessee a band of former Confederate soldiers has burned a black schoolhouse and threatened the schoolmaster with death. In Arkansas the rape of one white woman cost the lives of thirty people. In Alabama the blacks have had to take to flight and hide themselves in the forests. They had no other way of resisting their former owners who had joined together to force them to remain on the land and continue to work it without pay as in the days of slavery. There are even plantations where owners have been able to keep the blacks from learning that they are free.[10]

The only protector the blacks have is the "Freedmen's Bureau." The initial purpose for which this institution was founded was to aid black refugees from the South. The scheme was to put these unfortunate people to work on plantations abandoned by Rebel owners and confiscated by the government of the United States rather than allow the land to remain uncultivated; parcels of forty acres each were leased to them and it was provided that they might buy these later for a low price. Afterwards, following the end of the war, when the Bureau was extended to all the Rebel states, its nature and aims changed. Having been a charitable institution, it

[10] These atrocities were the work of secret terrorist organizations of which the Ku Klux Klan was the largest, most widespread and best known.

now became a political and judicial agency.[11] The Bureau still was in control of confiscated or seques- tered lands, and it undertook large-scale distribu- tion of food supplies to the starving people of the South, particularly the new freedmen. Finally, and most important, it was charged with ensuring the safety of the freedmen and with seeing to it that, in so far as possible, they were able to exercise their civil rights. Whenever a league of planters tried to force the blacks to work for ridiculously low wages or when the law, intervening to support their mach- inations, fixed wages at a ludicrously low level, the Freedmen's Bureau would step in between the freedman and his employer, safeguard the independence of the former and itself established a reasonable wage-scale. When a black person had a complaint against a white, or whenever a white sought to enforce a legal claim against a black, it was the Freedman's Bureau that took cognizance of the matter, acting by turns as judge and guardian in the interests of the freedman.

This paternalistic and benevolent institution is needed in the South. Nonetheless it has certain de- fects and disadvantages. The agents of the Bureau have been criticised for excessive zeal and for acting unfairly and exclusively in behalf of their wards. It

[11] The Freedmen's Bureau had been created by an act of Congress (March 3, 1865) and at first devoted itself almost entirely to the feeding and care of Southern refugees both white and black. A bill framed by moderate Republicans, extending the life of the Bureau and expanding its powers to counteract the various "black codes" of the former slave states, was vetoed by President Johnson in mid-February, 1866, though it eventually became law in late April, 1866.

is claimed that in certain localities where blacks and whites were already getting along fairly well together the Bureau's agents came as sowers of discord rather than as peacemakers. Occasionally they may have abrogated contracts that were equitable and encouraged the fatal propensity of some Negroes for laziness by giving them the foolish hope that the lands of their former masters were about to be carved up and shared out. Or again, they are blamed for using their authority arbitrarily and for handing down one-sided decisions in courts where there is a single judge and no jury; in a word, they are accused of upsetting the balance and the smooth functioning of governmental bodies.

But it is precisely in this realm that the Freedmen's Bureau has made its most vital contribution. Was it really thinkable that the blacks could be abandoned to the states' legal systems when they were denied even the right to testify in court, when the planters chained and whipped them as in the past, making them believe they were not yet free or arrogantly assuming the power to keep them at work for wages not exceeding five or ten dollars a year? The real failing of the institution is that it frequently lacks the power to protect those who depend on it. How can the former slave make an effective appeal to these unknown guardians who are often fifty miles away? In the month of September, 1865, a [white] man was brought before one of the "Provost's Courts" in Virginia and found guilty of having mistreated black people. "Ah!" said he, furious with rage, "if the war isn't over, why don't they tell us! We'll start all over again!" Elsewhere, in

Georgia, in the Carolinas, there were violent clashes between the quickly reconstituted state militia and the Federal agents of the Freedmen's Bureau; a certain Captain Healy was killed and dismembered. In South Carolina the "Home Guard," which had never been dissolved, set out to nullify the work of the Bureau by assuming judicial powers and by backing the planters' tyranny with armed force. Governor Perry of South Carolina has made no secret of his hopes: he urged his fellow citizens to abolish slavery in order to rejoin the Union; but once this formality was completed he warned the North to expect nothing further—"for," said he, "this is a white man's country, and a white man's government."* Why should we be surprised to hear an ex-Rebel talking this way when President Johnson himself did not hesitate to repeat this sorry commonplace borrowed from the partisans of slavery?

These crimes and disorders were not all to be attributed to the temporary tensions that always accompany a difficult transition. Most commonly they were the natural consequences of laws that people everywhere [in the South] were determined to keep in force or to make more stringent. In Alabama the constitutional convention, even when it was requested to do so by Governor Parsons, refused to grant to blacks the right to testify in court, with the result that the black continues to have no place in the courtroom except the dock. For example, a Negro is accused by a white man; twenty blacks swear that he is innocent, but he is condemned to be hung

* The same words were addressed by the President to the abolitionist Governor [Thomas] Fletcher of Missouri.

on the testimony of the one white man. Again, in Mississippi, Governor [Benjamin G.] Humphreys, elected by the people, assumed office by usurpation, not having been confirmed by the President, and, entering into conflict with the provisional Governor, Mr. Sharkey, sent to the legislature a message in which he advised them to enact laws that would ensure the perpetual inferiority of the blacks. A newspaper in the same state, the *Jackson News*, demands laws that will "make the ex-slaves constantly aware of their natural inferiority" and openly advocates Lynch for any "Northerner" who encourages the black man to resist his former master. Elsewhere, in Virginia, Unionists are persecuted, their crops are burned, their houses are pillaged, their horses' tendons are cut. The legislature of Alabama came close to enacting a law on vagrancy that was a real masterpiece of savagery—anyone found guilty, whether man or woman, was to be strung up by the thumbs for two hours at a time for three days and be given fifty lashes each day for good measure; for a second offense the punishment was to be doubled. This law formed part of a pattern of other measures which compelled the black to go on working on the plantation of his former owner and declared anyone who refused a vagrant. It is by a combination of ingenious expedients such as this that the Southerners hope to institute a sort of serfdom that will do for them all that slavery used to do.

They claim that the black man has a naturally lazy, easy-going disposition and that it is absolutely necessary to compel him—in his own interest—to resume his accustomed work. Otherwise freedom might mean only an idle life of luxury in which all human needs would be satisfied without labor. In the old days, when an industrious Negro had earned his freedom by the sweat of his brow, he often exclaimed: "Now that I'm a white man I don't have to work!" And he deserted the workshop or the cotton field for the open road and the saloon. But even if we ignore the fact that the poor black will be quickly undeceived of this infantile idea of life by cruel experience, aren't the whites the ones who have taught him to think this way by their example, treating labor as a shameful thing and freedom as the inevitable accompaniment of idleness and vice? Have they any right to blame him for the ignorance and lack of foresight they themselves have forced upon him? They complain that the black is not a human being, but a species of animal, a wild beast who knows nothing of religion, of the family or of moral obligation. If this be true, then who has reduced him to such a degraded condition? Who, if you please, has sold the wives of slaves, separated married couples, torn children from their mothers' arms and bred people in herds like livestock? Was that such a good school in which to learn the family virtues? So they are ignorant! Well, who closed the schoolroom door to them and the church door too, and who has taught them to make a clownish parody of religion? Who are the people who murmur and groan nowadays when the Federal government opens schools for freedmen in Virginia?

People may say what they will about the failings that tend to render the blacks unfit for freedom—the whites themselves are responsible for them and

ought to have to put up with any disagreeable results they may have. You must not expect to reap
wisdom, foresight, willing obedience to the law, the
spirit of order, the family virtues, conjugal fidelity,
where you have sown nothing but ignorance, oppression, brutality, and no sense of duty except an
abject cringing from the whip! If the public interest
requires that the blacks be forced to work, then let
the poor whites of the South—who do not have the
same excuse and who are born with the conviction
that they can live as idly as kings—let them too be
forced to work. They are even more demoralized and
unreclaimable than the blacks, for they are proud
beggars who must be fed because otherwise they would
tear down the governments whose bread they eat.

Finally, the freedmen are blamed for behaving
aggressively. But when they are provoked by daily
oppression, when their hopes have been raised by
the Civil War, by their hunger for land of their own
and a share of political power by the very promise
of real freedom that has been held out to them without being completely granted—how, considering all
this, would they not be tempted to take justice into
their own hands, if necessary by force? Colonel
[Samuel] Thomas, [Assistant] Commissioner of the
Freedmen's Bureau for the state of Mississippi,
wrote last year to General [Oliver O.] Howard
[Commissioner of the Bureau]: "If the local militia
is kept in service, I do not think the freedmen will
go on quietly cultivating the cotton fields. They are
enrolled [in self-defense bands] and are armed. It is
certain that there will be disturbances that will be
profoundly dangerous to social order."

Engraving   From *Harper's History of the Great Rebellion*

*General Oliver O. Howard, First Commissioner
of the Freedmen's Bureau*

Consequently he predicted that an uprising of ex-slaves could take place this year. The rumor is passed from one person to another that the Negroes of the South are armed, that they send to New York every day to buy large consignments of rifles and revolvers and, finally, that they have created a secret organization that must be snuffed out as soon as possible. People argue calmly about whether or not it is urgently necessary to exterminate them all.

The Democrats have been saying—as one might expect—that it is vital to give back the control of the military to the [white] people of the South so that they may be able to defend themselves against a black insurrection. The Radicals, on the contrary, say that it is more than ever the duty of the government to stand between the two races, to calm one by giving it its just rights and to control the other by forcing it to allow justice to be done. Otherwise, if they are simply left to settle accounts among themselves, there would be every prospect of a massacre such as took place in Santo Domingo,[12] only it would be a reciprocal slaughter of which the blacks would be the ultimate victims; slavery would undoubtedly have been abolished, but only by annihilating the whole black population.

Nevertheless, the influence of President Johnson in the Southern states has been gaining in strength. People are getting used to thinking of him as a protector sent by Divine Providence. The Radicals

[12] Refers presumably to massacres of white planters during the black uprisings that occurred during the period of the French Revolution. Many blacks, however, were later executed by the French.

have helped him by their very opposition, which allows him to use them as a bogey-man to frighten the Southerners. Their unbending harshness has taught the South to put a higher price on his mildness and to accept the necessity of following his lead in order to keep him as a defender. He himself is beginning to feel that he is strong enough to take command and he is finally using his authority to give some satisfaction to the Radicals.

For example, South Carolina and Mississippi hesitated to adopt the constitutional amendment abolishing slavery. Speaking in an authoritative tone which he should perhaps have adopted before, he peremptorily declared to the legislatures of those two states that he would not revoke the powers of the provisional Governors and would not recognize the elected Governors [James L.] Orr and [Benjamin G.] Humphreys until the amendment was ratified. North Carolina shrank from repudiating the Confederate debt, whereupon he sent by telegraph an imperious message to the Governor and the disputed measure was voted on the spot. Such docility contrasts sharply with the recent truculence of the Mississippi convention which began its work by validating acts passed by the legislature during the rebellion—that is to say, the very laws it had been summoned to annul. It contrasts too with the insolence shown by North Carolina in announcing loudly that it will use the rights being restored to it for the purpose of impeding, at whatever cost, the restoration of the Union.

Other states persisted in refusing to grant freedmen the protection they need when involved with the judicial process. Here public opinion was so adamant that Governor Holden [of North Carolina] was convinced—as he told his friends—that "the people will die before they will let blacks vote or testify in court." In Raleigh, North Carolina, one Unionist citizen declared at a Unionist meeting, to general applause, that he would kill himself and his whole family before he would see a Negro treated as his equal in a courtroom. But the President again made his stern voice heard; his commanding gestures and his copious threats of punishment balanced by copious promises of rewards carried the day, especially inasmuch as they were backed up by a pack of howling Radicals whom he threatened to unleash upon the South like powerful, bloodthirsty bulldogs. For the benefit of the obstructionists he pointed first to Messrs. Chase and Sumner, who want to give the blacks the vote, and then to the remorseless Thaddeus Stevens and his proposal to confiscate the property of all Rebels and use it to pay off the Federal debt. And the terrified Southerners groaned and grumbled, but they let the yoke be put over their necks.

This yoke, to tell the truth, was marvelously soft and light. In order to regain the President's good graces the Florida constitutional convention merely had to declare that, as a general rule, no one could be excluded on grounds of color from testifying in a case involving a colored person. The Mississippi House of Representatives also has accepted, though with great reluctance, an even more wishy-washy law extending the right to appear in court only to the interested parties—plaintiffs or defendants—but still refusing that right to other persons who might seek to testify in behalf of a member of their own race. President Johnson seems to think that these concessions are sufficient, for he has demanded nothing more for the protection of the freedmen.

Nevertheless, he drew closer to the Radicals. The prospect of the coming November elections had made both of them feel the need of joining in alliance against the secessionist Democrats who could be expected to take advantage of their disputes. Having by common agreement renewed the somewhat impaired unity of the great Republican Party, they presented themselves to the electorate in a compact and well-drilled body. President Johnson seemed at the zenith of his power and popularity. While the more extreme Republicans avowed what was perhaps only a half-sincere confidence in his intentions, the Democrats, to whom he had given so many unexpected pledges of sympathy, proclaimed him to be the greatest President the United States has had since Washington, sent by Providence to save the country from revolutionary anarchy.

Congress, however, was about to meet, and the Radicals had retained an imposing majority. By refusing to seat the elected representatives of the South they could overthrow the whole policy of legal restoration set on foot by the President and torpedo his ship just as it was entering the harbor. The outcome of a constitutional struggle with the two houses of Congress would always be uncertain, especially under the aegis of these republican institutions which give the President neither a definitive veto power nor the supreme power of dissolution, but merely a suspensive veto[13] for barely ten days, and this can be overridden by a two-thirds majority. It therefore seemed safer to reach an understanding, if possible, with those fierce Radicals who were about to become so dangerous.

It was no doubt in this hope that the President allowed one of his friends to circulate a kind of declaration of principles which he had outlined one day in a private conversation on the crucial question of freedmen's rights. According to the version published by this friend, Mr. [George L.] Stearns, Mr. Johnson said that in theory he was in favor of equal voting rights for the two races and that, if conditions allowed him to act as he wished, he would begin by granting political rights first to the black former soldiers of the Federal army and then to educated and wealthy colored men, making their right to vote subject to a property qualification that would later be lowered to the prevailing level [for whites]. Beyond this, he desired that liberty should not remain an empty word for the freed slaves, that their civil rights should be reliably safeguarded by law and that—last and most important of all—they should be admitted to the law courts as plaintiffs, defendants or witnesses on precisely the same footing as whites.

This profession of faith no doubt dealt with the main theoretical grievances of the Radicals against

[13] By "suspensive veto" the author means the "pocket veto" by which a President may prevent a bill from becoming law by withholding his signature provided that Congress adjourned before the expiration of the ten-day period. (See U.S. Constitution, Art. I, Section 7.)

the President; but they were certainly not disposed
to be satisfied by purely Platonic ideas locked away
in the recesses of the President's heart or given out
in a whisper in the form of an intimate conversation
of a purely speculative kind. For these reasons they
decided that when Congress reconvened they
would attempt to strike a decisive blow by peremptorily refusing to seat the newly elected senators
and representatives from the former Rebel states
who would be coming with the President's blessing
to knock at the doors of the Capitol.

Congress was then divided among three factions.
First, there were the Radicals, led in the Senate by
Mr. Sumner and in the House by Mr. Thaddeus
Stevens—they controlled a clear majority. Second,
there were the moderate Republicans, a less numerous group, lacking in cohesion and more in sympathy with the Radicals than with their opponents; in
the House they seemed to look for leadership to Mr.
[Henry J.] Raymond, a friend of Seward and his
confidential adviser on policy, while in the Senate
they looked to Mr. [James] Dixon or Mr. [James R.]
Doolittle, neither of whom, however, laid claim to
be a party leader. Finally, over against the Republicans of all shades of opinion, there was arrayed the
small rear-guard of Democrats, decimated, discouraged and diffident, but looking with some hope to
the future and ready to enlist under the banner of
President Johnson.

The Radicals arrived for the opening ceremonies
full of boundless confidence in their approaching
victory and determined to carry off at the very start
of the session a spectacular triumph that would also

be a great humiliation for the White House. To protect themselves against an invasion by elected representatives of the South they had the Test Oath, enacted by Congress in 1862, which obliges all officers of the government, whether civil or military, all judges and administrators and all members of Congress to swear a solemn oath that they have never borne arms against the national government, served the Rebel authorities in any capacity whatsoever nor voluntarily given any aid, support, counsel or encouragement to the Confederacy. Now, the elected representatives of the South could swear in good conscience that from that time forward they would support the Constitution and Federal government to the best of their ability, but they could not honestly swear that they had always been faithful when they had taken an active and public part in the rebellion. Even the most shameless perjury would not have solved their problem, for the act of July 2, 1862, declares that persons convicted of perjury are ineligible to hold any office of trust under the United States.

This retroactive oath consequently stood as an insurmountable barrier to the admission of the new senators and congressmen from the South, and the first thing the Democrats did when the session opened was to demand its repeal or modification. But the Republicans were so unwilling to heed them that they made haste to erect an even higher and more conspicuous barrier against a new "Rebel invasion" of the houses of Congress.

On December 2, 1865, on the eve of the reconvening of Congress, they all attended a great "cau-

cus"—this is the odd name given to the semi-official
meetings where the party delegations meet separately to rehearse their parts—in the very chamber
of the House of Representatives. There they adopted a resolution which Mr. Thaddeus Stevens was
instructed to introduce and bring to a vote in the
House the following day. It provided that a joint
committee was to be established by the two houses
to deliberate on the matter of the Southern representatives; this committee was to have fifteen members, nine representatives and six senators; it was to
look into the situation actually prevailing in the
former Confederate states and decide whether they
were ready to be readmitted to representation in
Congress.

Until its report was submitted and the issue decided by the two chambers, no representative from
the Rebel states would be received in Congress;
their credentials and all of their other relevant documents would be transmitted directly to the joint
committee. The Radicals had at last formulated
their own program and they were declaring war
upon the President.

The actors had learned their roles and the public
performance went off without a hitch the next day.
Mr. [Edward] McPherson, clerk of the House of
Representatives, in calling the roll, deliberately re-
frained from including the names of Southern congressmen. When Mr. [Horace] Maynard and the
congressmen from Tennessee—who, please note,
had been elected under a [state] constitution voted
into force by an assembly of Unionists—protested
against the omission, the reply they received was

that they had no right to speak because they were not members of Congress. Mr. Stevens even shouted, "There is no state of Tennessee!" Then, as soon as the House had organized itself and was ready to hear him, he read out the resolutions adopted the day before. And without debate nor any other sort of deliberation, without even deigning to answer the timid protests of the Democrats, he had them adopted on the spot by an enormous majority. The Democrats returned to the charge and sought to obtain for their Southern protégés at least the right of free entry onto the floor of the House. But even this harmless consolation was denied them, and the Radicals left the session proclaiming that they had won a great victory.

In the Senate, as in the House, they had only to show themselves in order to conquer, but in the Senate their strategy was somewhat different. Instead of a sudden, impetuous, bold attack, instead of the irresistible bayonet-charge led by Mr. Stevens at the same moment against the hapless Democrats, Messrs. Wade, Sumner, Wilson and the other leaders of the Senate methodically opened the battle with a withering fire from their heaviest parliamentary artillery and crushed the enemy under a mountain of resolutions, laws and propositions of all sorts. First, there was Mr. Wade's bill to grant the franchise to blacks residing in the District of Columbia, thereby setting a good example to the Southern states. Then came Mr. Wilson's bill "to maintain the freedom of the population of states declared to be in a state of insurrection or rebellion." Then a series of resolutions by Mr. Sumner

regulating the conditions under which the Rebel
states might return to the bosom of the Union, guaranteeing them a republican form of government,
imposing on them a new oath of allegiance, ensuring the enforcement of the [thirteenth] amendment
to the Constitution, modifying the numerical base
for determining the number of representatives from
Southern states and defining the obligations of Congress toward the loyal citizens of Rebel states. The
Radicals had come with a full armory of weapons,
with an arsenal of laws already drafted; they intended to have them adopted, and they would have to
be obeyed—what, then, was to become of President
Johnson's policy?

The country did not have to wait long for his
reply. The day after the opening session came his
message [on the state of the Union]. Here he elabo-
rated for the first time on the broad lines of his
policy with a moderation, a sincerity and a proud,
virile simplicity that only had the effect of showing
up the violence of the Radical attacks. He modestly
described the difficulties he had not been able to
overcome as well as those he believed he had got
the better of, condemning in solemn, severe tones
the policy that was seeking to impose military government on the states of the South and declaring
once again that the question of black suffrage must
be left to the states, though the national government owed the freedmen effective protection as
well as unsparing attention to their needs.

His cool imperturbability began to worry the
Radicals. They had been hoping to discover in the
President's message some provocative passage that

would provide a handle for their eloquence. Acting in its turn, the Senate had approved the Reconstruction Bill sponsored by Mr. Stevens, amending it only slightly, and the joint committee was already deliberating under the chairmanship of the bill's author[14] when the President sent the Senate a new message reassuring it on the condition of the South and advising it to restore political rights to the inhabitants of the former Rebel states. This was the spark the Radicals had been waiting for to set fire to the powder-magazine. In the Senate Mr. Sumner declared repeatedly and with great indignation that the President was an accomplice of the Rebels and that his message was intended to whitewash them. The storm broke at the same time in the House, and between the White House and the Capitol there began a series of charges and counter-charges that has just eventuated in an open rupture between the President and Congress.[15]

Of all the matters brought before the two houses, there were three especially that absorbed public attention and day by day acquired fresh importance from the ever-stronger antagonism between the Executive and Congress—the suffrage for blacks in the District of Columbia, the constitutional amendment modifying the apportionment of congressional seats and, finally, the extension of the powers of the

[14] Congressman Stevens.

[15] This does not refer to the move to impeach President Johnson, which began January 7, 1867, with a resolution introduced by Rep. James M. Ashley of Ohio initiating an inquiry by the House Judiciary Committee. Duvergier de Hauranne's book went to press before the middle of 1866.

Freedmen's Bureau. The black suffrage bill passed the House without any difficulty despite the President's announcement of his categorical intention to veto it and a popular protest vote by which opponents vainly sought to block the action of Congress. An amendment had, indeed, been offered, one that was wisely drawn and worthy in all respects of serving as a model to the legislators of the South. Its provisions limited political rights to three classes of colored people: those able to read the Constitution of the United States aloud, those who paid personal or property taxes and, finally, those who had served in the army of the United States. Unfortunately, a parliamentary blunder by the Democrats caused the amendment to be rejected without preventing the passage of the bill.

The question of the constitutional amendment was a more momentous one and was debated at greater length. It is well known that in the United States the number of representatives in Congress is based not upon the number of voters but upon the total population of the states. Nevertheless, in the states of the South, where half the population were slaves, the Constitution had provided that blacks would be counted for only three-fifths of their actual numbers. This was a handsome present to the slave-owners and gave to slavery a privileged political position. Thus South Carolina, with a tiny white population of 201,000 and an enormous black population of 402,000, wielded in the government of the Union a greater share of influence than the state of Connecticut, whose population amounted to 460,000 people.

This inequality was an integral part of the slave system, and it cannot subsist any longer now that slavery has been ended. If the Southern states want to hold on to their representation, or increase it, they need only to confer on blacks the right to vote; but it would be absurd today to enable them to preserve the power of a privileged aristocracy and to let them return as conquerors to this assembly where they ought to return only in defeat. For these reasons the idea has been advanced that the base of the national representation should be modified in such a way as simultaneously to apportion it more equitably and push the Southern states in the direction of radical reforms by giving them a strong interest for bringing them about.

Several different plans were put forward and competed for the approval of Congress. The simplest and most convenient provided for fixing the number of representatives for each state according to the number of voters rather than the total population; but this scheme had the serious defect of encouraging the states to broaden the franchise excessively by eliminating all conditions of age, wealth, domicile and [mental] capacity which still restrict political rights, thus lowering the intelligence and the dignity of the electorate in order to gain greater weight in Congress. Already women were agitating to secure final recognition of their rights, which have been so obstinately denied, and the senators were besieged by bearers of enticing petitions which they consigned to oblivion on the table of the Committee of Fifteen, side by side with those sent in by the black freedmen. Thereupon

Mr. Thaddeus Stevens proposed to retain the total population as the base for apportioning representation but with the proviso that those excluded from political rights by reason of race or color would not be counted. This version was the best of all, and it was the one that in the final outcome was adopted by the House. We shall see by what theatrical trickery the Radicals were able to make this vote seem like a national protest demonstration and a militant upsurge of sentiment against the President.

Mr. Johnson did not approve of the bill. He believed, perhaps not without reason, that it was wrong to play games with the Constitution and that the great abundance of amendments introduced and debated in Congress—this was the fourth since the beginning of the session—could have no other effect than to discredit the fundamental law of the land and undermine its authority in the popular mind. As for the particular question at issue, he believed that the simplest possible amendment was the best and that, if the Constitution were to be changed at all, it would be better to go ahead without delay and base the number of representatives on the number of voters. Unfortunately, he made the mistake of saying this to one of his friends in the Senate in a public exchange that was quickly published in the newspapers. The next day Thaddeus Stevens rose to denounce him. "This proclamation," said he, "this order issued to us by the man in the White House at the moment when Congress is considering legislation, is a violation of the privileges of the House. If, a few centuries ago, a king of England had done as much to his Parliament, it would have cost him his head. . . . But, gentlemen, it is not for us to trouble the President with our amendment; if Congress adopts it, we do not need to submit it to him nor plead for his gracious approval." Whipped up to an emotional frenzy, the House bounded forward under this stroke of the whip administered by such a strong hand; it adopted the amendment that very day and the President was forced to swallow the affront.

There remained the question of the Freedmen's Bureau. The Senate and the House had voted, under the influence of the Radicals, a law that transformed that temporary institution into a permanent and regular one. The states of the South were divided into twelve districts, each one occupied by a Commissioner to be duly named (like other high civil and military officers) with the advice and consent of the Senate. Under the direction of these officials there was to be a whole army of assistant-commissioners and supervisors—in all, some three or four thousand civil servants doing nothing but look after the welfare of the ex-slaves and refugees. At the same time the latter were to get the government's assurance that it would rent, sell or allot them the use of lands and turn over to them for three years the income from certain confiscated estates which they had been occupying since the end of the war. An immense and permanent almshouse was to be established in all the Rebel states for the profit of Radical propagandists and at the expense of the public treasury.

Yet of all the measures adopted by Congress, this was the most moderate and the most constructive.

The functioning of the Freedmen's Bureau was not founded upon ideal reasons or principles; it was the only effective protection that had been afforded the black population against the persecution of their former masters and President Johnson had recognized its practical utility when he played a part in setting it up. Perhaps in calmer times he might have been content merely to refuse his consent to several rash or exaggerated provisions of the new law and to demand that Congress revise them. But, wounded by the personal attacks of the Radical faction, irritated by so many bills and resolutions manifestly directed against his policy, he decided that this time he would retaliate and veto the measure. He called a meeting of his Cabinet and, except for Messrs. [James] Harlan[16] and Stanton, all agreed that he was right. His message was sent to Congress the next day. When the President withholds his signature from a law that has just been voted, the Constitution provides that it shall again be voted upon by the two chambers and, if it receives two-thirds of the votes, it becomes law regardless of his opposition. So the President was playing for high stakes. There was no doubt that the Radicals had a majority in both houses of Congress and, if they were able to pass the law over his veto [it was thought by many that] he would have no alternative but to resign the presidency or swallow, at whatever cost to his well-known pride, the humiliation of eat-

[16] Harlan was Secretary of the Interior and former senator from Iowa. Appointed to the Cabinet by President Lincoln early in 1865, he resigned in July, 1866, in protest against the Reconstruction policies of President Johnson.

ing humble pie and meekly obeying those he had been resisting.

He was saved by public opinion. Congress, which had been elected two years before in the heat of wartime passions, no longer represented as faithfully as it once had the real sentiments of the country. President Johnson knew very well that he had the support of the greater number and that, if some day he should suffer defeat, it would not be of long duration. The Radicals themselves, even while they were passing extreme measures, felt the ground being eroded beneath their feet and began to wonder anxiously whether the elections scheduled for the following November might not go against them. The President's veto, supported by noisy popular demonstrations, hence had the power to intimidate the moderate Republicans in the Senate who still hesitated to treat him as an enemy. At the last minute their courage failed them and seven Republican senators turned their backs on the law they had previously approved. Still, it would have needed only two more votes in order to pass, and it was known that the Republican majority of the House was prepared to reply to [that is, to override] the President's veto with an insulting challenge.

Nonetheless, this unanticipated setback for the Radicals was enough to reverse the fortunes of war. Their eloquent and fearless leader, Mr. Thaddeus Stevens, took his revenge in bitter words and by threatening an even more rigorous exclusion of Southern representatives. Senator Wade introduced a constitutional amendment making the President of the United States ineligible for a second term of office without concealing the fact that he intended it as a measure of retaliation against the author of the veto message. The Senate even allowed itself the pointless pleasure of rejecting *en masse* all the appointments to office lying under its jurisdiction.

President Johnson's victory was highly dramatic and humiliating for Congress. Without yielding, he had been able to sustain the terrible attack the Radicals had mounted against him. They had fired off all their big guns, used up all their ammunition, and President Johnson was still holding firm, just as strong as before.

To add lustre to his triumph, the Supreme Court, despite the efforts of the Chief Justice, Mr. Chase, to have it endorse Radical ideas, had just decided in favor of the constitutional theories of Mr. Johnson by declaring that the Southern states were not territories but members of the Federal Union and that they could restore their former judicial connections with the courts of the United States.

Finally, the veto seemed to have been welcomed by the people with unanimous feelings of approval. Everywhere large meetings were held; there were speeches, illuminations and general rejoicing. Delegations were sent to call on the President to congratulate him on his courage, and artillery salvos were fired in honor of his triumph. The Missouri legislature had earlier passed a resolution censuring the President; but now the people of Jeffersonville assembled in front of the state capitol in a tumultuous throng, forcing it to vote on the spot an artillery salute of twenty-one guns and an address in the President's honor.

No one yet knew what the country people thought, with their long history of support for the Republican policy and faithful, on the whole, to the Radicals. But the population of the big cities greeted the President's veto as a declaration of war against the blacks. Race hatreds suddenly burst into the open with unexpected violence. Mobs again began to attack colored people, to commit atrocities against them, to pillage their homes and set them on fire. For a short time it might have been thought that the country was on the verge of a race war, and Frederick Douglass, the chief spokesman of the black people, declared before a meeting where he came to speak under the protection of Chief Justice Chase, that the President's policy was leading straight to the extermination of the black race. At the same time, the news of the veto had stirred the enthusiasm and revived the hopes of the pro-slavery Rebels. They were only too happy to celebrate the conversion of President Johnson to their cause and declared themselves to be, under existing circumstances, the ardent defenders of the Federal Union against the rebellion of the abolitionists. One might have said that by a sudden miracle all the loyal states had been transformed into Rebel states and that, on the other side, all the insurgent states of the South had become the most zealously loyal members of the Union.

The President let his triumph go to his head. On Washington's birthday, meetings were to take place in all the cities of the United States to sing his praises. That evening an immense crowd gathered on the White House grounds. It was now the President's turn to take a defiant attitude toward his enemies, and he gave a speech in which all the furious eloquence of the former senator from Tennessee was again in evidence. He did not stop with celebrating his own past career in a tone of unheard-of arrogance and bad taste, but—labelling all the Radical leaders one after the other as secessionists and traitors—he invited the crowd to vent its most crude howls of abuse upon the three respected names of Thaddeus Stevens, Charles Sumner and Wendell Phillips. Then, picking up the gauntlet flung down in Congress by Thaddeus Stevens, he accused them all of wanting him dead and of having plotted his assassination; he even carried his extravagance so far as to offer his life to his would-be murderers if it would save the country. "If my head falls," he cried, "I want the whole American people to bear witness to my sacrifice! The blood of the martyrs never flows in vain!" However extreme and unjust one may suppose them to have been, the Radicals' provocations—even when they had unlimbered their most powerful verbal artillery—had never approached this level of violence: the President was repaying them with interest for the insults and slanders they had heaped on him.

Before long, he had occasion to repent. The crowd at the White House had received his sanguinary imprecations with wild applause. Carried away by the torrent of his demagogic oratory, President Johnson had doubtless forgotten that he was no longer merely a popular rabble-rouser speaking to an ignorant throng of backwoodsmen: he was the leader, the chief magistrate, of a great people, and his words were to resound from one end of the world to the other. Anticipating the deplorable effect such a speech was bound to have on public opinion throughout the country, the Secretary of War, Mr. Stanton, forbade the text to be transmitted by telegraph. The President was appealed to and, still excited by the success of his oratorical triumph, gave orders to ignore Stanton and send the messages. The next morning all the newspapers of the United States published his scandalous harangue and the astonished American people tried once again to imagine a natural cause for the President's fit of madness. The Democrats especially, who had been triumphant just the day before, now had no excuse to offer in reply to the Radicals' indignation. The [New York] *Evening Post*, the paper edited by the poet [William Cullen] Bryant, which up to that time had faithfully supported the presidential policy, declared that Mr. Johnson's speech dishonored him and his country, and that he owed it to public opinion to make a solemn apology. Thus the Radicals regained in a single day all the ground they had lost.

So this is where the parties now stand. No doubt they will arrive at some compromise after having continued for some time their rivalry in exchanging amenities. However bad their relations, the President and Congress have need of one another and will have to get along as best they can. The very day after the speech, it was resolved in a Republican caucus held at the Capitol that the party should profit from its advantage by offering the President the seating of the representatives from Tennessee as a pledge of reconciliation and harmony on condition that he himself accept the fundamentals of Radical policy. This had been the advice given to Congress by its own Committee on Reconstruction, even though it made no concessions regarding the absolute power of Congress and continued to insist on the total exclusion of the other Southern congressmen. In the Senate Mr. Wilson introduced a less stringent bill on the Freedmen's Bureau which would prolong its powers for only two years without adding to their scope; assurances are given that a law of this type could receive the President's approval. As for the amendment on [black] suffrage voted a month ago by the House, the Senate has shelved this bone of contention by a vote in which the most advanced Radicals joined with the most extreme Democrats. It was Mr. Sumner himself who led the fight against the measure and caused it to fail by introducing a bill, based on the constitutional amendment that abolished slavery, prohibiting "any oligarchy, caste or monopoly" and going on to provide that "no one may be deprived of civil or political rights on grounds of race or color." This was the same as proposing the immediate, absolute equality of the races. Mr. Sumner has convincingly demonstrated that nothing less than this far-reaching law would be consistent with the principles of the Declaration of Independence and the Preamble to the Constitution of the United States—and that, moreover, it flowed inevitably from the [constitutional] obligation imposed upon the Congress to guarantee a republican form of government to all the states of the Union, as well as from the power it

has to pass new laws providing for honest enforcement
of the constitutional amendment abolishing slavery.
But the Senate has decided to postpone still further
the granting of the equality which strict justice demands. It wants to remain in harmony with opinion
in the country.

It was in the same spirit of wisdom and moderation that the House of Representatives modified
and softened the law which was to protect the full
exercise of their civil rights by the freedmen. This
measure, at first proposed in the form of a constitutional amendment and thus beyond the power of
the President's veto, has now been passed, but only
as an ordinary law. It accorded the freedmen the
civil and judicial equality that Mr. Johnson himself
has advocated and it instituted special penalties for
recalcitrant judges and magistrates of the Southern
states. This time no one could accuse Congress of
overstepping its legal authority nor of violating the
principles of the Constitution. If it was still possible
for the extreme Democrats to condemn the measure
in the name of the absurd and incorrigible doctrine
of states' rights, which refuses to the Union any authority at all over the states that belong to it, it was
nevertheless solidly based upon the constitutional
amendment ratified last year which not only abolishes the name of slavery, but gives Congress the
power to watch over and protect the liberty of the
freedmen. The Radicals' position is so transparent-
ly correct that no one expected President Johnson
to refuse to sign the new law. Nevertheless he has
once again sent it back with a veto. But now the
great mass of public opinion is deserting him, and it

is to be hoped that Congress will no longer shrink back when confronted with his blind resistance.*

Such has been, up to the present time, the reply of the Radical Republicans to the White House speech. They have not even gone to the trouble of defending themselves against accusations so exaggerated and odious. Senator Sherman merely said, with superb disdain, that the President's insinuations were ridiculous and that he refused to talk about them. Mr. Thaddeus Stevens even carried irony to the length of saying that the speech had never been made and that it was nothing but a fabrication by the Copperheads for the purpose of discrediting the President. They sought to arrive at an honorable compromise without descending to useless recriminations. The one point they cling to and are unwilling to give up is their right to refuse to admit the Southern representatives to the Capitol and to impose on them whatever conditions they think proper. In that edifice they are impregnable and the President doesn't dream of attacking them there.

Thus Senator Wilson, who had shown so much wisdom and moderation by opening the path of reciprocal concessions for the President, has gone on to suggest resolutions that will oblige the Southern states—if they wish to enter the halls of Congress—

* It is now known that the Senate and House have indeed just overridden [late April, 1866] the President's veto, announcing that they are determined to stay in session until the month of November if their presence is needed to ensure the enforcement of the law. One may hope that Mr. Johnson will accept this with good grace and not place on Congress the solemn obligation of invoking the Constitutional process of impeachment against him.

to give full civil and judicial rights to persons of color, and even to accord the vote to those who know how to read, who have served in the Union army or are inscribed on the tax rolls. This is the kind of resistance Congress can use to overcome the obstinacy of the South. Already these efforts have not been fruitless. It is due as much to the Radicals as to the President himself that national authority is today seen to be triumphant, that the Southern representatives are kneeling in supplication before the doors of the Capitol and that the insurgents of yesterday are transformed into humble petitioners. It would surely be deplorable if the Radicals were to seize control of the government and attempt to apply their strict, inflexible principles to the states of the South without any mercy; but I see no reason to be sorry that they are making the latter expiate, by waiting a while longer, the crime that President Johnson has been too quick to pardon.

It is well that sitting beside those who govern there should be stern, rigorous critics who can recall them harshly to the path of duty. Were it not for the continuing opposition of the abolitionists, one can easily surmise where the well-known indifference of President Johnson toward the future and even the present existence of the black race would lead. He would have said: "Let every Negro on earth perish rather than lay a finger on the smallest privilege or the least important right of the states!" As he himself has said, he would have "formed a government of white men" under which the black race would have enjoyed not the least protection for its most elementary rights, and the abolition of slavery, praised as an act of true humanity and justice, would then have turned out to be nothing but extermination on an immense scale.

Yet "reconstruction" is going forward in consequence of the parliamentary struggles that have seemed to be obstructing it. All the while he has been battling Congress, the President has been undoing, one after the other, the temporary restraints he had placed upon the liberties of the Rebel states. One by one he revokes the provisional governors of Georgia, Mississippi, the two Carolinas; he gives Texas back its representative assemblies. Perhaps he would have done better to pursue another policy and lend an ear more often to the views of the Radicals; and the headstrong action he has just taken is an act of narrow-minded bitterness and blind anger. But it is still true that his policy, whether good or bad, has succeeded up to now, that even his mistakes can no longer easily prevent it from succeeding and that, after all, the Union has been saved. It would be reckless to turn the clock back and by so doing risk the dangers of a second experiment.

Throughout the entire course of this long and difficult process we have seen the parties maneuvering and attacking one another without respite, yet working together to forward the work of reconstruction. President Johnson has seemed to lean sometimes toward the Radicals, sometimes toward the Democrats and, on the whole, to hold the balance even between the two parties. At first he was heard to say harsh things, words full of threats that he has not carried out; then he was seen to turn toward the people of the South, offering them unhoped-for concessions and constituting himself their defender in order to be sure of mastering them. Then, when he saw they had committed themselves [to his policy], he made them feel the whip and the bridle while the Radicals behind him spouted fire and brimstone and prevented him from relaxing his severity. In this all-round hurly-burly each party played its own role and helped advance the common task. Even the vanquished and disorganized Democrats have contributed to the pacification of the former Confederacy by extending to them the same fraternal hand as in the past.

The credit doubtless belongs in great part to the remarkable man who was able to guide, along different paths, all these hostile armies and make them fight side by side against the common enemy. But the merit also belongs to the free institutions that permit all opinions to be expressed and to the national will to find a sure path amidst the struggles of the parties. These noisy political conflicts, the tumult of which may occasionally deafen the ears and disturb the meditations of statesmen, nonetheless provide the scales in which to weigh the hidden forces of public opinion, the school in which the people learn to shape their political ideas and come to self-awareness before taking action. In truth, on these solemn and perilous occasions, they facilitate much more than they hinder the work of those who govern; at the very least, they show leaders the road upon which they are setting forth and the kind of terrain it crosses; they reveal the obstacles to be met with along the way and the forces at hand for surmounting them. Finally, they make the leader listen

to the voice of the country itself instead of mounte-
banks and toadies. Nothing is more dangerous to
those who govern than to act amidst the silence and
solitude of their own thoughts. Therefore, despite
the daily embarrassment and turmoil of his relations with the parties, President Johnson should
congratulate himself on having met at every step the
warnings and opposition that have aided him.

I don't know why people imagine that mankind
becomes less prudent the more liberty it gains and
that the best way of leading men is to cover their
eyes and ears, as is done with unruly horses. If that
were true, President Johnson would have been
wrong to appeal to the people of the South at the
end of the war to resume the exercise of their former political rights and to invite them to enact for
themselves in their deliberative assemblies the reforms that he could have imposed on them by force.
He had confidence in the authority of reason and in
the conservative power of liberty.

Scarcely had the cannon fallen silent, while in
rural districts farms and villages set afire by the
Federal troops were still burning, when already the
citizens [of the South] had begun to hold their assemblies, to debate, to pass resolutions and to elect
municipal officials. The habits of "self-government"
survived every disaster. Neither the fall of the secessionist government nor the humiliation of defeat
nor the enemy invasion nor the conquest—not even
the famine and the misery that threatened the
Southern states—nothing could destroy this spirit of
independence and love of legal order. Beneath the
debris of ruined high society the community of

humble folk remained standing and came back to life by its own efforts. In a short time all was back in place: the people elected constitutional conventions and legislative bodies, and the man who only the day before had been carrying a rifle and wearing the Confederate uniform came peaceably to take his seat in an assembly to alter the laws of his state. Often he went there still a Rebel in the depths of his being, determined in advance upon an unreasoning resistance, but he came away preaching submission and national harmony: in the meantime he had estimated the needs, understood the dangers, weighed the interests and mastered the passions of the day. In less than a year the whole South had been brought under the rule of law and resumed the calm enjoyment of its liberties. This is the unique and wonderful spectacle American democracy has just given the world. What military dictatorship could have done as much?

An error that is unfortunately too widespread is to imagine democracy as the social state most vulnerable to revolutions and civil wars. There are those who love liberty so much that they even justify the worst excesses of popular government. I confess that I am not one of them, and that under no circumstances could I resign myself to seeing freedom turned into a carnival of bloodshed. Public murders, houses demolished, insurrections in the streets, which some people seem to regard as harmless amusements for the sovereign people, seem to me, on the contrary, to be serious arguments against political liberty if it could be demonstrated that liberty does indeed give rise to them.

There are several different ways of being an admirer of American democracy. Everyone recognizes its power, the scope it gives to all sorts of initiative, the boldness of the projects it encourages, and all agree that in this heterogeneous conglomeration there are to be seen the signs of a certain greatness. But then people hasten to add: "You are not sufficiently critical; you take no account of the neglected details nor of the individuals crushed under the mass; you simply enter all the injustices in the account-books, charged up to profit-and-loss, and only pay attention to the final balance. Your political theory resembles the morality of a railroad promoter who doesn't repair his equipment until it has caused the death of a lot of people, who thinks he has done very well if he has saved his company some money. You no more believe in the absolute value of justice than in the infinite preciousness of human life; you put a price on both of them in dollars and cents, and you weigh that in the same scales with cotton and salt pork. Your ideal of government has much less to do with liberty than with free competition. It is like the wind that blows on the fire and makes it rage more violently; but it makes society a battlefield always covered with the dead and dying." In our country such is, I believe, the opinion of most respectable people.

But this opinion is no longer valid. It is no longer correct today to see the Americans as nothing but powerful engines for getting work done, as a nation of vigorous, industrious beasts of burden, granting them the kind of admiration one has for a big stevedore or a champion of the prize ring. They have just given us the proof, after four years of the most terrible tests that the constancy and the liberty of a nation have ever had to meet, that they have other virtues besides animal courage and ruthless acquisitiveness. One would have to be blind not to see the perseverance, the sagacity, the devotion, the patriotism, and even the moderation and love of order they have manifested to the wonder of the world and the confusion of those who had predicted their downfall. I know of no greater spectacle than that of President Lincoln's re-election, which took place, so to speak, amidst the gunfire of the Civil War with all the calm, all the self-possession and all the serenity of the people's unshakable convictions. Do we have many such examples to offer?

The Americans have their faults, the seriousness of which I have no wish to deny. It is allowable to a Frenchman brought up in the school of our bourgeois manners to find the crudity of popular behavior shocking on occasion and to get tired after a while of the coarse intellectual victuals that please the democratic palate. But one must take care not to be too finicky, not to confuse simple distaste with justified criticism. An army making camp gives its first attention to firewood and cooking. Later, when the soup is ready and every soldier has firmly pitched his tent, then and only then can they worry about the pleasures of art and the refinements of thought. Meanwhile, people have to carry their rifles, swing their sledgehammers, cut down the forests, build cities, organize state governments, make laws and keep a close watch on the government and the national honor. The Americans are a new na-

Engraving, about 1860

French Line Pier, New York Harbor

From I. Eggermont, *Voyage autour du globe* (Paris, 1892)

tion, one still growing and developing—before we pass final judgment on them, let us wait for the perfection of their adulthood.

In the last analysis, the great merit of American democracy is that it excels in forming men and citizens. The freedom of a people is not to be found entirely in the outward form of its institutions; it is also and especially in the characters of those who practise it. It has been said that the Americans are coarse and greedy; no one has ever been able to deny that the very instability of the democratic character lends a prodigious dynamism to this whole nation in the process of being born; nor can one deny the self-confidence that is at the same time a strength and a virtue.

Have we not seen them in the course of this war heaping up millions upon millions, armies upon armies, multiplying their efforts tenfold along with their sacrifices, tormenting fortune so persistently that they have at length emerged victorious? The resistance of the Southerners—insane, criminal and heroic as it was—does it not itself show how much discipline the Americans are capable of accepting? And all this is bound up with the continual daily experience of liberty. Under the reign of real democracy the people do not see an enemy or a power foreign to themselves in the authority that governs them. The government has been brought forth from its own bosom, it returns there to be renewed and re-tempered without interruption. Since everybody has had a part in creating it, everybody comes running to its assistance whenever the government is in any kind of danger.

A glance is enough to measure the immense distance that separates this kind of society from ours. When the doors of the White House are thrown open to the multitude and the entire citizenry comes freely to shake the hand of the President they have elected, it is not a ridiculous or empty formality; it is the sign and symbol of the democratic unity between rulers and ruled. Authority is here honored not in the shape of a soldier in uniform or a prince in a royal mantle, but in the shape of a simple man of the people, a self-made man, a former plowman like Andrew Jackson, a lumberjack like Abraham Lincoln, a tailor's apprentice like Andrew Johnson. These great men of democracy have learned their statesmanship in the humble exercise of their everyday political rights; they owe their eminence only to the free election of their fellow-citizens. By degrees they have risen from township to county politics, from county to state office and from state to Federal government; it is solely by practical experience that their admirable political education has been brought to completion, that they have acquired the skills that astonish nations less expert in the art of liberty. No one will ever reproach them for their humble origin nor their lack of mastery of a theoretical science that is useless for making good citizens. Neither will anyone envy them their good fortune, for it is not a privilege of wealth or birth, nor even the monopoly resulting naturally from a superlative education. There are no prejudices barring the individual's way to success, and anyone can freely raise himself to the very pinnacle of society without colliding with those invisible walls, those jealously guarded class lines that linger on among us like stubborn ghosts surviving from the Ancien Régime.

The American government knows nothing of this fundamental defect of French society, this deplorable passion of envy that makes liberty so difficult to domesticate in our country. The rich and the poor are not up in arms against each other here like members of different races hostile to one another from birth. The words "aristocracy" and "proletariat" are here equally unknown. Everybody makes his way up from the mass of the people or is painlessly reabsorbed by them. Equality is not here an empty sham made necessary by the fear of a threatening populace sullenly seething with social hatreds. One sees no distinctions in people's manners, nor are there any in their inner feelings. So it is that Americans never feel that noxious sentiment of egoism which causes class dissensions and weakens the bonds of society. They are united in mutual independence instead of being divided under the weight of a common oppression.

How little we resemble them! With us there is an idol before which our democrats prostrate themselves and whose despotic power it is sacrilegious merely to discuss: this is modern centralisation, which is said to be a legacy of our glorious Revolution. The whole secret of this system consists of replacing the natural life of a people with an ingenious machine that imitates all the motions of living things. A centralised country is like a man who, though he has two good legs, thinks it better to tie them together and go about on crutches. Under such a regime it is to be expected that life drains out of the members and the body atrophies. Silence and repose are at last the sole desire and the sole need of the people. Let the slightest whisper of liberty be heard and it will overturn the whole startled world.

Meanwhile social antagonisms go on fermenting soundlessly. Sometimes the distant rumblings of a revolution are heard. The poor man would like to plunder the rich, while the latter thinks only of protecting his hoard, of barricading himself against the poor and keeping them far removed from power. The nation's entire political life revolves around the basest of human passions: greed, selfishness and envy. Conservatives, fearful that the democratic torrent may burst in prematurely, voluntarily throw themselves into the arms of a strong man whom they call upon to protect them. The lower classes acquire habits either of passive obedience or of licentious anarchy, of contempt for legal rights and orderly liberty, and they come to see their salvation only in some happy stroke of fortune that will allow them to gratify all their evil passions in one single day. By what name is such a society to be called? A great modern writer, who was preoccupied all his life by the future of democracy, a man whom no one will be surprised to hear quoted on the subject of America—[Alexis de] Tocqueville—has told us in imperishable words: "Such a society is not democratic but revolutionary."

Must we then despair of our ailing societies and see in the birth-pangs of liberty an eternal obstacle to liberty? If this were the true lesson of the realities we have before our eyes in France, it would be well to turn our thoughts away from it as much as possible and to think with hope about the great and heartening experiment the free democracy of America has just carried out for the happiness of the modern world.

Index to Volume Two

INDEX

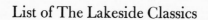

List of The Lakeside Classics

The Lakeside Classics